Hinduism
FOR
DUMMIES®

by Dr. Amrutur V. Srinivas

WILEY

Wiley Publishing, Inc.

Hinduism For Dummies®

Published by
Wiley Publishing, Inc.
111 River St.
Hoboken, NJ 07030-5774

www.wiley.com

Copyright © 2011 by Wiley Publishing, Inc., Indianapolis, Indiana

Published by Wiley Publishing, Inc., Indianapolis, Indiana

Published simultaneously in Canada

For general information on our other products and services, please contact our Customer Care Department within the U.S. at 877-762-2974, outside the U.S. at 317-572-3993, or fax 317-572-4002.

For technical support, please visit www.wiley.com/techsupport.

Wiley also publishes its books in a variety of electronic formats and by print-on-demand. Some content that appears in standard print versions of this book may not be available in other formats. For more information about Wiley products, visit us at www.wiley.com.

Library of Congress Control Number: 2011930297

ISBN 978-0-470-87858-3 (pbk); ISBN 978-1-118-11075-1 (ebk); ISBN 978-1-118-11076-8 (ebk); ISBN 978-1-118-11077-5 (ebk)

Manufactured in the United States of America

10 9 8 7 6 5 4 3 2 1

WILEY

About the Author

Dr. Amrutur Venkatachar Srinivasan was born in India in the village of Amrutur, Kunigal Taluk, in the southern state of Karnataka. He had eight years of formal education in Sanskrit, the liturgical language of Hinduism, followed by many years in the United States performing a wide variety of Hindu religious ceremonies of worship, weddings, housewarmings, and bhajans or kirtans.

His publication *The Vedic Wedding: Origins, Tradition and Practice* (Periplus Line LLC, 2006, www.periplusbooks.com) is widely acclaimed and won the USA Book News 2007 Best Book Award in the category of Eastern Religions. He has developed a contemporary format for Vedic (Hindu) weddings that retains all essential Vedic rites within a one- to two-hour ceremony, and in practice has blended this approach with those of other creeds in many interfaith weddings. See www.indianweddings.us.com.

He is a popular writer and speaker and has published/presented numerous papers on a variety of cultural, social, and religious issues in the United States and India. He has taught courses on the classical literature of India at the University of Connecticut and Wesleyan University. As the primary founding member of the Connecticut Valley Hindu Temple Society, he conducted pujas in private homes and delivered a series of lectures on the *Mahabharata* in the 1970s as part of a fundraising campaign for the temple project. He also founded the Raga Club of Connecticut in 2006 aimed at preserving and promoting the classical music of India. His latest publication, *Hindu Wedding: The Guide* (White River Press, 2010), is available in paperback format. It retains the Vedic ceremony in full detail, with some revision, and a CD with all mantras is included in the book.

Dedication

To the Hindu community in Connecticut whose support, encouragement, and confidence helped in making my commitments to the community deeper in the past four decades. And to my parents and to my village, Amrutur, both of whom provided a firm foundation in Hinduism. And to my dear wife Kamla whose constant and continuous support, encouragement, and guidance over the past four decades have been invaluable. For this project she was the first one who reviewed my drafts and maintained a dialogue that helped shape the submissions to Wiley. And to my daughters Asha and Sandhya whose unconditional love and support made everything possible. And finally to my grandchildren Sunil (3) and Naveen (1), both of whom opened my eyes to the real meaning of divinity in human beings. May God bless them to grow up and thrive within the framework of dharma.

Author's Acknowledgments

It is a pleasure to acknowledge the interest, enthusiasm, and hard work on the part of the Wiley team: Tracy Barr who received, read, and made the much needed modifications on the first drafts; Joan Friedman who copy-edited the material with care and led the project to its final shape; and Erin C. Mooney who provided overall direction to the execution of the efforts. These three ladies made sure that the focus was always on you, the reader. Also I must acknowledge Mike Baker at Wiley who was the first to contact me in October of 2009 to inquire about writing this book and helped shape a preliminary version of the contents. This project got on timely track due to the keen interest taken by my agent, Linda Roghaar of Amherst, MA.

My sincere thanks go to Professor Jeffery Long, Chair, Religious Studies, Elizabethtown College in Pennsylvania who took time to read a few chapters and offer useful critique and comments. I thank my friends Dr. Suresh Shenoy, Joseph Getter, Gregory Besek, and Dr. Deborah Willard who all readily agreed to read the early versions of some chapters and offered helpful comments. Thanks also to my family friends Priyamvada and Dr. T.S. Sankar, Sushma and Arvind Gupta, and architect Barun Basu for their encouragement and for sharing their knowledge and some photographs for possible use in the book.

Grateful thanks are also due to the following for providing permission to Wiley to reproduce illustrations, photos, and material for possible use in the book: Swami Harshananda of the Ramakrishna Math of Bangalore; Paramacharya Paliniswamy of Kauai Monastery in Hawaii; the Ramakrishna-Vivekananda Center in New York; Dr. Satyakam Sen; George Herrick; famous artist, illustrator, author, and film director Bapugaaru of Chennai; and Asha & Stephen Shipman.

Publisher's Acknowledgments

We're proud of this book; please send us your comments at http://dummies.custhelp.com. For other comments, please contact our Customer Care Department within the U.S. at 877-762-2974, outside the U.S. at 317-572-3993, or fax 317-572-4002.

Some of the people who helped bring this book to market include the following:

Acquisitions, Editorial, and Media Development

Project Editor: Joan Friedman

Acquisitions Editor: Erin Calligan Mooney

Development Editor: Tracy L. Barr

Assistant Editor: David Lutton

Technical Editor: Nishta J. Mehra

Senior Editorial Manager: Jennifer Ehrlich

Editorial Supervisor: Carmen Krikorian

Editorial Assistants: Rachelle S. Amick, Alexa Koschier

Art Coordinator: Alicia B. South

Cover Photos: © iStockphoto.com / Brandon Laufenberg

Cartoons: Rich Tennant (www.the5thwave.com)

Composition Services

Project Coordinator: Sheree Montgomery

Layout and Graphics: Corrie Socolovitch, Kim Tabor

Special Art: Chapter 7 illustrations provided by Swami Harshananda (Ramakrishna Math) and Bapu

Proofreader: Tricia Liebig

Indexer: Ty Koontz

Publishing and Editorial for Consumer Dummies

    Diane Graves Steele, Vice President and Publisher, Consumer Dummies

    Kristin Ferguson-Wagstaffe, Product Development Director, Consumer Dummies

    Ensley Eikenburg, Associate Publisher, Travel

    Kelly Regan, Editorial Director, Travel

Publishing for Technology Dummies

    Andy Cummings, Vice President and Publisher, Dummies Technology/General User

Composition Services

    Debbie Stailey, Director of Composition Services

Contents at a Glance

Table of Contents

Part II: The Hindu Pantheon and Its Religious Leaders 79

Chapter 6: Pantheism to Polytheism: From the One to the Very Many 81

Chapter 7: Hindu Gods and Goddesses 89

Part V: Delving Deeper into the Hindu Concept of Reality 287

Introduction

*T*here are a billion plus Hindus around the world today, and between 1.5 to 2.5 million Hindus in the United States. Perhaps your neighbor is a Hindu, or your child goes to school with Hindu children. Maybe your doctor or the guy at the gas station is Hindu. In just four decades, nearly 300 Hindu temples have sprung up in the United States alone. Still, Hinduism is not a household word in the Western world.

Mainstream Hinduism does not proselytize. Hindus have no interest in making you see their way because Hinduism's fundamental belief is that God has many names. Hindus believe your way may be just as good, and that you and they will meet at the end of the journey. Hinduism lets you be. With such a detached outlook, no wonder the faith remains a mystery to most. My aim with this book is to unlock that mystery and help you develop an understanding of this ancient religion.

About This Book

What does one have to do to understand Hinduism? How does one convey that the principal teachings of Hinduism are universal, positive, dynamic — and practical? Hinduism is perhaps the only religion that encourages you to have faith in your own faith. The concepts inherent in such a broad outlook on life need to be shared, which is what this book aims to do.

Some books written about Hinduism are either too highbrow or too elementary. As alternatives, you could learn about Hinduism by going to India and studying in an ashram under a guru (which is the expensive option), or you can go to a center near you — if one exists. What you more likely need is a comprehensive text that gives you an overall picture of the religion and then elaborates on the principal concepts in an informative and enjoyable manner. Look no further. You have come to the right place.

The chapters and the contents in this book are organized to help open the door to an understanding of Hinduism. There are certain facts and concepts that you need to know if you want to get a feel for this faith. Here are just a few examples:

  ✔ **Concept of time and history:** Given that Hinduism is the world's oldest religion and that even scholars cannot agree on precise dates for most milestones, dates are estimates. They can vary not just by a few years here or there but by centuries! The oral tradition of communicating and maintaining sacred findings lasted long after the invention of writing. That means few or no dated records exist before the Common Era. Further, Hindus believe that time is a continuum; there are no beginnings and no endings. This cyclical concept allows for a period of 4.32 million years divided into four *yugas* (subperiods), with declining values from one yuga to another. We are now in what is known as *Kali Yuga,* the last of the four, at the end of which a renewal takes place only to be repeated again — and again.

✔ **Geographical location:** The geographical location for thousands of years during which Hinduism developed was mostly the subcontinent of India. In the past couple centuries, more Hindus have settled in distant lands, like the United States, where the community is thriving.

✔ **Creed:** Hinduism has evolved from its core belief in One Supreme Being to a belief in the many representations of the same, from worshipping nature to worshipping deities in temples, distinguishing the Supreme Soul from an individual soul in one approach and maintaining no such distinction in another — all in parallel, all inclusive, all still flourishing, letting go of nothing. Even atheism is accepted.

✔ **The stories:** All of Hindu philosophy and theology is based in sacred scriptures called the Vedas and the Upanishads. But equally valuable lessons are learned through *puranas* (God stories from the ancient past) and through Hindu epic stories from the *Ramayana* and the *Mahabharata.* Stories — thousands of them — within more stories have helped keep the faith vivid, challenging, and alive through many thousands of years.

In this book, you can find out about all these points and more. Keep in mind that whenever I say "Hindus believe . . ." I don't mean that every Hindu believes — but that *most* Hindus *may* believe.

Conventions Used in This Book

The basic tenets and truths of Hinduism are mainly expressed in Sanskrit. Religious Sanskrit, sometimes referred to as *Vedic Sanskrit,* was used to write poetry (sometimes set to melody with precise rules for intonation) or to write aphorisms and chants (mantras).

In this book, I have avoided using Sanskrit lettering. (I include it only in Chapters 23 and 24 so that you can see how beautiful it is.) Instead, I use *transliteration,* meaning that I use the English alphabet to "spell" the Sanskrit words. Spelling Sanskrit words in English is always tricky because Sanskrit has more sounds than English does, and it's based on long and short syllables rather than stressed syllables. But to keep things as simple as possible, I have avoided using diacritical marks except in Chapters 23 and 24.

Also, when a name has been spelled a certain way (anglicized) for centuries, I have used the anglicized spelling. For example, I use Ganges instead of Ganga, Benares instead of Varanasi, and so on.

For historical dating, I use BCE (Before Common Era) or CE (Common Era) rather than B.C. and A.D.

Finally, I use italics when I introduce an unfamiliar term, followed shortly by an explanation or definition.

What You're Not to Read

My hope is that you'll find everything — both the essential information and the interesting side notes — endlessly fascinating. But because this book is designed to enable you to find just what you need to know when you need to know it, you can skip the paragraphs that appear beside Technical Stuff icons and the text within sidebars (the highlighted boxes) without losing continuity or impairing your understanding of the topic at hand. If you have to skip these bits in the interest of time, I recommend you come back to them at your leisure later. Although the information is supplementary, it often offers a historical or personal perspective of Hinduism.

Foolish Assumptions

As I wrote this book, I made a few assumptions about you:

- ✔ If you are not a Hindu, you take an interest in faiths other than your own that may help provide a glimpse of light in regard to some of the hard questions of life.

- ✔ You have friends, family, or colleagues who are Hindus and you want a better understanding of their faith.

- ✔ You are traveling to India and want to know more about Indian culture, which is largely built around the Hindu religion.

- ✔ If you are a Hindu, you should be on familiar territory, with a variety of useful information under one cover that can serve as a good reference for further exploration.

How This Book Is Organized

There's so much to know about Hinduism historically, geographically, religiously, and culturally that it can be overwhelming without a clear, easy-to-follow organizational framework. To help you find the information you need and understand the information you find, I've divided the content into chapters that each deal with a particular topic related to Hinduism, and then I organize these chapters into the following thematic parts.

Part I: Introducing Hinduism

I begin much the same way that ancient Hindu sages did, by first planting a seed that conveys all that is to come when it grows into a tree. Consider this part that seed. In it I provide a big-picture view of Hinduism. Here, you get a condensed history followed by core values, major denominations, and Hindu societal structure. With this information in hand (or mind), you're ready to explore the topics in the other parts.

Part II: The Hindu Pantheon and Its Religious Leaders

A topic of special interest especially to Western readers is the concept of polytheism. I present the evolution of this basic feature of Hinduism, beginning with pantheism, and then introduce you to Hinduism's many gods and goddesses and the various avatars. In this part, you can also find information about Hindu saints of lore whose contributions and teachings are in use to this day.

Part III: The Sacred Texts

Hinduism is probably the oldest religion in the world, beginning long before humans had developed any writing system. In this part, you discover what was revealed to the ancient sages and how these findings were kept intact through a systematic oral tradition. These revelations appear in a series of sacred texts, beginning with the Vedas and followed by the Upanishads. Other important texts include two epics, the *Ramayana* and the *Mahabharata,* and the most sacred scripture of the Hindus: The Bhagavad Gita.

Part IV: Hinduism in Practice

In this part, the rubber meets the road. Here, you find out how sacred thought and Hindu theology translate into what Hindus do from day to day. I explain how Hindus worship at home and at temples and how they celebrate their festivals. This part also includes the Hindu rites of passage from cradle to cremation and concludes with an examination of the Hindu penchant to travel to sacred places.

Part V: Delving Deeper into the Hindu Concept of Reality

For those who want to dive deeper into Hindu philosophical thought, this part explains the Darshanas, which examine six ways to "see" Reality; the Vedanta and the philosophies that emerged from it (Monism, Dualism, and Qualified Nondualism); and the Yogic path to attaining salvation. (Yes, in Hinduism, Yoga goes far beyond the exercises taught at your local yoga center.)

Part VI: The Part of Tens

Crisp, concise, and to the point: That's what you'll find in this part, where I share common questions, common prayers, and common pieces of advice. (Chapters 23 and 24 are also where I include examples of the Sanskrit alphabet. Consider it a bonus!)

Icons Used in This Book

In this book, I use icons to identify particular kinds of information:

This icon highlights traditional lessons or ideas and moral fables that Hindus learn from parents and elders, as well as familiar stories derived from the epics and puranas.

This icon highlights concepts, ideas, mandates, and more that come out of any of the Hindu sacred books.

There's a lot to know about a religion as ancient and vast as Hinduism, but not all of it is vital. I use this icon to highlight interesting but nonessential topics, at least during your first reading.

This icon highlights suggestions or comparisons I've included to help you understand the current topic or an idea that may be unfamiliar to you.

Information that appears beside this icon is important for your understanding of Hinduism. Beside this icon, you'll see key concepts, foundations of the faith, or other essential points that you'll want to remember.

Where to Go from Here

With all the objectivity I, as a Hindu and author of this book, can muster, I suggest you read Part I entirely to get a good overview of Hinduism. Then look at the Table of Contents to identify what struck you most when you read Part I. Perhaps you like the idea of festivals; if so, go to Chapter 16. If you're on your way to a Hindu temple, Chapter 15 is the one you're looking for. Attending a Hindu wedding? Go to Chapter 17. Maybe you are visiting a Hindu family; see Chapters 4 and 5. Or maybe you are a serious type or a student and you want to go deeper or study Hindu philosophy; head to Chapters 19 and 20. There's something here for everyone.

Upon reading this book either in part or as a whole, if you are inclined to explore further, I suggest you read the epics, the *Ramayana* and the *Mahabharata,* both of which cover every aspect of Hindu thought. Then I strongly recommend you read one speech: that of Swami Vivekananda delivered at the World's Parliament of Religions in Chicago on September 11, 1893. If you're in a hurry, just read the last four paragraphs of the speech. In order to do so, go to any search engine and type in "Vivekananda Chicago address."

Wherever you choose to begin reading this book, I hope you find passages that make you smile, wonder, and laugh. If you are a person of faith, I hope your faith in your own faith is enhanced after reading this book. If you are not a person of faith, you'll learn what makes people on the other side tick!

Part I

Introducing Hinduism

The 5th Wave   By Rich Tennant

"The core beliefs of Hinduism really changed my life. Prior to that, my core beliefs had more to do with not buying retail, avoiding day-old fish, and wearing my lucky necktie to the racetrack."

In this part . . .

How did it all begin? In this part, I introduce you to Hinduism. A little bit of history gets you started as you learn the origin of the word *Hindu,* what Hindus believe in, what their value system is, and the variety of Hindu denominations. It is true that Hindus worship many gods, goddesses, and even animals, and in this part you find out why. You also learn about the caste system and whether it is still in vogue today. I also introduce you to the key concepts of dharma and karma.

Chapter 1

A Quick Overview of Hinduism

. . . .

In This Chapter

▶ Seeing the broad view of life in Hinduism

▶ Reviewing the core beliefs

▶ Learning about Hindu gods, goddesses, saints, and sacred texts

▶ Appreciating modes of worship and societal structure

. . . .

*H*induism, the oldest and perhaps the most complex religion in the world, has its origin in India. It has survived as a faith for thousands of years despite many outside influences, including invasions and occupations of the land. Hinduism has always been interested in — and welcomed — ideas from anywhere. One of its earliest sacred scriptures, known as the Rig Veda, declares "Let noble thoughts come to us from all directions."

While absorbing into its bosom almost all good ideas from outside, Hinduism has been successful at keeping its own good ideas intact. Its focus has always been (and continues to be) inward; it has little interest in convincing others to embrace its values. Therefore, Hindu religious leaders rarely try to convert others. Hinduism firmly believes in both a supreme being and the idea that other belief systems are as valid as its own. This flexibility may be one factor that has led to the religion's survival over the millennia.

This chapter provides a very general overview of Hinduism, introducing you to the basic beliefs, ways to worship, and more.

The Hindu Worldview

Unlike Christianity, Islam, Judaism, and Buddhism, Hinduism has no founder. It has no single religious book, such as the Bible or Koran, as its basis. Nor is it an organized religion. Hinduism has no founding date. It has no hierarchy of priests and no organizational structure that relies on a powerful leader (such as a pope) at its head. There are no standard sacraments or rites of initiation accepted and practiced by all those who profess to be Hindus. With no such anchors, or even an expectation that the followers believe the same things, you won't be surprised to know that scholars have had a field day trying to assess Hinduism in a Western framework. Not only has that task been nearly impossible, but also it has led to hundreds of interpretations — some of which portray Hinduism as flexible, broad, and secular, and others that treat the religion with ridicule or doubt.

When it comes to ultimate values, Hindu thought has never recognized or accepted any boundaries, be they geographical, racial, or otherwise. According to the Hindu worldview, Truth is unquestionably valid universally. In fact, this belief leads to the universal outlook typical of Hindus.

Hinduism, the oldest of all religions, has a unique perspective on life. It excludes nothing! Hinduism has as its adherents a broad spectrum of people who span from the extremely orthodox immersed in elaborate ritual worship of the Almighty to those who openly declare that they do not believe in any god. In fact, Hinduism's view of the world is epitomized by this declaration from one of its sacred scriptures, the Mahopanishad (Chapter VI, Verse 72): "Vasudhaiva kutumbakam," which means "The whole world is a family." This fundamental belief helps Hindus feel connected with the world. The belief that there is but One Supreme Soul from which *everything* — all living entities and inanimate objects — emerged further strengthens the connection with the entire universe.

Devout Hindus worship many gods and goddesses. They worship cows, monkeys, snakes, trees, plants, and even tools. They worship mountains, rivers, and oceans. In the life of a Hindu, every day of the week involves worship of a minor or major god or goddess or the celebration of a festival. Religion is in the air for Hindus no matter where they are. The ideas and practices are at once complex and simple. But fear not. In this book, I help unravel some mysteries and still leave you with a sense of awe!

A broad set of key beliefs

Survey after survey reveals that more than 95 percent of Hindus believe in the existence of God. A broad set of beliefs stem from that most basic of beliefs, and they include the following (which I discuss further in Chapter 3):

✓ **Belief in the Supreme Soul:** This being is identified as Brahman, universal spirit. Brahman is the One who reveals himself in the minds of the sages and seers as the Supreme Consciousness. Hindus understand Brahman to be the only thing real in the universe. All else is therefore unreal, false or illusory, and untrue. Brahman sounds like an abstract entity but is entirely real in every sense — the one and only Reality. You can find out about Brahman and the other divine entities in Part II.

✓ **Belief that Truth is the goal of life:** The goal of life, according to Hindus, is to reach back to Brahman, the one Reality, by realizing our true nature. That goal is defined as *moksha:* liberation from repeated cycles of births and deaths. The goal is to realize unity, or oneness, with

Brahman. For that reason, the Hindu prays, "Asato ma sat gamaya," which means "Lead me from the unreal to the real."

✔ **Belief in the authority of the Vedas:** The Vedas are Hindu sacred books of knowledge, written in Sanskrit, the ancient and liturgical language of India. There are four Vedas: Rig Veda, Yajur Veda, Atharva Veda, and Sama Veda. Hindus believe that all four were revealed to Hindu sages. The Vedas contain hymns of praise to various gods, procedures for sacrificial rites and rituals, recommendations of cures for all ills, and musical chants appropriate at rituals. The Vedas are considered so sacred that the very definition of a Hindu is often stated as one who accepts/ believes in the authority of the Vedas. Part III is devoted to the Vedas and the other important Hindu sacred texts.

✔ **Belief in the idea that time is circular and not linear:** According to this concept of time, there are no beginnings and no endings; time is simply a continuum. Hindus define periods of time as cyclical in nature, with each cycle containing four subperiods known as *yugas:* Krita, Treta, Dwapara, and Kali. Added together, the four yugas total about 4.32 million years. At the end of each cycle, gradually declining time spans and human values lead to dissolution. Then another period starts, and the cycle repeats all over again. This view of time has helped in developing the ancient Hindu perspective on life — a perspective that allows for a tolerant view of events and people.

✔ **Belief in karma and karmic consequences:** *Karma* is action that relates to service, specifically service to society. Hindus believe that what we are today is the result of our actions in the past. It stands to reason that what we will be in the future depends on what we do now, this moment, and onward for the rest of this life.

✔ **Belief in the concept of dharma:** The root word for dharma is *dhr,* which means "to hold" or "to sustain," specifically within the context of maintaining harmony and balance in nature. Dharma or right conduct is so central to Hindu life that it encompasses everyone, irrespective of age, station in life, or caste. Each being has its own dharma consistent with its nature. A tiger's dharma, for example, is to kill and eat its prey. Yielding milk to sustain the life of the young is a cow's dharma. The dharma of humans is to serve.

The word *dharma* appears quite frequently in this book, much like the word *Veda.* That's because, in some ways, understanding the concepts inherent in these two words is vital to understanding the Hindu faith.

✔ **Belief in tolerance as the core value:** Ancient universities and religious centers in India attracted students and visitors from many parts of the settled world. They invited debate and inquiry into religious ideas. With this same spirit, modern Hindus accept all religions to be true and self-contained. A Hindu hymn asserts this view by comparing the various paths to God with hundreds of rivers and streams all mingling finally with the ocean.

These fundamental beliefs have paved the way for Hindus to develop a philosophical outlook on life. This outlook is based firmly on the belief in an intimate connection between the individual soul, called atman (or *Jivatman*), and the Supreme Soul, called *Paramatman*. Broadly speaking, these fundamentals comprise a code of behavior that continues to form the contemporary Hindu view of life.

A brief look at Hindu gods and goddesses

Early Hindu thought had a clear focus on the One Supreme Being. The Chandogya Upanishad — one of the sacred texts of Hindus — contains an eloquent phrase: "ekam eva adwiteeyam." It means, "There is but One without a second." Yet Hinduism ended up embracing a large number of gods and goddesses. This one-size-doesn't-fit-all realization provided an extraordinary variety of choice for individuals to worship. The One without a second doctrine, however, which holds that God and the universe are one and the same, remains fundamental and is still preserved. The simple prayer offered by Hindus at the conclusion of any worship, irrespective of the god or goddess being worshipped, sums it all up:

> You alone are our mother and father
> You alone are our sibling and friend
> You alone are our knowledge and prosperity
> You alone are everything to us
> My Lord, my Lord

Hindu mythology identifies three gods at the head of a hierarchy of gods. These three are

- Brahma, whose main function is to create

- Vishnu, who sustains the created universe

- Shiva, who is in charge of dissolution prior to the next time cycle of creation in an endless cycle

In simplistic terms, these three are sometimes referred to as Creator, Sustainer, and Destroyer respectively. Each of these major gods has a female consort also playing a major role:

- Saraswati, consort of Brahma, is the goddess of learning.

- Lakshmi, consort of Vishnu, is the goddess of wealth and well-being.

- Devi, Shiva's consort, represents the creative power known as Shakti.

Below these primary gods are a variety of forms of gods including the avatars of Vishnu (which I explain in Chapter 8). Many temples exist and continue to be built for Shiva, his sons (Ganapati and Murugan), the previous goddesses named, and the various forms of Vishnu. The concept and presence of Brahma is enshrined in the heart of every sanctified Hindu temple (see Chapter 15).

During the early Vedic period, nature gods such as sun, wind, fire, and dawn were objects of Hindu worship. (When was the early Vedic period? Different scholars offer widely differing dates, but probably between 1500 and 1000 BCE.) These Vedic gods are invoked and worshipped in household rituals, weddings, and temple rituals to this day. Except for the sun god, no temples exist for other Vedic gods. However, hymns of praise for these gods fill the revealed sacred scriptures.

The Vedic gods fall into several general categories:

✔ Nature gods, especially gods connected with weather and climate

✔ Planetary gods who feature in destiny and the composition of horoscopes

✔ Gods who rule over household health and wealth and community values

In addition, other gods and goddesses, who are regional and local, preside over small villages and towns; their patronage is sought during natural disasters such as floods, epidemics, and the like.

You can read much more on the subject of gods and goddesses in Chapter 7.

Hindu religious leaders

Hinduism is a more than 5,000-year-old culture, philosophy, and faith, so you can imagine how many religious leaders have contributed to it! The number is very large — perhaps thousands — and covers a broad spectrum of people. Chapter 9 provides details on Hindu religious leaders. For now, I briefly describe what the various Hindu religious titles mean:

✔ **Sages:** In Hindu parlance, a *sage* (or *rishi* in Sanskrit) is an extraordinary spiritual person who is totally devoted to seeking Reality and practicing austerities in remote environments such as caves and deep forests. Sages first "heard" the revelations that formed the basis of Hinduism (see Chapter 2).

A long list of such sages exists, and all Hindus who belong to the first three castes (see the upcoming section "Societal Structure") trace their origins to one of these sages of the ancient past. While performing rituals,

Hindus cite their lineage (called *gotra*) by referring to a set of sages (generally three, but sometimes five or seven) from whom they claim spiritual descent. You occasionally read about the Seven Sages called *Saptarshis* who are represented in the seven stars in the constellation Ursa Major.

Some names of ancient sages often cited in the scriptures are Vasishta, Vishwamitra, Atri, Jamadagni, Bharadwaja, Narada, Agastya, Markandeya, Garga, Kanva, Bhrigu, and Kaushika.

✔ **Gurus:** The word *guru* means teacher. Hinduism accords a special place for teachers in general but in particular for religious teachers. Each family has a revered teacher, and more often than not that teacher is also the founder of a particular Hindu sect and referred to as an *acharya*. For example, in the Srivaishnava denomination (more on denominations in Chapter 4), the most revered teacher is Ramanujacharya. Families belonging to this denomination would cite this guru in reverence at the conclusion of rituals and offer their allegiance to him.

A very well-known prayer is addressed to such gurus during daily prayers:

> I salute that guru who is Brahma, Vishnu and
> Shiva and who is verily the Brahman.

✔ **Swamis:** *Swamis* are religious leaders who belong to an order, such as the Ramakrishna Order. When such a leader is ordained, his name is prefixed with the title *Swami* and ends with *ananda* (meaning "bliss"). The ordained name replaces the given and family names. Swami Vivekananda and Swami Satchidananda are examples. Swamis set up missions and accept, train, and ordain disciples in order to continue their particular tradition. I say more about swamis in Chapter 2.

✔ **Monks and preachers:** To this general category may belong any and all persons who have a religious interest, talent, and perhaps some following. Monks and preachers may travel around, offer advice, preach, tell stories from the great epics, sing, chant, bless, and be a part of a community in general. Monks may also belong to an ashram as a celibate community, or they may live alone.

✔ **Priests:** Priests (also known as *purohits*) conduct worships regularly at temples and when devotees visit. They also go to private homes, upon request, to help families perform rituals and ceremonies. Hindu priests may marry.

✔ **Reformers:** Hinduism has had important reformers who have introduced various approaches to salvation over the past several thousand years. The most famous reformers are Shankaracharya (who introduced a philosophy of Nondualism known as *Advaita*), Ramanujacharya (who introduced the philosophy of qualified Nondualism known as *Vishishtadvaita*), and Madhvacharya (who introduced Dualism, known as *Dvaita*). I introduce you to all three — and their philosophies — in Chapter 20.

Why dates and other details in Hindu history may not be specific

The history of the Hindu religion can get a bit hazy simply because it's so very old. Here are some factors that make it difficult to pin down exact dates and other details about the religion's history:

✔ **The oral tradition:** The Hindu religion began with revelations "heard" by several sages over several centuries and then preserved through oral tradition — that is, a system of memorization. Much later, again at unknown dates, these revelations were compiled and put in writing. Does it surprise you that controversy exists about who did what and when?

✔ **Uncertain dates:** Scholars cannot agree about the period in which certain significant events in Hindu history took place — especially when the focus is events occurring more than several thousand years ago. For example, there is still no agreement on the period in which the most sacred scriptures of Hindus, the Vedas, were compiled.

Here's another example: Hindus believe that the end of the era known as Dwapara Yuga occurred when the Kurukshetra battle (which almost wiped out a whole royal race that ruled ancient India) ended. Some scholars claim that the sole surviving prince (known as Parikshit) ascended the throne at Hastinavati (present-day Delhi) around 3500 BCE. Other scholars place the date of the battle as anywhere between 500 BCE and 200 AD. The discrepancy here isn't a squabble about 100 or 200 years; we're talking about disagreements in the order of *thousands* of years.

✔ **Lack of hard evidence:** Some scholars have made extraordinary efforts to carefully note events recorded in Hindu epic histories and correlate them with the corresponding astronomical events mentioned, such as the position and phase of the moon, alignment of planets, and the like. But some of these astronomical events recur each century or two, so the scholars' conclusions may still be in some doubt.

✔ **Identical names and alternate names:** I'm not talking about identity theft here, but sometimes the name of a sage is taken by another sage centuries later. When that happens, it raises the question of which sage is being referred to. In addition, some sages are referred to by alternate names. For example, a well-recognized sage known as Veda Vyasa (whom I call "the Homer of India") is claimed, by some scholars, to be the same as sage Badarayana. Other scholars deny that identity entirely.

Keep these factors in mind as you read about the extraordinary saints, sages, scholars, and leaders whose contributions have molded the lives of billions of Hindus over the millennia.

Hinduism's sacred texts

Hinduism is not a faith that is based on one book. Very many sacred texts serve as the basis for the philosophy, rituals, and practices of Hinduism. These texts are mainly written in Sanskrit, but several major contributions are also to be found in other vernacular languages. The following sections provide a brief overview of these texts, and I provide much more detailed information in Part III.

Revealed texts: The Vedas

A basic Hindu belief is that the Vedas were inspired by what is known as *shruti,* meaning they were directly revealed by God and heard by sages performing intense penance. Accumulated over millennia, the Vedas form the basis of Hindu faith. The Sanskrit word *Veda* has its root in *vid* (to know), so the Vedas are the sacred knowledge of the ancient Hindus. They are recognized as *apaurusheya,* meaning that their origin is not traced to any individual and is, therefore, divine.

There are four Vedas, or Vedic traditions: Rig Veda, Yajur Veda, Sama Veda, and Atharva Veda. Each Veda is divided into three or four major sections, referred to as Samhitas, Brahmanas, and Upanishads. The word *Upanishads* literally means "something below the surface"; the Upanishads comprise the intellectual content of the Vedas and serve as the very foundation of Hindu philosophy.

Remembered texts: The Shastras, the epics, and the puranas

An equally voluminous literature known as *smrti,* which means "remembered" (as opposed to revealed), emerged, undoubtedly inspired by the rich shruti literature. The dates of these scriptures are equally uncertain. The remembered texts include Dharma Shastras (rules of right conduct), the two major Hindu epics (the *Ramayana* and the *Mahabharata*), and puranas (stories of gods); they consist of thousands of exciting tales to drive home the basic principles and values of Hindu thought. Their influence on the psyche of Hindus remains intact to this day.

The Hindu value system is embedded in the epics, puranas, and many other stories. In these texts, you find emperors, empresses, kings, queens, gods, goddesses, demons, festivities, holy rivers and mountains, prayers, devotional songs, weddings, births and deaths, successes and failures, the heights to which humans can rise, and the depths to which they could sink — all summed up in one word: life!

The Bhagavad Gita

The Bhagavad Gita ("Song of the Lord"), or simply *the Gita,* is considered very sacred by all Hindus and many Western scholars and devotees of Hinduism. The Gita is, in some sense, a Hindu manual for a spiritual life. Its story occurs just before the great Mahabharata War is about to commence, when the hero Arjuna decides to quit the battlefield. He suddenly realizes that a battle that pits brothers against brothers, students against teachers, and the young against the old makes no sense. He throws down his powerful bow and becomes silent and dejected. In a timeless moment, the Lord teaches Arjuna the meaning of duty and charges him that he has no choice but to fulfill his duty as a warrior to restore dharma.

The 18 chapters of the Gita have inspired millions of Hindus over the centuries. Not a day goes by in India when some aspect of the Gita is not evoked among the Hindu populace in the form of recitation, discussions, or enactment. This scripture is the subject of Chapter 13.

Key components of Hindu worship

Hindus worship in myriad ways, from simply closing their eyes and offering a short prayer to conducting elaborate ceremonies at home or in temples that last the whole day. I touch upon components of worship briefly here, and you can find the details in Chapters 14 and 15.

Devotions

For most Hindus, prayer is a daily event. Home altars are common in devout Hindu households. The orthodox may pray at least three times a day, first in the morning after *ablutions* (ritual washings), at midday before a meal, and in the late evening around sunset before supper. These prayers are known as *sandhya vandanam* and are a prescribed daily routine for young men who have been initiated into *brahmacharya* (meaning they are students of the Vedas) and their elders. I cite a few prayers here and offer more details about devotions in Chapters 14, 15, and 23.

Upon waking up, this prayer is addressed to Bhudevi (earth goddess):

> I salute you, whose bosom is represented by a range of mountains and whose clothing is the cosmic ocean, and beg your forgiveness for stepping on you.

Immediately after, looking at open palms, this prayer is recited:

> At the tip of my fingers resides Lakshmi
> At the center of the palms is Saraswati
> At the base of the palms is Govinda (Vishnu)
> So we should look at the palms in the morning

During bathing, this prayer invokes the sacred rivers:

> O Ganga, Yamuna, Godavari, Saraswati
> Narmada, Sindhu and Kaveri,
> May you manifest yourselves here and now.

To wish for a good day, Hindus say this prayer:

> May Brahma, Vishnu and Shiva along with the planets
> Sun, Moon, Mars, Mercury, Jupiter, Venus, Saturn,
> Rahu and Ketu grant this day to be a good day for me.

Before undertaking an important task during the day or before any religious function, this prayer is offered to Ganapati — an elephant-headed god who is Hinduism's lord of obstacles:

> O Lord of the curved tusk, immense being, blazing with the brilliance of a million suns, please help remove all obstacles to this undertaking.

One of the most well-known prayers to Vishnu declares that a mere remembrance of the almighty is enough to absolve one of all the shackles of life. So mere remembrance it is, and off we go! Thus prayers can be very brief.

Festivals: 365 days of Thanksgiving!

Festivals for Hindus are like a 365-day Thanksgiving! Pick up a Hindu calendar and pick a day, any day — you're bound to find a reason for a celebration somewhere in the Hindu world. Some festivals are celebrated at home, and some are out in the community. Some may be low-key and serious, and some may be grand and lively. But most involve community gatherings in the open or at temples, and all involve prayers, special foods, excitement, and fun.

The festivals are seasonal. Tied in with a lunar calendar, they land on different days but in essentially the same month of the common calendar each year. In the month of January, Hindus celebrate Makara Sankranti, which is devoted to the sun god. In February is a night of Shiva called Shivaratri. Spring festivals include Rama Navami: celebrations over a nine-day period of Lord Rama's birth and life. Krishna Janmashtami is a worldwide celebration of the birthday of Lord Krishna in August. Ganesha Chaturthi honors Lord Ganapati in September. In the fall, Hindus worship goddesses Lakshmi, Saraswati, and Durga with festivals including grand processions, musical performances, and feasting. The well-known festival of lights (Diwali) celebrated all over India and the rest of the Hindu world in late fall is a celebration of the triumph of good over evil.

In addition, colorful festivals are conducted regionally that exploit regional legends and flora and fauna. I cover a wide variety of festivals in Chapter 16.

Worship in temples and shrines

Any excuse will do for Hindus to show up at a temple to have *darshan,* which is "seeing" God. A new baby, a new job, a promotion, an approaching examination at school or college, or visiting family . . . you name it. Hindu families offer a plate of fruits and coconut and light incense sticks, and the priest goes through some rituals. Then the family prostrates in front of the deity, the priest blesses the family, and all is well.

In addition to the millions of such visits that take place every day, devout Hindus also observe the days and nights of special worship when the family must find its way to a nearby temple. The intent is the same (to "see" God), the routine is the same, and the effect is the same: a feeling of satisfaction and gratitude. The experience is at once complex and simple. I sort out this experience for you in Chapter 15.

Rituals to mark the stages of life

Hindu scriptures have prescribed rituals and ceremonies to mark 16 defined stages of life. These 16 cradle-to-cremation rituals are known as *samskaras.* They begin with conception and continue with rituals performed before the baby is born. After the birth, the childhood rituals continue, marking the naming of the child, the first feeding, the first haircut, and the piercing of the ears. The childhood rituals are followed by ceremonies that initiate the young into adulthood, followed by householder-related rituals that include the wedding. The final stages of life bring rituals that prepare the individual for retirement, followed by the rituals to bury or cremate the dead. You can find information about all these ceremonies in Chapter 17.

Societal Structure

Hindu society of the distant past was organized on the basis of societal functions that included

- Providing for the society's intellectual and spiritual interests
- Protecting the land against domestic and foreign enemies
- Conducting trade and commerce
- Tilling the land and performing manual labor

Creating a systematic way to provide for all these needs and functions — at both the individual and community level — makes logical sense. The fact that this system went awry with the stigma of caste and hereditary ownership is an unfortunate matter of history that Hinduism is stuck with.

Following are the four major castes as they are understood and practiced. Note the word "major" carefully. Many, many minor castes and subcastes exist:

- **Brahmin:** Spiritual and intellectual services
- **Kshatriya:** Defense-related services
- **Vaishya:** Trade and commerce-related services
- **Shudra:** Manual labor services

A lower caste, known as *untouchables,* also exists and includes people who undertake to do society's dirty work such as cleaning latrines, tanning leather, and so on. The existence of this lowest caste — the poverty, ill treatment, and prejudice against it — infuriated Mahatma Gandhi (the political and social leader who led the Indian independence movement and is considered the father of the nation) to the extent that he named the very lowest level *Harijans,* or "God's people."

In general, the sharp divisions among castes no longer exist in practice in India and the rest of the Hindu world. Except that sometimes they *do* still exist, especially in respecting family traditions!

Is the caste system still alive? The proper answer is a resounding *yes* — and *no!* Today, the system exists from one extreme (where the idea and practice are condemned with obvious disgust) to the other (strict observation, within reason — that is, not violating state and federal laws) and a whole lot in between. Hindus of all castes now sit together side by side in classrooms, buses, restaurants, and workplaces, and they can live in the same neighborhoods thanks largely to modern education and the laws of the land.

The caste situation gets complex when simultaneous loyalties are observed. For example, a person who is single may, in some situations, openly proclaim freedom from the caste requirements and in other situations (such as mate selection and marriage) declare obvious preferences. Internet sites that advertise available grooms and brides stating their preferences run the whole gamut. Be patient, and you will see a full treatment of this subject in Chapter 5.

Chapter 2

From Past to Present: A Condensed History of Hinduism

*H*indu. Not a household word, is it? At least not in the Western world. And *Hinduism* is much less so. But why? How did the history of an ancient people, who have lived, developed, and sustained the same civilized way of life in the same geographical location for millennia, slide out of view? Two or three thousand years ago, many visitors traveled from afar to study Hindus and their lifestyle. Some were scholars — notably Greek, Chinese, and Arab — who traveled the ancient land to write about Hindus in their own languages. Some were invaders who came with armies, occupied the land, stayed, and shared or imposed their own ideas about life. These historic developments took place long, long before Columbus set sail for India seeking silk, spices, and gold.

Christianity is named after Christ and Buddhism after the Buddha. What about Hinduism? Who is it named after? Who called them Hindus anyway?

First of all, what name can possibly describe an outlook so broad that it is all encompassing, all embracing, all inclusive, and respectful of every living creature and all of nature? Hindus think of their philosophies and practices as eternal and universal. The closest description of this lifestyle is contained in two Sanskrit words: *Sanatana Dharma. Sanatana* in Sanskrit means a concept that has neither a beginning nor an end. And the word *dharma* in Sanskrit is based on the root *dhr*, meaning that which holds a thing together leading to a set of spiritual laws or principles. Thus, Sanatana Dharma means "eternal law." And Sanatana Dharma is the name many modern Hindus prefer to substitute for Hinduism.

The word *Hindu* (and therefore the word *Hinduism*) did not originate with the ancient Indian communities flourishing on the banks of the river Indus in ancient northwest India. Those ancients did not identify themselves with a specific name. As it happened, the origin of the word *Hindu* is attributed to their neighbors, the Persians.

How far back do you have to go to find any trace of Hinduism? Are those traces likely to be in India itself, or could the origin have been outside India? The answers to these crucial questions are shrouded in doubt, debate, and controversy. Some scholars (generally of Indian origin) date the origin of Hinduism to be anywhere from 25,000 to 6000 BCE, while other scholars (generally Western) typically put the date between 4500 and 1200 BCE. Further complicating matters is the lack of much hard evidence related to the origin of Hinduism. Because Hinduism reaches so far into the past, in a continuously populated land, too few physical records or artifacts exist to draw a clear picture of the religion's beginnings or the beliefs of the earliest Hindus.

But no matter the dates, no matter the controversies, Hinduism is, without doubt, the oldest continuing faith to retain so many elements of its original beliefs and practices to modern times. In this chapter, I discuss the beginning and the growth of the religion, from the Indus Valley to Indiana and beyond!

Getting the Lay of the Land

The land I am referring to here is the ancient India whose history is essentially the history of Hinduism. Before you jump into that early history of India, it may help to get a few basic facts about the area. Figure 2-1 is a map of India showing the areas and geographical features that I mention in this chapter.

Covering nearly a million and a half square miles, modern India is populated by about 1.2 billion people; Indians speak 18 major languages with about 1,600 dialects. The climate varies considerably with cool winters and hot to very hot summers, but the real weather story in India is the monsoon season when rain dominates. A wet, hot, and humid climate does not lend itself to preserving ancient artifacts. This fact has been one of the roadblocks in terms of finding and preserving archeological treasures that could help unravel mysteries of the ancient past.

And just where did the name *India* come from? The answer to that question connects to the origins of the word *Hindu*. Sanskrit was the ancient language of the Hindus, and the Sanskrit name for the Indus River is *Sindhu*. The Ancient Persian language (the closest linguistic relative to Sanskrit) tended to change the initial S to H when it transposed Sanskrit names. So Sindhu became Hindu; thus the people who lived across the Indus River from Persia were called Hindus. The Greeks (who fought their way into the country in the fourth century BCE) took the Persian word, dropped the initial H, and added their typical "–ia" ending for the name of a country or abstract noun; hence: India. There you have it!

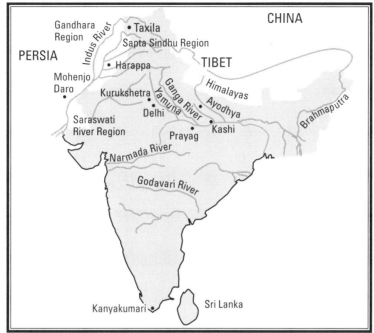

Figure 2-1:
Regions of importance to the early history of Hinduism.

From the Ancient to the Not-So-Ancient Past in India

The history of Hinduism, as we know it, is based on the history of the Vedas, considered to be the most sacred of the scriptures of Hindus (see Chapters 1 and 10). Beginning as part of a strong (and still dynamic) oral tradition, the Vedas were composed over an unknown number of centuries and finally written down. The authors of the Vedas called themselves Aryans. The Sanskrit word *Veda* has its root in *vid* ("to know"); the Vedas are the sacred knowledge of the ancient Aryans.

You likely define the word *Aryan* differently from how I use it in this chapter. In Sanskrit, the word *Arya* means "noble," and the whole of northern India where the Aryans lived was once called *Aryavarta.* The word Arya was also used in a religious context in addressing respected persons: *acharya* (meaning "revered teacher") is an example. In subsequent chapters, I refer to the Aryan people as Vedic or simply as Hindus.

In this section, I address a contemporary controversy in regard to the Aryans: Were they, or were they not, indigenous to the ancient land of India? I present the elements of an intense debate in regard to the beginnings of Hinduism between two groups of scholars:

> ✔ On one side are scholars who date Hinduism from 1500 BCE, linking it with an event called the *Aryan invasion.* (See the upcoming section "The Aryan invasion theory.") According to this theory, the earliest known *extant* scripture (one that is still in existence), the Rig Veda, was imported into India by invaders.

> ✔ On the other side are Indian and some contemporary Western scholars who believe that Hinduism and the Vedas originated on Indian soil, in the Indus Valley region. In other words, they believe that the authors of the Vedas were indigenous folks.

The Indus Valley civilization

In 1924, Sir John Marshall, director of the Archeological Survey of British India, announced that his assistants digging at Mohenjo-daro in the province of Sindh (now in Pakistan) had found evidence of a great ancient city. Mohenjo-daro was located on the banks of the Indus River. The diggings revealed a community of an estimated 30,000 people that enjoyed many modern amenities, including a municipal drainage system with sewers and houses with wells, baths, and indoor plumbing. Objects discovered in these houses included utensils and other household supplies, games (dice and chessmen), art (painted pottery and stone carvings), coins, fine jewelry (including gold and silver earrings, bracelets, and necklaces that would rival things you'd see in a Tiffany's display case), bronze and copper weapons, and a model of a two-wheeled cart. Later discoveries revealed a similar large city called Harappa further up the Indus with similar amenities.

These discoveries established (at least in Sir John Marshall's mind, at the time) that they represented, as did Egypt and Sumer in Iraq, one of the oldest of all civilizations, portraying an advanced civil society with an extraordinary infrastructure.

We know that these cities had disappeared by 1500 BCE; recent archeology and new technology (such as satellite imaging) confirm this fact. (Archeologists estimate that 2500 BCE was the peak of civilization at Harappa and Mohenjo-daro.) But what happened to them? Was there a natural disaster that wiped them out, or did a group of nomads (the invading Aryans?) from outside the vast subcontinent arrive, fight the natives, and destroy them all in order to begin their own settlements? One theory is that a huge flood may have destroyed them and wiped out the population. The debate continues.

Specifically, the controversy is centered on the connection, if any, between the development of Hinduism and the following:

  ✔ The people who lived in the cities and early settlements on the banks of the Indus

  ✔ The composers of the Vedas who called themselves Aryans

The questions that initiated the never-ending debate are these:

  ✔ Were any of these groups indigenous to India?

  ✔ Were any of them invaders (in other words, marauding newcomers)?

  ✔ Were they separate migrating groups — that is, the descendants of two or more migrations of Eurasian lineages out of Africa?

  ✔ Did the Aryans come into India from the northwest bringing the Vedas with them?

The puzzle is this: On the one hand we have an advanced civilization, an urban marvel, with no written documents beyond short inscriptions (as yet undeciphered) on a few hundred seals. On the other, we have what seems to be a tribal community of warring princes toting compositions of advanced spiritual and abstract thought. The first civilization flourished up to 1500 BCE and then faded away. The second group "arrived" near the same scene around the same time but did not build such cities for another thousand years.

We don't have firm answers to these questions, but the debates about them can be very emotional. Brace yourself to examine a few arguments and counterarguments.

The Aryan invasion theory

Based on the Bible, nineteenth-century Western scholars tended to date all historical events with respect to the year 4004 BCE, which was supposedly when the world was created. Meanwhile, *Indologists* of the nineteenth century (academicians who specialized in India and her culture, religion, and history), especially in the West, set a date of 1500 BCE as the true beginning of history in ancient India tied to an event they termed the *Aryan invasion.* This invasion of a nomadic people from central Asia to the northern plains of India was credited with bringing the sacred Vedas into India. Thus the civilization and culture of ancient Hindus originated, according to this theory, outside India.

This basic assertion was enough to motivate debate, discussion, arguments, claims, and counterclaims pertaining to its implications. Excavations in the Indus Valley (which I explain in the previous section) raised serious questions about the 1500 BCE dating as they portrayed an advanced culture there long before that date. Some seals and other structural evidence implied worships, specifically of fire, which in turn may support a Vedic-based civilization thriving at Harappa and Mohenjo-daro long before 1500 BCE.

Here are some broad arguments on both sides of the theory:

✔ Some scholars describe the ancient Aryans as nomads, driving herds of cattle. The same group of scholars also claims that the Aryans arrived in ancient India with chariots and horses, which they introduced to the natives. Another claim is that these invaders fought and destroyed city settlements and occupied land.

✔ Other scholars call the invasion theory a myth and take issue with the assumption that light-skinned warriors invaded India from their Central Asian homeland and brought civilization to dark-skinned natives. The assumption that these invaders brought with them sacred scriptures related to pantheistic nature gods similar to the gods of Greece and Rome is also challenged.

Following are a few points/counterpoints in regard to the key assumptions supporting the Aryan invasion theory:

✔ Archeologists estimate that 2500 BCE was the peak of civilization at Harappa and Mohenjo-daro. Yet scholars have traditionally claimed that the Aryans arrived in India around 1500 BCE — about 1,000 years after the Indus Valley civilization's peak.

✔ Nomads are nomads; they don't typically nomad around with horses and chariots. In addition, seals found at the Indus Valley excavations, dating circa 2500 BCE and earlier, show spoked wheels used in chariots, as well as toy wheeled carts.

✔ Any destruction of such large cities as those that existed in the Indus Valley was more likely caused by floods, climate change, or tectonic forces than by invaders. (The wholesale destruction caused by floods in Pakistan in 2010 by the same Indus River is a case in point.)

✔ Some scholars note that the Saraswati River system, east of the Indus Valley, is mentioned in the Rig Veda. The opponents of the Aryan invasion theory question how the visitors could have known about it if the Vedas were brought from outside India.

✔ Another useful source in this context is the *Avesta,* an ancient Persian scripture that scholars tend to date around the same time as the composition of the Rig Veda. It names two rivers (Harahwati and Harayu) and a river region (Hapta Hindhu). When Persians saw a Sanskrit word, they transformed the letter H to S. So we have then the rivers Saraswati and Sarayu and a region called Sapta Sindhu. River Saraswati is mentioned in the Rig Veda, Sarayu appears in the Hindu epic stories of the *Ramayana* (see Chapter 12), and Sapta Sindhu refers to the seven tributaries of the river Indus (Sindhu). Avesta also refers to the migration of Aireyas (Aryans) eastward.

✔ Some scholars argue that the Sapta Sindhu region, which was part of ancient India (and is now in modern Pakistan), may well have been the location where the Rig Veda was composed before 1500 BCE.

The debate continues to this day, and I cannot resolve it for you. Instead, I want to go back with you and meet Alexander the Great so that we can pick up the thread of our discussion of history. Follow me!

Then came the Greeks bearing no gifts

In 327 BCE, a visitor from Greece, Alexander the Great, started knocking on the doors of India. He fought his way through the northern regions of Gandhara and Taxila (Takshashila was its name in the ancient days) and crossed the Indus where he defeated the Indian king Porus. But Alexander had to retreat down the river because his army was too tired to go on.

This brief saga is a historic milestone in ancient India because it gives scholars a solid date. Alexander traveled with his own historians. Many of his troops wrote up their own accounts of the adventure. Although the original accounts are all lost, fragments survived through later writers and gave the Western world a glimpse of life in India that you read in history books today.

Alexander was not a former pupil of Aristotle for nothing. Upon capturing a group of what the Greeks called *gymnosophists* (naked philosophers), thinkers who are still found in India, he questioned them. Threatening them with execution for irrelevant answers, he set the eldest of them to judge the rest. According to Plutarch (a first-century Greek historian and biographer), the interrogation went roughly thus:

Question: Which are more numerous, the living or the dead?

Answer: The living, because those who are dead are not at all.

Question: Which produces the largest beasts, the earth or the sea?

Answer: The earth, for the sea is but part of it.

Question: Which is the cunningest of beasts?

Answer: That which men have not yet found out.

Question: What argument was used to persuade Sabbas (a local chief) to revolt?

Answer: No other than that he should live and die nobly (like a *kshatriya,* the Sanskrit term for warrior).

Question: Which is the eldest, night or day?

Answer: Day is eldest, by one day at least.

Question: What should a man do to be exceedingly beloved?

Answer: He must be very powerful, without making himself too feared.

Question: How might a man become a god?

Answer: By doing that which was impossible for men to do.

Question: Which is stronger? Life or death?

Answer: Life is stronger than death, because it supports so many miseries.

Question: How long is it decent for a man to live?

Answer: Till death appears more desirable than life.

This Q&A sheds some light on the penchant for knowledge of the ancients, on their sharp mindset and attitudes, and on the keen interest of visitors to India in learning Hindu ways and thought.

Alexander came and went, leaving a small contingent of Greeks under Seleucus to hold onto territory around Gandhara (modern Kandahar) and Bactria, now both in Afghanistan. Megasthenes, the Greek ambassador to the court of the Emperor Chandragupta Maurya, in his book *Indika,* notes that yogis of the time (circa 300 BCE) practiced peculiar austerities, subjecting their bodies to various tests of fortitude such as sitting still in one posture for a long time. These men were respected and consulted often on astrology, health, and religious matters by kings and the populace, and they were free to enter any household and receive food or other necessities. Megasthenes also noted that these yogis preferred voluntary death by fire to long illnesses they could not cure.

The Vedic period and expansion of Vedic culture

The Rig Vedic culture spread across northern India from the Sapta Sindhu region of the Indus tributaries in the West, down through the valley of the Ganges and its tributaries eastward. By the year 1000 BCE, the river banks were settled with towns forming city-states. The city-states were ruled by princes, each with his brahmin counselors, kshatriya (warrior) nobility, merchant class, and farmer/artisan/laborer class. (See Chapter 5 for a detailed introduction to these four castes.)

Gradually, the free and easy feudal state (which mirrored what was written in the Rig Veda) — where a person's class could be chosen and/or improved by individual ability — grew stricter. The Vedas were expanded into law books and philosophical commentary. The warrior class supported the king and the priesthood in setting up codes of behavior and rules of heredity, which became intertwined with religious doctrine and pollution laws. (People whose occupations associated them with unclean objects, such as working with leather or cleaning latrines, became viewed as "untouchables"; see Chapter 5.)

The reform period

As the priesthood expanded its rules and mandates in Sanskrit (a language that the average worshipper did not speak), a general mood of questioning arose. This movement against ritual was echoed in mainstream philosophical dialogues called Upanishads (see Chapter 11) and also in the contemporary reform movements of the Jains (under Mahavira) and the Buddhists (under Gautama Siddhartha, known as the Buddha or Enlightened One).

During the period from 500 to 100 BCE, which saw so much in the way of new thinking in other cultures (such as Greek thinkers from Pythagoras and Socrates to Plato and Aristotle), religious dogma and ritual came under question and debate. The immediate result was a turning away from the Vedas and organized Hinduism and a turning toward simple ethical practices and agnostic movements, using local languages to write down their tenets. Here are just two examples of how this reform played out even at the highest levels of Vedic society:

- Soon after the Greek ambassador Megasthenes' visit (sometime around 300 BCE; see the earlier section "Then came the Greeks bearing no gifts"), the Emperor Chandragupta Maurya abdicated and became a Jain monk.

- The Emperor Ashoka, following a particularly bloody victory in battle in 264 BCE, became a Buddhist.

The Darshana schools of theology

The period from approximately 500 to 200 BCE saw the establishment of the six Darshana schools, which set out to provide a rational basis to the search for salvation that religious ritual had promised to provide. In Part V of this book, I discuss all six schools, which helped revive faith in the Vedas and ushered a counter-reformation for mainstream Hindu beliefs.

Around this same period, a lawgiver named Manu codified the caste system (see Chapter 5) into the form it had until the reformations of the late nineteenth and early twentieth century.

The puranic period

Between 500 BCE and 500 CE, two famous Hindu epics — the *Ramayana* and the *Mahabharata* — were written down in the form that they more or less exist in today (see Chapter 12). Because the epics were favorite topics for storytellers throughout India, they existed for centuries in several editions (called *recensions*) that tended to have the flavor of different regions.

The Upanishads (philosophical treatises in dialogue form; see Chapter 13) and most of the puranas were composed in this period. The *puranas* are a mix of god stories, ancient royal genealogies, creation and destruction stories, rituals, and prescriptions for spells and charms. They represent Hinduism at street level and had mass appeal because they were written both in Sanskrit and local languages in a mix of poetry and prose.

The early modern period

Fast forward many centuries (this is a *very* condensed history, after all!): Between 1200 and 1600 CE the Mughal invaders established their rule over North India. An emperor named Akbar, who took the reins in 1556, invited debates between the various religious groups in his power: Hindus, Muslims, Sikhs, Jains, Jews, Christians, and Zoroastrians. He also commissioned translations of works from Sanskrit to Persian and from Persian to Sanskrit. During this period, the poet Kabir composed songs comparing names of God in different religions, and Guru Nanak Dev (1469–1569) founded the monotheistic religion Sikhism.

The British are coming!

European traders began arriving on the shores of India in the sixteenth century. In the seventeenth century, the British came to trade. They ended up staying on and on, eventually ruling India for three centuries. I outline this historic development very briefly here.

The East India Company

A royal charter issued by the Queen of England in 1601 approved a British venture to travel on the Indian Ocean and to trade. This charter was the basis for the founding of the East India Company (EIC). How this trading company expanded its influence under patronage from the British government and began to rule most of India is a fascinating story but outside the scope of this book. Suffice it to say that under the auspices of the Company, the men involved engaged in activities far beyond mere trading — activities that included everything a legitimate government would do.

The classical education of many EIC administrators had already led to an interest in the Sanskrit language and the establishment of the Asiatic Society of Calcutta, which sponsored and published lectures on language and Indian religious themes. Scholars from France and Germany began translating sections of the Hindu epics and classical poetry. The Germans established chairs in Indology in universities and translated many Hindu scriptures, which were included in a series edited by Max Mueller, the 50-volume *Sacred Books of the East* that was published in the late nineteenth and early twentieth century.

The missionaries get organized

As far back as a hundred years before the Company obtained its charter, Christian missionaries had begun to arrive in India. The sway of power the Company held on India and its relationship with the British government encouraged Christian evangelists further to target the people of India and attempt conversion. The primary aim of the Company was profit from trade; it did not directly support the missionaries. Nevertheless, the atmosphere and timing were right for the church to pursue its objective with considerable fervor.

Oxford University takes up Sanskrit

With this backdrop, Colonel Joseph Boden, a former officer of the East India Company, endowed a chair in Sanskrit at Oxford University in 1830. He did so with the specific purpose of supporting Christian missionary work in India. To this end, the occupant of the chair had the responsibility to provide education and the needed tools for missionaries on their way to India. Among these "tools," the highest priority was given to teaching Sanskrit and writing an authoritative dictionary.

Sir Monier Monier-Williams was appointed to this prestigious Boden chair in 1860. Monier had been born in Bombay (present-day Mumbai) to Colonel Monier Williams, who served as Surveyor General of the Bombay Presidency under the East India Company. The son studied Sanskrit and Hindu philosophy and wrote authoritative books on the subjects with the sole object of guiding missionaries deployed to India. His goal in mastering Sanskrit was, in part, to translate the Bible into that language. We don't know how much his efforts helped the missionaries or the converted; his work was mostly scholarly. His views on the need to encircle Hinduism in order to save Hindus were clearly not relished by people who had no reason to believe they needed saving. However, Sir Monier is best known for books on Hinduism that shine through as a labor of love, and he is especially renowned for his Sanskrit-English dictionary, which serves as a useful reference to this day.

The Bengal Renaissance

While the British were running things, Hinduism was undergoing another social, cultural, and religious reformation. Led by Bengali intellectuals such as the Tagore family, a new Hindu movement (lasting from about 1800 to 1900 CE) emphasized Vedanta (discussed in Chapter 20) in a form called *Brahmo Samaj*. The new Hinduism had leaders who tried to end the caste system and improve the status of women — crucial steps on the road toward an independent India, which would be realized in the twentieth century.

The reforms aimed at improving women's status included addressing marriage traditions. The practice of arranging marriages between children had taken hold in medieval times, when epidemics of plague and other fatal diseases were sweeping through India. Arranging the marriage of a daughter had been one of the necessary religious mandates for a Hindu householder, tied in with his chance of salvation. Girl babies were betrothed almost at birth and married at puberty, in the name of religion. The Bengal reformers were determined to end this kind of burden on women and to remove the restriction that forbade widows from remarrying.

Examining the New Hindu Wave

Hinduism is the oldest religion in the world. The dates are always debated, but scholars generally accept that a flourishing civilization existed along and around the Indus River as far back as 3,000 years before Jesus of Nazareth was born. The focus of these ancient people was to unravel the mysteries of life by raising and answering fundamental questions of life and death. Clearly, this focus was inward. The resulting philosophy, religion, and culture did not prescribe one scripture but instead many. It had no organization (and still doesn't). It did not identify one spiritual leader but many. It did not try to set up a single set of guidelines to follow but very many to suit different views and approaches. In short, Hindus have always acknowledged and accommodated life's vicissitudes the best they know how. They excluded nothing. And they left nothing behind, in terms of ways of worship.

Despite this universal approach and message of Hinduism, the religion long remained a mystery to people in the Western world. As the previous section explains, early interactions between Britain and India focused on trade and religious conversion. Gradually, however, the Western world was introduced to Hinduism and its key tenets. The following sections describe the people largely responsible for the new wave that swept into Europe and America starting in the late nineteenth century.

Spreading the message to "Sisters and Brothers" in America

In September 1893, the Western world got a clear glimpse of the ancient world of the Hindus when Swami Vivekananda addressed the World's Parliament of Religions in Chicago and opened with the words, "Sisters and brothers of America" to thunderous applause from the thousands in the assembly. That true Hindu feeling of inclusivity and intimate connection with humanity impressed the audience, and America, for the first time, heard the basic concepts of the Hindu approach to life from a Hindu. The message of Vivekananda has been reverberating ever since. The subsequent founding of the Ramakrishna Mission in India and the United States by Vivekananda has firmly established the study and understanding of ancient Hindu precepts and practices, which continue to attract thousands of devotees in the United States.

Vivekananda was unquestionably the greatest modern Hindu thinker and saint to bring a positive message of *Vedanta* (the divinity of the individual soul, the oneness of humanity, and the practicality of religious thoughts) to the West. In that speech delivered in Chicago in 1893, he was able to brush away centuries of obscurity to expound the philosophy of the Hindus. That speech is still read by Hindus around the world and continues to serve as a basis to explain Hinduism. You can read more about Vivekananda in Chapter 9.

Introducing transcendental meditation

In the twentieth century, a similar effort to share the Hindu philosophy was made by a Hindu sage called Maharishi Mahesh Yogi. His focus was not conversion but instruction about individuals and world peace. The basic tools he chose were from the Vedas, Hinduism's treasured scriptures. The message was that we are entitled to be happy if only we understand our own role in this world. He was spreading the most positive view of life enunciated by Swami Shivananda, who had declared to his disciples, "Bliss is your birthright." The medium the Maharishi used was instruction in the basic approach toward peace, first on a one-on-one basis and later to huge groups.

The early 1960s were ripe for new ideas about world peace, especially in Europe and the United States. The Maharishi believed strongly that world peace could be attained through meditation, and his technique known as Transcendental Meditation (TM) was made popular by celebrities such as the Beatles, the Beach Boys, Shirley MacLaine, Stevie Wonder, and Kurt Vonnegut.

The TM technique is based on Vedic texts and established rules to guide day-to-day living. The program took off, and the discipleship and contributions rose to such an extent that the Maharishi founded the Maharishi International University in Fairfield, Iowa, in 1974 to teach Vedic Science and Meditation techniques. In 2008, with more than 1,000 centers around the world and with all this accomplishment behind him, the Maharishi established a trust in the name of his guru, announced his retirement, and entered the *mouna* (total silence) stage preparing for the end of life, relinquishing his body a month later.

An epic portrayed on film: The Mahabharata by Peter Brook

The Hindu epic called the *Mahabharata* is the longest poem in the world with more than 100,000 couplets; it is 15 times the length of the Bible and 8 times the length of the *Iliad* and *Odyssey* combined. As I explain in Chapter 12, it tells the story of a bloody war that took place in a location called Kurukshetra in India's northern plains. The war arose due to a conflict between cousins (known as Kauravas and Pandavas) of the ruling race of Kurus. *Maha* means *great* in Sanskrit, and *Bharata* refers to the events in the lives of the ruling dynasty who were descendents of king Bharata. The stories of the Kauravas and Pandavas have had extraordinary impact on the lives of generations of Hindus. The *Mahabharata,* having taken place before the present age began, contains events, problems, failures, and successes, all of which parallel life as lived now. (As I explain in Chapter 1, Hindus believe we are now living in the last of four *yugas* — subperiods of time that collectively span about 4.32 million years. The *Mahabharata* took place in the third yuga.)

Avignon is a town in France 124 miles from Lyon. What can possibly be the connection between the ancient Indian town of Kurukshetra and Avignon in modern France? A play.

Although books about the *Mahabharata* have been written over the centuries, the epic did not truly impact the Western world until Peter Brook, working with Philippe Lavastine, a French professor of Sanskrit, and French writer Jean-Claude Carrière, crafted it into a spectacular nine-hour drama. In his *Mahabharata,* Brook transported the battlefield of Kurukshetra to the quarries of Avignon in France to the utter delight of the French, who packed the open-air auditorium for weeks in 1985. Then the play moved to the United States with limited engagements in Los Angeles and Chicago and at the Brooklyn Academy of Music.

The Hindu temple movement in the United States

Until the late 1950s, the immigration laws of the United States allowed immigrants based on a quota system. Under these laws, the annual quota for Britain was set at 65,000, while only 100 people were allowed to emigrate from India. With President John F. Kennedy's initiative, and at the urging of President Lyndon B. Johnson, Congress abolished the system entirely in 1965 and allowed up to 170,000 people worldwide to emigrate on a first-come, first-served basis. This law contributed to increasing the number of students entering the United States from India in the 1960s.

With the new immigration policy in place, many of these students (including me) were able to work, marry, raise children, and settle here in the United States. This development set in motion a series of sequential steps not unlike those taken by any other immigrant community. Yet there were some major differences with respect to this particular nationality.

First, Indian immigrants were not a homogenous group. We came from different states in India and spoke different languages. The language we used to communicate with each other was English! Second, a majority of us were under the impression that we would eventually return to India. For this reason, Indian communities in the United States were not so enthusiastic about setting up permanent institutions.

Do we need Hindu temples in the United States?

Temples belong in the "permanent institution" category. In ancient and medieval India, only kings or famous saints built temples. In modern India, the temple builders were millionaires. As ex-students, newly minted workers, parents, and mortgage-holders, none of us fit those categories. Also, serious concerns were raised by a few people about possible resistance from the so-called "mainstream" community. The fact that almost all U.S. residents were descendents of immigrants from a different era played no part in our collective thinking. Other concerns focused on the expenditures involved and the difficulty of maintaining a temple that would satisfy all the requirements appropriate to a Hindu religious center. However, not all Indian immigrants felt that way or considered the challenges insurmountable.

New York leads the way

A pioneering effort to establish Hindu temples in the United States began in the 1960s in New York City under the leadership of C.V. Narasimhan, retired United Nations Under-Secretary General. Dr. Alagappa Alagappan, a devout Hindu, working with Narasimhan, took the reins to organize and establish the Hindu Temple Society of North America, which was officially registered on January 26, 1970. The New York group chose the presiding deity to be Ganapati (who is also called Ganesha), the elephant-headed god. Any Hindu undertaking of an auspicious nature invariably requires worship of this deity, and so the choice was most appropriate for the very first sanctified temple in the United States.

The New York City temple was built, and deities (sculpted in India) were brought to Queens. In addition, artisans who were experienced in building temples were also brought to New York. The temple's consecration took place on July 4, 1977, and this established shrine continues to attract thousands of devotees each year. The Queens experience served as an inspiration to Hindu communities in other states, and today every state in the union either has at least one sanctified Hindu temple or has plans to build one. You can read more about temples in the United States and Canada in Chapter 15.

In the pages of Newsweek

Anyone needing proof that the new Hindu wave has made an impact on Western culture got it in 2009 when *Newsweek* magazine ran an article titled "We Are All Hindus Now" by religion editor Lisa Miller. Ms. Miller concludes the article asking us all to say Om. Why? Because according to her, America is no longer just a Christian nation, even though it was founded by Christians and 76 percent of Americans continue to identify themselves as Christian. Quoting the Rig Veda verse "Truth is One but the wise express it in different ways," she feels that we are more like Hindus in our views about God, our own selves, interpersonal relationships, and relationship with God. That different religions may lead to the same goal is acknowledged by 65 percent of Americans which, according to her sources, include 37 percent of white evangelicals. She also notes that more than one-third of Americans now choose cremation (a notably Hindu choice) over burial. So by all means say Om, and resume your reading!

Chapter 3

Hinduism's Core Beliefs and Values

A belief system defines the bedrock of a religion whose followers go about their daily lives working, raising families, and interacting with neighbors. Even though individuals may not be aware of it, every action they perform is based on a set of beliefs they learned from parents, teachers, and the community. Hindu children learn their codes of behavior by observing elders around them, listening to stories from their epics, attending traditional ceremonies at home and in the community, and participating in worship services at temples.

Unlike other organized religions, Hinduism does not have a single systematic, Sunday school–type of approach to teach its value system. Nor is there a simple set of rules like the Ten Commandments. Local, regional, caste, and community-driven practices influence the interpretation and practice of beliefs throughout the Hindu world. Yet a common thread among all these variations may be found in Hindus' belief in a Supreme Being and a feel for certain basic concepts such as Truth, dharma, and karma irrespective of an individual's caste, knowledge base, and educational background. Of course, belief in the authority of the Vedas (sacred books that I explore in Chapter 10) serves, to a large extent, as the very definition of a Hindu, even though how the Vedas are interpreted may vary greatly.

This chapter explains the core beliefs of Hinduism, including the Hindu concept of Truth/Reality; the nature of the soul and the Supreme Being, Brahman; and the spiritual goal of *moksha,* which means liberation within the context of attaining release from the cycle of deaths and rebirths.

Truth: The Foundation of Hindu Belief

The concept of Truth is at the intersection of philosophy and religion. Hindus, however, have traditionally made no sharp distinctions among Truth, religion, and Reality. They see these three concepts as deeply related and overlapping.

Hindu scriptures, epic stories, folktales, proverbs, and even ordinary conversations are full of subtle and not-so-subtle references to the concept of Truth and Reality. Consider these quotes from a variety of Hindu sources:

> From the Taittiriya Upanishad: "I shall speak the truth."
>
> From *A Hindu Primer: Yaksha Prashna*: "It is the truth of the good that causes the brilliance in the sun" and "What in one word is heaven? Truth."
>
> From the Rig Veda: "Truth is the base that bears the earth" and "Truth is One, but the wise express it in different ways."
>
> From the Brihadaranyaka Upanisad: "Lead me from the unreal to the Real."
>
> The Republic of India's national motto, taken from the Mundakopanishad: "Truth alone triumphs."

Each one of these statements emphasizes the high honor Hindus bestow on the concept of Truth. Yet to fully grasp this idea, you need to understand the Hindu concepts of Truth and Reality.

Truth is a multilayered concept. It is more than just being "right" or factual. It is even more than being ethical and moral. In fact, Truth is more than all those attributes combined. In Hinduism, Truth comprehends the natural laws of the universe. Truth is absolute and eternal. For Hindus, Truth is, in a word, God. Realization of the Truth is a Hindu's goal, and that means realization of the self, God, and Brahman.

Because Truth isn't a particular path or answer but the very essence of the universe, it is, therefore, the only *real* thing. It is Reality. In Hinduism, Reality is eternal; it doesn't change with time. Instead, it remains forever as is and as it always has been. As an example, consider this book you are reading. Is the book real? Of course it is — but only in a physical sense. Otherwise, it is not real because over time, the book will be gone! But the concepts such as dharma discussed in this book will remain eternal and therefore real.

Understanding Hinduism's Three Core Beliefs

Hindus are brought up to believe in God — in whatever form (Fire, Sun, Krishna, Rama, Linga . . .) the individual's family and community perceive God to be. At the practical level, a family's or community's godhead may be Vishnu, Shiva, or Devi (goddess) in one or more of their forms. (See Chapter 1 for an introduction to these primary Hindu gods.) But Hindus also hear and are aware of something deeper, the One.

Although educated Hindus and intellectuals undoubtedly know that the origin of their faith is rooted in the Vedas, all other Hindus, irrespective of their sectarian affiliations, are also aware of this fact. Many of them may not be able to recite even a single hymn from any of the Vedas, but the very word *Veda* generates an immediate reverence.

The concept of dharma is likewise held in great esteem. The word is used in common parlance in casual conversations to point out right from wrong.

The three core beliefs — belief in the Supreme Being, the authority of the Vedas, and a commitment to the concept of dharma — serve as a firm foundation on which all other beliefs and values that guide Hindus are built. I explain all three in this section.

Brahman: The one true (real) entity

That there is an entity that defies description, which excludes nothing, that can be seen and not seen, that can be conceived or not by Hindus in their quest for something beyond material well-being is ingrained in Hindu thinking. This Being is identified as Brahman, a universal spirit. Brahman is the One that reveals Itself in the minds of the sages and seers as the Supreme Consciousness.

Brahman is all-inclusive, encompassing everything in the universe. It has no form. (Don't mistake Brahman for the god Brahma or the caste of brahmin, discussed in Chapters 6 and 5, respectively.) Brahman, the pure and formless One, limitless and all-pervading, is everywhere. It is the divine essence and substratum of the universe containing being and nonbeing. It is the timeless entity from which all else issues and into which all else returns.

Brahman is the only thing real in the universe. All else is unreal, false, illusory, untrue, or has (at best) a dependent and relative reality in relation to Brahman. Although Brahman sounds like an abstract entity, it is entirely real in every sense. It is the Supreme Soul, Supreme Being, Creator, the One and Only Reality. This is the *pantheistic* doctrine — the doctrine that equates God with forces and laws of the universe — leading to the firm declaration *ekameva advitiyam*: "There is but one without a second." These attributes of Brahman are complex concepts and are less known and talked about by Hindus in general.

The root word for Brahman is *brh,* which means "to grow" and indicates infinite growth and expansion of the Being from barely visible living and nonliving objects at the lowest level (atomic) to the highest forms of life.

Belief in the authority of the Vedas

Ancient Hindus received their religion through revelation: the Vedas. There are four Vedas known as Rig Veda, Yajur Veda, Sama Veda, and Atharva Veda. Hindus believe that the Vedas are without beginning and without end. You may be wondering how a book can be described in that way. But the Vedas, in the eternal sense, aren't actual books. In 1893, Swami Vivekananda explained that the Vedas are "the accumulated treasure of spiritual laws discovered by different persons at different times." Being eternal, the Vedas existed before they were revealed to (or discovered by) the sages. (I introduce you to the sages in Chapter 1.)

Once revealed, the Vedas have been passed on from generation to generation for more than 5,000 years through the process of oral transmission.

On the basis of star positions and calendars used in the Vedas, some scholars are of the opinion that the Rig Veda (1,028 fairly short hymns of praise) in its oral form was composed around 6000 to 4000 BCE. (Most scholars trace them in their current, written form to around 1500 to 1000 BCE.)

A true test of a Hindu is his/her acceptance of the authority of the Vedas. Throughout this book you can see the extraordinary influence of the Vedas on every aspect of Hindu life. Chapter 10 is devoted to this most important of Hinduism's sacred texts.

Committing to the concept of dharma

In Hinduism, there are four personal aims to be realized or striven for during the course of a lifetime. These aims are known as *chaturvidha phala purushartha.* The first of these is dharma. The other three are *artha* (wealth, prosperity, reputation, fame), *kama* (sensory and aesthetic fulfillment), and *moksha* (liberation and salvation, covered later in this chapter). Hindus are obligated to practice artha and kama with dharma as the foundation in order to attain salvation and release from cycles of birth.

Happiness, prosperity, and the good life are legitimate human experiences for Hindus as long as they are within the framework of dharma. I need to point out that Hindus have no problem tolerating atheism, but when it comes to those who violate dharma, they will not look the other way! In a paper I wrote titled "Dharmo rakshati rakshitaha," I provide a much more detailed treatment of this unique Hindu concept. You can access this paper on my website: www.avsrinivasan.com.

Understanding dharma

Dharma is the first of four personal aims to be realized or striven for during the course of one's lifetime. It is central to Hindu life and encompasses everyone, irrespective of age, station in life, or caste. In a nutshell, dharma insists on each person performing his or her duty. This aspect is the key component of the Bhagavad Gita (which I discuss in Chapter 13) when Lord Krishna charges the hero Arjuna to perform his duty. Winning or losing is not the issue, but doing one's duty is.

So just what is that duty? It depends. At different stages in life, each person has a different role, which means different duties. Your duty as a child is very different from your duty as a young adult, which in turn is different from the duties that fall on the shoulders of a householder. Your duties continue to change until the end of your life.

How does a Hindu determine what his or her duties are at any given time? An individual may be able to define the boundaries of dharma through interacting and talking with others; reading Hindu sacred texts (the scriptures, the epics, legends, and mythologies); studying history and drama; and paying attention to the wide variety of stories heard throughout the formative years. These various experiences help constitute personal measures and yardsticks that a Hindu may use in making decisions throughout his or her life. In a sense, dharma forms the individual's conscience, and it is perhaps the only available light that guides individual actions.

Understanding dharma helps you understand the Hindu faith. Unfortunately, no single word in the English language adequately covers the meaning of this concept. Although I can use words such as right conduct, righteousness, moral law, and so on, to get a better appreciation of this term I recommend reading the two epics, the *Ramayana* and the *Mahabharata* (see Chapter 12), even in a condensed form in English. Cryptic statements about dharma made in Sanskrit aren't all that helpful beyond shedding a little light on how Hindu ancestors viewed this concept. Consider, for example, the following statements:

The one devoid of dharma is an animal.

Nonviolence is the supreme dharma.

Where there is dharma, there is victory.

These statements drive home how dharma should be central to all transactions in life. Mahatma Gandhi's nonviolence *(ahimsa)* movement, for example, was guided by dharma, and *ahimsa* is still practiced by his followers. The reference to victory in the last statement above is invoked by many while pondering whether to engage in or respond to major conflicts. Even political leaders use the concept of dharma in their debates. In 1970, a Communist party member of India's Parliament is reported to have explained his position on a bill by stating that his party preferred to die like Abhimanyu (a prince in the Mahabharata war who gets fatally stuck in an intricate army formation) than flee the battlefield.

Hindus keep in view these ideas about dharma, not only to guide their own lives but also in the course of raising children.

Avoiding the six temptations

Hindus learn early in their lives that there are six temptations they should try hard to avoid in order to stay on the path of dharma leading to moksha. The temptations are the following:

- ✔ **Kama:** Lust and desire for material possessions (Caution: The word *kama* in this context differs from *kama* in the context of the personal aims I introduce in Chapter 1. There it means love, beauty, aesthetic aspects, and so on. Here it is the opposite. Welcome to the world of Sanskrit, where context is paramount!)

- ✔ **Krodha:** Anger

- ✔ **Lobha:** Greed

- ✔ **Moha:** Delusion through unrealistic attachment to things, people, and power

- ✔ **Mada:** Egotistic pride

- ✔ **Matsarya:** Jealousy

These undesirable qualities play a major role in the daily life of human beings; thus the cautionary warning to remain alert to avoid these pitfalls.

Following your conscience

Although dharma is a key component of Hinduism, other cultures and people have also defined what it means to be a good citizen and a good person — and what to do when those two roles are in conflict. Aristotle, for example, said:

A good citizen is one who acts in accordance with the laws of the state. A good man is one who acts in accordance with the principles of virtue. . . . In the best state, however, laws will be in accordance with the principles of virtue and so there would be no distinction between a good man and a good citizen.

But what does one do when there is, in fact, a clear difference between the laws of the state and the demands of conscience — which in Hinduism are dharmic laws? Such cases result in an internal conflict. Such was the case when Mohandas Karamchand (known as Mahatma) Gandhi was asked to vacate his seat on a train in South Africa because he was not a white man, when Rosa Parks was asked to vacate a seat on a bus merely because she was black, and when Abraham Lincoln agonized over the need to go to war to preserve the Union.

When a Hindu faces a conflict that pits his or her conscience against prevailing laws or accepted standards of conduct, the conscience alone is the true guide that helps the individual choose what to do. That is precisely the reason Hindus train their conscience in dharma so that they may, when called on, have the benefit of guidance at crucial times.

Believing in the Existence of an Immortal Soul

A Hindu believes that the soul is pure, perfect, and holy. It is neither created nor destroyed. It is simply there. The soul has been, it is, and it will be. It is unbounded and free. Actions of the soul while residing in a body require that it reap the consequences of those actions in the next life — the same soul in a different body. A body is a mere medium. Depending upon the experiences and tendencies during one life, the soul finds itself next in a body most appropriate to those tendencies, and a new life begins. The process of movement of the atman from one body to another is known as *transmigration.* The kind of body the soul inhabits next is determined by karma. This is what Hindus (and others) mean by karma and karmic consequences; the concept refers to the "pre-history" of the soul.

The philosophical outlook of Hinduism is based firmly on the belief that there is an intimate connection between the *jivatman,* the individual soul, and the *Paramatman,* the Supreme Soul.

Transmigration, death, and rebirth

The human experience is like a coin; it has two sides. Life is one side, and the other is what we call death. The two come as a package. Birth and death are two aspects of life on this earth which no one, neither a pauper nor a monarch, has any control over. The born must die. That is inevitable.

The Bhagavad Gita (Chapter II, Verse 27) puts it this way: *jaatasyahi dhruvo mrtyu: dhruvam janma mrtasya cha,* which means "Death is certain to the one that is born and birth is certain to the one who dies."

Upon death of the body, the soul needs a residence in another body being born in order to experience the results of karma carried out in the previous body — unless, that is, it is ready for the final step of being absorbed in the Supreme Self.

But by *death,* the Hindu refers only to the body: Only the body dies, never the soul. At the World's Parliament of Religions in Chicago on September 11, 1893, Swami Vivekananda declared:

> *Here I stand and if I shut my eyes, and try to conceive my existence, "I," "I," "I," what is the idea before me? The idea of a body? Am I, then, nothing but a combination of material substances? The Vedas declare, "No." I am a spirit living in a body. I am not the body. The body will die, but I shall not die. Here am I in this body; it will fall, but I shall go on living.*

Final release from the cycle of death and rebirth

The Hindu's goal is to live a dharmic life in order to avoid rebirths so that the individual soul merges with the Supreme Soul. Merging with the Supreme Soul is liberation or salvation *(moksha)*; see the later section "Understanding the Goal of Life: Moksha." Upon release from the cycles of time, the soul merges with the essence of the Supreme Soul and becomes unbounded, pure spirit.

Karma and Its Consequences

Most people, Hindu or not, have heard of karma; you may even use the word in your daily conversations. But most people don't have a complete understanding of the concept of karma. In this section, I illuminate it for you.

Linking karma to character and willpower

Karma is action. I am writing this sentence; that is action. You are reading this sentence; that is action. You are thinking; that is also action. All such actions, 24/7 throughout a person's life, help build that person's character. The nature of such character depends upon the nature of the actions. The strength of this character translates into willpower. That willpower determines our actions as well as their effects on us, our families, and our society at large.

Swami Vivekananda reasons that heredity alone does not define our character and the resulting willpower. He illustrates this fact by pointing to a great man with a giant will: the Buddha. Without strength of character generated through the nature of action, how could one explain that the Buddha, son of a petty king, had half the world worship him? His giant will, accumulated from his own actions, helped him burst on society like a giant wave and change the world forever.

Could such giant willpower have been accumulated in a single lifetime, or even two? Hindus believe the answer is "No!" It must have taken ages and several lifetimes for this willpower to accumulate to such a degree.

Good karma versus bad karma

The soul moves on and on, carrying the consequences of its karma in one body on to the next. The body dies, but the soul does not; it continues on forever or until it reaches perfection, upon which it merges with the Supreme Soul and achieves salvation.

What we are today is the result of our actions in the past. It stands to reason that what we will be in the future depends on what we do now, at this very moment and onward for the rest of our life.

Although Hindus do not refer specifically to good and bad karma, they understand that actions during a lifetime influence what happens in later lives. Hundreds of stories from the Hindu epics are used to impress upon the young the need to pay attention to their actions. In practical terms, this view serves as a trigger to motivate service to themselves, to their families, and to society at large. Knowledge and understanding of another crucial Hindu concept, dharma, help serve as a torchlight to guide actions. Good action may be the result — an accumulated treasure that influences the next life.

In that context, one can similarly view bad karma and its consequences. The story of stealing Vasishta's cow, which I tell in the sidebar "Prabhasa, Vasishta, and Nandini the Cow," serves as an example. This simple fable also shows that even gods and demigods are not immune to consequences of their actions.

SACRED TEXTS

Prabhasa, Vasishta, and Nandini the Cow

This interesting story is found at the very beginning of the epic *Mahabharata* (see Chapter 12).

Once a group of higher celestial beings known as Vasus, all eight of them brothers, along with their wives went on a holiday. They were close to the *ashram* (monastery) of sage Vasishta. This ashram was an idyllic setting, indeed, with luscious grass and fruit and flowering trees. There the kings and their wives observed one of Vasishta's cows named Nandini (yes, they gave names to cows!), an extraordinarily healthy and handsome animal. One of the ladies wanted to have the cow, but the men, wondering why they, who were already immortals, needed a cow at

all, resisted her pleas. Still, the lady insisted. She had a friend on the earth, she said, and she wanted to give the cow as a gift. Persuaded by this story, one of the Vasus, Prabhasa, stole the cow and its calf, and the entire party fled the scene. When the sage Vasishta rose after his austerities, he noticed Nandini's absence and through his Yogic powers understood what had happened. He cursed all the Vasus to be born on earth as a consequence of their action. The Vasus fell at Vasishta's feet and begged forgiveness. The sage reduced the sentence to all but Prabhasa. Seven of the kings would leave the earth right after birth, but Prabhasa would have a long life and pay in full for the crime.

Breaking free of karma

A Hindu's ultimate goal is to end the suffering and bondage of karma and its consequences, no matter how many lives it takes. Successive lives led according to the principles of dharma elevate each next life, leading to higher and higher planes of existence until the individual's life is totally absorbed in realizing the self. Under such conditions, the soul breaks free of the bondage of life as we know it and is absorbed by the Supreme Soul. That is true freedom, known as *moksha* — the subject of the next section.

Understanding the Goal of Life: Moksha

The goal of life, according to Hindus, is to reach back to Brahman by realizing our true nature. Upon attaining this awareness, we achieve liberation (salvation, or *moksha*).

Brahman is *the* common element in each living being. Our differences come through the individualized body and mind each of us inherits. That feature — the inherited body and mind, which is far less important than the commonality (the Brahman in each of us) — makes us think, act, and feel different and makes us forget that we are the same.

The goal is to realize our unity, our oneness; it's the reason Hindus pray *asato ma sat gamaya* ("Lead me from the Unreal to the Real"). Hindus are urged to give up the unreal, realize the real, and experience freedom from bondage to the body. That freedom is bliss, and as the great sage Swami Sivananda (1887–1963) declared, "Bliss is your birthright."

What is the path toward this goal? The Bhagavad Gita reveals many paths, and I briefly cover three of them in this section. (I go into more detail about these three in Chapter 13.)

Each person has his or her own qualities, likes, dislikes, and preferences. Therefore, each person should be able to choose a path toward liberation that suits his or her own taste, mindset, persona, and interest. Hindus firmly believe that *any* path, however different, peculiar, crooked, or straight, leads to the same goal of reaching the One. Such freedom leads not only to the choice of a philosophy that works for the individual but also to the rejection of any philosophy that doesn't work for that person. The result may seem chaotic (and sometimes it really is!), but the underlying spirit of this approach cannot be denied. After all, the effort to achieve liberation is a personal affair, and no one else — including those who are near and dear to the individual — has any right to impose any restraint or constraint on that effort.

The path of duty

The Yoga of Karma is selfless service to society. *Yoga* means union — with God. Yoga of Karma is the approach, which in this case involves action — in other words, reaching that union through selfless action. Each of us inherits a role in society. Whatever that role may be, our successful performance in that role is essential to a successful society. The path of duty insists that we fulfill our roles with enthusiasm, with objectivity, and with passion — fully absorbed even while remaining detached. This concept, which I call *detached dynamism,* is truly Hindu.

Detachment in this context acknowledges the spirit of Karma Yoga, which wants you to lovingly focus on what you need to do. Hindus are urged to do their duty and not be attached to what may or may not be the outcome.

The path of knowledge

Another path toward moksha is defined as the path of knowledge, known as *Jnana Yoga.* Through this path, the individual strives to obtain knowledge of the Brahman through appropriate austerities such as through studying under a teacher with dedication to serve the Lord, and through service to other aspirants. The path requires a high level of intellect and determination. It involves rigorous self-discipline and dedication as the mind engages in unraveling complex issues pertaining to the self.

Individuals on this path cultivate such austerities as the practice, on a daily basis, of doing no harm, meditating deeply, controlling passion, avoiding harsh foods that aren't conducive to a healthy body, and so on. This path requires the mental capacity to go deep into the philosophies of life; for that reason it is most suitable for those with a scholarly or intellectual bent.

The path of devotion

The third path I present here is that of devotion, known as *Bhakti Yoga*. This path demands total, unconditional surrender to God with the individual completely absorbed in devotion to a chosen deity.

Normally, people who choose this path associate themselves with a temple, take part in worships, assist in maintenance of the shrine, and take an active part in the service, treating the deity as though it is a person with whom they are in love and to whom they have surrendered in a visible way. The most visible example is the Hare Krishna membership, which I discuss in Chapter 4.

Translating Beliefs into Core Values

Based on the set of core Hindu beliefs that I discuss earlier in the chapter, several values flow out. Such values are how the beliefs get translated into action and are visible in Hindu society on a daily basis. In this section, I introduce three such values, which are representative of a much larger group of values.

The joint family system: The more, the merrier!

In a joint family system, brothers, their wives and children, and unmarried sisters live with their parents, their paternal uncles, and the uncles' families, all under one roof. Sometimes there may be 15 to 20 people in one household sharing resources, problems, successes, and failures. Having so many family members under one roof can be a lot of fun (of course, not always!) — and there are never any babysitting issues! Free counseling is available 24/7 with no need for psychiatrists. This system is gradually vanishing in favor of the nuclear family, but the model is still the choice for business families and many others in villages and small towns in India.

Exercising tolerance

One fundamental aspect of Hinduism is its tradition of tolerance. Ancient universities and religious centers in India attracted students and visitors from many parts of the known world. These institutions invited debate and inquiry into religious ideas. With this same spirit, modern Hindus accept all religions to be true and self-contained. Hindu thought is ingrained with the idea that other ways of life leading essentially to the same goal may be equally good.

One particular Hindu hymn translates this way:

> *As the different streams, having their sources in different places, all mingle their water in the sea, O Lord, the different paths which men take through different tendencies, various though they appear, crooked or straight, all lead to Thee.*

Similarly, a verse *(shloka)* in the Rig Veda declares that "Flowers and bees may be different, but the honey is the same." And the Lord has declared in the Gita that "Wherever thou seest extraordinary holiness and extraordinary power rising and purifying humanity, know thou that I am there."

Showing respect for elders

Although every culture, every faith, and every society teaches its young to have respect for their elders, Hindus have made an art of this value. The outward signs are clear: In orthodox families, youngsters prostrate before elders, touching their feet. Men and women of any age prostrate this same way in front of holy men (and sometimes wash their feet). Even strangers who are elders are greeted by everyone, young and old, with the familiar sign of bringing palms together and bowing heads down. Standing aside and making way for older people is common. Blessings of elders in an assembly are invariably sought during special ceremonies such as weddings.

Many Hindu families (though not all of them) still adhere to what's called the *joint family system,* which means that the family cares for and attends to its elderly members at home. (See the sidebar "The joint family system: The more, the merrier!" in this chapter.)

Treating all life as sacred

Hindus grow up learning that any and every living being is part of creation, and all creatures share a certain mutual dependency. This value is clearly visible when you see Hindus offer worship (and/or showing respect) to trees, crops during harvest, monkeys, cattle, and even snakes.

Revering Bharat Mata (Mother India)

When the Pope arrives in another country, the first thing he does is kiss the ground. With this gesture, he shows respect for the host country. From a Hindu's viewpoint, this act is a familiar and fitting show of respect for Mother Earth. The feeling of connection between humans and the earth seems natural.

Hindus have a deity known as *Bhudevi* (Goddess Earth).They offer a prayer ("forgive me for stepping on you") begging her forgiveness. Before beginning any sort of construction, Hindus do a *bhumi puja* (worship of the earth) on the land. Before plowing a field, they offer prayers to Mother Earth. This reverence for the earth extends to identifying the entire country as a goddess: *Bharat Mata*, or Mother India.

Such connection and identification with the entire nation took firm hold during India's independence movement in the late nineteenth century into the twentieth century. During this movement, a poem known as *Vande Mataram* ("I Salute the Mother") by Bankim Chandra Chatterjee (1838–1894) became very popular and inspired thousands of young men and women to embrace the cause. In this poem, the country is visualized as goddess Durga (a symbol of female power). The song almost became the national anthem except for the compromise made by Hindu leaders to accommodate the sentiments of Indian Muslims in regard to idol worship implied in the poem. Nevertheless, the first two stanzas of the poem continue to be sung and used on some occasions because of the meaning and the beauty of the music to which it is set:

I bow to you Mother enriched with bountiful waters, bountiful fruits, cool winds, and great harvests. Rejoicing in the glory of moonlight, the whole country adorned with the beauty of trees and flowers, great sounds of laughter and pleasant speech — the Mother bestowing bliss (on the land and its people).

The implied belief is that an ecological balance is mandated and gratitude needs to be shown to preserve such balance through respect and/or worship. By specifying vehicles to gods and goddesses such as the eagle (Garuda) for Vishnu, a bull (Nandi) for Shiva, and a mouse for Ganesha, Hindus demonstrate the concept of acknowledging that all life is indeed sacred.

Chapter 4

Major Hindu Denominations

In This Chapter
▶ Reviewing the four major Hindu denominations
▶ Examining their core beliefs and practices
▶ Returning to the One

*H*indu denominations resemble, to a large extent, denominations in Christianity, Judaism, and other religions. That is, they are distinct communities of believers within the larger religious tradition. But differences are significant, complicated, and even confusing to an outsider. Whereas the denominations in, for example, Christianity differ (even vehemently) on how to interpret the Bible, what rituals to follow, or how to attain salvation (good works versus belief), they still all agree that God is God and Jesus is his son.

While all Hindu denominations agree that there is only one Supreme Being (Brahman) and acknowledge the Hindu Trinity (Brahma, Vishnu, and Shiva), they each prefer to believe that their own chosen deity, be it Vishnu (or one of his many forms) or Shiva or Shakti, embodies all the cosmic functions of creation, sustenance, and dissolution. Other differences, such as the individual's approach to worship and the relationship between the individual soul and the supreme soul, also play a major role.

In this chapter, I explain what led to the development of different Hindu denominations and also discuss their subsects.

The Origin of Hindu Denominations

As I explain in Chapter 1, Hinduism is based in the Vedas: eternal, sacred scriptures that were revealed to the sages and that outline the spiritual laws that Hindus follow — specifically the rules regarding how rituals and sacrifices are to be conducted. Early Hindus worshipped forces of nature, such as Surya (or Soorya), the sun; Indra, god of rain and thunder; Vayu, the wind god; and Agni, god of fire. The Rig Veda, the earliest known religious document (or *extant* scripture; see Chapter 2), is full of hymns of praise for these gods. (The Vedas are explained in detail in Chapter 10.)

Yet Hinduism proclaimed early its openness in allowing and welcoming different approaches to salvation. Therefore, it wasn't surprising that religious thinkers developed different schools of thought and choices of worship. These post-Vedic ideas sought alternate, more personal objects of worship in addition to (or instead of) the Vedic approach of rituals and sacrifices aimed at natural forces.

All these ideas and preferences served as the foundation of Hindu denominational thinking. Over time, in the post-Vedic era (500 BCE to 500 CE), and based on these choices, Hindus developed four major denominations, some with their own subdivisions:

- Vaishnavism (followers of Vishnu)
- Shaivism (followers of Shiva)
- Smartism (worship of Vishnu, Shiva, Ganesha, Surya, and Devi)
- Shaktism (worship of Devi, female power)

Note: The terms *Shaivite* and *Shaiva* are interchangeable; both words refer to someone who is affiliated with Shaivism. Similarly, the terms *Vaishnavite* and *Vaishnava* are interchangeable; they refer to followers of Vaishnavism.

Figure 4-1 shows the various denominations and their subsects.

All these denominations subscribe to the broad basic beliefs and principles of Hinduism, as I outline in Chapter 3; each denomination essentially accepts the authority of the Vedas. In addition, all four of these denominations emphasize devotion to *their* chosen deity as an essential requirement. Vaishnavism, Shaivism, and Shaktism each adhere to the strong belief that their god/goddess alone is the Supreme Being totally in charge of all the three primary functions: creation, protection, and destruction. Smartism, on the other hand, is more liberal and is based on *smrti* ("remembered") scriptures: the Puranas, epics, and myths. Smartas worship, in addition to Vishnu and Shiva, other deities: Ganesha, Surya, and Devi.

Vaishnavism, Shaivism, Smartism, and Shaktism have all developed their own literature and detailed procedures to guide devotees on a variety of worship services along with the mantras associated with each. Sophisticated devotional poetry describes in touching terms the typical loving relationship between the devotee and godhead, akin to that between lovers, with the pain of separation clearly spelled out.

The primary difference between Vaishnavites and Shaivites is in their approach to attaining salvation. Shaivites emphasize knowledge as the path to salvation, while Vaishnavites emphasize love of God and surrender to God as the path to salvation. The key word is "emphasize" because Shaivites also display love of their god, and Vaishnavites seek knowledge, too. It is most certainly *not* an either/or situation. This basic difference in emphasis, over time, led to choices of particular godheads by each denomination, and each denomination developed its own approaches and corresponding rituals to worship. These preferences created clear and unmistakable distinctions. Divisions and subdivisions within each of these main denominations have added further to the complexity. On the whole these divisions are accepted and tolerated much the same way you would find Catholics and Protestants each observing their chosen paths without any hindrance from the other. Hindus tend to simply accept these choices and continue with a remarkably detached outlook.

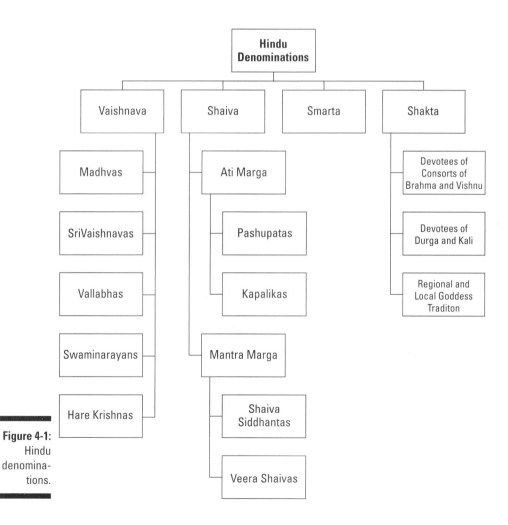

Figure 4-1:
Hindu
denomina-
tions.

In addition to the denominations and subdenominations that are presented next, a great variety of monks, saints, and *sadhus* (pious men or renunciates), over centuries, have developed their own ways of worship through simple community-based gatherings, prayers, and devotional songs. These highly localized efforts are popular, provide a sense of togetherness, and lead their audiences to a state of joy and exaltation.

Following Vishnu: The Vaishnavas

Vaishnavas are Hindus who worship Vishnu and his incarnations, principally the avatars Krishna and Rama. (An *avatar* is a physical manifestation of the godhead; see Chapter 8.) They may also worship other gods, including, for example, a deity known as Satyanarayana, who is believed to be a combination of the Hindu Trinity (Brahma, Vishnu, and Shiva). In addition, Vaishnavas worship the female consorts of Vishnu, including Lakshmi, goddess of wealth and wellbeing; Bhu Devi, the earth goddess; Sita, wife of Rama; and Radha, beloved of Krishna.

For Vaishnavas, salvation means that upon death of the body, the individual soul arrives at Vishnu's heaven called *Vaikunta.* In Vaikunta the soul is united with the Supreme Soul — Vishnu himself — even as it retains its own individuality. This assumes that the individual has lived a meritorious life deserving of such a union. According to Vaishnavas, the individual soul does not *merge* into the soul of the almighty; it *unites* — a subtle difference you will note when (in Chapter 20) I discuss the philosophies developed by the saints who established each of these denominations.

In this section, I outline the worship traditions of the Vaishnavas, as well as the various subsects of this denomination.

Worship traditions

The distinctive mark of Vaishnavas is what orthodox men may wear daily on their foreheads after morning *ablutions* (ritual cleansing): Three vertical lines, two white and one red, that are drawn on the forehead (see Figure 4-2). These lines are known as *Nama.* The red center line is known as *Sricharanam,* a symbol of the goddess Lakshmi. The outer lines represent the feet of Vishnu. The marks you see in Figure 4-2 are the type worn by a Tengalai SriVaishnava, a subsect of Vaishnavas. These marks are applied on 11 other places on the upper body and both arms; it's quite a sight to see. (Women and non-orthodox Vaishnavas don't wear these marks, although they may wear only the central red mark during religious events.)

Figure 4-2:
The mark worn by orthodox Tengalai SriVaishnava men.

Vaishnavas are known to install intricately carved sculptures (typically stone) of the deities, decorate them lavishly with colorful clothing and flowers, and perform elaborate 16-part ceremonies of worship (called *Shodasha Upacharas;* see Chapter 15) offering a variety of cooked foods, fruits, and so on.

Vaishnava subsects

Vaishnavas are further divided into subsects, which differ in philosophy pertaining to the relationship between the individual soul and the Supreme Soul, worship different forms of Vishnu, and look to different sacred scriptures for guidance. In this section, I introduce you to all the major Vaishnava subsects.

Your eyes may start to cross as you read this material — the distinctions among these groups of Hindus can be tough to keep straight! If you can come away from this section with just a sense of how one underlying belief (in the worship of Vishnu) can manifest in myriad forms of worship and philosophies, your reading will be rewarded.

The Madhvas

The Madhvas are named after their spiritual leader, Madhvacharya, who lived around 1200 CE. Madhvacharya was a proponent of Dwaita philosophy (Dualism), which maintains that an individual soul is distinct from the Supreme Soul. (The philosophy of Nondualism makes no distinction between the individual soul and Supreme Soul. I explain Dualism and Nondualism in much more detail in Chapters 9 and 20.)

Subsects based on Krishna worship

A form of Vishnu that plays an important role in Vaishnavism is Krishna, an avatar of Vishnu — especially his portrayal as a playful cowherd adored by local milkmaids. Krishna's flute-playing attracts young women, and he enchants them with songs and pranks that would make lovers today blush. Such intense interaction between the lovers is interpreted as divine love, not erotic love, and was portrayed in an extraordinarily beautiful and sophisticated poem called the *Gita Govinda* composed by Jayadeva in the twelfth century CE. The poem evokes the joy of lovers being together, as well as the pain of their separation. You can read more by looking for a copy of *Song of Love: The Gita Govinda,* translated by George Keyt.

The Hare Krishnas

A Hindu saint named Chaitanya (1486–1533) established the subsect known as the Gaudiya Vaishnavism of Bengal. Chaitanya was regarded by his followers as an incarnation of both Krishna and his beloved, Radha. Followers of Chaitanya viewed the love they shared with the Lord as mirroring the love between Krishna and Radha. The result was an expression of love for the Lord that bordered on infatuation, which was evident in worshipful prayers and dances performed at temples and on street corners.

Today, Chaitanya's followers head the Hare Krishna, or the International Society for Krishna Consciousness. The West became aware of this subsect during the 1970s, when saffron-clad young men with shaven heads began collecting money for Krishna at U.S. airports. Dedicated to a *semimonastic* (somewhat cloistered) lifestyle, this group has built beautiful temples worldwide and practices the intricacies of Vaishnavite rituals with devotion and grand style.

The Vallabhas

Another noteworthy movement that also focused on Krishna worship was founded by the intellectual Vallabhacharya (1479–1531). His approach to the worship of Krishna does not call for any self-denial or practices such as, for example, fasting. The approach is obviously a bit easier for the average person to follow, and it maintains that this world is not illusory but real. Scholars have described this approach as the way of enjoyment that occasionally has led to irreligious and corrupt tendencies.

The Swaminarayans

Under the leadership of Swaminarayan (1781–1830), another movement emerged that was somewhat corrective in nature to the Vallabha movement; it encouraged a more puritanical approach to worship. With an emphasis on *asceticism* (rigorously abstaining from self-indulgence and being fully absorbed in meditation and worship), Swaminarayan claimed that he, not Vallabhacharya, was the true incarnation of Krishna, and he attracted a large following.

Centered mainly in the state of Gujarat in western India, the movement now is a popular organization whose tight-knit followers build huge temples around the world with guidance from their current head and guru Pramukh Swami Maharaj.

The SriVaishnavas

Vaishnavas who owe allegiance to the eleventh-century Hindu saint named Ramanujacharya are known as SriVaishnavas. They worship Vishnu and his different incarnations. Ramanujacharya advocated the Vedantic philosophy of *Qualified Monism*: the belief that Brahman has attributes, a major departure from Shankaracharya's thesis of Nondualism and Brahman with absolutely *no* attributes (see Chapter 20).

Ramanujacharya made no distinction among different castes. (I outline the Hindu caste system in Chapter 5.) In fact, he sought the help of his disciple Pillan, a shudra (fourth in the hierarchy of castes), to have an authoritative commentary written on a sacred scripture in praise of Vishnu known as *Tiruvaymoli,* which combines Tamil and Sanskrit. (Tamil is the language of the southern India state of Tamilnadu.) Including a nonbrahmin in an intellectual task was an extraordinary step a thousand years ago!

The Ranganathaswamy temple at Srirangam in the state of Tamilnadu in South India is the origin and center of this sect. The Sri Ranganatha Temple in Pamona, New York (`www.ranganatha.org`) replicates the original temple at Srirangam and diplays the principal emblems and symbols of the SriVaishnava tradition.

Divisions based on paths to salvation

After the death of Ramanujacharya in the twelfth century CE, SriVaishnavas considered and debated the concept of surrender to the almighty stated in the Gita:

> *Abandon all duties and surrender to me.*
> *I shall absolve you of all sins. Fear not.*

Bhagavad Gita, Chapter XVIII, Verse 66

This verse, which seems to provide a direct approach to salvation, has been a subject of interpretation by scholars over centuries. Does surrender imply no effort on the part of the devotee? Is that even possible? The debate led to two schools of thought:

- **The Cat School:** This school concluded that surrender to the Lord is total and requires no effort on the devotee's part. Everything depends on God's grace, and all a devotee needs to do is simply put faith in it. This school is also called the Southern School and is known as *Tengalai* (meaning southern).

Southern refers to the town of Srirangam in Tamil Nadu, which is south of the town of Kanchipuram where the school known as *Vadagalai* developed. The Tengalai and Vadagalai classification is unique to SriVaishnava brahmins known as *Iyengars,* most of whom live in the Indian states of Tamil Nadu and Karnataka. (See the next section.) The corresponding sect in Shaivite brahmins is known as *Iyers.*

✔ **The Monkey School:** Also dubbed the Northern School, this school believes that effort on the part of the devotee is a prerequisite for obtaining the Lord's grace.

Why name these schools of thought after cats and monkeys? Consider the way kittens and baby monkeys are transported by their mothers. A kitten is picked up by its mother. As the kitten lies limp in her mouth and trusts her totally, all is well — no effort on the kitten's part! The baby monkey, on the other hand, clings tightly to its mother as they both move along branches and trees. The baby monkey feels fear and must make considerable effort to reach other destinations safely.

Iyengars

Iyengar (or Ayyangar) is an important subsect of SriVaishnavas that came into vogue about ten centuries ago. In the Tamil language, the word *iyengar* refers to five duties. An orthodox Iyengar is required to undertake these five duties:

✔ Getting the marks of a conch and discus (symbols that appear on a Vishnu deity) branded on their shoulders by an *acharya* (religious head).

✔ Wearing the namam mark on the forehead (refer back to Figure 4-2) and 12 other locations on the upper body.

✔ Adding and using the adjective *dasan* as an ending to the last name. (*Dasan* means "servant" in Tamil, as in servant of the Lord.)

✔ Learning and chanting mantras used in a variety of Vaishnava worships.

✔ Performing a detailed worship every morning.

Being devotees of saint Ramanujacharya, Iyengars are followers of the Qualified Monism philosophy.

The branding ceremony takes place under the direction of an ordained acharya. Metallic emblems of a conch and disc are heated until red hot and are pressed on the top left side of the left arm (conch) and top right side of the right arm (discus) to make permanent impressions. This action qualifies as an initiation into the fold and is performed by authorized religious heads only. It serves to openly proclaim the individual's religious affiliation, and it denotes certain privileges and authority to perform formal rituals both at home and at temples.

Following Shiva: The Shaivas

The Shaivas or Shaivites are followers of the god Shiva. Their denomination is known as Shaivism. In this section, I touch on the broad spectrum of worship traditions within Shaivism, and I introduce you to the two primary subsects: Ati Marga and Mantra Marga.

Worship traditions

Shaivas vary in their worship practices according to the form of Shiva they revere: Shiva as Rudra (storm god), Shiva as Pashupati (lord of animals), Shiva in a ferocious form known as Bhairava, Shiva as an ascetic, or Shiva as one of the Hindu Trinity.

A note of caution is in order. As you read about the variety of sects and subsects within Shaivism, keep in mind that the practices described are confined to strict adherents of these subsect approaches. What do the large majority of Shaivite householders do? They go about their religious life by offering daily worship to Shiva, visiting a Shiva temple, fasting on days prescribed by their denomination, and taking part in a Shiva-oriented festival. Life for them is normal without any of the extremes you read about next.

Shiva worship has been continuous since prehistoric times. Its popularity increased starting around the first century CE as an alternative to more prescriptive approaches to Hinduism. Shaiva religious practices run the gamut from one extreme to another, from celibacy and total withdrawal to profane graveyard and Tantric cults. (*Tantric cults,* commonly understood to involve a combination of religion, astrology, spells, charms, and occult rites, emerged around the fifth century CE, centering around *Bhairava* [a ferocious version of Shiva] and *Bhairavi* [a ferocious form of Shakti]. These cults allowed for physical and sexual freedoms as ways of opening a path to self-awareness.)

For a Shaivite, salvation means that the soul, upon death of the body, arrives at the abode of Shiva called *Shivaloka.* Shivaloka is believed to be located on Mount Kailash in Tibet.

You can recognize orthodox Shaivites much the same way you do Vaishnavites: by the markings on the face (and arms and upper body as well). The difference is that Shaivite markings use three white horizontal lines drawn from left to right on the face using ash (see Figure 4-3). The markings are known as *Vibhooti* and are believed to represent the three qualities inherent in humans: Sattva (noble), Rajas (vibrant), and Tamas (inert).

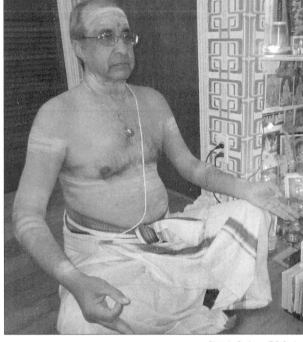

Figure 4-3:
Three broad, horizontal marks made from ash mark Shaivite men.

Photo by Professor T.S. Sankar

Shiva is often portrayed as a *lingam* — a stone pillar — or as Nataraja, the lord of dance, in a dancing stance (see Figure 4-4).

Figure 4-4:
Shiva in his dancing form, Nataraja.

Other deities included in Shaivite worship are his sons, Ganapati (also called Ganesha) and Murugan (who goes by many names).

Subsects of Shaivism

I now introduce you to two primary subsects of Shaivism within its broad umbrella. One of them is known as *Ati Marga* (extreme path) and originated at a time way, way back before the Vedic period. The second one, known as *Mantra Marga* (ritualistic path), developed later, past the Vedic period. Adherents to these practices are almost always men.

What do these two subsects have in common? Both paths revere the example of Shiva in his ascetic aspect: celibate, living away from civilization, eating very little, covered with ash, wearing animal skins as clothing, and in deep meditation.

What do the followers of these two approaches do that is different from each other and why? I begin with the first group.

The pre-Vedic approach: Ati Marga

I begin with the pre-Vedic Ati Marga subsect. Within this subsect there are branches known as *Pashupatas* and *Kapalikas.* Although both groups want to disassociate themselves from society, they differ in practice in how they go about it. In addition, there is a branch called Veera Shaivas or Lingayats. I introduce all three here.

Pashupatas

Pashupatas follow some deliberate (some may think almost outrageous) steps aimed primarily at disconnecting themselves from society. Their thinking is that, because the bonds between an individual and his family, caste, community, and society at large are strong, extraordinary efforts need to be made to cut them. These extraordinary efforts involve inappropriate laughter, singing or dancing uncontrollably, making uncalled-for advances toward women, taunting others, speaking incoherently, and so on.

Pashupatas appear to perform these acts with a passion, and the objective is accomplished when persons exposed to their pranks gladly withdraw. Mission accomplished! Links are destroyed. Freed thus, the Pashupata can now resort to austerities through Yogic practices with the hope of acquiring magical powers (such as immunity from heat and cold and from extreme pain inflicted on the body) on the path to union with Shiva.

These practitioners have been seen in and around the famous pilgrimage center Kashi (in the holy city of Benares in North India), where Shiva is worshipped 24/7. Here they practice what appear to be strange austerities such as gazing on the sun, standing on one leg for months and years, and lying on beds of nails. These recluses have helped fill pages in *Ripley's Believe It or Not* and in travelers' tales of the mystic East.

Kapalikas

Shaivites who embrace this approach live on the edge of society, naked and covered with ash, observing asceticism on cremation grounds. They carry a staff with a skull attached to the top and a begging bowl made of a human skull. To please their deities (Shiva in the form of Bhairava and his equally ferocious consort Bhairavi), they worship them with blood and offerings of meat, alcohol, and bodily fluids obtained through ritual lovemaking. This subsect has all but vanished in India except in the city of Benares.

Veera Shaivas or Lingayats

The Lingayats are Shaivaites who worship Shiva in the form of a *lingam,* a stone pillar. They wear a metal replica of the pillar as an amulet around the neck. They generally reject caste distinctions and accept women as equals.

The post-Vedic approach: Mantra Marga

The post-Vedic approach, called Mantra Marga, is a branch of Shaiva philosophy and lifestyle generally practiced by South Indian and Sri Lankan Shaivite Hindus. It started as ritual-based worship, and the emphasis shifted to devotional *(bhakti)* approach, similar to that of the Vaishnavas.

Shaiva Siddhanta philosophy, which is part of Mantra Marga, is *Dualistic:* It makes a distinction between the individual soul and the Supreme Soul (see Chapter 20). The adherents follow an intense three-fold daily practice through methods that include the following:

- ✔ Purifying the body with total commitment to a spiritual path.

- ✔ Seeking divine energy in the body through such rigorous yogic practices as Kundalini Yoga. This is a rigorous and very powerful form of yoga which, through intense practice under guidance from a competent teacher, allows the life force within the body to move up the spine. In the process, the aspirant may obtain some magical powers. (See Chapter 21 for details.)

- ✔ Awakening the soul with one's own intellect, breath control, and visualization of Shiva's trident.

Like the Vaishnava *alwars* (poet-saints), Shaiva saints known as *nayanars* created stirring Tamil poetry attracting a large following. The best example of a Shaiva Siddhanta center in the United States today is the Kauai monastery in Hawaii.

Integrating Vaishnava and Shaiva Ideas: The Smartas

Smartas are brahmins who follow *smrti* texts: post-Vedic scriptures that are considered to be "remembered" (as opposed to *shrutis,* which are considered "revealed" or "seen"). Smartas have special interest in adhering strictly to the concepts of dharma (see Chapter 1). This denomination successfully integrates the ideas contained in the Vedas with those of the post-Vedic literature (texts that came later than the Vedas), bridging Vaishnavism and Shaivism.

Smartas worship five gods and goddesses: Ganesha (Ganapati), Durga, Surya, Shiva, and an avatar of Vishnu (of the devotee's preference). The worship traditions largely resemble those of the Vaishnava sect. The followers believe that the individual soul aspires to merge into Shiva as a river merges into the ocean.

The followers of Smarta tradition generally adhere to beliefs propounded by the renowned Adi Shankara (788–820 CE), an *acharya* (religious guide) known for his *Advaita* (Nondualism) philosophy, which makes no distinction between the individual soul and the Supreme Soul (see Chapter 20).

Worshipping Devi, the Female Power: Shaktas

A unique feature of Hinduism is that the adherents worship both gods and goddesses. Hindus whose main worship is directed to a goddess are called *Shaktas.* The word *Devi* is a generic term for the goddess, although the same word is used as an ending to the name of any goddess: For example, *Lakshmi Devi* means the goddess Lakshmi. Two forms of Devi predominate in these worships, and I introduce them here.

In one approach, Hindus revere the concept of Mother and the associated love and compassion. They recognize the female partner of any male godhead as the creative aspect of (and support of) her consort, be it Brahma, Vishnu, or Shiva. Examples of this form of Devi are the goddesses Mahalakshmi, Saraswati, Sita, Radha, and a host of others who are worshipped by millions of Hindus around the world. Earth is worshipped as Bhumi Mata, Mother Earth.

In the other (even more common) approach, Devi is associated with awesome strength and power in her own right. She is recognized most often in this aspect as the goddesses Durga or Kali.

Both these aspects of Devi — motherly and powerful — represent to the Shaktas all that is beautiful, fearful, and awe-inspiring in nature and the universe.

Ritual worship of goddesses such as Lakshmi and Saraswati includes a ceremonial offering of clothing, ornaments, sanctified water, fruit, flowers, incense, and food. This is also true of the public worship of Durga in her benign aspect. However, worship of other forms of Shakta goddesses (either

Devi or many regional and village patroness goddesses) may include offerings of sacrificial animals.

Returning to the One

All these denominational divisions, subdivisions, and sub-subdivisions — as well as the multiple theological systems and practices that arise from them — get so complicated, interconnected, and thoroughly mangled/tangled that you may be tempted to throw up your hands and entirely abandon the attempt to understand. Well, you wouldn't be the first!

Sir Monier Monier-Williams, a nineteenth-century British scholar and expert on Sanskrit and Hinduism (see Chapter 2), likened the complexity of Hinduism to a fig tree. He said:

> *It is a creed based on an original, simple, pantheistic doctrine, but branching out into an endless variety of polytheistic superstitions. Like the sacred fig-tree of India, which from a single stem sends out numerous branches destined to send roots to the ground and become trees themselves, till the parent stock is lost in a dense forest of its own offshoots, so has this pantheistic creed rooted itself firmly in the Hindu mind, and spread its ramifications so luxuriantly that the simplicity of its root-dogma is lost in an exuberant outgrowth of monstrous mythology.*

True. But the thing you need to remember is that, behind all the variations, the fundamentals are always in the background and remain the same.

So despite all these denominations, subsects, and sub-subsects, the "root-dogma" is not quite lost. How else can we explain the simple prayer offered during worship by Hindus irrespective of what god or goddess is the object of worship?

> *You alone are our mother and father*
> *You alone are our sibling and friend*
> *You alone are our knowledge and prosperity*
> *You alone are everything to us*
> *My Lord, my Lord*

So there you are: back to *The One!*

Chapter 5

The Structure of Hindu Society

*T*he caste system: Everybody has heard of it — especially people in the West. They tend to shake their heads in disbelief, and why not? No one, anywhere, can defend any system that directly or indirectly led to centuries of discrimination against human beings. Not only is such discrimination illegal in civil societies, but it's also unethical and immoral in a social or theological context.

In India, the caste system began as a way to fulfill all of society's needs. Inspired by the verses in the Rig Veda and the Bhagavad Gita, its intent was to create a balanced and, therefore, ideal community. Yet the introduction of hierarchy and subsequent scramble for hereditary power made caste distinctions rigid and restricted mobility between castes.

In this chapter, I examine the origin of the caste system, its original intent (which, believe it or not, wasn't a bad idea), its development over the centuries, and its status today in the world of Hindus.

Looking at the Caste System's Origins

All societies have some sort of system in which people are classified based on education, culture, and income levels. In the West, this system is seen in terms of *lower class, middle class,* and *upper class.* Even so-called *classless* societies (for example, communist nations) have class divisions, though their governments may deny it and claim that everyone there is equal.

Caste versus class: What's the difference?

As it turns out, not much. The word *caste* originates from the Portugese word *casta,* which translates as "class"! So the real difference between *class* and *caste* is mainly one of perception. The word "class" is simply more palatable to those who look askance at the same type of system when it's called a "caste" system. In other words, the word "class" doesn't have the stigma associated with it that the word "caste" does.

Of course, semantics don't make a bit of difference to those on the receiving end of discrimination. Bottom line: Whether you call it caste or class, any system that promotes the oppression of entire groups of people is unacceptable.

In India, these divisions didn't just occur spontaneously. They were inspired by the Hindu scriptures and were implemented as a way to create a society in which all the needs of the community were addressed and all people assumed roles vital to the life of a community in an equitable manner. In this section, I give you an overview of the system as it was intended.

The source of the concept: The Bhagavad Gita

The scriptural basis for the Hindu societal structure — the Bhagavad Gita — points to societal functions and associated qualities. Lord Krishna proclaimed the structure in Verse 13 of Chapter IV:

> *I have created a fourfold system in order to distinguish among one's qualities and functions.*

In their discussions of the caste system, Hindus refer to this verse to indicate a god-mandated social order. This passage is the often quoted source of the concept.

The participants in this social structure are distinguished by their individual qualities, as well as the functions they take on. The four functions and corresponding identities were broadly defined as

✔ Spiritual/priestly

✔ Warrior

✔ Trade and agriculture

✔ Manual labor

But as time passed, the functional classification began to be associated with the word *caste,* and Hindus began thinking in terms of *upper* and *lower castes.* That shift in thinking (and speech) was the beginning of a problem that has remained for centuries. When the "upper" castes declared menial tasks (such as cleaning toilets, sweeping streets, tanning leather, and dealing with meat products) "impure," it only got worse. And a new class came into being: the untouchables, the lowest of the low. What began as a benign concept was corrupted by human intervention, interpreted with a twist, and the situation continued to deteriorate from there.

The Sanskrit word used to describe the caste system is *varna,* whose literal meaning is "color"; it is interpreted to mean categorizing functions and/or groups.

Seeing the original purpose of the system

Any civilized society defines itself and makes its mark on the rest of the world by how well it performs in the areas that impact the quality of life for its citizens: areas such as manufacturing, trade, commerce, education, agriculture, infrastructure, and health. The wellbeing of its people depends on the skills they possess to maintain and improve their standard of living. In addition, the moral standing of a nation needs to be on par with its material wealth so it can be respected as a leader of the family of nations.

With this background, I look upon Lord Krishna's proclamation regarding a societal structure as an expression of the need for extraordinary skills. By matching task and talent at all levels, an efficient system is created. Ancient societies defined these tasks much the same way we do now.

Based on the passage quoted in the previous section from the Gita, ancient Hindus defined four functions essential for any successful society. Agriculture, defense, and trade and commerce comprised the first three essential tasks. The fourth function emphasized the need for a nation's spiritual prowess to match its physical prowess. Who should perform these functions? The Hindu answer was that those whose inherent skills matched the task should perform each function; in that way, each person could earn a livelihood and contribute to society's wellbeing. That was the original purpose of the varna system.

In explaining the varnas further, Lord Krishna refers to the four functions as duties to be performed by persons with appropriate qualities *inherent to their nature.* He then names the four groups. Following is the passage in question, Verse 41, Chapter XVIII of the Gita. The words in parenthesis are mine.

> *The duties of Brahmanas (priestly class), Kshatriyas (warrior class) and Vaishyas (trade and commerce class) as also Shudras (agricultural and manual labor class), are distributed according to the Gunas (qualities) born of their own nature.*

Each group is thus charged to perform a role in society in a way that reflects its own qualifications and strengths.

The caste system is both simple and complicated. The rest of this chapter explains its complications. But in what way is the system simple? It's simple if you view the duties prescribed in the Gita as shared responsibilities that each person undertakes depending entirely on his/her own skill levels. It requires an extraordinary objectivity to focus only on one's own task and pay no attention to any other function — very hard to do. But the success of the system depends on total commitment to the role accepted. Keep in mind that the Gita does not restrict movement among groups (assuming, of course, that the individual develops the appropriate qualities to perform another task and prefers to make the shift). Only when humans got their hands on the system did birth become the criterion to determine caste. (Keep reading to find out more.)

Introducing hierarchy into the system

The Bhagavad Gita is not the only scriptural reference to the caste system. The Rig Veda (see Chapter 10) also refers to the four castes (brahmin, kshatriya, vaishya, and shudra) when describing the infinite embodied spirit — the Supreme Self, called Purusha. The Rig Veda states that the brahmin was his face (head; thought center), the kshatriya was his arms (power of protection), the vaishya was his thighs (power of acquisition and distribution), and the shudra issued from his feet (power of support and movement).

The Rig Veda's description associating different parts of Purusha to the different groups is open to interpretation. A positive interpretation would be to accept that no part of a body is inferior to any other part: Each has a clear and distinct function. Successful functioning of the body demands that all parts perform their assigned functions efficiently and harmoniously. A negative interpretation is that the placement of shudra at the feet and brahmin at the head somehow dictates hierarchy, with the brahmin caste being the highest and shudra being the lowest. I discuss the implications of this interpretation in the upcoming section "The Great Confusion about Castes."

Defining the Main Castes and Subcastes

In this section, I explore each of the four main castes by discussing the qualities associated with the people fulfilling each duty. (Chapter XVIII, verses 42, 43, and 44 of the Gita define these qualities.) I also examine the practical function of each caste within Hindu society.

Although the Gita prescribes four societal groups, some Hindus speak of just two classifications: brahmins and non-brahmins. The non-brahmins are the other three castes. But in truth, the caste system is much more complex than two or even four classifications. Each caste has its own subcastes, perhaps numbering in the hundreds. This extraordinary layered arrangement has lasted for centuries, and I briefly touch on its complexities in this section.

Brahmin: The priestly/intellectual class

Serenity, self-restraint, purity, forgiveness, uprightness, knowledge, realization, and belief in God are among the essential requirements to take on the role of brahmin.

The associated "job description" is that the individual serves as a gatekeeper of knowledge of Brahman, provides intellectual advice to governing bodies, and offers priestly services and religious leadership. In addition, any society needs people who can grapple with the fundamental questions of life, such as Who are we? Why are we here? What is our role in society? What is our connection with the Supreme Being? What is the Truth?

The particular group of people who specialize in such inquiries, who search for truth, who have the training to judge issues with logic and without emotion, and who base their conclusions on experience are defined as brahmins.

Kshatriyas: The warrior class

The requisite talents for kshatriyas are physical prowess, courage, splendor, firmness, dexterity, determination not to flee from battle, generosity, and lordliness. The associated function is to provide defense-related services to protect the country from external aggression or internal strife. This group needs to specialize in the science of arms, ammunition, strategies, tactics of warfare, and so on.

Vaishyas: The trade/commerce class

The vaishyas are people who specialize in trade and commerce in order to procure goods and services so that the society as a whole can lead a life of plenty and enjoy the good life. Modern-day vaishyas are primarily traders and entrepreneurs.

Shudras: The agricultural/labor class

A society needs a group of people to offer manual labor services such as tilling the land, working in the fields, raising cattle, and growing crops to feed the society. The shudras perform this function. I need to point out that while manual labor defines the shudra caste in concept, in practice this caste include everyone not belonging to the other three castes, except for the untouchables (people performing the most menial labor, such as sweeping streets and tanning leather).

Craftsmen of all sorts (smiths, tailors, barbers, launderers, and the like) are identified with their trade name for the caste and may choose not to identify themselves as shudras. Their affiliations are with profession-based subcastes in the non-brahmin category, as I explain in the next section.

Subcastes and sub-subcastes: The jatis

Each of the four castes has developed its own divisions and subdivisions. These subgroupings, sometimes called *jatis* (pronounced *jaa-thees*), are based on people's trade, location, occupation, and/or area of expertise. *Jati* also refers to birth. Thus the association of caste with birth/heredity came about. Here are just a few examples:

Would you like to be a brahmin?

Why not? No one can prevent you. What does it really take to be a brahmin if one wishes to do so? That question was put to the warrior Yudhishtira by the *Yaksha* (a nature spirit) in a famous episode in the epic the *Mahabharata*. When asked how one becomes a brahmin — whether it is by birth, character, the study of the Vedas, or education — Yudhishtira replies, "It is neither birth nor education, nor even the study of the Vedas. *Without doubt*, it is character alone that marks a Brahmin." (The italic is mine.)

Yudhishthira's answer is crisp, clear, and unambiguous: *Vritta* (character) alone determines a brahmin. What is Yudhishthira's definition of a brahmin's character? "He is known as a Brahmin . . . in whom truthfulness, liberality, patience, deportment, mildness, self control, and compassion are found." This long list of attributes may be looked upon as components of character.

More recently, in the twentieth century, Swami Vivekananda declared that "Our ideal is the Brahmin of the spiritual culture and renunciation . . . I mean the Brahmin ideal-ness in which worldliness is altogether absent and true wisdom is abundantly present. That is the ideal of the Hindu race."

Do you still want to be a brahmin?!

✔ **Subcastes based on location:** Many such subcastes exist. Here are just two of them.

- *Gujarati brahmins:* Brahmins from the state of Gujarat who have 84 subcastes of their own and are not normally allowed to intermarry!

- *Kanuj brahmins:* Brahmins from a city called Kanyakubja, who are divided further into more than 150 sub-subcastes!

✔ **Subcastes based on trade:** These subcastes identify themselves simply as "nonbrahmin" (rather than affiliating with a specific caste). Again, I offer just a few examples of the many that exist.

- *Kayastha:* The writer caste, which has 12 further divisions

- *Barhai:* The carpenter trade, which has 7 divisions

- *Khatris*: Shopkeepers and dealers in cloth, silk, and so on

✔ **Subcastes based on line of study:** Some Hindus' last names are the names of these brahmin subcastes (to emphasize their affiliations).

- *Rigvedi:* Expert in Rig Veda

- *Yajurvedi:* Expert in Yajurveda

- *Dvivedi:* Expert in two Vedas

- *Trivedi:* Expert in three Vedas

- *Chaturvedi:* Expert in all four Vedas

✔ **Subcastes based on occupation:** Like the tradesmen, members of these subcastes identify themselves with their pursuits and may or may not identify themselves as brahmins. Here are just three examples.

- *Jyotisha:* Astronomer/astrologer

- *Pauranika:* One who recites puranas

- *Ojha:* Exorciser of demons

The Great Confusion about Castes

Beginning with the simple concept of a four-fold functional responsibility/divide, the social system referenced in the Bhagavad Gita deteriorated to a system of upper and lower castes. An additional blow was delivered with the association of caste with birth and function *(jati),* leading to hundreds of subcastes.

In this section, I explain why the caste system evolved from a fairly sophisticated approach to addressing how to create the optimal community to a system that built rigid boundaries.

Mistake 1: One class is superior to another

The original intent and classification of the different varnas must have sounded logical and worked well — until a compilation of what became known as the "laws of Manu" *(Manava Dharma Shastra)* around the fifth century BCE. (According to legend, Manu was the first man and a great sage, but there is no agreement among scholars regarding when he lived.) This Manava Dharma Shastra became the basic law book for Hinduism up to the twentieth century. (Indian civil law has amended a number of Manu's constraints, such as inter-caste marriage and widow remarriage.)

Popularly referred to as *Manu Smrti*, this manual prescribes hard and fast rules about the Hindu code of life. Two rules in particular are the most problematic:

- ✔ In the tenth chapter of his book, Manu says explicitly that a brahmin who meets high standards of scholarship, practices codes of right conduct, and excels culturally is superior to people of other castes.

- ✔ Manu's doctrine forbids mobility among the four castes. In other words, the caste you're born into is the caste you're stuck in.

Manu's "laws" dealt a severe blow to the original intent of the social order, and it was downhill from there! This view lent credence to claims that the castes were not equal, and a hierarchy was conceived in which brahmins were considered the highest caste, followed by kshatriyas, then the vaishyas, and last the shudras. Also, keep in mind that each caste also has its own hierarchy of subcastes! The idea of hierarchy caught on, and the original intent of the caste system was lost.

Even though mobility between functions was restricted, under certain circumstances Manu allowed downward mobility to brahmins so that they could become soldiers, farmers, and so on. Such pandering to the so-called "upper" caste provided ammunition to those opposed to a social order meant to be centered on responsibility/functionality. The idea of function was thus abandoned in favor of class.

To add insult to injury, the group of people who undertook tasks of cleaning, tanning leather, sweeping streets, and so on were dubbed *untouchables,* and the rest is history.

Gandhi's definition of the lowest caste: God's people

Mahatma Gandhi, who was a vaishya (not a brahmin), never condoned the caste system as practiced but was especially outraged by the way the so-called untouchables were treated. He proclaimed that everyone should call the lowest caste *Harijans* (God's people). He said that caste has nothing to do with religion in general and Hinduism in particular. Gandhi asserted that It is a sin to believe anyone else is inferior or superior to ourselves; we are all equal in the eyes of God. Commenting on untouchability, he said that it is the touch of sin that pollutes us, and never the touch of a human being. None are high and none are low for one who would devote his life to the service of others. The distinction between high and low is a blot on Hinduism which he maintained must therefore be obliterated.

Because of Gandhi's proactive involvement in eradicating caste barriers, patriots who worked closely with him during the Indian independence movement in the early twentieth century came from all castes. They walked with him, protested the British government with him, dined with him, and went to jail with him.

Mistake 2: Using the caste system to justify discrimination

When I was growing up in a village in South India, I was aware of the caste system in full force. For example, if a brahmin — any brahmin — were walking down a street and a shudra were coming in the opposite direction, the shudra would move to the side of the street and pause with a show of respect until the brahmin had passed. These displays of subservience were expected, and they were done; nobody thought anything of it. Looking back, I can now clearly imagine how the shudra must have felt.

One time, I observed a brahmin landlord summon a shudra whose responsibility it was to grow rice on a piece of the brahmin's wetland . One of the conditions of the agreement was that no phase of the work could begin without express permission of the landlord. In this instance, however, the shudra had harvested the crop without obtaining the brahmin's permission. When the landlord heard about it, he became furious — hence the summons. The individual shudra arrived with a group of his elders, and they all entered the compound of the landlord's residence. I cannot even now forget the scene of the landlord chasing the tenant around the courtyard and beating him with a stick while everyone sat on the floor and watched. It would appear the brahmin made the point as to who was the boss! Painful to watch and painful to recall — even after so many years. Fortunately, today such incidents are not likely to happen and, and if they did, the landlord would be in jail.

There are two important things to note about events like this:

- ✔ In this particular incident, the brahmin did not possess, even remotely, the qualities prescribed for that function (listed in the earlier section "Brahmin: The priestly/intellectual class"). This fact indicates that the underlying foundation of the caste system — that the function someone would perform was determined by innate qualities — had been perverted.

- ✔ Tolerating such atrocities resulted in complete distrust of the social order, which in turn led to legislation at federal and state levels to protect the "lower" castes. After India gained its independence from Britain in 1947, the new government introduced what was the equivalent of an affirmative action program, making considerable differences in the lives of non-brahmins. (I explore these programs in the next section.)

Figure 5-1 illustrates an example of the power structure of the bygone days between a brahmin and a shudra.

Figure 5-1:
A brahmin and his shudra servants.

© Margaret Bourke-White/Getty Images

The Caste System Today: Alive and Well — and Changing

As I write these words, India has been an independent nation for 60+ years, more than 1 billion people in the world are Hindu, and India is experiencing an economic boom due largely to outsourcing from the West. Given these facts, you would think major changes in the structure of Indian society would be underway. Hindus in India now enjoy largely improved lifestyles complete with modern appliances, better houses, shopping malls, gleaming cars, faster trains, more airplanes, more recreational facilities, fancy restaurants, fancier hotels, lavish weddings, more lavish parties, birthday bashes, and — would you believe it— Halloween! They are creating a near-perfect imitation of America, and yet the caste system simply won't go away.

In this section, I explore what steps have been taken in very recent history to combat the atrocities of the caste system and what issues remain to be addressed.

Passing laws to address the inequalities

When India won its independence from Britain in 1947, one of its first acts was to craft a constitution to reflect its guiding principles. Article 15(1) of the Indian Constitution (which came into effect in 1950) says that the "State shall not discriminate against any citizen on grounds only of religion, race, caste, sex, place of birth or any of them." And Article 15(4) stipulates that the State can make "special provision for the advancement of any socially and educationally backward classes of citizens or for the Scheduled Castes and the Scheduled Tribes." (Note that the term "backward classes" refers to non-brahmins, and "Scheduled Castes" refers to those lower than nonbrahmins in the caste hierarchy, such as untouchables.) From just these two examples, you can see that the leaders of the newly independent India took rapid steps to correct the caste system's atrocities.

An affirmative action program was instituted to allow opportunities to lower castes that before had simply been out of reach. For example, in the education arena, nonbrahmin students are now offered "reserved seats" that allow them to enroll in a college or university by meeting minimum standards. The same principle has been applied to filling state and federal government jobs. These protections apply, even more forcefully, to classes lower than the nonbrahmins, meaning the untouchables. In addition, nonbrahmins can seek public office in certain demographic constituencies reserved only for them, so they are guaranteed a voice in the government.

To the credit of the people of India, these programs have succeeded beyond expectation without a major civil conflict. And the society is better off for them. Nevertheless, some questions arise regarding whether these policies should continue, as the next section explains.

To continue the policy or not?

Because the number of available university seats and government jobs is limited, the result of India's affirmative action policies has been denying admission and/or employment to qualified candidates. This situation has led some people to call for the affirmative action policies to be discontinued.

Looking beyond caste

Representatives from every cross-section of India's society, irrespective of caste or class, joined together to bring their voices and talents to bear to achieve India's independence and construct the laws of the new republic. Here are just a few key examples:

✔ When India became a free republic in 1947, there was absolutely no resistance in electing nonbrahmin Dr. Rajendra Prasad (1884–1963) as the first president of independent India. His vice president was a brahmin: the philosopher-statesman Dr. Sarvepalli Radhakrishnan (1888–1975).

✔ Bhimrao Ramji Ambedkar (1891–1956), an untouchable, rose to prominence in independent India to become Law Minister and the architect of India's Constitution. With advanced degrees from Columbia University and London School of Economics, Ambedkar was a prolific writer who was extremely critical of the caste system.

✔ A vaishya, Kamaraj Nadar, Chief Minister of the state of Tamilnadu, was a fighter in India's independence movement and an influential politician in the Congress party. He was posthumously awarded the highest civilian honor, Bharata Ratna, by the Government of India in 1976.

On one hand, more and more communities are scrambling to get on the lists of subcastes that qualify for special consideration under these policies, so it would appear the need for the policies still exists. On the other hand, people argue that the policies themselves are discriminatory and should be abandoned.

Following are several milestones in this continuing debate:

✔ In 1979, the Indian government issued a report from the *Mandal Commission* (which studied the quota system mainly relating to reserved seats in government-aided colleges and government jobs). The report recommended that the number of reserved seats be increased from 27 to 49.5 percent.

✔ In 1990, a Delhi University student named Rajiv Goswami attempted self-immolation in protest against implementation of the Mandal Commission report.

✔ In 2008, the Supreme Court of India ruled that such reservations cannot exceed 50 percent. In response, several states ruled that they will pass their own legislations to alter that restriction of 50 percent.

Hunger strikes, attempts at self-immolation, legislative actions and inactions, protests, and more protests continue to keep the issue alive. (Even Indians' T-shirts join in the conversation, touting such declarations as "Merit is my caste, what is yours?" and "Quotas? The Cure Is Worse Than the Disease.")

Recognizing the reality of caste today

The reality is that the caste system — and the debate surrounding the policies issued in regard to it — won't just go away. The 5,000-year-old Indian culture refuses to give up caste in its private life even while it dances boldly with modernity in public. The responses to caste run the spectrum from honor killings to avenge inter-caste marriages to love marriages where caste considerations are thrown to the wind. However, in public life modern Hindus mix freely while, for example, traveling in public transportation systems, sitting in a classroom with other students, or standing in line to attend an event. If you were to attend a village council meeting, you would notice that the council members include men and women from different castes. A spirit of live and let live has emerged.

Fluidity among castes

However, even today, there is essentially no movement between castes. Considering the perception that the brahmin caste is superior, for example, you might think that people would rush from other castes to learn Sanskrit and the Vedas that could serve as a stepping stone toward becoming a priest. Yet that hasn't been the case. (Lack of interest is one reason, but another is economic: A priest's position may not produce enough income to enjoy a good standard of living.)

So the economic conditions rule, and society turns to the familiar. I give you two examples: When religious ceremonies need to be performed in a family (a variety of rituals from birth to death including, of course, a wedding), the overwhelming preference is to invite a priest, who is almost always a brahmin. In addition, the priests serving traditional temples are, with rare exception, all brahmins.

Holy matrimony: The caste-based choice of spouse

In India today, being socially connected with persons of other castes is acceptable in many circles. But when it comes to intimacy that may lead to matrimony, many families still confine themselves to others within their castes.

Not only can the family's opinions and preferences to adhere to one's own caste (and, in fact, subcaste) be overwhelming, but other important aspects of life also come into focus. Language — even a difference in dialect — can play a role in selecting a mate. Food habits almost always become a factor as well, because whether a family eats meat or not may be a big issue. (In some cases, even eating onion can be an issue.)

Nevertheless, some couples decide to marry outside of their own caste. As in any part of the world and any culture, love between two individuals can supersede any other considerations.

A quick peek into the matrimonial columns

Hundreds of websites are devoted to advertising available, eligible Indian men and women interested in meeting and learning about each other (sometimes with families involved in the discussions). These ads are popular both in India and abroad. An ad may specify everything but the name of the potential spouse being sought! For example, it may list the caste, subcaste, food habits, complexion, and so on of the mate being sought. At the other end of the spectrum, some ads simply declare "caste no bar," which means the seeker's preference includes all requirements listed and the mate's caste is not one of them.

Following are two fictional examples that represent typical ads:

Master's degree, youthful male, handsome, 45 years, fair complexion (wheatish), approaching six-figure income, willing to move, looking for a beautiful, fun-loving Hindu girl in her 30s. Caste no bar.

Parents of a handsome boy, 27, Master's degree in Engineering from America, looking for a slim, beautiful Brahmin girl (non-Koushika) from a noble family. Bio-data with horoscope may be emailed to urthe1@wedspace.com.

Caste no bar! This small but significant phrase may well be the flag of the future. The key has been education, which improves the economic status of individuals. Such upward mobility is consistent with the practice of Hinduism (as the contemporary surge in temple building in the West and the millions who converge on pilgrimage sites can testify).

Part II

The Hindu Pantheon and Its Religious Leaders

The 5th Wave   By Rich Tennant

THE PROBLEM WITH BEING RAISED IN THE SOUTH, AND THEN BECOMING A HINDU.

In this part . . .

How did *pantheism* (a belief that the universe as a whole is God) yield to *polytheism* (a belief in many — in the case of Hinduism, thousands of — gods)? In this part, I present how Hindus have been able to maintain both of these concepts simultaneously. I describe the sages and saints who were the beneficiaries of revealed knowledge conveyed through the oral tradition from one generation to the next for centuries. I also discuss the gradual transformation toward a personal god and respect for individual choice leading to the Hindu pantheon. I present a whole pageantry of gods, as well as the divine descents (avatars) of god Vishnu who came to restore and uphold dharma.

Chapter 6

Pantheism to Polytheism: From the One to the Very Many

*T*he one thing about Hinduism that most confuses, puzzles, and even annoys people from monotheistic religious traditions is the concept of multiple gods. How, they wonder, can there be more than one God? And why can't Hindus simply accept what half of the world believes in — a single God?

I want to begin this discussion by defining two key terms I use in this chapter:

- ✔ **Pantheism** identifies God with the universe. This is the Hindu's "One without a second" — Brahman, the Supreme Soul — and it includes everything and excludes nothing. This identification brings with it a reverence for all forms of life.

- ✔ **Polytheism** is belief in multiple gods or multiple personifications of God, which allows an individual to make a choice to worship more than one deity based on family traditions or any other consideration.

In this chapter, I help you make sense of the Hindu belief in both a Supreme Soul that encompasses everything and the multiple gods and goddesses who are the objects of worship by millions of Hindus around the world. By the time you complete this chapter, you'll see how these seemingly contradictory ideas actually form a cohesive and complex understanding of the universe and all that is in it.

Understanding Pantheism

If you were to listen to conversations taking place in Hindu households, you'd hear things like the following :

"God only knows."

"My husband is just finishing up puja (worship) to God. He will call you later."

"It is all in God's hands."

But I said that Hindus believe in many gods. So why don't they say something like, "Rama (or Krishna or Govinda or Lakshmi) only knows" or "My husband is just finishing up puja to Shiva and Ganesha . . ." or "It is all in Ayyappa's (or Durga's or Kali's) hands"?

Even when Hindus are worshipping a multiplicity of gods, they are fully aware of God in the most fundamental sense — the One.

Conceiving the whole universe as God

In Hinduism, God is All and All is God. This belief does not exclude or deny anything.

Some people confuse pantheism with atheism, but as you can see, Hindu pantheism is not atheistic. India and Hinduism represent a civilization of many millennia in which the same people have remained on the same soil, worshipping the same land, the heavens above it, and every body of water and natural phenomenon in sight *and* imagined. These people have also accepted nearly every idea of a sacramental nature that has entered from other sources. In Hinduism, *Om Swasti* (which means "All is holy!").

Ancient Hindus observed, with a sense of awe and reverence, life-sustaining natural forces such as the sun, wind, rain, fire, and so on. Hinduism, like many ancient religions, began with reverence for nature and nature gods. This early form of pantheism attributed special powers and presence to forces of nature, such as these:

✔ **Time keepers:** The sun, moon, dawn, stars, and constellations

✔ **Weather controllers:** Storms, thunder, and lightning

✔ **Sustainers:** Rivers, seas, lakes, fire, earth, air, trees, herbs, and animals

Early Hindus bathed in the rivers. Lifting a handful of water and looking at the sun, they offered the water to him. They built a fire and made offerings to the fire. They revered trees. They even invoked the gods of skill they imagined must reside inside tools and weapons.

From this early reverence emerged more sophisticated philosophical ideas regarding the unseen power *behind* the visible universe. This power is Brahman; Hindus consider Brahman the Universal Essence. This power is the Supreme Spirit. It is the Absolute. It is immutable. It is greater than the greatest and smaller than the smallest. Brahman is the answer to the question: What is that, by knowing which, everything else is known? Hindus describe it as *Satchidananda,* meaning existence, knowledge, and bliss all blended into That. It defies description such as "I" or "Thou." It has no beginning or end. It includes everything and excludes nothing. It has no emotions. It is simply That.

Do you want to know how many gods there really are in Hinduism? A tale from the Brhadaranyaka Upanishad should make it all clear! A disciple asks his guru how many gods there are, to which the sage replies, "303 and 3003." Not understanding the answer, the disciple asks again. "Sir, how many gods are there?" And the sage answers, "33." The disciple questions the guru a third time, and the sage settles on 6. Growing more perplexed, the disciple asks a fourth time, and the sage says, "3." The disciple begs, "Sir, how many gods are there?" The sage's reply: "One and a half!" Almost beside himself, the disciple pleads, "Sir, how many gods are there?" Finally the sage declares, "One!"

Although this tale is certainly amusing, the sage's answers are not puzzling to the Hindu. If he believes that all life is sacred, that belief is just one short step away from attributing divinity to all life (including animals and trees) and all things (like lakes, rivers, the seas, the mountains, and so on). After all, they *all* emanate from the One!

Visualizing the many embodied in the One

Early Hindu thought had a clear focus on the one Supreme Soul identified as Brahman. Yet Hinduism ended up embracing a large number of gods and goddesses. Why? After all, Hindus could have stayed with that earlier sophisticated, abstract concept of the universe, the Supreme Spirit. But they didn't. They needed more than philosophy in grasping the ups and downs of life. They needed something less abstract — a visual representation to focus on.

By definition, Brahman is expansive and delights in variety. Brahman, remaining itself, projects itself into two: Purusha (which for now you can consider the male) and Prakriti (which you can call female). Out of these two emerged *everything:*

- ✔ Every living being, from the lowest cell to the highest gods and the Hindu Trinity consisting of Brahma (not Brahman!) the creator, Vishnu the preserver, and Shiva the destroyer (who completes the time cycle in order to begin the process of renewal).

✔ Every nonliving thing, from the barely tangible (wind, air) to the immovable (rocks, earth), from atomic-level materials to huge space shuttles, and every "thing" in between.

Underneath all this philosophy persists the belief that the many are the components of the One. Based on that belief, a human can reach the One by attempting to reach the components first and then expanding that reach. For example, the love between an individual and a family may become wider and wider until it involves more families, the community, and finally the entire universe. This is what some monks are able to accomplish; they reach a point where they do not distinguish between one person and another even though they may feel special love for, say, their own disciples.

Nearly every religion has begun with a form of pantheism and moved on to the concept of a savior god or an abstract God or a code of ethics. In India and within Hinduism, pantheism (one god) never lost hold. Of course neither has polytheism (many gods) or even atheism (no god). But polytheism is the most common and widely accepted form of Hindu worship.

Polytheism in Practice

Only a rare Hindu would tell you that he or she prays to or worships a single divine entity. Most Hindus think of, pray to, and worship more than one god or goddess. In Hindu homes, it is common to see pictures, emblems, and small replicas of a variety of gods. In addition, there may be a small, sealed brass or copper vessel containing water from a sacred river, such as the Ganges. When families set up an altar at home, the arrangement includes multiple pictures and small metallic or clay statuettes of gods and goddesses. Likewise, only a rare Hindu temple has a single deity.

This section explains some of the practical aspects of polytheism, like how Hindus choose which gods to worship. It also provides a broad overview of how various divinities are incorporated into home altars and temples.

The cosmos, the Brahman, the Hindu Trinity . . . Hinduism casts a wide net. No restrictions. The choice is yours, say Hindus. For them, religion is an intensely personal affair, between you and your maker as you perceive it. The Hindu philosophy insists that all people are free to go on their own paths toward liberation within the constraints of family and community and by fulfilling the sacraments (rites of passage; see Chapter 17) appropriate to age.

Deciding which gods to worship

For Hindus, deciding which gods to worship is not difficult. In most cases, the decision is driven by two main considerations:

> ✔ The denomination you belong to
>
> ✔ Family practice, inherited over centuries

In addition, local/regional influences and practices come into play. I sort out all three factors in this section.

Following your denomination's lead

As I explain in Chapter 4, Vaishnavites, Shaivites, Smartas, and Shaktas have their own preferences when it comes to which godhead to worship. Vaishnavites, for example, worship Vishnu and his incarnations, as well as his consorts. Shaivites, on the other hand, worship Shiva and his sons, Ganapati and Murugan.

What causes confusion in non-Hindus, however, is the cross-allegiance evident in this apparently contradictory practice. For example, a Vaishnavite Hindu may pray to Shiva's son Ganapati. Or a Shaivite may show great reverence while visiting a Vishnu temple. Hindus accept this as normal because Lord Ganapati (or Ganesha) is believed to be the remover of obstacles. Likewise, a Shaivite might worship Rama (a form of Vishnu) because of Rama's attribute of strictly upholding dharma.

What you have to remember is that these aren't like rival sports teams during a championship match, where cheering for one means booing the other. Hindus take the intertwined nature of the deities and denominational allegiances all in stride.

The family rules! Going with family tradition

The other major determining factor in the selection of godhead to worship is usually the family tradition. These traditions involve the temples your family has attended; the allegiances your family has to other temples, gods, and goddesses; the *gurus* (religious leaders of the family) whose counsel and blessing your family has received; and more.

When I was growing up

When I was growing up in a village in South India, my family worshipped at the Keshava (a form of Vishnu) temple at one end of the street, but we also were attached to and occasionally worshipped the village goddess known as Pattaladamma, whose temple was located on the outskirts of the village. In addition, we owed strict allegiance to Lord Venkateshwara (another form of Vishnu) in Tirupati, 150 miles away in a neighboring state. This multiple affiliation remains intact today and is common among Hindu families. (If you have determined that my family is Vaishnavite, you are right!).

For example, gurus of the Smarta tradition worship RajaRajeshwari (a form of the goddess Devi) or Ganapati (Ganesha), and those who are connected with that guru would follow suit.

Looking at regional allegiances

Hindus have a wide choice when it comes to which godhead(s) to worship. (Be sure to read Chapter 7 if you have any doubt.) Yet even with the large variety to choose from, many Hindus also worship local deities *(gramade-vatas)* of regional lore — especially goddesses. The *gramadevatas* are minor but very important local deities (goddesses) who are looked upon as guardians of a town or village. Their temples are generally located at the very edge of town and face outward as though keeping an eye on evil forces that may bring harm to the town. People who believe that cholera, plague, or small pox are brought about by evil forces especially look to these goddesses for aid. The gramadevatas are usually addressed by attaching the word *amma* ("mother") to a name. For example, Mariamma is a preferred goddess to appease in case of small pox. Devotees often believe that bad things happen to a community when a goddess is angered by some failings in sacrifices and so must be appeased. For more about the worship of these local deities, head to Chapter 15.

Multiple gods at temples and home altars

Early Hindus wanted to give a form to the life-sustaining natural forces: a human form, a handsome form, a strong form that they would long to see and worship. If the form looked like a mere human, another pair of hands could be added to the visualized image/sculpture (or more than just one additional pair of hands as in the case of goddess Durga, or four heads as in the case of Brahma) to denote a superhuman form. This process of creating something superhuman may well have been what led to the worship of idols — many different forms of them.

Hindus enjoy looking at, praying to, and worshipping a variety of symbols and images. In orthodox SriVaishnava families, for example, at the altar is a sacred object known as Saligrama kept covered in a silk cloth. The Saligrama is usually a set of two small, very highly polished, nearly spherical black stones. These stones come from the riverbed of the sacred river Gandaki in Nepal. They're considered sacred and worthy of worship because, on these black stones, you can see finely etched grooves that were made by water worms. These grooves resemble Lord Vishnu's discus. Extraordinary care is taken to protect the stones: they're opened only during daily worship and are covered right after the worship is over.

A word about the use of images: Hindus know that the image being worshipped is nothing but a step that helps them focus on God. Some families make a small clay or wet turmeric image of a human form right on the spot before a worship begins, install it, and offer worship to it. All such steps allow them to rise from one component of truth to the next higher one until they finally reach the Truth. For more information on worship traditions at home and at temples, go to Chapters 14 and 15, respectively.

Worshipping the cosmos in its entirety

Hindus integrate the many different aspects of their tradition — the multiple gods, the image worship, and the original pantheistic doctrine originating in the Vedas — in a way that encompasses the totality of existence.

Consecrating a temple: Why it took 20 years

On October 22, 1978, I attended the consecration ceremony of the entrance tower to the Venkateshwara temple in Pittsburgh. I applauded the efforts of the Hindu community there. On my return flight to Connecticut, I resolved to duplicate the efforts in Pittsburgh. As it turned out, that was a tall order. Although we now have a magnificent temple in Middletown, Connecticut, it took us 20 years to sanctify it!

Why so long? Simply put, it was because of the wide variety of views held by Hindus *in any region* in regard to god, goddess, temple, and worship. Upon discussing my views and plans with a group of close friends, the reactions varied from "Why do we need a temple? I can pray in my own home!" to "It is truly God's work, and we should build a temple and install deities."

Note the word *deities* — plural. You are not likely to see a consecrated Hindu temple anywhere with only a single deity. Even home altars have pictures and metal replicas of several gods and goddesses. Nor will you ever see a plain tower at the entrance or on the top of a *sanctum* (main shrine). Every tower depicts animals, humans, gods, and goddesses — and in a variety of colors!

At our temple in Connecticut, the name of the presiding deity is Satyanarayana. That choice was relatively easy because this particular godhead is believed to be a combination of the Hindu Trinity (made up of the creator Brahma, the protector Vishnu, and Shiva, who is in charge of completion of each time cycle). Satyanarayana is worshipped by different Hindu sects.

For every presiding deity in Vishnu form, Hindus add two consorts, which makes a total of three deities. But we didn't stop there because the overwhelming view of the group was that we should also install a statue of Ganesha (Ganapati), the remover of obstacles, a popular god. And Hindus also worship nature in the form of Nine Planets (*Navagrahas*) installed together as one group. So far, our tally was five deities and five separate sanctums.

We were not done yet! Some in our community (much like in *any* Hindu community) grew up worshipping god Rama, some Krishna, some Venkateswara, some Shiva, some others Ayyappa, some Durga, and some Muruga. So we ended up adding seven more deities and seven more sanctums! In all, if you visit the temple at Middletown, you will see 12 sanctums — unless, of course, more are added by the time you arrive!

The most visible aspect of this interplay comes about during the declaration of intent in each important ritual. The *subject* (the performer of the ceremony — for example, the father of the bride in a Hindu wedding) specifies the location of the event and the precise time based on the position of the sun and moon, the season, the year, the month, the fortnight, and the day of the week. As a part of the ceremony, sacred rivers are invoked in a cleansing mode. Fire is lit, and herbs and *ghee* (clarified butter) are offered in a gesture of gratitude and surrender of material possessions. Add to this the Hindu practice of worshipping planets, trees, plants, and animal vehicles that support or convey a god or a goddess, and you have the vast cosmos covered in every detail.

Hinduism is like a vast ocean holding in its sway all people, from the highest gurus with sophisticated knowledge of the Brahman to the simple villager who gets "high" intoxicated in the worship of a local goddess. Throughout it all, Hindus fully subscribe to the mandate that the goal of their religion is to be near God and become one with the Universal Soul: to be and to become.

Hindus today still possess the desire to dive deep into fundamentals of their religion. You will note them when you hear about efforts to build a temple to nothing but the sacred symbol *OM,* which is believed to represent Brahman (see Figure 6-1), or when you see a temple in which the presiding deity is Light, or when you meet Hindu monks who declare that serving mankind is truly worshipping God.

Figure 6-1:
The sacred
symbol, OM.

Hinduism is a vast ocean of ideas and practices, indeed.

Chapter 7

Hindu Gods and Goddesses

Hindus on their way to worship a deity call the event a *darshan,* meaning an auspicious visit to "see" God. And they do visualize and "see" many gods.

The word *Hindu* and the idea of multiple gods and goddesses are synonymous. When people of other faiths think about Hinduism, the images that come to mind must be the variety of idols and pictures depicting deities. As I explain in Chapter 6, it is a rare Hindu household that has only one picture or one statue of the god the family worships. Most families — from the poorest to the most affluent — have multiple representations of gods in their homes, including on calendars; in pictures of temples; or as icons made of metal, wood, plaster of Paris, paper mache, and even plastic.

This chapter introduces you to Hinduism's key gods and goddesses, from Brahman, the One Supreme Soul, to the gods that comprise the Hindu Trinity (Brahma, Vishnu, and Shiva), and many others besides. I also explain how you can identify the gods and goddesses you see in pictures and statues, and I describe where Hindus believe their gods reside.

Starting with the One Supreme Soul

Early Hindus had a clear focus on the One Supreme Soul, identified as *Brahman,* referred to in the Chandogya Upanishad as the "One without a second." Brahman is the sole, self-existing, Supreme Universal Soul. It manifests itself without limit, creating, destroying, and re-creating forever and ever. In other words, Brahman *is* the universe and all the forces in it.

Unlike the conceptualization of God in monotheistic religions such as Christianity, Brahman does not interact in human lives. The Brahman is simply there, forever, the pure spirit of the universe, and the goal of Hinduism is to reach back to that Brahman.

The root word for Brahman in Sanskrit is *brih,* meaning "to grow" or "to burst forth." This fact is the basis for the saying that Brahman is expansive. ("All indeed is this Brahman," says the Mandukya Upanishad, a sacred Hindu scripture.) The word *brih* is gender-neutral, meaning it is not a masculine or feminine word. That is why I refer to Brahman as "It" instead of "He" or "She."

Out of this entity issues every visible and conceivable object, from the lowest level of a cell, to all that we see in nature, to demigods and spirits and a variety of gods. At the apex of all these aspects of Brahman are three principal gods and their consorts. These gods are defined as *Trimurti* and sometimes referred to as the Hindu Trinity:

- Brahma, the creator. (Note that Brahma is *not* the same as Brahman.)
- Vishnu, the preserver or pervader.
- Shiva, who is in charge of the process of destroying all creation before another time cycle begins.

While these gods and their functions appear distinct, Hindus believe that they constantly exchange these roles as situations demand. In addition, any interaction between humans (or other creatures) and the divine starts at the Trimurti level and below, meaning visualization of physical representations of these gods and other demigods in worship. I discuss these three gods in more detail later in this chapter.

The Trimurtis share in the tasks of creating, caring for, and completing the lifecycle of a timespan of four yugas. A *yuga* is an era. As I explain in Chapter 1, there are four yugas:

- Krita Yuga, which lasts $432,000 \times 4$ years
- Treta Yuga, which lasts $432,000 \times 3$ years
- Dwapara Yuga, which lasts $432,000 \times 2$ years
- Kali Yuga, which lasts $432,000$ years

A complete cycle from one creation to another therefore lasts about 4.32 million years. Hindus believe that our present age is Kali Yuga.

Identifying Gods by Their Portrayals

The first time you look at a picture of a Hindu deity in a book or on an Indian calendar, or the first time you see the sculpture of a deity, your reaction may be "Wow!" That's because such representations often feature the following:

- ✔ A multitude of colors.

- ✔ More than a single pair of arms. Hindu gods typically have four arms, but the goddess Durga (shown in Figure 7-1) may be portrayed with eight or ten or eighteen!

- ✔ A variety of weapons and/or other paraphernalia in the hands.

- ✔ Specific gestures (called *mudras*) represented by the hand and arm positions.

- ✔ A variety of animals serving as conveyance vehicles or symbols.

- ✔ A variety of markings on the face.

- ✔ Elaborate decorations.

- ✔ Other deities that appear in the same setting. Some gods have one or more associated deities (a consort or two, a sibling, or a companion animal, for example) and a group of worshippers standing nearby.

All these elements may seem confusing to a non-Hindu, but for a Hindu, they make the god instantly recognizable. Figure 7-1, for example, shows a representation of the goddess Durga, whom you can read about in the later section "The Feminine Divine."

As you try to comprehend this busy and complex portrayal, keep in mind the Hindu's desire to see divinity in superhuman form. The goal is to feel the presence of a higher power that invokes a certain level of reverence. To the Hindu, these complex portrayals most certainly accomplish that function.

The very first thing to note when you look at a picture or sculpture of a male deity is the type of mark that has been applied to the forehead. It's your first clue in classifying its sectarian identity. (As I explain in Chapter 4, Hinduism has four major denominations and myriad sects and subsects.)

- ✔ **The mark of Vishnu:** Male gods that are forms or incarnations of Vishnu (such as Rama, Krishna, and Venkateshwara) typically carry three nearly parallel vertical lines known as Nama drawn on the forehead; the two outer ones in white, about two to three inches apart, and the center one in red. With minor variations, this symbol is typical of the Vaishnava denomination; the attending priest normally has the same pattern applied to his forehead. See Chapter 4 for more details about this marking, as well as a photograph of it.

✔ **The mark of Shiva:** The mark worn by a male deity who is a form or incarnation or son of Shiva (such as Murugan or Ganapati) consists of three horizontal white/gray lines (made with ash) that span the entire width of the forehead. The mark is known as *Vibhooti,* and you can see a photo of it in Chapter 4. The priest at a *sanctum* (holy space) of the Shaivite denomination will draw the same three horizontal lines on his forehead, and sometimes on his arms and upper body. The three lines are believed to represent the three qualities inherent in humans: Sattva (noble), Rajas (vibrant), and Tamas (inert).

Figure 7-1:
Portrayals
of Hindu
deities are
complex —
and
beautiful.

Brahma, the Creator

Brahma, shown in Figure 7-2a, is the first member of the Hindu Trinity. He is often shown emerging from a lotus flower growing out of god Vishnu in his form as Narayana, floating on the vast causal cosmic ocean.

Hindus consider Brahma to be the Golden Embryo from which all the forms in the universe developed. He was, according to Hindu mythology, the first ever person, and all beings are considered his progeny; he is therefore referred to as Lord of Progeny *(Prajapati).*

Figure 7-2:
(a) The four-headed Brahma; (b) Saraswati, the goddess of learning.

Attributes of Brahma

Brahma has the following attributes in visual representations:

- He has four heads. The heads face each of the four directions, and they are believed to represent the four Vedas (Hindus' most sacred texts), the four yugas (which I explain earlier in this chapter), and the four divisions in the Hindu societal structure (see Chapter 5).

- He has four arms. He may be shown holding a rosary (representing the counting of time) or a sheaf of grass, ladle, or water pot, all of which are used in Vedic sacrifices. He also holds a book, which represents knowledge.

- The palm of one hand faces forward in a gesture called *abhaya mudra,* which means "fear not."

- He is sometimes portrayed as seated on a swan.

- His consort is Saraswati, the goddess of learning. The next section has more information about goddess Saraswati.

There are very few temples for Brahma; you learn the reason in Chapter 18. Those that do exist include a temple in Pushkar in the state of Rajasthan, India, and one in Angkor Wat in Cambodia. Based on the *vastu shastra* (a Hindu architectural manual), a space for Brahma is reserved at the center of the base of the main sanctum in every Hindu temple. In addition, an outline of Brahma is included at the center of the shrine in every sanctified Hindu temple. This image helps locate all sanctums in the temple with reference to Brahma's location. However, while other sanctums are built and the specified deities are installed (see Chapter 15), Brahma is there only in spirit.

Brahma's consort: Saraswati, the goddess of learning

The goddess Saraswati is the consort of Brahma the creator and is worshipped as the goddess of learning, wisdom, speech, and music. Hindus offer prayers to Saraswati before beginning any intellectual pursuit, and Hindu students are encouraged to offer prayers to her during the school/college term and especially before and during examinations!

Saraswati is portrayed as a beautiful, white-clad goddess, exemplifying serenity and wisdom. She has four arms and holds a *veena* (lute), a pearl rosary, and a manuscript. She is sometimes seated or riding on a swan or peacock (see Figure 7-2b).

Annual festivals to celebrate Saraswati emphasize Hindus' recognition of the need to acquire *jnana* (wisdom) as an indispensable tool of life. The very first stanza in the great Hindu epic called the *Mahabharata* (see Chapter 12) is an invocation to Saraswati:

> *Upon saluting Narayana and Goddess Saraswati,*
> *as well as the noblest of men, Arjuna, shall one undertake the study.*

Vishnu, the Preserver

Vishnu is the second member of the Hindu Trinity; he maintains the order and harmony of the universe periodically created by Brahma and periodically destroyed by Shiva (to prepare for the next cycle of creation). Vishnu is worshipped in many forms and in his several *avatars* (incarnations, which you can read about in Chapter 8).

In the Vedas (one of Hindus' most sacred texts), Vishnu is an important, somewhat mysterious god. Less visible than many of the nature gods that preside over elements, such as fire, rain, and storms, Vishnu is the *pervader* — the divine essence that pervades the universe.

Vishnu and his forms are worshipped primarily (but not exclusively) by Vaishnavites and Smartas. (See Chapter 4 for details about these Hindu denominations.)

Attributes of Vishnu

Through the ages, whole treatises, stories, and poems have been written on Vishnu's attributes. Here are just the highlights:

✔ He has an erect, forward-looking stance and wears a benevolent expression on his face.

✔ He is dark blue in color. On his chest is a jewel, and a five-row garland of flowers or jewels hangs around his neck.

✔ He has four arms. He holds his lower right hand in an *abhaya mudra* (gesture), meaning "fear not." In his upper right hand, he holds the *discus,* a circular, saw-toothed weapon useful in battles fought to preserve dharma. The upper left hand holds the conch, which symbolizes victory and the five elements (air, ether, water, fire, and earth). His lower left hand holds a mace, which represents the power of knowledge and protection. Sometimes the lower right hand simply points to his feet, suggesting surrender by the devotee.

✔ His vehicle is the eagle Garuda.

Divinities related to Vishnu

Vishnu is more often recognized and worshipped by other names (Venkateshwara, Balaji, Srinivasa, Satyanarayana or Narayana, and Jagannath) and through his ten avatars, which I discuss in detail in Chapter 8. Here, I explain the divine forms Vishnu takes and two of the avatars, Rama and Krishna, which have developed large followings over the centuries.

Vishnu as Venkateshwara, lord of the seven hills

Venkateshwara is worshipped by all devout Hindus irrespective of their special and regional affiliations. The very name (which is a combination of *Venkata* and *Ishwara*) may also imply a unification of Vaishnavite and Shaivite beliefs. (See Chapter 4 for details about these beliefs.)

The most famous shrine to Venkateshwara is at Tirupati on the crest of the Seshadri Hills in the southern Indian state of Andhra Pradesh. Here he gives *darshan* (blessed sight) to millions of devotees from all parts of India and the world. Venkateshwara's blessings and his worshippers' generosity have been so abundant that a university, a hospital, and a host of other institutions are all funded by the temple and managed under its direction.

Vishnu as Narayana

Narayana is another name for Vishnu, identified as one whose abode is the primeval waters. As Narayana, floating in the primeval ocean, Vishnu has two forms:

✔ An infant lying on a lotus leaf, foot held in mouth, signifying time with no end and no beginning.

✔ Vishnu reclining, dreaming, on the serpent *Ananta* (whose name literally means "endless") while Lakshmi, his wife, holds his feet.

Vishnu as Jagannath, lord of the universe

In Chapter 16, I describe a chariot festival in the Indian state of Orissa that is centered around this form of Vishnu (and his avatar Krishna). Jagannath's brother Balabhadra and sister Subhadra also feature in this event.

Vishnu as the avatar Rama

Rama is the prince of Ayodhya whose story is told in the Sanskrit epic called the *Ramayana* ("The Story of Rama"). Hindus have moved this hero up to the status of a major deity because they revere the qualities he represents: the ideal qualities of a king, spousal love, fraternal devotion, and the proper relationship between subjects and their king.

The historical dating of the reign of an actual prince of Ayodhya by the name of Rama is uncertain, although recent excavations claim to have found the structure raised over his birthplace.

In pictures and statues, Rama is represented as a young warrior holding a bow who is flanked on the right by his brother Lakshmana (who also holds a bow) and on the left by his wife Sita, a beautiful woman with a mild expression. Also in the grouping is his faithful servant, the monkey god Hanuman, who kneels at Rama's feet. Figure 7-3a shows the *Ram Parivar,* the iconic grouping of Rama's attributes that is immediately recognizable to Hindus.

Figure 7-3:
(a) The Ram
Parivar; (b)
Krishna, the
cowherd.

Hanuman, the devoted servant

Like Rama, Hanuman, the monkey god, is featured in the epic called the *Ramayana* (see Chapter 12). Hanuman has earned his own path to deification and has many temples built for his own worship. His qualities are dedication, loyalty, courage, intelligence, and determination. Anecdotes featuring Hanuman are often used in Hindu households to encourage the younger generation when they are not living up to their potential. Elders cite the time when the monkey leader Jambavan cajoled Hanuman for not recognizing his inherent extraordinary strength. Hanuman was then inspired to help Rama in countless exciting incidents leading up to the battle of Lanka. Hanuman went searching for Rama's beloved wife Sita, who had been kidnapped and hidden in Ravana's palace. He located her and assured her of rescue. Before leaving, he set fire to the city. During the final battle between Rama and Ravana, Hanuman was sent to bring an herb to help revive the wounded Rama, Lakshmana, and many of Rama's soldiers. Not sure which herb was the right one, Hanuman lifted the entire mountain and brought it to the battlefield. These feats of strength, devotion, and lively courage have endeared Hanuman to many and brought him followers and temples in his own honor.

Vishnu as the avatar Krishna

If the name of one Hindu god is known and recognized throughout the world, it is Krishna, the eighth avatar of Vishnu. The form of Krishna most familiar to Hindus is that of Gopala or Govinda, a handsome young cowherd with a cow close behind and a flute held at his lips (see Figure 7-3b). His head gear is crested with a peacock feather, he is a cloud blue color, and his clothing is saffron. Another popular depiction shows him embracing his lover, Radha, in a circle of adoring dancing milkmaids *(gopis)*.

Students of the Bhagavad Gita (see Chapter 13) know Krishna as the charioteer friend, cousin, and mentor of Arjuna. Students of the epic *Mahabharata* (see Chapter 12) know him as the pivot around which hundreds of ugly events occurred — events that were resolved through his intervention and guidance. But most of all, Lord Krishna's promise to humanity that he will return to save the world whenever dharma declines has sustained Hindu belief in the Supreme Being over thousands of years.

Krishna is also the divine child as described in the story of his birth (which you can read about in Chapter 8). For his devotees, Krishna is a delight because of his playful, childish pranks. Hindus enjoy recalling how, when baby Krishna ate mud and his mother asked him to open his mouth, she saw the three worlds (earth, ether, and heavens) revealed.

Vishnu's consorts

Vishnu has two consorts: the goddesses Lakshmi and Bhu Devi. Bhu Devi is the earth goddess, who was rescued from the primeval ocean by Varaha, Vishnu's third incarnation — an avatar in the shape of a boar (see Chapter 8).

Lakshmi (also known as *Mahalakshmi,* meaning "great goddess Lakshmi") is the goddess of good fortune, wealth, and wellbeing. She is depicted as a beautiful female form with four arms, standing or seated on a lotus and holding lotuses or showering gold pieces; see Figure 7-4. She is sometimes flanked by two elephants. She is also referred to as Sri (pronounced *shree*) and Kamala, among many other names.

Figure 7-4:
Lakshmi.

The goddess Lakshmi bestows both wealth and wellbeing on her devotees. She is the consort of Vishnu, a role she plays in every incarnation. For example, she is Sita, wife of Rama; Rukmini, wife of Krishna; and Dharani, wife of Parashu Rama, another avatar of Vishnu. As I explain in Chapter 12, she was one of the 14 precious items recovered during the *Amritamanthana,* the famous churning of the milky ocean, and she emerged with a lotus in her hand.

A wide variety of prayers describing her various attributes are found in the *Sri Sukta,* a series of hymns in praise of Lakshmi. The practice of worshipping Lakshmi is a testimony to the importance ancient Hindus placed on the practical aspects of life. For example:

> ✔ Hindu practice includes meditating first on Lakshmi upon waking up in the morning. Hindus open and hold their palms up together and recite the following:

> *At the top of the hands resides Lakshmi*
> *And at the center Saraswati*
> *And at the base resides Govinda.*
> *Thus we should look at our palms in the morning.*

✔ Among the days of the week, Fridays are most auspicious for the worship of Lakshmi. Hindus light lamps or turn on lights at dusk on Fridays to welcome Lakshmi.

✔ At temples where an image of Lakshmi has been installed, an elaborate ceremony of worship to Lakshmi takes place on Friday evenings.

✔ In traditional South Indian weddings, musicians perform a special song in praise of Lakshmi as the bride enters the wedding hall with her entourage because, on her wedding day, the bride is considered to be the embodiment of the goddess herself.

In addition, as goddess of wealth, Lakshmi holds a special role for merchants and businesses, especially at Diwali. This annual festival of lights coincides with New Year in many parts of India (see Chapter 16). Merchants and businesses use this special day of celebration to offer worship to Lakshmi, to close the books for the year, and to make preparations for the new fiscal year.

Shiva, the Destroyer

Shiva, whose name means "auspicious," is the third member of the Hindu Trinity. He is tasked with the unmaking of the universe in order to prepare for its renewal at the end of each cycle of time (at the end of the fourth yuga). A key point to remember about Shiva is that his destructive power is *regenerative*: It's the necessary step that makes renewal possible.

How Shiva got his blue throat

The Amritamanthana, or the churning of the milky ocean, is a story from the *Mahabharata*. (You can read about the whole story in Chapter 8.) The story goes that the serpent Vasuki, used as a churning rope, was so tired and sick from the repeated action of churning that he vomited the most potent poison into the ocean of milk. Fearing the destruction of the world through this pollution, Shiva immediately drank the poison. He himself would have succumbed were it not for the timely intervention of Parvati, his wife. Parvati held Shiva's throat tightly to prevent the poison from entering into his body. It is said that the arrested poison turned Shiva's throat blue. Another name for Shiva is *Nilakanta,* meaning "blue-throated."

The power of Lord Shiva's eternal penance (he is depicted as always in deep meditation, the disturbing of which causes major havoc) is such that Hindus customarily invoke Shiva before the beginning of any religious or spiritual endeavor. Hindus believe that any and all bad vibrations in the immediate vicinity of the worship venue or practice are eliminated by the mere utterance of Shiva's praise or name. Shiva and his forms are worshipped primarily (and mostly) by Shaivites and Smartas (see Chapter 4).

Shiva is represented as Rudra, the howler among the Vedic gods (whom I introduce in the later section "Gods and Goddesses of the Hindu Firmament). He is red with a blue throat and four arms. In his hands he holds a trident. Above his brow is a crescent moon, in his hair is the River Ganges, and around his neck is a snake and a necklace of *rudraksha beads* (prayer beads) or pearls. He owns a spear called *Pasupata* (the herdsman's staff). Shiva's vehicle is a bull named Nandi. The most identifiable of his features, however, is his third eye, which he almost always keeps closed. When it does open, it is a disaster to anyone within its gaze; they simply burn away instantly. See Figure 7-5 for a representation of Shiva.

Figure 7-5:
Shiva.

Forms of Shiva

Millions of devotees around the world worship Shiva. Each year, a certain night in February is devoted to celebrating *Shivaratri,* the "great night of Shiva" (see Chapter 16). Shiva has many forms, from a simple stone representation (called a *lingam*) to an ash-covered *mendicant* (beggar) deeply absorbed in meditation. Here are four forms of Shiva to remember:

Shiva worshipped in the linga form

Temples to Shiva, including wayside shrines and other sanctums, invariably present the deity in the sculptural form of a *lingam* (or *linga*): a stone that represents a phallus or a pillar. The Sanskrit word means "gender." This ancient representation of the generative organ crosses all cultures from the Stone Age onward and demonstrates the very ancient lineage of the worship of Shiva. Devotees accept this simple elemental form as symbolic of fertility, growth, and strength.

- ✔ **As Kaala or time, the destroyer of worlds:** At the end of Kali Yuga, the fourth age of the world (which Hindus believe we are in right now), evil threatens to overtake all of creation. Shiva, as Nataraja (Lord of Dance), performs the dance that undoes all forms and ends the yuga. This iconic image of Shiva shows him within a circle of fire with one leg raised and one resting on a recumbent body; Shiva holds a drum in one hand and a flame in the other. (See Chapter 4 for a picture of Shiva as Nataraja.)

- ✔ **As ascetic:** In this form, Shiva spends eons in deep meditation, in his abode called Mount Kailas (or Kailasa) in the Himalayas. He is clothed in animal skins, his body is covered in ash, his hair is bound up on top of his head, and he sits with legs folded in the well-known yoga stance. His eyes are closed, shielding the unwary from his terrible third eye.

  Several stories and dramas portray attempts to distract Shiva from his meditative trance. Most such stories end in disaster. An example is the tale of how the gods attempted to help Parvati, daughter of the mountains (Himalayas), tempt Shiva. Cupid *(Kama),* the lord of desire, was sent on this errand with his bow made of five flowers, but he was burnt to a cinder when Shiva opened his third eye. In time, Parvati was able to overcome Shiva by her power of true devotion.

- ✔ **As Pashupati, the herdsman (or lord of beasts):** Shiva has an ancient task in which he roams the wild jungles using his healing powers for animals.

- ✔ **Shiva the Terrible (Bhairava):** Shiva's task as destroyer of a universe that has reeled beyond help at the end of the fourth era (the Kali Yuga) is helped by his role as midnight haunter of graveyards, a fearful being, controlling the forms of death and decadence.

The consorts of Shiva: Parvati and Sati

Both Parvati and Sati are Shiva's consorts. Parvati (whose name literally mean "the daughter of the mountain," referring to the Himalayas) is a peaceful, domestic form of the goddess known as Devi. (Devi's other forms are described in the upcoming section "The Feminine Divine.") Parvati created Shiva's son Ganapati (or Ganesha) — the elephant-headed god — from her bath lotions, turmeric paste, and skin rubbings because she needed a guard for her chamber door.

Sati, worshipped as a paragon of virtues idealized by Hindu women, was a daughter of King Daksha. According to legend, when Daksha organized a great ceremony of sacrificial rituals, he did not invite his illustrious but questionable son-in-law because he had heard about Shiva's occasional association with strange, dark spirits that tended to disrupt such rituals. In anger and shame over such disrespect for her husband, Sati threw herself into the ritual fire. Enraged and grief-stricken, Shiva disrupted Daksha's sacrifice and then took up Sati's body over his shoulder and moved north. As he traveled, Sati's body fell to pieces in places that are now associated with Sati or with pilgrimage. Shiva sank into deep meditation in the mountains until he was finally revived by Parvati's devotion. This story is considered the origin for the practice of *suttee,* or the voluntary burning of widows on their husband's funeral pyre. The practice was never sanctioned by the Vedas or basic Hindu scriptures and is now outlawed.

Shiva's sons

Shiva has two sons: Ganapati and Murugan. Ganapati is worshipped as the lord of obstacles. He is invoked by most Hindus before starting any auspicious undertaking; they pray for a smooth and flawless performance of the task at hand. Murugan is worshipped mostly by *Tamilians* (people who speak the language Tamil). I relate stories of these two sons of Shiva in this section.

Ganapati: The remover of obstacles

Ganapati is referred to reverentially as *Maha Ganapati* ("great Ganapati)" but is equally well-known as Ganesha and also known as *Vighnaraja* ("lord of obstacles"). Lord Ganapati occupies a very special place in the hearts of Hindus. Most Hindu households have a picture or statue of this godhead, and it's not uncommon to see small replicas of Ganapati hanging from rearview mirrors of cars and trucks! The elephant head is the obvious clue to identifying this godhead.

The form of Ganapati with his elephant head and portly belly invokes enormous reverence *(bhakti)* among Hindus. Consider these examples:

✔ Most Hindus, except for the Vaishnava denomination (generally speaking), believe that worshipping Ganapati first before any worthwhile undertaking is a must so that their task is blessed to proceed toward a successful conclusion. Most concerts of Indian classical music, for example, begin with a composition in praise of Ganapati.

✔ Every September, a special festival is held throughout the Hindu world to make images of Ganapati in clay; color them in gold, yellow, pink, and red; worship the same image for ten days; and at the end perform what's called a *visarjan* by immersing the image in a body of water. The festival is especially popular in the Indian state of Maharashtra. To this day, the festival takes place in grand style attracting millions to Maharashtra's capital Mumbai. This religious fervor unites Hindus everywhere as no other festival has. Read more about it in Chapter 16.

Murugan

Shiva's second son, Murugan (or Muruga) is a popular deity worshipped by Hindus, especially Tamilians, around the world. He is known by several names: Skanda, Kumara, Kartikeya, and Subrahmanya.

He was created when Shiva, disturbed by Kama Deva (Cupid) at the bequest of Parvati, opened his third eye and reduced Kama instantly to ashes. The ball of fire emanating from Shiva's fury fell into a pool in Saravana, a forest of arrow-like grass in the Himalayas. Six sparks of fire turned into six babies, who were nursed by six mothers. When Parvati gathered the six babies and made them into one, the child was known as *Shanmukha* ("six faces").

As interesting as Shanmukha/Murugan's birth is, his story really begins with the havoc caused by an asura known as Taraka. Hindus believe that *asuras,* which are like demons, are power-seeking deities that acquire enormous strength through their devotees' austerities and prayers. They generally long for supremacy over the *devas* (gods), tormenting humans and creating havoc during sacred ceremonies. They also are not easy to defeat. Taraka set out to conquer the entire universe and nothing, it appeared, could stop him. But Murugan became a general of Shiva's army, and his mother Parvati gifted him with a powerful lance called *Vel.* He and his army destroyed Taraka in a six-day battle (which is now celebrated on the sixth day in October–November), and the devas were liberated.

How Ganapati lost and gained his head

Ganapati's mother, Parvati, asked Ganapati to guard the entrance to her apartments and admit no one while she took a bath. When Shiva, Ganapati's father, tried to enter, Ganapati stopped him. No amount of persuasion or threats helped, and a furious Shiva cut off Ganapati's head. A grief-stricken Parvati demanded that Shiva find a way to restore the boy's life. Shiva instructed his staff to find anyone, human or animal, sleeping with its head pointed in the southern direction, and to bring that creature to him. As it happened, the first creature to be found sleeping with its head toward the south was an elephant, whose head was duly severed and brought to Shiva. Shiva positioned the new head onto the body of Ganapati and, lo and behold, the boy came alive as the handsome elephant-headed god.

The Feminine Divine

A unique feature of Hinduism is the worship of goddesses as well as gods. Lakshmi, Saraswati, Sita, Radha, and a host of other goddesses are worshipped by millions of Hindus around the world. Earth is worshipped as *Bhumi Mata,* Mother Earth. The aspect of mother and the associated reverence, love, compassion, and respect are clearly implied in these rituals.

The female form, especially in the case of the deities I list in the previous paragraph, is generally accepted as representing a role supportive of a male deity, be it Brahma, Vishnu, or Shiva. In temples throughout India and abroad, sanctums of female consorts usually flank those of the major male deities, even if the goddesses have a substantial personal following themselves.

At the same time, the female form is associated with *shakti,* awesome creative strength and power — a resource that the gods recognize and depend on. This is particularly true of regional forms of Parvati, the wife and consort of Shiva. These forms include Durga Devi and Kali, which I discuss in detail next.

Durga Devi

Durga Devi is *the* goddess who signifies the shakti aspect in all its implied creative and destructive power. The mission of Durga is primary, not supportive, and therefore her actions are not typical of a female consort. Because of this independence, she is powerful, even frightening at times, with an unusual spirit to fight fiercely in order to restore *dharma* (moral order). Yet, while Durga is at once a terrifying *Shakti Mata* ("powerful mother") to her adversaries, she is full of compassion and love for her devotees.

The story of Durga's birth

The manner in which the manifestation of Durga came about is unlike that of other goddesses. When the demon Mahisha Asura conquered the heavens and drove Indra (lord of gods) out of his kingdom, the gods began to descend to earth. Brahma and Shiva knew they could not bear this assault on dharma anymore. All the gods and demigods visited Vishnu to discuss the news of Mahisha's onslaught and the resulting lack of balance between forces of good and evil. The recounting of events angered the assembled gods so much that bolts of light began to issue from their bodies. The fusion of these lights gave birth to a feminine form known as Durga, who was gifted with immense power. Each part of the goddess was formed from bolts of light emanating from individual gods. For example, her face came into being by Shiva's light, her hair from Yama's light, her arms from Vishnu's light, her feet from Brahma's light, and so on! In addition, the gods offered her a variety of weaponry: a trident from Shiva, a discus from Vishnu, a conch from Varuna, a spear from Agni, a bow and quiver full of arrows from Vayu, a thunderbolt from Indra, a noose from Yama, and more.

Fully armed, Durga roared with anger and the three worlds (the earth, ether, and heavens) shook. There ensued a fierce battle between her and the asura forces of Mahisha. Thousands of asuras were slain in the gruesome battle, and the enormous loss of his army brought forth Mahisha himself to the battlefield. He had supreme confidence that he could never die in battle because he had, through his own penance, received a *boon* (gift) from the gods that no man could kill him ever. He was immensely satisfied with that boon because he had never thought to include freedom from death at the hands of a woman! Mahisha assumed several animal forms in an attempt to overcome her, but finally Durga slew Mahisha by stomping on him and driving a trident through his heart. Thus ended the saga of Mahisha, which restored dharma, returned the three worlds to order, and restored the balance of good against evil.

Durga's attributes and festivals

Durga is visualized as a beautiful, powerful female divinity riding a lion and fully armed in all her hands (refer to Figure 7-1). Festivals to celebrate Durga each year emphasize Hindus' recognition of the need for strength to protect dharma. In worshipping Durga, Hindus celebrate the feminine principle for its strength and fortitude as well as compassion, and they seek her grace and blessings.

Kali, the destructive power of time

Kali is the terrifying aspect of Durga. While Durga is strong and even violent in action, a militant power against evil, she is beautiful in form. Kali, while basically attractive, has some ugly attributes in her battle against evil and against illusion.

Kali's appearance is fearsome: She is dark in color to represent that, at the end of the fourth yuga, all forms dissolve into a dark night and all colors disappear until the next creation. Her tongue hangs from her mouth to indicate a loud laugh. She stands on a corpse that represents what is left of the non-existent or destroyed universe. Although she is clad in space (that is, naked), she wears a necklace of skulls and a belt of arms. She has four arms, two of which hold a head and a sword; the other two are positioned in the "fear not" and the "giving of boons" gestures *(mudras)*.

The boon that Kali offers is that knowledge and perspective pertaining to the passage of time, with no illusions, remove fear. This understanding allows bliss to be granted by Kali's giving hand. She is frightful because of the illusion that must be abandoned and the fear that such a loss entails, but Kali destroys despair.

Village goddesses

It is not uncommon to see simple temples on the outskirts of villages to house a village goddess. These temples are, more often than not, planned, constructed, and maintained by castes other than brahmin (see Chapter 5). These goddesses, unlike major Hindu gods and goddesses, are believed to demand and receive animal sacrifices, such as chickens, lambs, and buffalos. The devotees believe that bad things happen to a community when a goddess is angered by some failing in sacrifices, and so the goddess must be appeased. These goddesses are looked upon as guardians of a town or village, and their temples generally face away from the towns they protect as though keeping an eye on evil forces that may bring a disease or similar harm to the town. People who believe that cholera, plague, or smallpox are brought about by evil forces look to these goddesses to ward off the evils and protect their community.

Gods and Goddesses of the Hindu Firmament

The gods named and described in this section, and many others connected with households and communities, are found in the Rig Veda, the earliest book of Hindu sacred scripture (see Chapter 10). Known and revered as the *Vedic gods,* they are invoked and worshipped daily in all household and many temple rituals. As such they are basic to the living, ritual culture of Hinduism. Except for Surya the sun, these gods have no temples built to them or personal following, although Hindus revere them deeply.

The Vedic gods fall into these general categories:

- ✔ Nature gods, especially gods connected with weather and climate
- ✔ Planetary gods who feature in destiny and the composition of horoscopes
- ✔ Gods who rule over household health and wealth and community values

Although separated and categorized here for convenience, all these areas of human concern are considered to influence each other in the Hindu universe.

Indra and the Vedic storm gods

Indra, the king of heaven and lord of the gods, wields a thunderbolt and brings rain. He is a hero and a warrior mounted on a white horse or immense white elephant. His bow is the rainbow, and he resides in Amaravati ("immortal city") near the mythical Mount Meru. His wife is Indrani (also called

Sachi). More hymns are addressed to Indra than to any other god in the Rig Veda because he is the chief of gods and provider of rain.

Legend has it that with all this adoration and his position as the head of all gods, he became arrogant. Thus, when the folks in Lord Krishna's kingdom offered worship to a local hill known as Mount Govardhan instead (on Krishna's advice, no doubt) because they recognized the true source of rains, Indra became furious and sent continuous rain, thunder, and lightning to scare the populace. Krishna came to their rescue and held up the entire mountain to shelter them from Indra's onslaught. It was then that Indra understood the source of the problem — his own arrogance and Krishna's plan to teach him a lesson. He begged Krishna to forgive him. Lord Krishna forgave Indra and allowed the worship of Indra on that particular day in winter at a festival known as *Bhogi.*

Indra is not the only Hindu god associated with weather. The weather above the earth is controlled by Vayu (wind lord), the Maruts (storm gods), and the fearful deity called Rudra, the howler, who was later associated with Shiva.

Varuna, who is lord of the waters that circle the earth and rivers, is also seen as affecting the waters of heaven.

The sun and planets as rulers of destiny

The planetary gods are the *navagrahas* (literally, the "nine planets"):

- **Surya,** the sun, is a golden warrior arriving on a chariot pulled by seven white horses; his color is gold or copper; his favored grain for offering is wheat.

- **Chandra,** the moon, is a gentle sage dressed in white, riding a deer or a three-wheeled chariot; his color is pearl white; his favored grain is rice. The moon, also called Soma, is the timekeeper who counts out the years; he is also the cup of immortal ambrosia from which the gods drink periodically and which then fills up again.

- **Angaraka,** or Mangala, the planet Mars, is a young warrior armed with a spear; his color is red; his favored grain is red or *toor* lentil.

- **Budha,** the planet Mercury, is a gentle sage; his color is green; his favored grain is moong lentil.

- **Brihaspati,** the planet Jupiter, is the guru of the gods; his color is saffron yellow; his favored grain is peanuts or chic peas.

- **Shukra,** the planet Venus, is the guru of the asuras; his color is diamond white; his favored grain is a small bean.

- **Shani,** the planet Saturn, is the son of Surya and brother of Yama, judge of the dead; his color is dark blue; his favored grain is sesame.

✔ **Rahu,** the eclipse, is represented as a mouth that threatens to swallow the sun and moon. His image in temples, a head with no tail, never faces that of the sun or the moon. His color is smoke grey; his favored grain is urad lentil.

✔ **Ketu,** the comet, is the unlucky trailing tail with no head attached; his color is khaki green; his favored grain is horsegram.

These deities are invoked in rituals and are also studied avidly by astrologers who provide horoscopes at the birth of a child. (Ancient Hindus believed that the position of planets at the precise moment of birth launched a life into a dynamic system and that the subsequent fortune of that person depended upon the initial conditions of the total system.) Many Hindus today continue this custom, seeking astrological advice before undertaking a task or a journey or any important step in life, or exchanging and studying horoscopes in the proposal stage of an arranged marriage.

Worship of nature has always been an important aspect of Hindu prayer. During sacred ceremonies, Hindus invoke sacred rivers and fire, and they refer to the year, month, day, season, position, and phase of the moon and integrate all these to specify time and space. This procedure is called *sankalpam.* (See Chapter 17 for more information on worship rituals.)

Agni and the Vedic gods of home and community

Agni, the fire god, holds a special place in Hindu ritual to this day as

✔ **The sacrificer:** The priest who performs the ceremony as specified in the Rig Veda (Book I, Hymn 1, Verse 1)

✔ **The sacrifice:** The ritual fire and the offerings made into it.

✔ **The witness:** The one who sees all rites. For example, Hindus consider Agni to be the witness to a wedding.

The Sanskrit word for the fire ritual is *homa* (related to the word for "home") or *havan* (related to the word for "oven").

Not long ago, the fire initiated for Hindu wedding rites was kindled from the bride's parents' home fire and carried carefully with her to her husband's home. A beautiful hymn from the Rig Veda tells how the daughter of the sun went to marry Soma, the moon god. The description of her escort is a catalogue of the household virtues and guardian deities of the early Vedic world:

- **The Ashwins,** twin heavenly horsemen who heal horses and cattle
- **Mitra,** god of friendship and god of contracts
- **Varuna,** here referring to divine law
- **Aryaman,** the personification of family honor
- **Bhaga,** the personification of ancestral share of property
- **Pusan,** the guardian of the roads and nourisher
- **Purandhi,** abundance
- **Matarisvan,** spark of conception
- **Dhatar,** sustainer
- **Destri,** a form of Saraswati (goddess of learning) associated with easy birth

Many of these household deities, some better known than others, are still invoked during Vedic wedding fire rituals today.

Discovering Where the Gods Reside

Where can all these Hindu gods be found? The heavens? Special worlds? Mountaintops? Yes! Hindus sum it all up by saying that God is everywhere. Still, Hindus recognize special abodes for gods. The belief is to allow for a gradation of higher worlds to accommodate both the divinities and humans (including insects, animals, and so on) and lower worlds for subhuman and demonic types.

Thus, Hindus speak of a total of 14 worlds called *lokas* with the earth situated in the middle. In a simpler version, there are three worlds. I explain both mythologies here, starting with the simpler version.

Introducing the three worlds

Hindus define three worlds inhabited by people and gods:

- The physical world of the universe (known as *bhur* in Sanskrit).
- The world of atmosphere *(bhuvas)*.
- The realm of the gods *(svar)*. The Sanskrit word *swarga,* for heaven, comes from this root word.

Humans live in the physical world, performing actions and enjoying the world within the framework of acceptable codes of conduct. Gods descend to this world in some form whenever there is an unacceptable imbalance between good and evil.

The world of atmosphere exists above the physical world. Here live the demigods and spirits, such as Indra (god of thunder, lightning, and rain), Rudra (destroying and dissolving power), and Vayu (the wind god).

The realm of the gods is above the world of atmosphere. In this topmost world resides Vishnu, along with other major gods such as Rita (the god of righteousness), Dyaus (the god of the sky), Varuna (the god of the waters), and Mitra (the god of day). This location up above is popularly referred to as *Vaikunta,* to which a departed soul can enter if conditions are right.

Magnificent mountains are also identified as abodes of gods. For example, Mount Meru is considered to be the abode of Brahma and Indra. Shiva is believed to reside in Mount Kailash in Tibet.

Looking at all 14 worlds

In another version, Hindu mythology recognizes worlds above and below the earth. Specifically, the six worlds above the earth are the preferred ones for the soul and the seven below are to be feared.

The lowest of the higher worlds is the earth *(bhu).* The six worlds above the earth are called *bhuva, suva, maha, jana, tapa,* and *satya.* The highest, not surprisingly, is the abode of Brahma and is known as the world of Truth *(satya loka)* reached after successfully passing through the worlds of a hierarchy of gods as the result of living a purer and purer life on earth.

Below the earth are the seven hells called talas: *atala, bitala, sutala, talatala, rasatala, mahatala,* and *patala.* These hells are inhabited by those who need to undergo suffering based on the level of their condemnable actions while on earth. The lowest is considered an abode of demons and serpents and is reached successively through a hierarchy of hells due to worsening lives on earth birth after birth.

Chapter 8

The Avatars of Vishnu: The Divine Descent

Whenever there is decline of dharma, O Arjuna,
I shall manifest myself in order to restore it.

Bhagavad Gita, Chapter IV, Verse 7

This pledge was given by Lord Krishna — an incarnation of the major Hindu god Vishnu, the preserver — to a warrior prince named Arjuna. The key word here is *dharma,* which (as I explain in Chapter 1) is a fundamental part of Hinduism that roughly means moral order. Hindus are realistic about the concept of dharma. They know that evil forces have always been at work, are currently at work, and will continue to be at work in the future. What Hindus focus on is balance — balance between good and evil, tipping toward the good.

When that balance is (or is likely to be) disturbed to such an extent that human efforts are inadequate to restore normalcy (or a state of dharma), Hindus believe the time is right for a divine descent in some form. This divine manifestation, whatever shape it takes, is known as an *avatar.* In this chapter, I explain what an avatar is and what conditions must exist for an avatar to appear, and I describe the ten avatars of Vishnu.

Understanding the Role of an Avatar

Avatars play a key role in Hinduism. The literal meaning of the word *avatar* is "descent," and it's usually understood to mean divine descent. Thus, avatars are savior forms of a god that descend to earth to intervene whenever help is needed to restore dharma and peace.

In the Bhagavad Gita (see Chapter 13), immediately after Lord Krishna speaks the words that appear at the beginning of this chapter, he then proclaims:

> *In order to protect the pious and destroy the wicked*
> *I am born again and again from one age to another.*

> Bhagavad Gita, Chapter IV, Verse 8

The main function of an avatar is to preserve dharma through every *yuga* (eon) in order to bring stability and save Vishnu's followers and the three worlds (earth, heaven, and the intervening ether) from the consequences of evil or ignorance.

The avatar concept is essentially Vaishnavite (refer to Chapter 4) and is central to understanding the nature and worship of Vishnu.

The conditions essential for incarnations

The conditions that result in the appearance of an avatar may vary from an imminent danger to a perceived one — that is, a danger perceived by the gods before humans realize the threat. This danger may not materialize for years, but to meet the eventual challenge, an avatar may be in order. For example, the boar avatar, Vahara, was generated by Vishnu to save the earth, which had been dragged down under the ocean. This was a single, immediate danger. In the case of the avatars Rama and Krishna, the avatars were born into earthly existence for the long range of time it required for them to prepare for and to accomplish their tasks (always the restoration of dharma). The later the yuga, the worse the case of *adharma* (loss of dharma) and the longer the task.

Thus, every avatar discussed in this chapter has addressed an imminent or perceived danger to a large group of innocent people, perhaps the whole earth, or even the three worlds (which include the worlds of space and heaven where the gods reside; see Chapter 7). Vishnu assumed the form appropriate to the need and the age and fulfilled the promise to "protect the pious and destroy the wicked."

Decline of dharma on earth

In the Hindu concept of cyclical time, the first *yuga* (world age) is the most righteous, and each of the remaining three yugas is less righteous than its predecessor. (See Chapter 7 for an overview of the four yugas.)

I describe here a Hindu scenario of decline of dharma and its consequences. As each age progresses, there is a general and gradual decline in dharma. People forget to offer sacrifice to the gods, the incense of their love and devotion fails to rise to the heavens, the gods weaken, the good forget, and the bad remember and try to claim their *boons* (earned blessings; I describe this scenario in the next section). As a result the balance of dharma begins to falter, and the sun and moon fall down. The Vedas (the most sacred Hindu scriptures) disappear. At this point, an avatar descends. Keep this basic scenario in mind as you read the stories in this chapter.

Eventually, the final cataclysm occurs at the end of Kali Yuga (the fourth age), presided over by the last avatar Kalki, bringing about the end of the cycle and the dissolution of all forms back into Brahman. After a dark period of rest, Brahman dreams the gods and the worlds back into being again, and the cycle resumes.

Plea from a devotee

A fundamental characteristic of Hindu gods is their readiness to come to the rescue of their devotees. Gods respond to a plea, or they recognize a peril and work with a responsible human being to end it. This response is always the result of genuine appeals, strict penance, and extraordinary distress. Therefore, a human being's rigorous penance to a particular godhead almost always results in a divine appearance and the grant of *boons* (blessings) sought by the aspirant.

Occasionally, however, boons bestowed into the wrong hands are actually the root cause of the trouble. For instance, many Hindu demons and ambitious kings, as the stories go, attached themselves as serious devotees to gods of their choice and engaged in deep penance and austerities. In doing so, they pleased the gods, who almost always offered the devotees boons the devotees could choose. This offer was like a blank check, and the demons sometimes made fantastic requests. The boon-giving gods felt an obligation to reward the correct behavior even though they were aware that such boons could lead to trouble, crisis, and danger later. The gods then had to figure out a way to bring back order and normalcy by getting rid of the very person who had received and misused the boons.

The descent of the savior

How does an avatar descend to earth? In cases where the perceived danger has not yet occurred, the avatar may begin by being born as a human whose upbringing and training prepare the baby to be ready to address a calamity when it does occur. Rama and Krishna, two of Vishnu's ten avatars (see the next section for details), are great examples. In the following stories, I show that the very first avatar of Vishnu was a tiny fish, followed by the forms of a tortoise and a boar; the descents progressed upward in what would appear to be an evolutionary pattern to human forms.

Not all divine presence on earth is identified as an avatar even though, in the strict sense of the term, it may well be. A *consort* (female companion) of a divine being may also be born about the same time as the birth of the avatar on earth and marry him in human form; the two then live through all the ups and downs a human couple would experience. These extraordinary personages may not always be recognized as avatars. Goddess Lakshmi, for example, was born as Sita and married the form of Vishnu called Rama.

The Ten Incarnations of Vishnu

The ten incarnations of god Vishnu have taken place during times of extraordinary stress and continue through the present age. These ten avatars are Matsya (fish), Kurma (tortoise), Varaha (boar), Narasimha (man-lion), Vamana (dwarf), Parashu Rama (Rama with an axe), Rama, Krishna, Buddha, and Kalki. These ten, known collectively as *Dashavatara* (literally "the Ten Avatars"; see Figure 8-1), are recognized as avatars in traditional Hinduism. They are described in the Garuda Purana and the Bhagavata Purana, two popular compendiums of god stories, genealogies of kings, prescriptive passages for rituals, and moral stories that have conveyed Hindu beliefs down to street level for centuries. I introduce each of these incarnations of Vishnu in order in the following sections.

I want to emphasize that the ten avatars cover the timespan of four yugas (one complete time cycle). One cycle spans a time period of 4.32 million years. One thousand such cycles equal a single day of Brahma, which is 4.32 billion years long. (Brahma's night is just as long.) Keep this in mind as you read the stories.

As you read the following sections, notice the evolution of the avatar forms. The ten avatars evolve over time to match the needs of the age and the level of threat. When the avatars take on human forms, from Vamana onward, they are born into human life — for better or worse. While preparing for their destined role, they suffer through all the ills that mortal men experience. They also incur a few very human flaws along the way, which have to be paid back in earthly punishment. The human avatars are not doppelgangers (twins of their real selves) or bionic heroes, even if their powers can be seen as extraordinary. Krishna will eventually die a real, sad death.

Figure 8-1:
The ten avatars of Vishnu.

Matsya: The big fish story

According to Hindu mythology, when the time cycle nears its end, the creator, Brahma, begins his great sleep for a single Brahma night. At the end of each such cycle, certain treasures need to be retained for the next cycle to function. These treasures are, in order of importance:

✔ **The Vedas:** When Brahma goes to sleep, he swallows the sacred texts called the Vedas (see Chapter 10) so that, upon his awakening, they are available for the folks in the new age. (This is why Hindus call the Vedas eternal!)

✔ **The Seven Sages:** *Saptarshi* (or Sapta Rishi), the Seven Sages of Hindu legend, are the seers who will preserve and explain the Vedas in the new age to come. They form the constellation L. Ursa Major, the Big Dipper. The sages' names relevant to the current age are Atri, Bharadwaja, Gautama, Jamadagni, Kashyapa, Vasishta, and Viswamitra. These names differ in separate scriptures and other writings that refer to the constellation.

✔ **Seeds of all the vegetation in the entire world.**

I present to you now the first avatar of Vishnu, Matsya, who descended when a demon stole the Vedas from the sleeping Brahma.

A demon known as Hayagriva was aware that the end of the previous cycle was nearing and didn't want to perish with everything else. He schemed to steal the Vedas so that he, too, would remain eternal. Hayagriva hung around the sleeping Brahma, waiting to find a way to grab the sacred texts. He got his chance. When Brahma had a huge yawn, the Vedas almost came out. Hayagriva grabbed the Vedas, devoured them himself, and then hid himself in the ocean. The deluge to end the time cycle began, and the Vedas were in the belly of Hayagriva. Now there was, as they say on Wall Street, a crisis of major proportions. It was time for Vishnu to descend.

Vishnu assumed the form of a fish, Matsya. Needing the assistance of a human to carry out the task, Matsya found King Satya Vrata (Manu, the progenitor for the coming age) standing waist deep in a local river, beginning his morning prayer. When Satya Vrata picked up a handful of water to offer in salutation to the sun god, he found a tiny fish in his watery palms. The fish spoke to the king, asking for protection from other big fish in the river. Hindu kings obliged anyone in their kingdom who sought protection, so Matsya found itself in the palace fish tank. Soon the fish outgrew the tank and was placed in a palace pool. When the fish outgrew the pool, King Satya Vrata realized it must be some sort of divine intervention and sent the now large fish to the ocean. There, Matsya commanded the king to assemble a boat. Into this boat he was to gather the Seven Sages, their wives, animals, and all seeds, and — after they had been recovered — the Vedas. Soon after, Matsya spotted Hayagriva, killed him, and recovered the Vedas, which were safely placed in the boat. The big fish pulled the boat to higher ground, and all was well.

Kurma, the tortoise, lends his back

Here is another story during the same deluge in which Vishnu appears as a tortoise.

Many precious, life-sustaining items had been lost in the cosmic ocean, and any continuation of life would be impossible without their recovery. One such item was the all-important vessel containing nectar that fed the gods and gave them immortality. The sun and the moon had also disappeared into the ocean. The gods became weaker and weaker because of the loss of nectar. Every element and being that helped sustain life was missing somewhere in the great ocean of milk. It was clear that unless something was done soon, the world would come to an end — again.

Brahma, Vishnu, and Shiva (the three primary gods who are considered the Hindu Trinity) met and conferred to determine how the lost gods and the heavenly bodies, as well as the all-important nectar, could be restored. It was clear that the only solution was to churn the cosmic ocean of milk. This huge undertaking required enormous power. It was the opinion of the trinity that the help of even the demonic forces was essential in this endeavor. But what about the consequences, such as the possible theft of the nectar and resulting immortality for the demons? Any concern about protecting the nectar from the demons was balanced by the need to recover the lost life-sustaining elements.

After the demons agreed to cooperate, only the mechanical details were left to be worked out. What about the rope? What could serve as a churning rod? How would the churning rod rest secure on the ocean floor?

At this point, Vishnu decided to take the form of a huge tortoise. A huge monolithic mountain described in the epic the *Mahabharata* as Mount Mandara offered himself as the churning rod. And the huge serpent Vasuki volunteered to be the rope. The gods held the tail of the serpent, the snake wound itself around the mountain, and the demons held its head, and all was set for the great churning of the milky ocean. (In Sanskrit literature, the churning is called *Amritamanthana*.)

The gods stood on one side, the demons stood on the other, and they pulled in opposite directions toward a common goal. The churning was successful. Out came, among the very many precious items, the sun and the moon, the goddess Lakshmi, a jewel worn by Vishnu, celestial dancers, a wish-fulfilling tree, the cow of plenty, many of the special weapons of the gods, medicine and poison, god Indra's elephant and horse, and finally the physician carrying the pot of nectar. The tortoise avatar had fulfilled its mission.

What happened to the nectar? Did the gods share it with the demons? Heavens, no! In fact, they schemed to hide it in four places in northern India: Prayag, Hardwar, Ujjain, and Nasik. Stay with me, and I'll come back to this part of the story when I introduce Hindu festivals in Chapter 18.

Varaha, the boar, rescues the earth goddess

In his third incarnation, Vishnu takes the form of a wild boar who subdues and kills a demon named Hiranyaksha who had the audacity to drag the entire earth down to his own underworld, the bottom of the ocean. The fantabulous tale recounts that Vishnu in this form fought the demon for a thousand years, finally destroyed him, and heaved the earth up again on the boar's tusks to her rightful place above water.

Narasimha, the man-lion, uses his claws

Vishnu's fourth avatar is neither fully man nor fully animal, but a combination of the two: a man-lion.

There was a king known as Hiranyakashipu who had "conquered the world" and thought that he was a god and need not accept any higher authority. Hiranyakashipu had a son named Prahlada. Prahlada grew up revering the god Narayana, a form of Vishnu. When the king learned of this he tried to convince Prahlada that none was more worthy of worship and more powerful than Hiranyakashipu himself. The king claimed that he had successfully persuaded all his subjects to honor and worship him as god. Prahlada knew not only that the king's subjects hated the king's arrogance but also that his own love of god Narayana was beyond question. Further persuasion, appeals, and threats led the king nowhere.

One day, as he argued with his son, the king grew angrier and angrier. He asked, "Where is your Narayana? Show me." Prahlada replied gently, "Father, he, the Lord of the Universe, is everywhere, don't you see?" Beside himself, the king pointed to a nearby pillar in the palace hall and asked, "Son, is he in this pillar?" Prahlada replied, "Yes, of course, father. Didn't I tell you? He is *everywhere!*"

Immediately, the king swung his mace and dealt a severe blow to the column. Lo and behold, a form — half man and half lion — emerged! It was Narasimha, one of the ten incarnations of Vishnu. The roaring Narasimha had had enough of the king's abuse of his subjects and his son. He lifted Hiranyakashipu up, sat down on the threshold to the palace, laid the king down on his lap, and with a lion's sharp claws tore the king's belly apart. End of story. But wait, why the lap? Why claws? Why on the threshold?

Earlier, as a devotee of Vishnu, Hiranyakashipu was one of those ambitious kings who had asked and received a *boon* (a blessing from the gods) which granted that he could not be killed by a human or animal, inside or outside, or by any weaponry. That's why the form that Vishnu took was neither that of a man nor an animal but a combination of the two. It's also why Narasimha killed the king on a threshold (neither inside nor out) using mere claws (not a weapon). Many Hindu stories involve such matching of wits!

Vamana, the dwarf, takes three giant steps

In his fifth incarnation, Vishnu assumes the form of a dwarf, Vamana. This story pertains to another powerful demonic ruler known as Emperor Bali who was a pious devotee of Hari (Vishnu) and ruled his empire without swerving from the path of dharma. All was well until Bali desired to displace Indra as chief of the gods.

With Bali's intention proclaimed, the *devas* (gods) panicked and appealed to Vishnu. Vishnu agreed to be born as the avatar Vamana, a dwarf. As a young *vatu* (a boy from the brahmin caste who is devoted to the study of the Vedas), Vamana traveled to the kingdom of Bali. Bali felt honored by this visit and attended to the young fellow. Bali encouraged Vamana to ask for anything he wished: land, cows, elephants, palaces, gold, and so on. Vamana said he wouldn't need any of those things because he was a simple bachelor. All he wanted was space that could be covered by no more than three paces. Bali was astonished.

It was then that Shukra Acharya, the guru of the demons, came in and warned Bali about the real identity of Vamana and urged him not to go through with this gift. But Bali was overjoyed to realize that Lord Vishnu himself was in his land. Besides, how could giving a measly three steps' measure of land cause any harm? So Bali agreed to the request, only to be taken aback when Vamana grew and grew and grew until, with one foot, he covered the whole sky. His other foot covered the entire earth. There was still one more measure to get. Where could Vamana put his foot now? Bali offered his own head, and Vamana simply put his foot on Bali's head and pushed it all the way to the netherworld below. Mission accomplished! Everybody and everything went back to normal.

Parashu Rama and the revenge of the clerics

In his sixth incarnation, Vishnu takes the form of an angry sage, Parashu Rama, who intervenes when one caste tries to overtake the others. (See Chapter 5 for an overview of the Hindu caste system.) The warrior caste (called *kshatriya*) lost its self-control and attempted to control the clerics (brahmin class) and bully the populace it was supposed to protect.

In response to the warrior caste's bad behavior, Vishnu was born as Parashu Rama, or Rama with an axe. (The axe was given to him by the god Shiva.) Parashu Rama was born the son of a brahmin sage, and his purpose was to rid the world of the warriors altogether. The reason? He wanted to avenge the merciless death of his father at the hands of a kshatriya. In addition, Parashu Rama concluded that the kshatriyas had become tyrants over their people rather than protectors. A fearful carnage erupted, and all the kshatriyas were destroyed. (Is it surprising that there are no temples for Parashu Rama?)

Rama and the ideal of kingship

After Parashu Rama destroyed the kshatriya caste, Vishnu then returned as the avatar Rama, who was himself a kshatriya (a warrior prince). Rama, the seventh avatar of Vishnu, is also known by the name Shri Ramachandra and, in Hindi, as Ram.

Rama is the hero of the great Hindu epic called the *Ramayana* (see Chapter 12). He is portrayed as the ideal son, a strict adherent to dharma, an ideal brother and husband, and an ideal king. Thousands of generations of Hindus have read or heard the hundreds of stories in the epic. Immense satisfaction and catharsis are still derived by recalling the trials and tribulations of this young prince.

The primary motivation for the appearance of this avatar was the rising menace of demons. These demons aimed their destructive activities at monasteries, where sages practiced austerities and studied the Vedas. The most famous demon was Ravana, a ten-headed king.

Rama's stepmother, who wished to replace Rama with her own son as crown prince, convinced her husband, the king, to send the young warrior Rama into exile. She was cashing in on a boon the king had given her. The exile lasted 14 years, during which Ravana abducted Rama's beloved wife Sita. Rama assembled a rescue force including an army of monkeys and other allies acquired during his exploits in exile. With the aid of the monkey brigade, Rama built a bridge from the southern tip of India to Ravana's kingdom, called Lanka. (A key character in this episode is Hanuman, the monkey hero, who served Rama and became his devotee. More about him in Chapter 7.)

A fierce battle ensued between Rama's army and that of Ravana. Finally, Lanka was set ablaze by Hanuman. Ravana and Rama dueled with many weapons, and Rama prevailed. Rama's exile ended, and he returned to his kingdom. A long period of ideal rule began, known as *Rama Rajya*: a phrase still associated with peace and plenty.

The birth of Krishna, the eighth avatar

The descent of this avatar of Vishnu was driven by a severe breach of all that defined a kind and able king. The cruel tyrant Kamsa ruled a region in the western part of India. In this incarnation, Krishna was the eighth child born to Kamsa's sister Devaki and her husband Vasudeva.

Kamsa was a cruel ruler, but he celebrated the wedding of his beloved sister Devaki to Vasudeva with a great deal of pomp and enthusiasm. With great pleasure and satisfaction, after the wedding was over, he decided to take them in his own chariot to their new home in town.

On the way, a voice from above taunted Kamsa and warned him that the eighth child born to Devaki would bring about his end. A furious Kamsa decided to kill the couple right then and there. As he drew his sword, Vasudeva pleaded with Kamsa to spare their lives and pledged that as soon as a child was born, Kamsa could choose to let it live or die. Kamsa thought no harm would come from this arrangement, but for his own peace of mind, he made sure the couple was jailed. Devaki had many children, and the parents suffered the pain of losing each one as Kamsa made sure that all the babies were killed soon after they were born.

During Devaki's eighth pregnancy, Kamsa increased security and put Vasudeva in chains. When the eighth son was born, Vasudeva heard a voice that instructed him to take the baby to a cowherd named Nanda in a nearby town called Gokul. Vasudeva was to exchange the baby for a newborn baby girl. Suddenly, Vasudeva's shackles came undone, and he was free. Vasudeva feared that he would be stopped by the guards, but to his further amazement they were all sound asleep and Vasudeva walked out and reached Nanda's home. There he found Nanda's family asleep, and he was able to leave his child there and bring back the baby girl.

Of course, the first thing the baby did upon arrival at the prison was to cry. The sound awoke the guards who hurried to inform the king. Kamsa was surprised that the baby was a girl. Girl or boy, the child had to die. Kamsa picked up the baby by its feet with both hands to smash it on a rock. But lo and behold, the baby simply flew up and disappeared. And Kamsa, once again, heard the taunting voice, which now proclaimed: The boy who will kill you is growing up in Gokul.

Many stories are centered on Krishna's childhood in Gokul: Kamsa's failed attempts to kill him; his baby pranks; playing his flute; his teasing of the *gopis* (milkmaids) as a young lover; and so on. Finally, Kamsa insulted the adult Krishna during an encounter, and after that direct confrontation, Krishna killed him.

Thus, the principal mission of this avatar of Vishnu was complete when Krishna was still a young man. However, Krishna's role in restoring dharma continued through the end of the famous battle at Kurukshetra, which you can read about in Chapter 12.

Buddha, the ninth avatar

Some Hindus saw the Buddha — the ninth avatar of Vishnu — as a precursor of the end of days, or as a warning that the Vedas were in danger. Some saw him as a reformer who brought attention back to what mattered more than mere rituals: the quest for Reality. Buddha himself was the perfect human, beyond all temptations, intent on promoting dharma.

Buddha was born more than 2,500 years ago as Siddhartha Gautama, son of king Shuddhodhana of the city of Kapilavastu at the foot of the Himalayas. He was brought up as a noble prince in luxury learning the appropriate military arts, as well as the philosophical knowledge available at the time. Everything in his life was ideal with joy, happiness, wealth, great parentage, and friends worthy of a prince. Legend has it that he saw no misery around him having lived inside the great palace. Everyone was nice, and everything was at its very best; the king made sure of it. The prince married and had a male child, but he had never seen the world outside the huge palace.

One day he happened to be out of the palace alone, and he saw what he had never seen before in his life. For the first time he saw a very old man who was lean, bent, helpless, and miserable — completely different from the adults he had been exposed to in the palace. On another such outing he saw a beggar and a sick man agonizing. A few days later, he saw a dead man being carried off to the cremation ground. Talking to people on the street, he learned that every human being must experience these stages in life, and it came as a shock.

This experience was enough for the prince to leave his family when he was around 29, walk away from the palace, and begin to meditate on the realities of life. This contemplation and deep meditation made him realize that true happiness can come only when we break the cycle of births and deaths. Thus enlightened, he taught that the root cause of all suffering is desire and offered an eightfold path for people to follow: right thought, speech, effort, living, action without motive, understanding, concentration, and thoughtfulness. It was this enlightenment that made Gautama the Buddha. His principal message may be summarized this way: Do good, be good, and that will lead you to the Truth and allow you to experience freedom from birth and death.

Buddha, the Enlightened One, as an avatar of Vishnu? A total surprise to Buddhists! This adoption by Hindus, according to some scholars, was aimed at reaching a compromise with Buddhism itself.

Kalki: The tenth avatar yet to come

The world is now in what Hindus call the fourth and final age, named Kali Yuga. Hindus expect that during this yuga, moral order will continue to decline and evil will steadily increase. Sometime during this age, the tenth avatar, named Kalki, will appear in the sky sitting on a white horse and armed with a sword. When Kalki arrives, Hindus believe that all wickedness will be destroyed and moral order will be restored in order to usher in a new age of purity. The new age will be the very first age (the first of four yugas), and the cycle of time will start all over again.

The ten manifestations at a glance

To help you keep track of the ten avatars of Vishnu, I offer Table 8-1. I show in the first column the age in which the avatar manifested, followed by the name of the avatar in the second column. The next column lists the name of the individual(s) who initiated or helped the action that followed. The last column describes the task the avatar undertook, the action performed, and/ or (briefly) the story.

Table 8-1		The Ten Avatars of Vishnu	
Age/Yuga	*Avatar*	*Agent*	*Action/Story*
Krita (First)	Matsya the fish	Satya Vrata (sometimes referred to as Manu)	**Rescuing the Vedas:** King Satya Vrata saved a small fish, which became enormous and retrieved the Vedas from the belly of a sea monster. Satya Vrata was told to build a boat and fill it with the Seven Sages plus seeds of all plants to be saved; the boat was pulled to dry land by the fish avatar.
Krita (First)	Kurma the tortoise	Gods and demons	**Amrithamanthana (churning the milky ocean):** Kurma supported Mount Mandara in the churning of the ocean of milk to retrieve amrita, the food of immortality.
Krita (First)	Varaha the boar		**Saving the earth:** Varaha restored the earth, which had been carried down to the depths of the sea by demon Hiranyaksha.
Krita (First)	Narasimha the man-lion	Prahlada	**Saving a devotee:** The man-lion appeared out of a pillar of fire to kill arrogant king Hiranyakashipu, who could not be killed by god, man, or animal.
Treta (Second)	Vamana the dwarf		**Saving the three worlds from demon king Bali:** Vamana requested as much land as he could cover in three paces. His third giant step pushed Bali down to the hell of Patala (the underworld).

(continued)

Table 8-1 *(continued)*

Age/Yuga	Avatar	Agent	Action/Story
Treta (Second)	Parasu Rama (Rama with the axe)		**Massacring the kshatriyas:** When the warrior caste tried to control the brahmins, angry sage Parasu Rama destroyed all the kshatriyas.
Treta (Second)	Rama, the hero of the epic *Ramayana*		**Destroying the demon king Ravana:** As a kshatriya, ideal king Rama defeated Ravana and established a model kingdom.
Dwapara (Third)	Krishna, hero of the epic *Mahabharata* and the *Bhagavad Gita*	Arjuna	**Destroying the cruel king Kamsa:** Krishna was born to Kamsa's sister Devaki, in spite of the king's vow to kill all her children. As a young man he killed Kamsa (and also helped the Pandava princes defeat their evil cousins).
Kaliyuga (Fourth)	Buddha, the Enlightened		**Destroying illusion:** As Buddha — yes, that same Buddha! — the ninth avatar of Vishnu came to test humans' faith in the Vedas and the gods.
Kaliyuga (Fourth)	Kalki, avatar yet to come		**Restoring a new cycle of ages:** The tenth avatar will arrive on a white horse to destroy evil and restore a new cycle, beginning again with Krita (the first) Yuga.

Chapter 9

Revering the Role of Religious Leadership

. . . .

In This Chapter

▶ Finding out what priests, swamis, and gurus do

▶ Studying the characteristics of great Hindu leaders

▶ Learning the impact of saints and sages on Hindu philosophy

. . . .

> *What is the path?*

*I*n the *Mahabharata,* a Hindu epic that I discuss in Chapter 12, a Yaksha (nature spirit) dwelling in a forest posed that question to Yudhishtira to probe his spiritual strength. The question really means: How should one lead a life on earth? How does one lead a spiritual life? How does one attain salvation? Yudhishtira replied simply:

> *What great men have followed — THAT is the path.*

The reply bypasses the complexities of scriptures, competing philosophies, and ritualistic approaches. A simpler route is to observe the life led by a great person, accept to learn from and follow that exemplary person, and thus seek the path toward knowledge and salvation. Who are such great men (or women)? They could be kings, warriors, or learned men or women, but in this context they're holy persons whose guidance and grace are sought for such an important quest.

Legend after legend from ancient India portrays kings and emperors rushing down from their thrones to greet and offer obeisance to a guest clad in saffron — a holy man. (The color saffron is associated with sacrifice and renunciation.) Centuries later, this practice continues with Indian presidents and prime ministers showing respect to religious leaders, occasionally conferring with them and seeking their counsel. Even in the United States today, it is not uncommon for a community of Hindus to show special respect to these visiting gurus and swamis in saffron robes.

This chapter introduces you to the centuries-old Hindu tradition of revering saints, swamis, and gurus. I define what each of these words means to a Hindu and list some of the great men who are considered saints, swamis, and gurus. Also, Hindu families look to religious teachers for guidance on how to learn and practice the faith and have special relationships with these teachers, who are more accurately called *preceptors*. I explain what this word means and why the relationship between student and teacher is so vital to Hindus.

Priests, Gurus, and Swamis: Spiritual Leaders of Hinduism

Within a Hindu community, different people have different interests related to their religion. Therefore, each person's relationship with his or her religious leader is unique. Here are just a few examples of the types of interaction between Hindus and their religious leaders:

- Hindu intellectuals may seek the guidance of *seers* (mystics) and philosophers, and some intellectuals may choose to attend *discourses* (lectures) and contribute to discussions and journals focused on religious topics.

- Other Hindus may prefer to visit a swami or *guru* (teacher) and may support that leader with cash or in-kind contributions.

- Some Hindus find fulfillment worshipping at a temple, participating in and helping with daily or weekly services.

- Others obtain peace by joining a group that conducts daily or weekly programs in which a leader, knowledgeable in Hindu devotional songs, leads the group in singing such songs accompanied by musical instruments.

- Some Hindus may associate themselves with a yoga center (where physical exercises and meditation techniques are taught) and visit it when the founder or the leader addresses the disciples and daily visitors.

- Others are completely satisfied simply consulting a priest for advice regarding an upcoming wedding or domestic ceremony (such as a naming ceremony for a baby).

To meet the variety of needs, a corresponding cadre of religious leaders has sprung up over time. Chief among them are priests, swamis, and gurus. The following sections describe who these key religious leaders in Hinduism are, explain how one becomes such a religious leader, and identify the more renowned leaders.

Priests: Leading services in temples and serving the community

Priests are usually from the brahmin caste (refer to Chapter 5) and are trained in *agamas:* procedures involved in temple rituals and domestic rituals. More often than not, priests learn how to conduct rituals from a father or uncle. Some also get formal schooling in Sanskrit and scriptures. Priests are almost always employed by temples.

Hindu priests are known as *pujaris* or *purohits.* Their main function is to perform daily and weekly services to temple deities with or without the presence of devotees. In addition, they must keep the *sanctums* (the holiest spaces in the temple where the deities reside) clean and stocked with materials needed for performing the *puja* (worship).

Unlike their counterparts in other religions, Hindu priests do not generally deliver sermons. Their expertise is essentially in performing rituals.

Many priests become *family priests,* which means they guide and lead families during major ceremonies such as weddings and housewarmings. In such situations, a rapport and mutually supportive relationship develops between the priest and the family. For this reason, priests are also an indispensable part of a Hindu community.

Swamis and gurus: Training and inspiring young people

The word *guru* literally means "teacher." *Swami* translates as "master," a title for a religious leader. I use these two words interchangeably in this text, so wherever you see one word, assume that the other is implied as well.

Swamis are spiritual leaders who teach, train, and guide others not only by delivering sermons, discourses, and lectures but also on a one-on-one basis. If a swami belongs to an order, such as the Ramakrishna Order, he serves that order as an authorized, ordained swami who is part of a global organization, and he is governed by rules, regulations, and guidelines set up by the parent organization. Swamis may or may not be attached to a temple, and they may have their own ashrams/centers of learning, as I explain later in this section.

Understanding the concept of master and disciple

Having this book in your hands now means you are interested in religion — in particular, Hinduism. Suppose you were interested in more in-depth information about Hinduism; you'd read advanced treatises on the subject and deepen your understanding of basic concepts. But if your interests were to run even deeper — if you wanted to be spiritually illumined, in other words — then, to follow the Hindu approach, you would have to go beyond books.

Hindus make a distinction between intellect and inner spirit in the context of religion. Even though studying advanced books on spirituality undoubtedly sharpens the intellect and adds to your knowledge base, your inner spirit remains less than fulfilled without some guidance from someone who has lived and is living a spiritual life. Such a person, who can guide you and lead you to the state of perfection, is known as guru. You, the disciple, are a *shishya* — if and only if the swami or guru accepts you and determines that you are, in fact, prepared. There is a saying among Hindus: When a student is prepared, a guru appears!

Establishing ashrams

A swami or guru needs a space in which to teach his disciplines. Such a space may be an *ashram:* a hermitage (secluded space) often located far from populated areas. (Think park-like locations, such as forests, river banks, and hills.) It usually has residential facilities for students and visitors. At ashrams of the ancient past, the students (children from nearby communities) lived an austere life with the guru and sometimes his family. They served the guru and obtained a disciplined and rigorous training in the faith.

If the leader resides at the ashram, then at the end of each day, disciples gather to listen to a *satsang,* which roughly translates as "holy meeting" or "auspicious gathering." A satsang serves as a meeting between a religious leader and his/her followers when devotional songs and chants are offered, followed by a sermon.

Starting in the 1960s, several swamis who settled in the United States from India established ashrams and took Western and Hindu disciples. Several such thriving ashrams can be found in the United States today. Ashrams in the United States are often called *religious centers.* More often than not, they offer programs in yoga, meditation, and *Ayurveda* (the traditional medicine of ancient Hindus, which defines the health of a human being based on the extent of balance among three principal components: the body components, the extent of lubrication of joints, and digestive ability).

Studying at an ashram

At ashrams, the swamis have strict daily routines for the disciples, for themselves, and for visitors. Training takes place with rigor and vigor appropriate to the level of the trainees. Gurus may conduct classes devoted to topics selected from scriptures and are available to answer questions of a spiritual and theological nature.

Keep in mind that studying and staying at an ashram, paying for classes, or volunteering do not require conversion to Hinduism.

For serious disciples, training also includes Sanskrit, Hindu scriptures and philosophy, and Hatha yoga (which emphasizes physical exercise). A disciple may have the goal of being ordained as a monk into the same Hindu order that the swami belongs to, and he may wish to stay with and serve the swami and the ashram (living a *monastic* life). Such followers perform assigned tasks, including teaching.

In the upcoming section "Initiating Hindu monks," you find out more about how one becomes a Hindu monk. First, I introduce you to four Hindu religious centers in the United States so you can get a sense of their variety.

Yogaville (Buckingham, Virginia)

Satchidananda Ashram, also known as Yogaville, was founded in 1980 by Swami Satchidananda (1914–2002), who is shown in Figure 9-1.

Figure 9-1:
Swami Satchidananda with the author at the Hindu Temple in Connecticut, 1989.

Originally established in a quiet corner of Connecticut, the ashram moved to a 500-acre plot of land on the James River in Virginia. A beautiful interfaith temple in the shape of a lotus was also built; it's known as Light of Truth Universal Shrine (LOTUS). Swami Satchidananda's Integral Yoga approach (a combination of physical, mental, and spiritual practices) is an attempt to synthesize all the Yogas (see Chapter 21) toward development of the body, mind, and soul.

A man of extraordinary simplicity, full of charm and grace, Swamiji mended many lives. He took many youths under his wing and brought them back to a path free of drugs and alcohol. Many of his disciples around the world continue his legacy, bringing honor to a great man of peace. For more information about the center, visit www.yogaville.org.

Hindu Monastery (Kauai, Hawaii)

Another organization doing yeoman service to young people is the Hindu monastery on a beautiful 353-acre property in Kauai, Hawaii. The emphasis here is *Shaiva Siddhanta,* which means Shaivite traditions (see Chapter 4) that are practiced in South India and Sri Lanka. The disciples do not study the Bhagavad Gita. The monastery publishes a high caliber journal known as *Hinduism Today.*

Only single Hindu men (or converts to Hinduism) under the age of 25 are eligible for monastic training at this center. An impressive order of monks (see Figure 9-2) have dedicated themselves to a monastic life offering regular programs of instruction and training. This monastery is currently under the leadership of Satguru Bodhinatha Veylan Swami. For more information about the monastery, visit www.himalayanacademy.com/ssc/Hawaii.

Figure 9-2:
Monks at the Hindu Monastery in Hawaii.

Photo by Himalayan Academy

Arsha Vidya Gurukulam (Saylorsburg, Pennsylvania)

This *gurukulam* (which means "residential center under a guru") focuses on teaching Vedic scriptures through regular program offerings on its campus, as well as online. Under the leadership of Swami Dayananda Saraswati, the gurukulam has an excellent staff that includes additional ordained monks. Two temples and a bookstore allow for training in chanting and learning the basics of Hindu philosophy. Visit www.arshavidya.org to find out more.

Maharishi University of Management (Fairfield, Iowa)

The Maharishi University of Management is a fully accredited university founded by Maharishi Mahesh Yogi in 1971. The university's uniqueness is its emphasis on developing a knowledge of one's own self as a basis for all studies. Transcendental Meditation is part of each student's life. Students may earn basic and advanced degrees in traditional subjects, as well as degrees in Vedic Science. Visit `mum.edu` to find out more.

Initiating Hindu monks

Some ashrams are *monasteries;* they are specifically concerned with the training and ordination of young men for a celibate life as monks. These ashrams are usually run by recognized orders.

A serious aspirant can be initiated into an order of Hindu monks if the student is prepared and the guru blesses it. Preparation may differ from one order to another, but the fundamentals remain the same. In general (there are exceptions), a knowledge of the Vedas and the Bhagavad Gita (sacred texts that I explain in Part III) and an extraordinary commitment to serve human beings anywhere at any time irrespective of any other consideration are minimum requirements. Above all, the blessing of the guru is essential.

To become a monk, a student is initiated into *sanyas,* which means "renunciation." The student takes part in procedures and ceremonies that are held in the open and under the direction of the authorized head of the order of monks. Upon initiation, the individual's life is dedicated only and entirely to the service of others.

Generally, the new monk gives up his or her birth name and assumes a name chosen by the guru. For example, in the Ramakrishna Order, the names of monks begin with the title *Swami,* and the new name ends with *ananda* (joy).

After ordination, the monks sometimes continue as residents of the monastery. Sometimes, in India, they may become wandering *mendicants* (those who live essentially on alms, giving an opportunity for the donors to gain spiritual merit).

Several U.S. and European centers offer disciples the opportunity to be initiated into sanyas. The Hindu Monastery in Kauai is one example.

What It Takes to Become a Spiritual Leader

Concern for the welfare of humanity, extraordinary interest in personal salvation, and a general disinterest in material life are the primary drivers that influence an individual to first seek a spiritual leader who can guide the aspirant to be a good disciple. If the apprenticeship works out, the disciple may advance to a higher state of renunciation, totally absorbed in self through deep meditative states and devoted to learning and service. The guru — and only the guru — can decide the future of the disciple and bless him with a mission to lead others. Thus, a new leader is born.

In the case of almost every Hindu spiritual leader, what stands out is the leader's intense desire to know God. To realize that desire, spiritual leaders exhibit the following characteristics or actions:

✔ They have acquired spiritual wisdom through penance. (See the next section for an explanation of penance.)

✔ They have risen above worldly life; a sense of detachment is evident.

✔ They have extraordinary love for humanity and creatures.

✔ They exhibit qualities of fearlessness, confidence, and a balanced mind.

✔ They lead a chaste life. In each category of spiritual leaders, you will find most are unmarried, although some may have families.

✔ They exhibit extraordinary self-control. The best of Hindu monks have always kept the mind and the body finely tuned with the constant practice of yoga, meditation, and the study of scriptures.

✔ They are dedicated to the concept of Truth in everything they do.

Knowledge of Brahman, the ability to communicate complicated and abstract concepts to disciples, an interest in teaching, the acceptance of personal sacrifice, depth, devotion to serving humankind — all these qualities add up to an extraordinary, complicated, and yet simple personality that befits an ideal Hindu spiritual leader. (Notice what characteristic is *not* on this list? Being a member of the brahmin caste; see Chapter 5.)

A Sanskrit verse sums up the personality of the masters:

> *Hard as diamond and soft as a flower*
> *Who can know the mind of the great?*

Meaning? Spiritual leaders are hard as diamonds when it concerns studies and training and soft as flowers in relations with other souls.

So how do people attain this state? Through penance and renunciation. The following sections explain these concepts.

Probing the idea of penance

The Hindu concept of *penance* encompasses dedication, study, service, apprenticeship under a guru, practicing austerities prescribed by the teacher, and training the mind to concentrate. Through these actions, an aspirant attains the state necessary to become a spiritual leader. See my detailed discussion of Raja Yoga in Chapter 21 to find out much more.

Looking at the concept of renunciation

Individuals who long for a spiritual life have little interest in what others would call normal life. They don't hate normalcy; they just don't feel its pull. They are, in a manner of speaking, above it. Setting up a household doesn't interest them. They choose to remain celibate and direct their energy at examining deeper aspects of life and death. They are *renunciates:* They engage in meditation, breath control, and yogic postures, and they eat frugal vegetarian meals. Their primary goals are the following:

✔ **Seeking personal salvation:** Normally the focus of renunciates is personal salvation. They realize that they are born in this world and bliss comes from striving to reach back to Brahman and end the cycle of births and rebirths. As such, they prefer to keep to themselves, and they may not be accessible to anyone. Although you may get the impression that renunciates don't care about this world, that is only partly true. They know they're part of this world, but their interest is seeking Truth. Therefore, all their activities are oriented toward that single goal.

✔ **Serving humankind:** A guru may direct renunciates to take on a spiritual task in the so-called "real world." Such an assignment brings the future leader into contact with people at large in big cities. Depending upon the guru's domain of interest and/or influence, he may (either at the request of a community or on his own) decide to send one of his disciples to a town, city, or village to set up a center to serve people. The new center serves the specific needs of the community (education, drug rehabilitation, caring for the sick and the elderly, and so on), and the renunciate is part of the community as a religious leader. The choice of who goes where is entirely up to the guru.

Mythological and Ancient Saints

There are religious leaders, and then there are religious leaders. Some leaders with extraordinary knowledge, analytical skills to delve deep into scriptures, and a magnetic personality, attract disciples of high caliber. They have all the characteristics of spiritual leaders mentioned in the previous section, and more. Such gifted and inspired individuals came along in ancient and modern India, and their contributions have changed thousands of lives and unraveled the mysteries of many a scripture. They effected reformations and insights that refreshed and validated Hindu thought over millennia. The result is a dynamic religion that has never ceased to satisfy a wide range of believers.

Ancient sages (wise persons) were known as *rishis* (pronounced *rushis*). The rishis are the most revered of all the spiritual leaders mentioned in Hindu legends, epics, and puranas.

Legend has it that these ancient sages were revered by either their own peers or by royalty and were recognized with special titles. These designations have come down to us and are acknowledged as such through stories notably in the Hindu epics. The special titles are the following:

- **Deva rishi:** A sage honored by gods, or god-like

- **Brahma rishi:** One who has realized Brahman

- **Raja rishi:** A king with spiritual wisdom

- **Maha rishi:** A great sage

- **Param rishi:** A sage who has realized God (Paramatman)

- **Shruta rishi**: A famous sage

- **Kanda rishi:** A sage who has heard by revelation a section of the Vedas

Any of these rishis may be honored with the title or description of *saint*. This title is honorific and not attached to any system of canonization.

Hindus in general, and brahmins in particular, may proudly claim that they are spiritual descendents of a particular rishi. This connection serves as an identification of a particular Hindu family with a sage and is referred to as *gotra*. The gotra is used during religious ceremonies to publicly proclaim the family's lineage.

Among the legendary rishis, a few made indelible marks on ancient societies and played major roles in Hindu stories, such as Puranas and epics. These rishis influenced events and helped restore dharma (moral order or balance; see Chapter 1). I introduce you to some of them in the following sections.

The Seven Sages

Hindu mythology refers to the Seven Sages (*Saptarshis* or *Sapta Rishis*) who are eternal, much like the Vedas, and are preserved at the end of each cycle of time. (As I explain in Chapter 1, Hindus believe that time is cyclical; at the end of the last eon, all of creation is destroyed so it can be reborn. But the Vedas are preserved, always.) These sages are often known by the following personal names: Bhrigu, Angirasa, Atri, Vishvamitra, Kashyapa, Vasishta, and Agastya. (Some scholars suggest other names: Jamadagni, Bharadvaja, Gautama, Atri, Vasishta, Kashyapa, and Vishvamitra.)

The Seven Sages are believed to be represented in the seven brightest stars in the constellation Ursa Major. They are considered eternal, immortal guardians of dharma, and their task is to teach the Vedas to the new world after each cosmic recreation.

Narada

Narada muni is a familiar sage in the sacred mythological literature of Hindus. (*Muni* is another name for a sage.) Considered a one-man postal service, Narada traveled a great deal and collected information, which he freely disseminated. His efforts caused rivalries and fights but occasionally had life-changing effects. Hindus refer to him humorously as a gossiper extraordinaire! Narada was a sage nevertheless and kept good company, visiting the gods Vishnu, Shiva, and Brahma frequently, collecting information from them and conveying it to them. Called a *deva rishi* (divine sage), Narada traveled the universe preaching dharma, motivating people to have *bhakti* (love of God), visiting kingdoms, and sharing information among and about friends and rivals.

The Darshana philosophers

We know the names of six ancient philosophers who helped develop sophisticated approaches to seeing reality in the Hindu context: Gautama, Kapila, Jaimini, Badarayana, Patanjali, and Kanada. (By "ancient," I mean they lived perhaps 1,500 to 2,500 years ago.) But other than their names, we don't know much about them. What little we *do* know comes courtesy of commentaries on these philosophers' complicated ideas, which were written some centuries later. I write about these philosophers in Chapter 19.

More Recent Saints

In this section, I introduce you to principal saints whose more recent contributions to Hindu philosophy are recognized by scholars and laymen alike. (By "more recent," I mean within the past 1,200 years or so. Remember that the Hindu religion has been around for a very, very long time!)

The acharyas

The spiritual leaders in this section are known as *acharyas* ("great leaders"). They argued about the nature of the relationship between individual souls and the Supreme Soul and helped found the Hindu denominations that I describe in Chapter 4.

Here I introduce you to Shankara, the founder of Advaita (Nondualism); Ramanuja, the founder of Vishistadvaita (Qualified Nondualism); and Madhva, the proponent of Dvaitha (Dualism). Keep reading to find out a bit about each acharya and his philosophy.

Shankara (788–820 CE)

Very little is known about Shankara's personal life. Even his year of birth is in doubt, with dates varying between 508 BCE and 788 CE. (The latter date is the one most scholars seem to agree upon.) He was born at Kaladi, a town in the present-day Indian state of Kerala. It is said that by the age of 10, he had already mastered the Vedas and was engaging scholars in debate and discourse. He was a prolific writer and the founding father of the philosophy known as Advaita: Nondualism.

I explain this philosophy in Chapter 20, but here's the abbreviated version: Advaita emphasizes that there is only one Reality, which is Brahman. Brahman (the Supreme Self) and the individual *atman* (soul) are one.

Although Shankara and his followers worshiped Shiva and forms of Vishnu (leading to a denomination known as Smartism; see Chapter 4), the focus of Advaita is *jnana* (spiritual knowledge). This knowledge removes the individual's ignorance pertaining to his or her individual soul's true identity with the Supreme Soul.

In his short life (he lived only 32 years), Shankara fought to restore Hinduism on the basis of the Vedas by countering what he saw as a decline of spirituality and an emphasis on materialism. Referred to as *Adi Shankara* ("the first Shankara"), this reformer toured India from north to south and established four major centers, known as *maths,* to teach Advaita. The centers are: Badrinath in the north, Puri in the east, Shringeri in the south, and Dwaraka in the west. To this day, these four centers are managed by acharyas referred to as *Jagadguru Shankaracharya.* The first part of that name, *Jagadguru,* means "preceptor (teacher) of the universe." The second part identifies the acharyas as spiritual descendents of Adi Shankara.

Ramanuja (c. 1017–1137 CE)

Ramanuja, popularly known as Sri Ramanujacharya, was born in Sri-Perumbudur in the southern state of Tamilnadu in the year 1017. He studied Vedanta (a topic I cover in Chapter 20) and became the chief proponent of a philosophy similar to Shankara's but with a qualification. This philosophy became known as Vishishtadvaita, or Qualified Nondualism. The emphasis in this approach is to balance the need for spiritual wisdom with passionate devotion to God through surrender.

A devotee of Vishnu, Ramanuja wanted his followers to experience the bliss of God's love. His reasoning was that this relationship was possible only if the individual remained distinct from Brahman. According to Ramanuja, total identity of the individual with Brahman dilutes what could otherwise be a beautiful, loving dependence. (Dependence requires two; when that distinction is lost — when you become one with Brahman — the dependence is lost as well.)

Ramanuja's intention was to merge reason with faith. Therefore, while accepting Shankara's insistence that Brahman is Reality, he reasoned that it was not the *only* reality. Instead, he allowed for the relative realities of individual souls and matter.

Ramanuja developed a following when he settled down at Srirangam in Tamilnadu and led the SriVaishnava movement, which became and continues to be an important Hindu denomination (see Chapter 4). Later he moved to Melkote in the state of Mysore (now in Karnataka) and established a famous shrine for Cheluva Narayana (a form of Vishnu). You can find out more about this shrine in Chapter 16.

Madhva (c. 1199–1278 CE)

Madhva was a Vaishnava theologian born near Udupi in the present state of Karnataka. At school, he proved to be more an athlete than a scholar. He excelled in sports activities and left school to study Hindu scriptures at home. During this period, he developed an intense desire for a monastic life.

At 25, he took vows of renunciation and devoted himself to advanced studies of Shankara's Nondualism (the Advaita Vedanta philosophy). Soon after, he developed his own approach to Vedanta, interpreting it in a different light than did Shankara and Ramanuja. Madhva maintained that the individual self and the Supreme Self are indeed distinct. This doctrine of difference, known as Dvaita (Dualism), emphasizes differences between (1) the Supreme Self and an individual self, (2) all the individual selves, (3) the Supreme Self and matter, (4) the individual self and matter, and (5) one substance and another. This last item in the five differences appears obvious, but it is quite a subtle concept. Nine substances are included in this concept: earth, water, light, air, ether, time, space, soul, and mind. I discuss the impact of this view in relation to the Hindu view of reality in Chapter 19.

Madhva interpreted liberation to mean experiencing the bliss of the Lord through surrender to a deity. The famous Udupi Krishna shrine in the western Karnataka town of Udupi is testimony to this devotion.

Nineteenth-century saints

Much closer to our own time, several nineteenth-century philosophers, monks, and preachers were able to sort out the different philosophies and condense them so that they could be taught and learned by thousands. Because of their efforts, the world is full of well-established and active monastic orders that offer instruction and train Hindu monks in a systematic manner. The following sections focus on four such saints: Ramakrishna and Vivekananda, shown in Figure 9-3; Shivananda; and Ramana Maharshi.

Figure 9-3:
Rama-
krishna (left)
and Vive-
kananda
(right).

Photos by Ramakrishna-Vivekananda Center of New York

Ramakrishna (1836–1886)

Sri Ramakrishna Paramahamsa was an extraordinary saint of the nineteenth century. He served as a priest at the famous Kali temple at Dakshineshwar near Kolkata (Calcutta). His goal was to see God, be with God, and serve God. He had no other interests. He was a poster child of the devotional approach, surrendering himself to Mother Kali's image, worshipping her, begging and weeping and longing to actually see her in person.

As a boy, he showed little interest in school. At the sight of anything divine, he easily lost himself in deep meditation. He sought solitary places to think and meditate, and he stayed in that state for hours. In his teens, he frequently considered becoming a monk, but he rejected the idea as selfishness. He preferred to work to benefit mankind.

His knowledge, devotion, and rigorous practice attracted young men who sought his advice on spiritual matters, and in this way, Ramakrishna laid the foundation of modern Hinduism — unintentionally! Those drawn to him soon became his disciples. His wife, Sharada Devi, became his disciple, serving him and his other disciples. Many famous people began to take notice of this extraordinary Hindu saint. Word got out, and seeds were sown for what would become the now-famous Ramakrishna Mission, which has spread throughout the world thanks to his first disciples. His most famous disciple was Narendranath Dutta, who became known to the West as Swami Vivekananda.

Vivekananda (1863–1902)

Vivekananda was born Narendranath Dutta. The Duttas were a well-known, philanthropic, educated Calcutta family. As a young man, Vivekananda was keen on serious matters. He read books on history and literature and marveled at divine creation. He was attracted to the intellectual approach of the new Brahmo Samaj philosophical movement, which urged its followers to reject rituals and image worship and worship the Eternal instead. The Brahmo Samaj was a group of intellectuals under the leadership of Raja Ram Mohan Roy, who took serious issue with the increased emphasis on rituals in Hinduism. The Samaj was alarmed that the true spirit of the Vedas was giving way to superstitions and mindless practices. They condemned child marriage and *sati*: the practice of persuading a childless widow to sacrifice herself on her husband's funeral pyre. (This practice has been illegal for a couple of centuries now.) Brahmo Samaj became a force to be contended with in nineteenth-century Bengal.

Vivekananda never married and remained celibate to conserve his spiritual energy. But he did not follow the usual route to seeing God and seeking *moksha* (salvation). Distracted by the suffering of his countrymen, his personal salvation took a secondary role. He was focused on societal issues such as poverty, hunger, sickness, loss of confidence, and lack of self-respect that plagued Indians living under British rule.

Vivekananda believed that what India needed was to uplift its people, improve their living standards, and make their lives more bearable. He also believed that the way to accomplish these goals was through technology. So he journeyed to America to seek technology and assistance in order to improve the lives of Indians.

In the West, in exchange for the technology he needed to uplift India, he shared the dynamic message of the Vedas. He taught America the man-making message: "You are divine, not sinners! It is a sin to call you so. Get rid of your fears. Bliss is your birth right. Seek the One. Attain perfection. Learn the nonduality philosophy, Advaita, which insists Thou art That (*tat tvam asi*)." He encouraged Westerners to choose a path suitable to their personalities: *Karma* (selfless work in the service of humanity), *Jnana* (developing pure intellect to serve humanity), or *Bhakti* (total surrender in devotion). He also urged them not to identify themselves with their bodies and told them to be strong. He said, "I want muscles of iron and nerves of steel and a mind made of the same material of which the thunderbolt is made. Strength is life and weakness is death."

In 1893, Vivekananda electrified the World's Parliament of Religions in Chicago, and religious leaders around the country took notice of the refreshing and bold approach to presenting the Hindu viewpoint. The Chicago Speakers Bureau set up a three-year tour of lectures and visits to Unitarians and other enthusiasts.

In 1897, Vivekananda established the Ramakrishna Mission, an Indian philanthropic organization that still flourishes today.

Shivananda (1887–1963)

The religious organization and ashram called the Divine Life Society owes its origin to a sage known as Swami Shivananda Saraswathi. He set the principal goals of aspirants as follows: serve, love, meditate, and realize. Each of these goals represents a yoga path: Karma, Bhakti, Raja, and Jnana, which I cover in Chapter 21. Swami Shivananda considered that birth as a human was precious and the goal of life ought to be realization of God and termination of the incessant cycle of births and re-births. To this end, he developed a series of steps an aspirant needs to take to keep fit, study, and serve.

Established in 1936 at Rishikesh in the Himalayas, the Divine Life Society now has 17 major centers around the world helping mankind lead a spiritual life. To understand the ideology and read about a variety of subjects focusing on leading a life full of meaning and joy, go to the Society's website: www.dlshq.org.

Ramana Maharshi (1879–1950)

Born in a brahmin family, Ramana Maharshi fell in love with a pilgrimage center not far from his place of birth in Tamil Nadu. Somehow, the name Arunachala, a town dedicated to the worship of Shiva, created an ecstatic feeling in him, and while still in his teens, he decided to proceed there and settle down.

He stayed in a large cave-like opening under the Shiva temple, a location that suited his preference to be alone and to ponder the fundamental questions of life. While there, he became absorbed in deep meditation. His main thought was to understand "Who am I?" His conclusion was that a repeated inquiry of that fundamental question would reveal the truth — that is, that he (or any other aspirant) is the pure soul of the nature of *Satchidananda* (existence/conciousness/bliss). This became his emphasis and message to others who sought him.

He had little interest in developing a discipleship but, as it turned out, many people did gather around him. As a result, an ashram was constructed in his name at Thiruvannamalai.

Part III
The Sacred Texts

The 5th Wave   By Rich Tennant

"Here are the Vedas and the epics. These need to be back by Friday. Failure to return them will result in a 5 cents a day charge and an endless cycle of deaths and re-births."

In this part . . .

Do Hindus have a Bible? Who is the equivalent of a pope for Hindus? You may be surprised to discover that you can't so easily equate Hinduism with monotheistic religions. Hindus are not people of the book. They are a people of *many* books. Their sacred scriptures, called the Vedas and the Upanishads, serve as the foundation of all Hindu thought, theology, and philosophy. In addition, Hindu children grow up listening to the thousands of stories from two great epics, the *Ramayana* and the *Mahabharata,* and the god stories from the puranas. The awe inspired by the events and episodes in these tales prepares them to receive higher knowledge from the scriptures. In this part, I explain the different scriptures and show how the sequence of such learning has worked for thousands of years to keep this unorganized religion (with no single, central authority) intact.

Chapter 10

The Vedas: Centuries of Accumulated Treasures

In This Chapter

▶ Learning about the revelations: The four Vedas

▶ Understanding the nature and content of each Veda

▶ Following the impact of the Vedas on Hindu life through the centuries

*T*he Vedas are unquestionably at the root of Hindu thought, religion, and culture. Hindu writers like to refer to the period when spiritual truths were revealed to Hindu sages as *Krita* or *Satya Yuga,* the age of truth, which is the first in the great time cycle I describe in Chapter 7. When exactly was the age of truth? Estimates of the historical dates vary considerably. The belief is that the Vedas were first heard by these early sages as they did penance on the banks of the Indus River, probably more than 5,000 years ago.

The Vedas are poetic in nature and comprise the earliest religious thought of the Hindus — and perhaps some of the earliest religious thought of mankind as a whole. The revered nature of the Vedas is such that the Vedas are occasionally referred to as *Brahman,* which is why these sacred scriptures are considered eternal. (As I explain in Chapter 1, Brahman is Hinduism's God — eternal, all pervading, the One without a second.)

In this chapter, I introduce you to the Vedas: the scriptures that were preserved and transmitted through the oral tradition. I present all four Vedas and discuss the scope and the focus of each.

Getting Acquainted with the Vedas

The word *Veda* in Sanskrit simply means "knowledge": sacred knowledge of Hindu spiritual laws. In terms of reverence, the Vedas are to Hindus what the Bible is to Christians. That is where the comparison must end, however, because the Vedas, for ancient Hindus anyway, were not books at all. All

Vedic knowledge was regarded as spiritual truths preserved through systematic chanting and transmitted orally from generation to generation. When this knowledge was finally classified and compiled centuries later, the result was not just one but four Vedas:

- ✔ Rig Veda: A book of hymns praising Vedic gods
- ✔ Yajur Veda: A book of hymns related to sacrificial rites
- ✔ Sama Veda: Mantras or chants set to music for use in worships
- ✔ Atharva Veda: Largely magic spells and charms

The Vedas, which are considered by Hindus to originate with the gods, belong to a class of texts called *shruti,* meaning that they were revealed to and received ("heard" and "seen") by several *rishis* (Hindu sages) at several time periods. For centuries, the Vedas were transmitted carefully and orally from generation to generation. The "seen" aspect comes from the word *drishi* meaning "to see," which refers to the fact that the sages not only heard what was revealed but also had visions of the concepts that helped them articulate what had been heard. It is from these visions that these sages derived their designation as rishis.

The following sections go into more detail about the origin of the Vedas and explain why they are the most sacred texts in Hinduism. For a discussion of the content of each Veda, go to the later section "Delving Deeper into the Four Vedas."

Originally memorized in oral form, the Vedas were ultimately written down in the sacred language of Hindus: Sanskrit. Today you can purchase books in Sanskrit along with English translation and commentaries from scholars. The text that I most often refer to in the English language is that of Ralph T.H. Griffith, which is now available online along with Sanskrit transliteration and translation.

Next, I introduce you to some key concepts in the Vedas, explain how important the Vedas are to Hindu rituals, and help you understand why the Vedas have so much authority.

Illuminated by some unknown, unearthly light

"Whenever I have read any part of the Vedas, I have felt some unearthly and unknown light illuminated me. In the great teaching of the Vedas, there is no touch of sectarianism. It is of all ages, climes and nationalities and is the royal road for the attainment of the Great Knowledge. When I am at it, I feel I am under the spangled heavens of a summer night."

Henry David Thoreau, (1817–1862), author of *Walden*

Taking a peek at core ideas of the Vedas

The topics the Vedas deal with cover a lot of ground, from praises to a chosen deity to magic spells cast to curse a foe. All the Vedas except the Sama Veda are in the form of hymns in Sanskrit. The Sama is set to music. Without guidance from priests and gurus (discussed in Chapter 9), one cannot grasp the intonation of chants, let alone absorb the meaning of the verses. Where instructions to perform specific domestic ceremonies and rituals are given, their proper interpretation needs to be learned. Traditionally, priests perform these tasks. Today plenty of resources are available for all to learn them. Even then, however, guidance from a teacher goes a long way to helping the faithful appreciate the depth of thought and meaning, use the proper pronunciation, and enjoy the experience.

Even a casual reading of any of the four Vedas reveals the frankness, with no hint of taboo or inhibition, with which ideas are presented. Unabashed comments about truth, beauty, man-woman relationships, rites, sacrifices, and more are offered. Nothing is held back. Everything is open.

The link between the individual and the world

Much is written and talked about concerning personal salvation in Hindu philosophy. The general impression Westerners have of Hindus may be characterized as "navel gazing" — that is, focusing inward, disconnected with the world and contemplating the hereafter. Some Hindus may fit that description, but the Vedas do not support that approach to life. In fact, the Vedic view of life is precisely the opposite. The Vedas and Upanishads (see Chapter 11) insist on focusing on the "here" and not the "hereafter." Their logic is that the life led "here" according to the injunctions of the Vedas will take care of the "after" admirably!

In addition, the connection of the individual with the vast globe comes through the Veda's emphasis on your duty to raise your family but at the same time to be aware of the commonality with a larger family. One learns from the Atharva Veda that "This world is to be loved"— *ayam lokaha priyamataha* (Book V, Hymn 30, Verse 17). This sentiment is supported in the declaration, "This world is a family" (Mahopanishad, Verse 71; also see Chapter 24).

Different perceptions about God

One of the remarkable things about the Vedas is that the revelations allow for a wide variety of perceptions about God and ways to reach God, based on the individual's needs, interests, and approaches. For the intellectual, there is the formless, the absolute, the One. The action-oriented folk can find a heroic Vedic god to worship, such as Indra (god of thunder and lightning), Surya (sun), Varuna (god of rain), Agni (fire), a bountiful Mother form such as the earth goddess (Prithvi), or a healing goddess (Saraswati).

While the variety of revelations fulfills specific needs as they arise, devotees have never lost sight of the basic truth of the oneness inherent in these different forms of God. Someone can visualize, for example, Indra clad in arms, ready to help his devotees fight their adversaries (be they demons or cruel kings). But that same person may, in an advanced state of mind, also accept the One, the Supreme, which does not have a physical form. Hindus see no contradiction in a variety of such representations. In Hinduism, the way a person visualizes a god can evolve and advance if the mind so desires and is prepared. Confusing? Perhaps, until you allow for the Hindu thinking that accepts *any* path you choose to reach your spiritual goal. All paths are valid, and no one may judge.

The message of hope

What exactly is the message of the Vedas that inspired so many: the sages who ensured that the message was preserved through the ages; the great Hindu reformers, such as Shankara, Ramanuja, and Madhva; and the modern reformers, like Ramakrishna and Vivekananda (see Chapter 9)? This message is what Vivekananda called the message of hope, a "man-making message" full of inspiration to strengthen the mind and maintain a positive outlook.

In the Vedas, life and living are looked upon as grand, ritualistic celebration. In the following list, I cite verses I have selected from several Vedic sources. These verses summarize the ancient Hindu outlook on life: joyous, vibrant, open to ideas, respectful of nature, and praising the idea of oneness.

In the list, I include details like book number, hymn number, and verse number so that you can find more information and additional commentaries if you so desire. I've paraphrased translations available in various references.

- God is infinitely compassionate. *Rig Veda, Book II, Hymn 34, Verse 5*

- Let noble thoughts come to us from every direction. *Rig Veda, Book I, Hymn 89, Verse 1*

- Like joyous streams bursting from the mountain, our songs . . . *Rig Veda, Book X, Hymn 68, Verse 1*

- That holy world I would know where spiritual power and ruling power move in harmony. *Shukla Yajur Veda, Book XX, Verse 25*

- May there be concord with our own people and concord with foreign peoples . . . *Atharva Veda, Book VI, Hymn 52, Verse 1*

- To Ushas, goddess of Dawn, in reference to Surya, the sun: Like a maiden, in pride of beauty . . . smiling, youthful and brightly shining, Thou uncoverest thy bosom before him. *Rig Veda, Book I, Hymn 123, Verse 10*

- To the Supreme Soul: Thou art man, Thou art woman, Thou art boy, Thou art maiden; Thou art the old man tottering with the staff; Thou existeth on all sides. *Atharva Veda, Book X, Hymn 8, Verse 27*

> ✔ By self dedication one obtains consecration, by consecration one obtains grace, from grace one obtains reverence and from reverence is truth obtained. *Shukla Yajur Veda, Book XIX, Verse 30*
>
> ✔ To him who knows this God simply as One . . . In Him all deities become the One Alone. *Atharva Veda, Book XIII, Hymn 4, Verse 15*

Revelations through poetry

By transmitting the wisdom of the Vedas in poetic meter, the sages made it memorable. And close examination suggests that the poetry in the Vedas is sophisticated, by any measure, even when the topic is down-to-earth. In Book X, Hymn 85, Verse 7 of the Rig Veda, for example, is a beautiful description of the bride Surya, the daughter of the sun god Surya.

> *Thought was the pillow of her couch; sight was the unguent for her eyes. Her treasury was earth and heaven when Surya went unto her Lord.*

> Translated by Ralph T.H. Griffith, 1896

The Vedas in religious practices

Hindus find in the Vedas a great variety of gods that they can praise and adore, as well as specific ideas pertaining to the almighty God and to youth, love, valor, joy, strength, concord, and duty. All these ideas served as the basis for developing the rules to be followed in domestic ceremonies. (You can find information about many Hindu gods and goddesses in Chapter 7.)

The *Grihya Sutras* literature outlines domestic rituals: procedures to be observed in performing weddings, for example. This literature is full of mantras borrowed from the Vedas that have lasted in essentially the same form all these centuries. Agni (the fire god), for example, is simply praised in the Rig Veda (Book I, Hymn 1, Verse 1) but is invoked and offered sacrifices in almost every domestic ritual celebrating such events as weddings and pre- and post-natal ceremonies. (Chapter 17 covers these rituals.) Agni is believed to serve as a witness to weddings; therefore pledges and vows are exchanged in front of Agni.

Recognizing the authority of the Vedas

The Vedas have a sacred position in the spiritual life of Hindus for a number of reasons:

 ✔ The belief that these truths were revealed to great sages of the ancient past

 ✔ The reverence shown in the Vedas to nature and the cosmos

✔ The care with which the ideas were preserved and transmitted from generation to generation

✔ The beauty of the poetry and the breadth and depth of its scope

Because of the Vedic messages that life in its fullness should be perceived in a positive, energetic, loving manner, they are revered by intellectuals and ordinary people alike. As a result, acceptance of the authority of the Vedas has served as a measure by which a Hindu is defined.

Delving Deeper into the Four Vedas

Here are the relevant statistics and facts about the structure and content of the Vedas:

✔ **Rig Veda:** This Veda has 10,552 mantras or stanzas organized into 1,028 hymns in 10 books (called *mandalas,* or cycles). The Rig Veda includes mantras that focus on spiritual ideas and thought processes.

✔ **Yajur Veda:** This Veda consists of 1,975 stanzas. It includes verses and text that are action-centered in order to develop the mind.

✔ **Sama Veda:** This Veda contains 1,875 stanzas, which include mantras pertaining to energies and *prana* (vital breath).

✔ **Atharva Veda:** This Veda contains 5,987 stanzas, not all of which are in the form of poetry. Chants, spells, and charms aimed at developing a perfect body are collected in the Atharva Veda. It also differs from the other Vedas in that the ideas found here are not particularly religious.

All told, the four Vedas contain a grand total of 20,389 mantras. If you dig deeper, you'll note that some of the mantras from the Rig Veda are simply lifted and repeated in one or more of the other Vedas. For example, most of the verses in Sama Veda are from the Rig Veda.

Each Veda is also divided into essentially three major sections:

✔ **The Samhitas:** The collections of mantras singing the praises of one or another god of choice are known as *Samhitas.* Most mantras are poetic, but some passages are written in a sort of rhythmic prose. The Sama Veda mantras are meant to be sung and are set to fixed melodies.

✔ **The Brahmanas:** This part of the Vedic literature explains the mantras of the Samhitas in a simple manner and describes the application of the mantras in sacrifices. From the Brahmanas, you learn the types of rites appropriate to an occasion, the necessary mantras, the requisite qualifications of the performer, and the steps involved in the ritual.

✔ **Aranyakas:** The Aranyakas are known as *Forest Treatises* (literal meaning) and comprise certain chapters in the Brahmanas. They were judged to be so deep, potent, and inspiring that nothing but the solitude of a forest was considered adequate for their study.

Each Veda has its own Brahmanas, and each Brahmana has its own Aranyakas. The Aranyakas are a link between the world of rituals contained in the Vedas and the world of philosophy contained in the Upanishads.

Next, I offer more detail about each of the four Vedas, as well as important appendices to the Vedas that help devotees understand them.

Rig Veda: The hymns of praise

The Sanskrit word *Rik* means praise. (When the Sanskrit word Rik is combined with Veda, the grammatical rules produce RigVeda. In English we split the word but retain the first part as Rig.) The Rig Veda Samhita is a collection of hymns that can be classified in three separate categories:

✔ Praises/prayers to gods

✔ Philosophical reviews of such concepts as Truth and the origin of the universe

✔ Topics of a certain secular and semi-religious nature, such as weddings, wars, and generosity

The Hymn of Creation

The Hymn of Creation from the Rig Veda (Book X, Hymn 129) has some parallels to the opening of the Book of Genesis:

At that time there was neither nonexistence nor existence; neither the worlds nor the sky, nor anything that is beyond. What covered everything, and where, and for whose enjoyment? Was there water, unfathomable, and deep? Death was not there, nor immortality; no knowing of night or day. That One Thing breathed without air, by its own strength; apart from it, nothing existed. Darkness there was, wrapped in yet more darkness; undistinguished, all this was one water; the incipient lay covered by
void. That one thing became creative by the power of its own contemplation. There came upon it, at first, desire which was the prime seed of the mind, and men of vision, searching in their heart with their intellect, found the link to the existent in the nonexistent. . . . There were begetters; there were mighty forces, free action here and energy up yonder. . . . The gods are later than this creative activity; who knows, then, from where this came into being? Where this creation came from, whether one supported it or not. He who was supervising it from the highest heaven. He indeed knows; or He knows not!

The hymns of prayer are addressed to a variety of gods, principally nature gods. The Rig Veda also mentions Truth, which is regarded as God, and all the gods mentioned are considered aspects of that one Truth.

The Rig Veda contains one of the most sacred prayers for Hindus, the Gayatri, which expresses a longing for intellect and enlightenment. This mantra is considered so sacred that a father whispers it into his son's ear during a ceremony known as *Upanayanam* (see Chapter 17), an initiation sacrament.

In the Rig Vedic period, life was considered worth experiencing in all its glory, with the emphasis being on the "here and now." Thus, the Rig Veda features many prayers for a strong body, wealth, and long life.

Yajur Veda: The mantras of rituals

The Yajur Veda is the book of knowledge containing mantras and methods pertaining to conducting sacrificial rites. It borrows heavily from the Rig Veda, arranging the mantras in the form of liturgical texts. There are two major versions of the Yajur Veda:

- ✔ Shukla Yajur Veda, which is pure and referred to as *white*
- ✔ Krishna Yajur Veda, which is *black* or *mixed*

This classification is based on the fact that the white Yajur Veda contains only mantras pertaining to specific rituals, while the black Yajur Veda includes liturgical guides in prose.

What does sacrifice mean? What is sacrificed? To whom is the sacrifice addressed and toward what end? To understand the answers, you need to understand the word *yajna* (pronounced "yagna"), which means ritualistic sacrifice to gods with a specific intent. (The word *yaga* has the same meaning.) The objective or intent of a yagna may be to pray for children, wealth, long life, a safe journey, cure of a disease, and so on. In practice, Hindus have integrated these sacrificial rituals into wedding and other ceremonies, which you can read about in Chapter 17.

The Hindu rite of sacrificial offering, or yagna, has two modes:

- ✔ **Inner yagna:** The inner yagna is a process through which an individual intent on making a sacrifice quietly brings the mind to focus and concentrates on the inner flame or light. The sacrifice itself consists of meditating and symbolically offering each part of one's body to the god of choice (a family deity, a cosmic power, the god Vishnu or Ganesha or Shiva, and so on). The devotee prays for strengthening and purifying each body part. The process includes a focus on vital breath, the key to life. An appropriate mantra hails this *prana* (vital breath). This process constitutes the inner sacrifice. In this approach, the sacrifice is symbolic, and this approach is suitable for those trained in rigorous concentration, meditation, and focus.

✔ **Outer yagna:** The inner yagna approach is not suitable for the untrained. But the same concept can be translated into actionable steps, such as building a fire in an altar (the equivalent of the inner flame), offering symbolically your material possessions (grains, clothing, and so on), and uttering appropriate mantras that declare that these possessions are in fact God's and not yours. These actions can be seen as a sacrifice known as *Agnihotra,* meaning an offering into Agni (the fire god).

The Brahmana that corresponds to Yajur Veda is known as *Shatapatha* (100 paths) and is a prose equivalent of rituals in the Shukla Yajur Veda. It covers a wide variety of topics, including myths of creation; the end of the yugas; and details pertaining to the construction of altars with such minute details as sweeping and smearing with cow dung.

Sama Veda: The book of songs

The Sama Veda is special in that the hymns, most of which are from the Rig Veda, are set to musical scales and sung by specialists at important religious ceremonies. These hymns are pleasant to hear and add another dimension to the mantras. The Sama Veda is considered sacred because Lord Krishna himself (see Chapter 7) stated in the Bhagavad Gita that, among all the Vedas, he is Sama Veda. References to Sama can be found in the Rig and Atharva Vedas.

Sama literally means "sweet song that destroys sorrow." The entire treatise is divided into sections that are devoted to songs in praise of Agni (fire), Indra (thunder and lightning), and Soma (the moon). Other classifications include songs that are appropriate to be sung at a contemplative location, such as a forest, and songs appropriate to be sung in towns and villages.

Atharva Veda: The mantras of charms

Get ready to charm your friend and hex your foe! Atharvan was a legendary Hindu sage credited with having discovered fire, and he's mentioned in the Rig Veda as the one who brought Agni to life (Rig Veda Book X, Hymn 21, Verse 5). The Atharva Veda describes procedures to build a fire altar, including details such as sizes of bricks to be used and the utensils needed to perform the fire ceremonies. This Veda concerns itself with life on earth.

Within the Atharva Veda are hymns *(suktas)* that fall into certain categories:

- **The Bhaishajya Suktas** give a glimpse of diseases of the time (assumed to be caused by germs, transgression of nature's laws, angered gods, sinful acts, and demonic forces) and recommended cures through herbs, physical therapy, and prayers. This insight into health sciences is assumed to be the basis for the now famous system of traditional Indian medicine called Ayurveda.

- **The Ayusha Suktas** contain prayers for long life offered as blessings during special ceremonies of coming of age of the young.

- **The Paushtika Suktas** list prayers for adequate rain for growing crops and for building houses.

- **The Abhicharika Suktas** focus on spells aimed at destroying enemies.

- **Prayaschitta Suktas** take care of rites that undo evil effects caused by omission of certain mandated religious duties, such as not fulfilling a vow.

- **The Strikarma Suktas** deal with aspects of love and marriage.

- **Rajakarma Suktas** deal with political issues, including prayers for victory in war and expressions of love for the country. The information about warfare includes such details as how to make hollow arrows filled with poison to assure quick death of the enemy.

- **The Brahmanya Suktas** serve as a link between hymns in the Rig Veda and corresponding considerations of a philosophical nature dealt with in the Upanishads. This Veda abounds in charms and spells.

The Brahmana that corresponds to this Veda is known as *Gopatha,* attributed to a sage of the same name. The text covers creation; the worlds of Agni (fire god), Vayu (wind god), and Surya (sun); the science of serpents; demons; and evil spirits.

Spells and charms, Atharva Veda style

Here are some examples of the types of charms and spells that you can find in the Atharva Veda.

For securing a woman's love: "As the wind here tears the grass, so do I tear thy mind, that thou woman mayest love me and not be averse to me."

A charm against a cough: "Just as the soul, with its desires flies swiftly to great distances, so shall thou fly forth."

A curse against a curser: "Avoid us O curse, much as a spreading fire avoids a lake! But strike him that curses me just as lightning hits a tree."

The Vedangas: Components of the Vedas

Because the Vedas were considered difficult to understand and because of the archaic language and the differences in styles and meters, the ancients developed a set of assists that are known as *Vedangas,* which literally means "limbs of the Vedas."

The Vedangas are actually appendices that help unravel the intricacies of the Vedas by examining them in six different ways:

- **Phonetics** *(Shiksha),* dealing with correct intonation and pronunciation of the mantras.

- **Grammar** *(Vyakarana),* explaining the roots of words used in the mantras along with identification of gender, declension, and so on to aid in unraveling what was meant. This is especially important because Sanskrit words may mean different things depending on context. A good example was taught to me when I was in middle school learning Sanskrit: The word *lavana* could mean either a "horse" or "salt"! So if someone says in Sanskrit *lavana maadaaya,* meaning "bring lavana," the context becomes crucial. If the person asking the question is eating, obviously the correct translation has to be salt!

- **Prosody** *(Chandas),* dealing with meters in which the mantras need to be chanted.

- **Etymology** *(Nirukta),* which may be looked upon as a glossary or dictionary of terms, words, gods, and goddesses.

- **Astronomy** *(Jyautisha),* whose purpose in context is to define times appropriate to the performance of sacrifices depending upon the planetary movements and positions.

- **Religious practice** *(Kalpa),* containing four sections that delineate details pertaining to Vedic sacrifices, rules of classification (caste) in society, construction of altars needed in Vedic rituals, and domestic rites.

Preserving the Vedas

As I note earlier in the chapter, the Vedas were revealed to different sages at different times. That's why the language, style, and content differ among the Vedas and appear inconsistent. The Vedas are preserved and revered as is. If you believe in miracles, the survival of this vast collection of sacred literature, which is the very basis of Hinduism, must be one. The following sections explore how this ancient knowledge has been preserved and passed down through millennia.

You can read about the Vedas in books, articles, and blogs. You can listen to some chants on the Internet. You can Kindle, Google, and Nook the Vedas. If you visit Hindu temples, you may hear priests chanting Vedic mantras. But don't expect to ever hear the last word on the history, content, or meaning of the Vedas. Scholars continue to argue about all these aspects.

The oral tradition lives on

One reason the Vedas have survived intact is perhaps due to the mnemonic system devised by the sages to ensure accuracy in transmission. Schooling the young in ancient times meant teaching the Vedas, including intonation, proper pronunciation, memorization, and recitals. Families were assigned different Vedas, and it was their duty to chant them at home regularly, often, and at special ceremonies. This system assured preservation of the sacred verses in the form we see today.

Orthodox Hindu families continue to teach their children to learn to recite the Vedas. Priests who learn their craft chant in a melodious voice, and so the art and science of the Vedas are preserved. The Maharishi International University in Fairfield, Iowa, even offers a degree in Vedic Science. All this confirms the confident declaration by the scholar A.A. Macdonell, who said as far back as 1899 that "The Vedas are still learnt by heart as they were long before the invasion of Alexander, and could now be restored from the lips of religious teachers if every manuscript or printed copy were destroyed."

To assure the Vedas' survival, the youth (mostly bachelors), particularly in brahmin families (members of the priestly caste; see Chapter 5), are initiated into what is called *dwija* or "second birth" during a born again–type ceremony (see Chapter 17). After the ceremony, they are asked to undertake the study of the Vedas. The ceremony begins with establishing sacred fire in an altar to make offerings to specific deities, depending on the particular Veda to be studied. The chanting begins by acknowledging the name of the sage to whom the mantra was revealed, the deity to whom it was addressed, and even the meter of the composition. In this manner, no important particulars regarding a mantra are ever lost.

Integrating the Vedas into rituals

Clearly the ancients were determined to preserve the sacred knowledge of the Vedas and thought of yet another method of preserving the sacred scriptures. Name a Hindu ceremony, and you will find mantras from the Vedas integrated into the rituals. Orthodox Hindus perform daily rituals invoking Agni, the fire god, and make offerings. Daily functions in Hindu temples invariably involve chanting Vedic mantras in a variety of worships. Ritual baths given to images of deities involve chanting Rig Veda mantras (Purusha Suktam, for example). Sama Veda chants are sung to please the deities being worshipped.

Chapter 11

Gaining Higher Knowledge with the Upanishads

In This Chapter

▶ Entering into the philosophical domain of the Upanishads

▶ Moving the emphasis away from rituals

▶ Admiring the parables that probe the depths of Hindu thought

▶ Understanding the ways to know the One

Dr. Sarvepalli Radhakrishnan (1888–1975), the second President of India, once said that the Upanishads disclose the working of the primal impulses of the human soul, which rise above racial and geographic differences.

As I explain in Chapter 10, the Vedas are a body of sacred knowledge for Hindus. The Upanishads may then be regarded as the crown of that body because they constitute the maturity of all the ideas taught in the Vedas. In addition, the focus of all Upanishadic knowledge is on the mind and beyond. The Upanishads show little interest in rituals. They indicate that you do not need to believe in anything without proper understanding and, more importantly, without any personal experience. The approach to life and belief in the Upanishads is to question, doubt, analyze, debate, discuss, and not rest until the doubt is clarified or the question answered and awareness results.

The Upanishads are a sort of stepping stone to the Hindu philosophy of Vedanta, which I cover in Chapter 20.

Becoming Familiar with the Upanishads

The Upanishads are part of the Hindu literature called *shruti*, which means "revealed," and they are written in Sanskrit. They were revealed, just like the Vedas (see Chapter 10), to different sages at different times. They are considered philosophical appendices of individual Vedas. Scholars do not agree about either a date assigned to their composition or how many Upanishads existed to start with. (Hindu scholars assign the date between 2500 and 2000 BCE, whereas Western scholars assign 1000 to 500 BCE.) One hundred and eight separate Upanishads have been preserved, but only 12 are considered major. They are: Katha, Isha, Kena, Prashna, Mundaka, Mandukya, Taittiriya, Aitareya, Chandogya, Brhadaranyaka, Kaivalya, and Svetasvatara Upanishads.

These 12 Upanishads are at the forefront because of commentaries written on them by several thinkers (including the sixth-century saint Shankaracharya; see Chapter 20), which essentially served as a stamp of approval.

The Upanishads vary in length — some have only a few hundred words while others are quite lengthy — as well as in style and tone, containing verses and/or prose. Some include parables in dialogue form between, for example, a teacher and student(s).

In addition to the twelve major texts, several other Upanishads are classified according to the god they glorify. Fourteen Upanishads are considered *Vaishnava* because they glorify Vishnu, while 14 Upanishads are *Shaiva* (honoring Shiva), and 18 are *Shakta* (glorifying Shakti).

Next, I explore the type of knowledge contained in the Upanishads, as well as their primary focus.

Seeking hidden knowledge

Hindus consider the knowledge hidden in the Upanishads to be superior to the knowledge propounded in the Vedas. A proper description of *Upanishad* is that it is the source of a secret, higher knowledge that leads one on the path to reach the Supreme Self by removing ignorance and cutting off the bonds that cause repeated births and deaths. (See Chapter 3 for a primer on Hindu beliefs about the life cycle.) The knowledge in the Upanishads is considered secret because it is taught only to those who are fit to receive it.

To understand the spiritual journey one must undertake to receive this knowledge, imagine this scenario: You're climbing some rock-cut steps to an ancient temple on a hill. But this temple is not devoted to a deity, and it has no priests. It has no bells to ring, and you do not bring any offerings beyond yourself in body and spirit. As you climb, at each step, one after another, you discard a dogma. You reject ritualistic approaches. You sweat through the futility of pride and vanity and settle for humility. You seek satisfaction beyond pleasure of the senses — something deeper.

As you climb higher and higher, you recognize that ignorance of your real nature is the source of all problems, so your goal is to destroy ignorance. Another step up and you realize that you do not need to abandon anything but simply remain detached! As the ancient Hindus said, real knowledge and infinite joy are yours, and they didn't mince words. (The ancients used superlative words to describe the stated goal of humans, such as *bliss, perfection,* and *dreamless sleep.*)

With the next step, you realize that simply believing is not enough; you must experience bliss and perfection yourself. Yourself. One more step, and you rise above mere intellect and stand on the threshold of a mystic experience with your heart and intuition tuned to that experience. Experience and only experience counts here on this hill.

The *sanctum sanctorum* — the holiest of holy places — at this temple contains bliss. Yes, bliss. That is what the ancient Hindus considered worth living (and dying) for. Bliss is your birth right, proclaim the Upanishads. Your interest is nothing but spiritual illumination. You have entered the temple of the Upanishads. You have reached the source of joy. Now you can begin your earnest inquiry into the ultimate Truth.

 Many Hindus believe that scriptures such as the Upanishads can be learned only from a competent teacher. In fact, the belief is that many people are not even aware of the Self, and most who hear of it are not able to understand it. Therefore, anyone who learns of the Self is deemed intelligent. Anyone who speaks with true awareness of it is considered special. And the person who understands it is considered truly blessed.

Realizing the Upanishads' focus

The premise in early Hindu scriptures was that the main problem facing mankind is ignorance — specifically, ignorance pertaining to the Supreme Self or Paramatman (the true nature of the individual self or atman). The same problem persists today! So the prescribed cure was/is obtaining knowledge of Brahman, which would be an intellectual enterprise.

As the ancient sages got deeper and deeper into this inquiry, however, it became evident that intellect alone was inadequate to the challenge. The Katha Upanishad states without any ambiguity that the Paramatman cannot be attained by intellectual prowess nor by study of books. Instead, the heart needs to be purified, and the seeker needs to be as a child and immerse himself in a pure meditative state to recognize Reality. That, the Katha Upanishad said, is the Truth.

 Each Upanishad reports the findings of a different sage through his own individual experiences. This fact is important because the seers had no intention of making names for themselves by being coherent, logical, and systematic in their revelations. This fact has two consequences:

✔ We don't know much about the sages themselves. What they decided to share is preserved and taught, but they remain in the background.

✔ The language and organization of the Upanishads is considered by some as erratic and archaic in nature (just as it is in the Vedas). So don't look for a logical treatment of topics with a clear beginning and end.

Nevertheless, the discoveries are precious because they deal with extremely complex issues pertaining to spirituality, and we can take much from them just the way they are. Through the Upanishads, you can get a glimpse of Hindu thought pertaining to such concepts as Reality, Brahman, the Supreme Soul, and the universe.

Studying Key Lessons in the Upanishads

The four Vedas are fairly action-oriented. The Vedic sages developed processes that focused on deities with human forms — processes that asked devotees to engage in worship by following certain rules and procedures. The sacrificial rites known as *yagnas* that took place in ancient ashrams were elaborate, involving the participation of a large number of visiting families under the direction of priests. The ancients also observed strict rules on how to construct fire altars and yagna halls (similar to auditoriums but considerably more modest; seating was usually on the floor). The mechanics of performing these rites became so complex that doing so required training, which led to a special cadre of priests. As a result, the *yajamana,* the person who wanted to perform these rites and who footed the bill, was reduced to a mere onlooker while priests performed the rituals on his behalf. The rituals became systematized . . . and a bit mechanical. The original purpose of immersion in prayer and offerings, slowly but surely, became a performance in a large community event.

During the post-Vedic Upanishadic period, sages no longer tolerated this situation. Instead, they longed for intellectual pursuits aimed at understanding the most basic ideas of spirituality:

✔ Who or what is God?

✔ What relationship does God have with what we can see around us and what we cannot see?

✔ What is a human's goal while alive?

✔ What is Truth? What is Reality?

✔ How do these concepts (God, Truth, Reality) affect individuals?

The urge was to reject formal rites and choose approaches that lent themselves to inquiry into fundamentals. Contrary to popular belief, this movement was led and supported not entirely by *brahmins* (priests) but also by princes, kings, and *kshatriyas* (the warrior class; see Chapter 5). A few women also actively participated in debates, discussions, and deliberations.

In their attempt to answer the fundamental questions over long and different periods of time, the sages came up with not just one but multiple answers, which should not be surprising. Complex questions tend not to have simple answers. The answer depends on the context of questions posed by the aspirant sage. In addition, the sages who went into deep meditation to probe into life's persistent questions reported what they visualized and heard, and it was left to those who later heard these reports to provide an interpretation of what had been revealed. The interpretations and commentaries continue to this day. For these reasons, the subject and subsequent analyses have remained complex.

In the following sections, I walk you through the key points and corresponding lessons to be learned from the Upanishads.

Understanding the key questions

In other chapters, I discuss Hindu concepts of reality, Brahman, the universe, the Supreme Soul, the individual soul, and of course God. In the Upanishadic context, these concepts may be understood through an approach as follows:

- **Universe:** The universe includes everything we see and don't see.

- **God:** At a fundamental level, the Upanishadic view is that God equals Brahman.

- **Supreme Soul** (*Paramatman* in Sanskrit): This is the Supreme Consciousness. The Hindu goal of life, according to one approach, is for the individual soul that resides in a body *(atman)* to merge upon death with the Supreme Soul. (There are, of course, other viewpoints about the goal of life and the relation between these souls.)

- **Reality and Brahman:** The world that we see with our eyes is dynamic. The sun rises and sets. So does the moon. Human and other beings are born, live, and die. In one's lifetime, even neighborhoods may change, decay, and be replaced. So a question the ancients focused on was this: Does anything remain the same, forever, through cycles of time (when the world comes to an end only to be renewed later to begin the next cycle)? The answer was a definite "Yes." The entity that is real, the ancients said, is Brahman.

- **Consciousness:** Hindu sages recognized planes of consciousness for a human being. At the lowest level is simply being awake. At the highest state, known as *samadhi,* the person attains the transcendental and ecstatic state in which all thoughts cease, all speech ceases, and perfect silence is all there is, even as the individual is fully alive.

Are these concepts related, and if so, how? And what does it matter to us in our life here on this earth and hereafter?

Keeping these definitions in mind, the Upanishadic quest may now be summarized as seeking answers to these two specific questions:

✔ There is the permanent, everlasting, omnipresent, omniscient, all-encompassing Brahman. And then there is also the universe. Are they connected and, if so, how?

✔ There is the individual soul and the Supreme Soul. Is there a connection between these two and, if so, what is it?

Notice the distinct difference between the two questions. The first one tries to find a connection between the concept of an entity called Brahman and the outward expressions of what we understand as the universe. I call this the *outward dilemma.* The second question relates to things that cannot be seen: On one hand is what I feel or believe is inside me (that is, my soul), and on the other hand is the Supreme Soul. The question is how is my soul connected to the Supreme Soul? I call this the *inward dilemma.* The next two sections discuss each dilemma.

The outward dilemma: Are Brahman and the universe connected?

The sages sought to answer these questions: Are the two entities — Brahman and the universe — connected? And if they are connected, what is the nature of that connection?

This dilemma was examined by Upanishadic sages who came up with not one answer but three! Why three? The answers were dependent on the meditative state of consciousness of the sages at the time of revelation. All the answers are relevant and may in fact indicate an evolutionary nature in the relationship between the universe and Brahman. I examine each answer in turn.

The first view

Consider a variety of clay pots used as utensils. All the pots are different, but they're all made of clay. If the utensils (forms) represent the universe, then the clay is Brahman (substance). The sages saw here a duality: Brahman and the universe are and are not the same! One is part of the other, so they are the same. But one (the universe) is the outward expression of the other (Brahman), so they are not the same!

Take a look at these statements explaining this relationship between Brahman and universe, which I've selected and paraphrased from two Upanishads:

✔ Look upon the head of Brahman as heaven, the eyes as the sun and the moon, the ears as the directions themselves, the air as the breath, the heart as the universe, and the feet as the earth (Mundaka Upanishad).

✔ Things that we see and do not see are all filled with Brahman. All that is, flows from Brahman. Yet It still is the same (Isha Upanishad).

The second view

The second answer did away with the word "and" between the universe and Brahman. There is Brahman, and that is that. The Mundaka Upanishad uses the analogy of several rivers with different names flowing into the ocean and losing their individual identities. This analogy shows how wise men attain the Supreme Being, freed from their individual names and the forms associated with their bodies. The essential oneness is the emphasis in this view.

The third view

In the third view, Brahman defies description. This view is illustrated by the tale of a student pestering his master to teach him the nature of Brahman. Repeated inquiries brought the teacher to say that he, the master, is teaching, but the student doesn't appear to follow. Finally comes the answer that Brahman is silence!

The sound of silence

W. Somerset Maugham, the British author who in 1944 wrote the best-selling novel *The Razor's Edge,* took his title from the Katha Upanishad. The particular passage he chose the title from refers to the path to salvation as the razor's edge, which is hard to tread and difficult to cross.

Maugham experienced an extraordinary yet tumultuous career; he wrote more than 70 books, had failed personal relationships, and served in the first World War. He considered himself a stowaway at heart and always had a desire for peace. So in 1938, at age 63, he traveled from ashram to ashram in India seeking inner peace. He was increasingly irritated by repeated chants of mantras he heard during these visits that he likened to parrot babble. In the presence of the sage Ramana Maharshi (see Chapter 9), however, he endured long bouts of silence. After one such session, when he complained that he felt weak and sick, he was informed that "Silence is also conversation!"

Reconciling the answers

Although each answer is different, each is right for the particular seer because it reflects his and only his intuitive, mystic experience. These answers are not theories intended to state an immutable law applying exclusively to all situations. The view depended on the state of consciousness of the seer. Each answer is consistent and compatible with the plane and level of consciousness of the sage who experienced it. As the sages' consciousness reached higher and higher planes, the answer evolved correspondingly.

The process may be described this way: At the highest plane, absorbed in meditation, the consciousness of a sage rises above physical perception. In this state, both objects and the ideas associated with them vanish from the sage's state of consciousness. All thoughts cease. Time and space lose their meaning. If you were to ask someone in this state what is the relationship between Brahman and the universe, nothing comes out because, on this plane, the real questions are not about the connection but are even more basic: What Brahman and what universe? Silence explains it perhaps.

At the intermediate plane, where a fraction of the highest state is still functional, the answer will be similar to the relationship between clay and the individual pots, focusing on the essential oneness.

At the lower plane, in a normal state, the clay vessels are simply dubbed as mere physical or palpable forms of the real — that is, the basic all-encompassing clay. There is and there isn't any connection between the two!

The inward dilemma: Knowledge of self

The world outside of us has always presented a dynamic kaleidoscope of color, movement, heights, and depths. Awesome mountains and oceans, days and nights. A seemingly endless chain of births, deaths, and all the varieties of human experience. Fascinating. And changing constantly.

But what about the world *inside* each of us? Hindus have always found this world equally fascinating. This inner world has no less variety than the outer world: emotions (joy, sorrow, fear, pleasure, hope, and despair) and thoughts (sublime, ugly, and beautiful), sensations and feelings both pleasurable and otherwise, likes and dislikes, consciousness of varying depths, and so on. These things are also always changing and are equally complex.

The inner dilemma explored this question: With all this excitement forever changing in the inner world of each being, is there anything that does *not* change? The sages answered that yes, there certainly is an unchanging entity: the soul. The soul exists in everything, animate and otherwise.

Some scholars translating the very first verse in the Isha Upanishad declared that the whole world is pervaded by what is called the Self. The Self (with a capital S) resides in everything, even rocks, stones, and trees, as well as birds, beasts, and humans. Hindus called the individual souls *jivatman* or simply *atman.* In addition to the individual souls, there is the Supreme Soul. What exactly are these souls, and what is the connection, if any, between these two?

The Vedas and Upanishads teach that the Self is deep inside us, so deep that individuals may not even be aware of it. The Self never changes and is always there, silent and witnessing everything. To know this Self was a quest that led to the inward dilemma. In fact, the ancients who lived in different countries and spoke different languages all seemed to have the same spiritual goal. The words they used, though in different tongues, all meant *Know thyself.*

Through parables and dialogue, the Upanishads teach how such a quest was undertaken by those who wished to know the Self. These parables instruct the aspirant through, as I characterize them, a series of careful steps:

✔ **Step 1:** The first task is to point out what Hindus call the *original error,* which equates the body with the Self. While the body changes, suffers, delights, and finally dies, the soul dwells inside us but never dies. Therefore, the Self cannot be the body.

✔ **Step 2:** The next task then makes clear that the Self is not the senses. The senses we experience (touch, smell, sight, sound, taste) can change. In addition, some people may experience a total loss of one or more of these senses, and there is visible change. Therefore, the Self cannot be the senses either.

✔ **Step 3:** The next point makes clear that the Self is not the mind. In a dreamless and very deep sleep, the conscious mind is simply not there. But the Self is never *not* there!

Through this exercise, it becomes clear that the Self is none of the above. The sages experienced the Self when they reached a state of meditation so deep that they were beyond all thought.

Are there two realities?

You may be tempted to conclude that each of us has this inner light, as it were, totally independent of other such selves. But that assumption is equivalent to assuming that the shining moon is the source of light, even though it is actually a mere reflection of the real source, the sun. Similarly, said the sages, the individual selves (atmans) are nothing but the reflection of the Supreme Soul, the Paramatman.

While the outward dilemma leads us to Brahman, the inner dilemma leads to the atman. Both are realities, which raises a final question: Are there two realities?

The answer from the sages was a resounding "No." Brahman and atman are one and the same! That realization led to a *maha vakya* (great saying): *Tat Tvam Asi* ("Thou art That!"). So we are back to the One, and that One is you!

A Few Parables and Great Utterances

The great utterances such as "Thou art That" are driven home in the Upanishads through a variety of dialogues, parables, riddles, and inquiries. Following are a few examples from various Upanishads. I selected these in particular to illustrate how ancient Hindus taught these complex concepts.

Know thyself (Atmaanam Viddhi)

Hindus insisted on the need to know the infinite because the infinite is the Self and a source of joy. The finite is considered to be mortal, and all possessions, including wealth and relationships, are nothing compared to the knowledge of the One.

Gnothi Seauton, which was carved into the lintel on the temple of Apollo at Delphi, meant exactly "Know Thyself." Ancient Greeks went to this temple for advice.

In the Brihadaranyaka Upanishad, King Janaka puts certain questions to sage Yajnavalkya to understand the nature of the Self. The question-and-answer session goes like this:

What serves as light for beings? The light of the sun.

What serves when the sun sets? The light of the moon.

What serves when both are set? Fire serves as light.

And when the sun and moon are set and the fire is out? Sound serves as light.

And when no sound is heard? The Self will serve as light for beings.

Who is such Self? That One dwelling inside the heart lotus, within sense organs, and serving as light — of the intellect.

God is in you: Thou art That

As I explain in the earlier section "Understanding the answers: Are there two realities?", Brahman (the Supreme Soul) and atman (the individual soul) are one and the same. These stories convey that idea.

Lunchtime lesson

Here is a story from the Chandogya Upanishad. Two sages are at lunch, and a young man knocks on the door and asks for some food. The sages ask not to be disturbed because they are having lunch. The young man asks, "Respected sages, what God do you worship?" Surprised at this impertinence, the sages nevertheless reply, "Vayu, the wind god, also called Prana, the vital breath." The boy tells them that the whole world took shape in that vital breath and that Prana does indeed pervade every living being visible and otherwise.

Now the sages are angry at the intruder, and they tell him off: Of course they already knew that, they say. They didn't need the boy to tell them about Prana! Not put off, the boy enquires for whom did the sages prepare the food. Their answer: for Vayu, our deity. The boy then informs them that the very Vayu is pulsating in his hungry body. "And by denying food to me, you are indeed denying food to your deity!" This declaration opens the eyes of the sages, who readily invite the boy to partake in their food.

The invisible essence

This is another tale from the Chandogya Upanishad. Young Shvetaketu asks his father to teach him about the Self. The father tells the son to fetch a fruit from the Nyagrodha tree. When the son brings back the fruit, the father instructs him to break it open and asks, "What do you see?" The boy replies that he sees extremely small seeds inside the fruit. "Break just one of them," says the father, "and tell me what you see." The son reports that he sees nothing. "Surely you know that this big tree cannot come out of nothing," says the father. He explains: "In that subtle essence that is not visible is the whole of the tree. That is the Self. And that, my son, That art Thou."

Lose yourself in Brahman

The Mundaka Upanishad compares the Upanishads to a bow. It asks us to bend the bow (learn the Upanishads) and, with mind absorbed and heart full of love, draw the arrow of worship (focus on the One) and hit the mark, the imperishable Brahman. Lose yourself in Brahman as the arrow loses itself in Brahman.

Truth — it shall set you free

Om Tat Sat. Om. That is the Truth. The Creator, the Preserver, and the Destroyer (see Chapter 7) are represented in the sounds A-U-M (rendered as Om) in that Hindu chant which precedes every other chant.

Here's another story from the Chandogya Upanishad. The young Satyakama wanted to seek a guru and learn about Reality. He knew that the first thing a guru would ask was about his identity, his *gotra* (the sage from whom he is descended and with whom he identifies). So Satyakama asked his mother Jabala about his gotra. The mother confessed that she did not know who his father was because she bore him while serving as a house maid in different places. She suggested he introduce himself as Satyakama Jabala.

The son agreed and proceeded to an ashram and prostrated in front of the guru there. When the question arose about his identity, the boy told the whole truth. The sage was astonished — and pleased. He declared that only someone born with a good lineage would dare tell an unpleasant truth, and accepted him as a student. Usually, non-Hindus (and many Hindus too) assume that a brahmin (a member of the priestly caste) is someone born in a brahmin family. This story illustrates that real worth, rather than heredity, determines who is a brahmin.

Hindus consider themselves as descendents of a sage and identify themselves with the name of that sage, which accordingly is their gotra. A child carries his father's gotra.

Da, Da, Da: Self-control, charity, and compassion

The spiritual life requires development of those qualities that lead to a balanced life. In this parable from the Brihadaranyaka Upanishad, understanding the predominant tendency that needs a corrective action is presented as the final test.

Prajapati, the creator (lord of progeny), had three types of sons: gods, humans, and asuras. (Think of asuras as anti-gods.) They all studied under their father.

When the gods' studies were completed, they asked for Prajapati's instruction. Prajapati simply said "Da" and asked whether the gods understood what he meant, to which they replied, "Yes, you told us to have *damyata* or *dama* (self-control) because we are likely to be unruly."

Then the humans completed their studies and asked for his instruction. Again, Prajapati simply said "Da" and asked whether they understood what he meant. The men said, "Yes, you told us to do *datta* or *dana* (charity) because we are likely to be avaricious."

Finally, the asuras completed their studies and asked for instruction. Prajapati simply said "Da" and asked whether they understood what he meant. The asuras said, "Yes, you told us to have *dayaadhwam* or *daya* (compassion)."

So Da Da Da (dama, dana, daya) is God's voice like thunder asking us to have self-control and be charitable and compassionate. (In an Indian context, thunder is welcome as it represents the sound of the monsoon season arriving to bless and refresh the land.)

Core Messages

In this list, I have collected what I consider a core message or two from each of the major Upanishads, and I indicate in parentheses the Vedas with which they are connected.

- ✔ **Katha Upanishad (Yajur Veda):** Your body is a chariot. Let the Self ride it with your intellect serving as the driver of the chariot, using the mind as reins to control the horses (which are your senses) on the road of desire. With a steady mind and a pure heart you will reach the goal of immortality.

- ✔ **Isha Upanishad (Yajur Veda):** Whatever is in the universe, at the very heart of it dwells the Almighty. That and only that is the Reality. Learn to rejoice in that, reject vanity, and never covet someone else's wealth.

  This message impressed Mahatma Gandhi so much that he declared that in case the Upanishads and associated scriptures were all reduced to ashes and if only the first verse of this Upanishad — which declares that Brahman exists at the very heart of everything in the universe — were left intact in the memory of Hindus, Hinduism will survive.

- ✔ **Kena Upanishad (Sama Veda):** The eye of the eye, ear of the ear, mind of the mind, speech of the speech, and breath of the breath is nothing but the Self.

- ✔ **Prashna Upanishad (Atharva Veda):** The Hindu chant Om is Brahman. With a little understanding of Om, a person returns to earth after death. With a greater understanding, he reaches, instead, the celestial world. With a complete understanding, he sees what the seers see. Then he can reach Brahman.

  Note: The Hindu mystic symbol for Om (which you can see in Chapter 6) is considered a combination of the Hindu trinity.

- ✔ **Mundaka Upanishad (Atharva Veda):** The disciple asks, "Master, what is it by knowing which all else is known?" The master answers, "There are two kinds of knowledge classified as lower and higher. Knowledge of the Vedas constitutes lower knowledge. It is the higher knowledge by which one knows the changeless reality."

- **Mandukya Upanishad (Atharva Veda):** Your life consists of three states: waking, dreaming, and dreamless sleeping. In the waking state, you experience pains and pleasures. In the dream state, you experience subtle impressions of past deeds, and the third state, the dreamless deep sleep, is a state of bliss with neither strife nor anxiety. But there is a fourth state in which you are neither conscious nor unconscious, beyond the senses, beyond knowledge. Here you are at peace.

- **Taittiriya Upanishad (Yajur Veda):** May your mother be a god to you. May your father be a god to you. May your teacher be a god to you. May your guest be a god to you.

- **Aitareya Upanishad (Rig Veda):** The Self dwells in our eyes while awake, in our mind when we dream, and in our hearts while in the state of dreamless sleep. If upon waking from the three states, we see none other than the Self, we can then say that we know Brahman.

- **Chandogya Upanishad (Sama Veda):** The Self is smaller than a grain of rice, smaller than a mustard seed. Dwelling in the lotus of my heart, the Self is larger than the earth, greater than the heavens, greater than all the worlds.

- **Brhadaranyaka Upanishad (Yajur Veda):** Just the way silk threads issue out of a spider and sparks issue out of a blazing fire, so do all the senses, all worlds, all gods, and all beings issue from the Self. That Self is known as the truth of the Truth.

- **Kaivalya Upanishad (Atharva Veda):** Practice sitting on a clean spot in solitude, keeping the spine in a straight posture aligned with the head and the neck. Try to be unaware of the external world and enter your inner world. Imagine yourself bowing down in reverence to your beloved teacher. Gradually imagine entering the lotus of your heart and begin to feel the presence of the ever pure, ever blissful Brahman.

- **Svetasvatara Upanishad (Yajur Veda):** May that divinity who is the supreme Lord and Master, the supreme deity all know simply as God, the One that is at once adorable, beyond any action and form, and unequalled without better or superior, the Self-knowing and strong Shakti, without birth or limit, creator and Mahatma, the One who lives in my heart, in my mind, and in my thoughts bless me today. To know That is for me to become immortal.

Chapter 12

Living with the Epics and Puranas

Throughout India and the world, almost all Hindus recognize and understand the implication of two words that non-Hindus may never have heard: *Ramayana* and *Mahabharata*. These are the names of two great Indian epics.

Ramayana, the earlier of the two epics, tells the story of Prince Rama (an avatar of Vishnu; refer to Chapter 8). In the epic, you find out about his 14-year exile, which began on the very day of his scheduled coronation; the abduction and subsequent rescue of his wife Sita; his defeat of her abductor, the demon king Ravana; and his eventual triumphant return.

The second epic, the *Mahabharata,* is a tale of jealousy and rivalry between royal cousins; it rivals any soap opera you've ever seen. This story involves banishment and secrecy and culminates in a terrible battle that must be won.

In this chapter, get ready to sample these stories of love, hatred, jealousy, greed, sex, violence, scandals, cheating, the hell of war and its aftermath, and political intrigue, but also extraordinary kindness, duty, courage, and decency. These tales encompass so much that Vyasa, the composer of the *Mahabharata,* said this:

> *What you read in this treatise may be found elsewhere*
> *But what is not here won't be found anywhere else.*

After you read this chapter, which presents highlights from these epics, you can judge for yourself whether he was right.

While the epics are this chapter's main focus, I also introduce compilations of religious and secular stories and wisdom called the *puranas,* which instruct and influence Hindu thinking and conduct much as the epics do.

Approaching the Epics

The epics belong to the class of literature known as *smrti* (remembered), which is different than *shruti* (revealed) literature such as the Vedas and Upanishads (see Chapters 10 and 11). Hindus refer to the epics by the Sanskrit word *itihasas,* which means "history of the people."

The oral narrative literary tradition was as important in India as it was in all early civilizations. Even though writing existed in Hindu society, the spoken word had greater significance than the written word. In India, much of the sacred *(shruti)* and popular *(smriti)* literature remained in the oral tradition long after the invention of writing.

The *Mahabharata* and the *Ramayana* are composed in verse and, like epic poems in many other cultures, center around a grand theme; involve a cast of heroic characters; and convey the values, history, and mindset of the culture in which they were composed.

In the following sections, I explain important facts about these epics and discuss the ideas and events you find within them. For a summary of the stories themselves, head to the later sections "The *Ramayana:* A Clear Case of Good versus Evil" and "The *Mahabharata:* Good, Bad, Ugly, and Everything In-Between."

The theme: Good versus evil

The subtle and not so subtle theme running throughout the *Ramayana* and *Mahabharata* is the idea of dharma (refer to Chapter 3), which must be protected if a society is to survive. Violate dharma and you create an imbalance in the universe between good and evil. If that imbalance reaches a tipping point in the wrong direction, all is over. The epics illustrate dire consequences that result in war and large-scale loss of life, limbs, and property, raising fundamental questions about life on this planet.

As I mention in Chapter 3, Hindus believe that as time progresses (through the periods known as *yugas*), dharma becomes more and more imbalanced until the imbalance becomes so great that the universe is either brought back to normalcy by an avatar (Chapter 8) or destroyed in preparation for the next cycle of yugas. You can see this growing imbalance in the epics.

The *Ramayana* takes place, according to legend, in Treta Yuga, the second of the four yugas in the current time cycle. During this period, the value system was higher than it is today; the stories support that fact. In the *Ramayana,* although evil exists and dharma is violated, the imbalance is less pronounced than in the *Mahabharata.* The latter takes place in the Dwapara Yuga, the third period in the time cycle, when the deterioration and decline in dharma are apparent. The result is a war marked by wholesale carnage that almost wipes out an entire royal race and more. In the *Ramayana,* the evils are simpler and countered by relatively simpler means. Consider these examples:

- ✔ Prince Rama's stepmother, Kaikeyi, uses her *boons* (wishes granted by her husband, the king) to banish Rama from his kingdom. She then tries to install her own son on the throne. But the son never sits on the throne; instead, to make clear that he is only ruling until Rama can return, he places Rama's sandals on the throne as he rules in Rama's absence. His actions are in stark contrast with the vindictive and vengeful behavior of the royal cousins in the *Mahabharata.*

- ✔ In the *Ramayana,* the demon king Ravana abducts Rama's wife, Sita, but treats her with respect. Her total devotion to Rama provides a shield. But in the *Mahabharata,* enmity between the Kaurava princes and their cousins, the Pandavas, turns mighty ugly. The attitude of the Kauravas toward the Pandava wife Draupadi is marked by cruelty and denigration. She is dragged into an assembly hall, spoken coarsely to, and nearly stripped before the entire assembly.

You can read more about these tales in the later sections of this chapter.

The scope: Life in its entirety

The Hindu epics portray the greatest heights to which human beings can elevate themselves, as well as the depths to which they can sink. They depict life's most joyful and most heartbreaking moments . Name an emotion or issue that most humans experience, and you'll find it experienced there. Love, hatred, jealousy, intrigue, joy, sorrow, deceit, politics, morality and religion, concerns of the elite, the worries of the common people, the technology of warfare, the rules and regulations of government, the restrictions imposed on the governing and the governed — you'll find it all portrayed in the lives of the heroes of the *Ramayana* and the *Mahabharata.*

One could argue that epics in general and the Hindu epics in particular can be summed up in a few words: the art of being human. Hindus went one better and summed up the whole thing in a single word: dharma.

The narrative style: Stories within stories

An unmistakable feature of both epics, but especially the *Mahabharata,* is that the narrative doesn't progress simply from beginning to end. Instead, the narrative is interrupted by any of the following:

✔ Philosophical questions

✔ Secondary narratives told as cautionary tales

✔ Events occurring behind the scenes of the main event

✔ Details supporting or backing up a statement or question posed by a main character

For example, an episode starts, and then right in the middle of the action, the story is interrupted by a philosophical question that causes the narrative to veer off in a new direction.

In an episode from the *Mahabharata,* for example, while her husbands (yes, she has five!) are away hunting, Draupadi is alone except for a maid servant and a house priest. A passing king named Jayadratha gets a glimpse of her and decides he must have her as his queen. He comes right out and asks her to be his wife. Upon her refusal, he abducts her.

In what turns out to be a ridiculous extreme in objectivity, the house priest, instead of kicking and screaming at the outrage, politely and firmly brings up the issue of the legality of the abduction! The priest warns Jayadratha that the *kshatriya* (warrior) code requires that Jayadratha carry off Draupadi only after defeating her husbands in battle. According to the wise man, the abduction is legal only if the wife is won in combat. Protocol is important: Jayadratha must also announce his intention before witnesses!

Upon their return, the husbands learn of the abduction and race after the abductor. The irony continues. Still following the requirements of the kshatriya code, Jayadratha asks Draupadi to identify the individuals who are in hot pursuit. Because she must follow dharma as well (forget the indignation of being stolen from her home), Draupadi promptly starts naming names. She's so thorough, in fact, that 19 verses in the epic are devoted to her answer!

When you hear or read the stories in the epics, don't skip over the asides to get to the "good stuff" (the action). The information conveyed with the secondary narratives is just as important as the main narrative, if not more so. Here, for example, the point is that even in the throes of a cruel abduction and desperate pursuit, following a certain code of conduct is the governing parameter.

The Ramayana: A Clear Case of Good versus Evil

Ramayana means "the Story of Rama." Rama was the seventh avatar of Vishnu (refer to Chapter 8). Composed by the poet Valmiki, this epic is written in Sanskrit and has 24,000 couplets. (A *couplet* is two lines of verse that are linked thematically or rhythmically and that generally convey a complete thought.)

The couplets are in the *Indra-vajra meter* (11 syllables to the half-line), and the chapter endings are written in *Jagati meter* (12 syllables to the half-line).

The epic is divided into seven books, or *kandas:* Bala Kanda (Childhood), Ayodhya Kanda (City of Ayodhya), Aranya Kanda (The Forest), Kishkindha Kanda (Province of Kishkindha), Sundara Kanda (Beauty), Yuddha Kanda (War), and Uttara (Aftermath). The books are arranged in a sequential order following the life of Rama from his childhood through his training to be the future king; then his exile, trials, and tribulations in the forests, war with the demon king Ravana, and triumphant return to his kingdom (and subsequent developments).

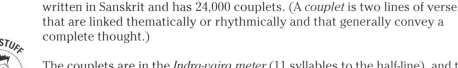

A tale of a robber turned sage

The *Ramayana* is attributed to the poet Valmiki. Although he is the author of this extraordinary epic, Valmiki was not the product of a famous *gurukula* (school) or tradition of learning, nor was he a *brahmin* (a member of the priestly caste; see Chapter 5). He derived his name and true occupation only after an encounter with the sage Narada, who I introduce in Chapter 9.

Prior to his meeting with Narada, Valmiki was a highway robber known as Ratnakara who supported his family by robbing travelers on their way to and from pilgrimages. One day, Ratnakara encountered the sage Narada and ordered him to surrender all his possessions. Narada, who had none, asked why a man would lead such a lowly and despicable life, accumulating sins. Ratnakara explained that it was through thievery that he was able to support his family. The sage asked whether Ratnakara's family supported his mode of livelihood. Although he thought so, the robber was persuaded to go home and ask.

The family members, upon learning how Ratnakara earned his living, were disgusted. They were most unwilling to share in this bad karma and warned him that, while it was his responsibility to maintain them, they refused to share the consequences. So Ratnakara went back to Narada, who advised him to pray to the Lord asking for forgiveness and to find salvation. Salvation is what he found, all right! His penance was deep. He was so completely absorbed in his meditation that Ratnakara lost total awareness of his body, and ants built an anthill around him. Months later, he awoke in response to a divine voice and came out of the anthill. From that point, he became known as Valmiki because the Sanskrit word for anthill is *valmika*. Valmiki became a saint and, upon sage Narada's suggestion, undertook to compose and write the story of Rama's life. The result of his efforts is the *Ramayana*.

The story of Rama, the ideal king

Rama, the hero of the *Ramayana* and avatar of Vishnu, is worshipped by Hindus in every part of India and thus serves as a unifying force. He married Sita (an avatar of Lakshmi) and lived the life of a human, suffering the associated consequences in order to demonstrate the need to adhere to and uphold dharma. He led an ideal life, fulfilling his duties (without compromise) as a son, brother, friend, husband, warrior, and ruler. In the *Ramayana,* evil is overcome by good. The following sections share the highlights of the *Ramayana.* In each section heading, I note the book *(kanda)* within the epic where you find the particular story.

Queen Kaikeyi earns two boons (Bala Kanda)

King Dasharatha of Ayodhya (the capital city of Dasharatha's kingdom) had three queens. The first queen was Kausalya, who gave birth to Rama. (Some Indian scholars date his birth at 4439 BCE.) Dasharatha's second queen, Sumitra, had two sons, Lakshmana and Shatrugna. His third queen, Kaikeyi, also had a son, Bharata.

Kaikeyi was a strong and brave girl who accompanied the king on his exploits. On one such occasion, Queen Kaikeyi noticed that a wheel on Dasharatha's chariot was about to come off. She jumped down and held the wheel fast, preventing a bad accident. The king immediately gave her two boons in return for saving his life. Kaikeyi accepted the offer and said she would ask for her boons later. Unbeknownst to Dasharatha, the boons she would later request would break his heart.

Rama is ready to be crowned (Ayodhya Kanda)

When Rama was 25 years old, King Dasharatha made elaborate preparations to install his first son as *Yuvaraaja* (crown prince). Upon hearing the news of Rama's coming coronation, Queen Kaikeyi at first felt happy. But then her maid, Manthara, sowed seeds of jealousy by fabricating a web of dire consequences for her mistress and her son Bharata if Rama was crowned and his mother, Kausalya, became queen mother. Kaikeyi decided to cash in the two boons the king owed her. These were her two demands: that her son Bharata be crowned king, and that Rama be exiled for 14 years. Despite his shock at Kaikeyi's demands, King Dasharatha could not take back his word.

The day and the hour set for the coronation arrived, and outside, all was ready for the happy event. But within the palace, Kaikeyi had already sent for Rama to tell him what the king could not bear to do. To Rama, Kaikeyi said, "I want you to relinquish the planned coronation and go into exile, leaving all the paraphernalia for use for the installation of Bharata." Remarkably, Rama did not show the slightest disappointment or sorrow and agreed that the king's promise to Kaikeyi must be fulfilled. Thus began the 14-year exile driven entirely by jealousy and greed.

The brothers do their dharmic duty (Ayodhya Kanda)

When Bharata arrived on the abandoned coronation scene, he discovered that Rama, his devoted brother Lakshmana, and Rama's faithful wife Sita had already departed and the king had died of shock soon after Rama's departure. Refusing to be crowned, Bharata rushed to the forest in search of Rama.

In the forest, Rama's party heard sounds of an approaching crowd. Recognizing the flag of Bharata's approaching army, Lakshmana believed that Bharata was coming to kill them. Of course, Lakshmana's doubts were unfounded. After failing to persuade Rama to return to Ayodhya, Bharata begged Rama to part with his sandals, which he planned to install on the throne. He himself would serve the empire as a figurehead until Rama returned.

The story continues with the exiles journeying down into the deeper regions of southern India.

Note the elements at play up to this point in the story: Dasharatha's fatal anguish, Rama's cheerful withdrawal, Kaikeyi's greed, and the evil counsel of Manthara. Add to this another extraordinary response, that of the young prince Bharata, which gives us a glimpse of the heights to which human nature can rise.

Stirrings in the forest (Aranya Kanda)

Rama, Sita, and Lakshmana arrived at a very peaceful area called Panchavati and decided to spend a few months there before moving further south. Trees full of flowers and fruits, a nearby river, hills in the distance, and singing birds suggested an ideal location to build a good cottage, enjoy the serenity of nature, and live at peace. These very forests, however, were also home to *rakshasas,* a tribe of demons. Rakshasas were generally a bad lot, and some had special powers such as the ability to transform themselves into whatever form they wished. They created havoc and pretty much got what they wanted one way or another.

One day, an ugly *rakshasi* (female demon) named Shurpanakha (which means "sharp-clawed") saw the handsome Rama and fell in love with him. She transformed herself into a beautiful woman and asked Rama to join her and be a part of her life. Rama refused, but by no amount of persuasion could he convince her to leave him alone. When Shurpanakha realized that the lovely Sita was in her way, she became very angry and sprang on Sita with her ugly nails. The brothers cut off her nose, and Shurpanakha ran away wailing. End of story? No. It's just the beginning!

The rakshasas seek revenge (Kishkindha Kanda)

The news of the rakshasi's disfigurement reached her brothers Khara and Dushana, who set out to kill Rama and Lakshmana. Wave after wave of demons appeared, yet despite their magical powers, they were all killed by

Rama and Lakshmana, who were experts in archery and martial arts. Finally, the bad news reached the rakshasa supreme commander, the ten-headed king Ravana, in his palace in Lanka (modern Sri Lanka). Ravana, the eldest brother of Shurpanakha, was shocked to learn that Rama, almost single handedly, could defeat and kill so many of his troops and their commanders.

That beautiful Sita should be yours (Kishkindha Kanda)

Ravana was advised to proceed with caution, but when he heard from his sister how beautiful Sita was and that Rama's wife should belong in Ravana's harem, he decided to act. So Ravana and his friend Maricha devised a scheme, not to fight Rama but to lure him away from Sita so that the lovely lady could be kidnapped!

Their plan: Maricha would assume the form of a golden deer so beautiful that Sita would want it for herself, and Rama would be persuaded to go after it. The deer would then draw Rama deeper and deeper into the forest and, at an opportune time, would shout loudly, pretending to be Rama in trouble and ordering Lakshmana to come to his rescue. When Lakshmana responded, Ravana would kidnap Sita and fly away to Lanka.

I must have that adorable deer (Kishkindha Kanda)

A beautiful golden deer made its appearance near the cottage. Sita fell in love with the exquisite animal and begged Rama to get it for her. Despite Lakshmana's warning that this might be a rakshasa trick, Sita would have none of it; she wanted the deer for a pet. So off went Rama, pursuing the deer deeper and deeper into the woods, until the false cry for help reached Sita and Lakshmana. The distressed Sita ordered Lakshmana to rescue Rama. Lakshmana, however, knew that Rama would not have cried for help. Now certain that the whole thing was a rakshasa trick, he refused to leave Sita alone, fearing for her safety.

The line in the sand (Kishkindha Kanda)

Sita was furious. Desperate and fearing for Rama's safety, she began to question Lakshmana's possible motives for staying. Lakshmana, who regarded Sita as a mother, was shocked at her suggestion that he wanted to have her if Rama were to die. Hurt, Lakshmana agreed to go look for Rama. Before he left, however, he drew a line right outside the front door of the cottage with a powerful mantra and asked her to stay inside and never cross the line. After assuring her that no one else would be able to cross that line, off he went with a great deal of hesitation and hurt.

The aged and needy mendicant must be served (Kishkindha Kanda)

The rakshasa plan had worked up to this point: Rama was in pursuit of the golden deer, and Lakshmana was in pursuit of Rama. The time was right for Ravana's next move. Having disguised himself as an aging wandering *mendicant* (a pious man, dependent on alms) in saffron robes with a begging bowl in his hands and chanting away, he appeared in front of the cottage. In those days, the custom was to show kindness to monks and the like who came asking for food. Dire consequences in this life and the next could ensue for the careless housewife. So Sita put together a plate of fruits and nuts and held it out to the "monk" while staying behind Lakshmana's line in the sand.

Ravana instantly knew the power of that line and that he could not cross it without risking his life. He begged Sita to bring the plate to him as he sat under a tree nearby to eat. Sita had no choice. Believing him to be a holy man and a gentle soul, she crossed the line and the next moment found herself in the rakshasa's embrace and flying away south on his chariot.

The devious scheme worked. Lakshmana reached Rama, who was just getting ready to return after killing the elusive deer (which, upon death, had transformed back into Maricha). Rama was shocked to see Lakshmana and realized that something really bad was afoot. He scolded Lakshmana for leaving Sita alone in the cottage. Both hurried back only to find their worst suspicions fulfilled.

Big Bird was watching while Sita was kidnapped (Kishkindha Kanda)

As Ravana hurried through the skies, an ancient giant bird named Jatayu, king of eagles, was watching. Sita asked Jatayu to tell Rama that she was being kidnapped and taken to Lanka by its king. Not being able to bear seeing this lady in distress, Jatayu flew up to face Ravana. The two fought ferociously, and with his powerful beak, the ancient bird inflicted serious damage on Ravana's flesh and to Ravana's chariot, pieces of which fell to the ground. But in the end, Ravana cut off Jatayu's wings, leaving the bird helpless. Ravana reached his palace and issued strict orders to his guards and staff to treat Sita with respect but to watch her carefully.

The monkey brigade to the rescue (Sundara Kanda)

The brothers Rama and Lakshmana began to look for Sita. Following signs of strewn flowers from Sita's hair and other clues, they located the dying Jatayu from whom they got the full story. The brothers performed the bird's funeral ceremony, chanting appropriate mantras as if the ancient bird were their own father. Moving ever further south, they were advised by witnesses to seek a monkey king named Sugriva a few miles down the river.

Sugriva and his faithful minister Hanuman agreed to help in return for aid in a local quarrel. They revealed that they had seen a weeping lady crying out the names of Rama and Lakshmana and that they had also collected a sash of jewels Sita dropped when she saw them. Rama closed his eyes and asked Lakshmana to examine the jewels to make sure that they were indeed Sita's.

Lakshmana opened the sash and confirmed that he recognized the anklets as those he used to see while prostrating in front of his elder brother's wife each morning to receive her blessings. Seeing the familiar jewels, Rama could not hold back his tears.

Hindu boys are taught to look upon each woman as a mother; as such the proper posture is a bowed head. Sita was like a mother to Lakshmana, and in the absence of his own mother, Sumitra, he treated Sita as a mother — with a great deal of respect.

The search begins in Lanka (Sundara Kanda)

Hanuman proceeded to Lanka to find Sita and make sure she was alive and well and to assure her of Rama's plan to rescue her. After a great deal of searching, Hanuman found Sita sitting under a tree in a palace garden.

Of course, finding her was one thing, but convincing her that he was a messenger of Rama was another matter altogether because Sita was in a land where things were not as they appeared. Hanuman was able to ease Sita's suspicions by showing her Rama's signet ring, which Rama had given him should he need to prove his legitimacy. Hanuman assured Sita that rescue efforts would begin in earnest upon his return to Rama. After delivering the message and receiving a jewel from Sita to assure Rama that he had in fact met her in Lanka, Hanuman set off.

Hanuman burns Lanka (Sundara Kanda)

Being a monkey, Hanuman wanted to have some fun before he left Lanka. He also wanted to see the king. So he began to create havoc in the city, which resulted in his arrest and appearance before Ravana. Upon questioning, Hanuman told the truth as to why he had come to Lanka, and he urged the king to surrender to Rama and beg his forgiveness.

Ravana's first impulse was simply to kill the monkey and be done with it. However, persuaded by his kind brother Vibhishana, Ravana realized that a king does not kill a messenger. So instead, he ordered that Hanuman be released, but only after pieces of oil-soaked cloths had been tied to Hanuman's tail and set on fire. This punishment suited Hanuman, who promptly jumped from building to building in the city, causing huge fires before he drenched his tail in the ocean and flew back to Rama.

Let's build a bridge and march to Lanka (Yuddha Kanda)

Now the task before Rama and Lakshmana was to assemble an army of all the allies they had gained during their march south to attack Lanka. They did so and, with help from the monkeys, built a bridge by throwing rocks into the sea between southern India and Lanka. When the bridge was completed, the entire army marched across it into Lanka. A fierce battle ensued, which lasted for days. At one point, the magical arrows of Ravana made the heroes Rama and Lakshmana lose consciousness.

Hanuman moves a mountain (Yuddha Kanda)

Upon seeing the heroes unconscious, the attending medic ordered Hanuman to fetch an herb known as Sanjeevini from a faraway hill. Hanuman promptly flew to the hill, but he could not locate the herb so he simply plucked the whole hillock and brought it to the battlefield. The revived heroes fought hard, killed Ravana, and rescued Sita. Before returning, they crowned Ravana's wise brother Vibhishana as the new king of Lanka.

Triumphant return to Ayodhya (Yuddha Kanda)

By the time Rama, Lakshmana, and their allies had defeated Ravana and rescued Sita, the 14 long years of exile were over. The time had come for Rama to go back home and ascend the throne to relieve Bharata of the burden he had carried all these years in Rama's stead. The party, accompanied by Hanuman and other allies, returned to Ayodhya to an extraordinary welcome from the family and citizens. Bharata and the citizenry waited anxiously to receive the returning hero. Some scholars have established that Rama's coronation took place in 4400 BCE.

The well-known Hindu festival of lights called Diwali commemorates this triumphant return and coronation (see Chapter 16).

The Epilogue: Rama Rajya (Uttara Kanda)

Rama's coronation set the stage for what has been known to millions of Hindus for centuries as *Rama Rajya,* a synonym for a period of ideal kingship and righteous rule according to dharma. But after many years of happy life together, Rama and Sita endured another trial and separation.

Sita had to endure three tests of purity. The test by fire (literally) occurred when she was rescued in Lanka and her chastity was questioned. She agreed to step into a fire that Rama made Lakshmana build. She emerged untouched by the flames. With this proof, all were happy and returned to Ayodhya.

The second test occurred when Rama the crowned king learned about a local washerman upbraiding his wayward wife by using Sita as a bad example of a wife who had lived under another man's roof but was allowed to return home. Although Rama was sure of her fidelity, he was forced, as upholder of dharma, to send her into exile to a forest hermitage. She lived under the protection of sage Valmiki and gave birth to twins, Lava and Kusha.

Twelve years later, when Valmiki attempted to reunite the family, Sita was asked to undergo another test of purity. This time she asked the earth, her mother, to take her back if she spoke the truth. The earth opened and accepted her. Sita never faltered in her devotion to Rama or questioned his motives, which she understood. In spite of her trials she was (and remains) a symbol of strength of mind.

Modern scholarship tuned to women's studies occasionally questions the attitude that required the faithful Sita to endure so many tests of purity. Much debate and discussion occur even now in Hindu families that question the wisdom of this act by Rama. It has remained a sore point, not only among women but among Hindus in general.

The importance of the Ramayana

Hindus remember Rama for the ideal life he led: a boyhood devoted to learning skills appropriate to royalty, his youth full of love and devotion to the family, an extraordinary ability to accept hardships and challenges with grace and dignity, his leadership and compassion toward his followers, and above all a remarkable sense of duty and loyalty toward elders in the family. Hindus want to remember Rama so often in their daily lives that many, particularly in the north, use "Ram Ram" to greet each other!

Hindus bless young men to grow to be like Rama, Lakshmana, Bharata, and Hanuman. Elders bless young women to grow up like Sita — full of love, flawless character, and strength.

The Mahabharata: Good, Bad, Ugly, and Everything In-Between

The word *Mahabharata* means "the great history of the descendents of Bharata." Composed by sage, philosopher, and poet Vyasa, it is the longest poem in the world, having over 100,000 couplets in the same meter as the *Ramayana,* with only a few prose passages. This work is 15 times the length of the Bible and 8 times the length of Homer's *Iliad* and *Odyssey* combined.

The *Mahabharata* is divided into 18 books or *parvas*: Adi Parva (Beginnings), Sabha Parva (Assembly), Aranya Parva (Forest), Virata Parva (named after King Virata), Udyoga Parva (Mission), Bhishma Parva (named after the patriarch Bhishma), Drona Parva (named after the preceptor/teacher Drona), Karna Parva and Shalya Parva (named after the warriors of the same names), Sauptika Parva (Sleep), Shanti Parva (Peace), Anushasana Parva (Instructions), Ashvamedhika Parva (Horse Sacrifice), Ashrama Vasika Parva (Retirement), Mausala Parva (Mace), Mahaprasthanika Parva (Great Journey), and Swargarohana Parva (Ascent to Heaven).

The sacred scripture Bhagavad Gita, which you can read about in the next chapter, is included in Chapters 25–42 of the Bhishma Parva.

The author's origin

The author of the *Mahabharata* is Vyasa. He is India's version of Homer. Vyasa is well-known in Hindu literature as a sage, philosopher, and poet. His original name was Krishna Dwaipayana, and he was the son of sage Parashara and a fisherwoman named Satyavati. Vyasa is so highly regarded by Hindus that he is referred to as *Bhagavan Vyasa* meaning Lord (God) Vyasa.

Here is the story of Vyasa's origin: Satyavati was a beautiful woman, but she reeked of fish as she plied a ferry boat on the banks of river Yamuna near present-day Delhi. One day, sage Parashara saw her and persuaded her to be intimate with him. Satyavati was respectful but afraid. The sage assured her that no harm would come to her and that, through his powers, she would become fragrant. As the boat reached an island, he created a thick fog to give them privacy. A baby boy, named Krishna Dwaipayana (he was so named because he was dark [Krishna] and born on an island [Dwaipayana]) was born who, upon birth, announced that he wanted to be an ascetic. He bade them goodbye, promising his mother that he would come to her whenever she summoned him in her mind. That son was Vyasa.

Shocked with the beginning? Remember these events took place in the third time cycle, and values were declining. Wait till you read the rest!

The story of the Kuru Kingdom

The *Mahabharata* is the story of envy, jealousy, and greed between the royal cousins of the Kuru Kingdom that culminated in a terrible war. The war almost destroyed the whole race, which left the victors wondering whether the cost of victory was too high. On one side were the 100 sons of Dhritarashtra, known as Kauravas. On the other side were the five sons of Dhritarashtra's brother Pandu, known as the Pandavas.

Hindus have long enjoyed the amusing way in which the great epic *Mahabharata* begins. It appears that the author Vyasa was looking for someone to act as a stenographer to write down the story as Vyasa recited the poem. He asked for advice from Brahma, who recommended that Vyasa meditate on Ganapati. When Ganapati appeared, the elephant-headed god set the condition that, when the dictation began, the poet must not stop the telling until its end. Vyasa countered by asking Ganapati to make sure he understood the meaning of each stanza composed before he wrote it down! This matching of wits produced the great epic.

In this section, I summarize the main stories presented in the *Mahabharata*. As with the *Ramayana* earlier in this chapter, in each section heading I indicate which book *(parva)* the story comes from.

Bhishma's terrible vow (Adi Parva)

The patriarch Bhishma, in his youth, was a powerful, scholarly lad and the son of the late King Shantanu and Ganga, the river goddess. During one of his outings, Shantanu fell in love with a beautiful girl and asked her to be his wife. When the king approached her father to seek permission, the father wanted to be sure that her progeny would inherit the kingdom. But prince Bhishma would be the legitimate king after Shantanu, so the king could not agree; he returned to the palace full of grief. When Bhishma learned this, he swore never to marry (therefore never producing heirs) so that Shantanu could marry the girl of his dreams. The name of that girl was Satyavati — yes, the very same Satyavati who gave birth to the *Mahabharata's* author, Vyasa!

Shantanu and Satyavati had two sons. Upon Shantanu's death and with the help of Satyavati, Bhishma raised these future heirs to the throne. The first son died in battle. The second son married two princesses, Ambika and Ambalika, but he also died childless. The Kuru race had come to an end without any progeny.

Extreme measures to save a royal line (Adi Parva)

Satyavati asked Bhishma to marry either Ambika or Ambalika, but he refused to break his vow. Conferring with Bhishma, Satyavati summoned her other son, Vyasa, and begged him to consider producing progeny with Ambika and Ambalika. Vyasa, concerned about his rough appearance, was hesitant to have any such relationships. But he realized the consequences if the race simply ended, so he obeyed his mother and saved the Kuru race from extinction. His sons, the heirs to the throne, were Dhritarashtra and Pandu.

One hundred sons from one: The Kauravas (Adi Parva)

Dhritarashtra was born blind, and Pandu was born pale. Pandu ruled the kingdom under the guidance of Bhishma. Dhritarashtra married a princess known as Gandhari from the town of Gandhaara (present day Kandahar in Afghanistan). Gandhari blindfolded herself so that she would not see what her husband could not, and she lived all her life in self-imposed blindness. Dhritarashtra and Gandhari had 100 sons and one daughter, known as the Kauravas. You need to know only two: Duryodhana, the eldest, and his brother Dushasana.

Five sons from the other: The Pandavas (Adi Parva)

Pandu married two princesses: Kunti and Madri. Unfortunately, he bore a curse that he would die if he tried to be intimate with his wives. The wives suffered a great deal and were helpless until Kunti remembered she had received boons that allowed her to meditate on any god, and that god would give her a son. Thus five sons were born, known as the Pandavas: Yudhishthira, Bhima, Arjuna, Nakula, and Sahadeva. The Pandava boys grew up intelligent and active. They excelled in sports and were loved by all.

The Kauravas were a jealous lot, always suspicious of their cousins and afraid they might usurp their blind father after Pandu's death. The seeds of jealousy that were sown in the boys' teens grew into a huge tree that is the *Mahabharata*.

The beginnings (Adi Parva)

Bhishma employed a famous expert in warfare, Drona Acharya, to teach all the princes. The Pandava boys trained well and met all challenges, excelling in each test of physical strength, endurance, and accuracy. Among them all, young Arjuna stood apart.

Do you see that bird in the tree? (Adi Parva)

One day the teacher hung a wooden model of a vulture on a branch of a tall tree. He asked each boy to aim for the bird. Just before each was ordered to shoot it, Drona asked, "Do you see the bird?" Everyone said yes. But when asked what else they saw, everyone except Arjuna said they saw the tree, the sky, their brothers nearby, and so on. Only Arjuna told the teacher that he could not see anything but the bird's head. This type of training was imparted by the great teacher to prepare them to be great kshatriyas, rulers of the land.

From pranks to hatred (Adi Parva)

What started out as innocent pranks and sibling rivalry got more and more serious as the cousins reached their teens. Duryodhana attempted to kill the Pandavas. For example, he tried poisoning Bhima once without success. Another time Duryodhana presented the brothers and their mother, Kunti, with a palace made of *lac,* a highly flammable material. The Pandavas found out and arranged to have an escape tunnel, enabling them to flee to safety when the fire was set and the structure burned to the ground. They cleverly left six dead bodies behind. The Kauravas assumed the charred remains were those of the Pandavas.

Competing for a bride: The Swayamvara (Adi Parva)

Upon escaping the fire, the Pandavas moved to the kingdom of Panchala. They disguised themselves as brahmins (members of the priestly caste) and tried to develop a strategy to survive. They settled in a modest house and tried to lie low, but more problems and opportunities always presented themselves, altering the course of their lives.

In those days, kings with marriageable daughters held a competition to determine the most suitable husband. These games were usually quite rigorous and required extraordinary skills and physical prowess. Drupada, the king of Panchala, had a beautiful daughter named Draupadi who was ready to choose a brave man who could meet the challenge the family set out.

The challenge in this case was to hit a target (the eye of a wooden model fish) suspended high above the ground. The requirements were to (1) lift the steel bow that was in a box, (2) string the bow, and (3) shoot the target with five arrows in succession. A fourth requirement was that the groom should be from a noble family.

Many princes, including the Kauravas, had come to take part. Draupadi, dressed in silk and jewels, arrived with her brother to witness the proceedings. At the appointed time, the assembled princes stepped forward and, one after another, tried their luck. Many could not even lift the bow. Those who could were unable to string and shoot. No kshatriya (warrior) could do it.

Someone then asked whether a brahmin could try! Despite the confusion and shouts from those assembled — after all, how could a brahmin accomplish a feat that no kshatriya had been able to manage? — the king claimed that the announcement had not referred to caste and therefore anyone could try. Arjuna, in disguise, walked up to the bow and circled it three times, praying in reverence. Not only did he pick up the bow, but he strung it and hit the target using the five arrows in succession.

The assembly was in chaos, but the challenge had been won. Draupadi garlanded Arjuna, and the Pandavas returned to their simple abode with the new bride.

Kunti's and Madri's sons: Children of Vedic gods

Pandu lived under a terrible curse all his adult life. While he was hunting in a forest, he heard stirrings behind a bush and shot his arrows, killing two deer making love. It so happens these deer were a sage and his wife in disguise. The sage, before dying, cursed that Pandu would die if he was intimate with his wives. Kunti and Madri knew this and carefully avoided any intimacy with their husband. Pandu felt terrible that there would be no progeny from his side of the family. But Kunti had a secret that she revealed to her husband: She had received boons at the age of 9, from a royal sage, that she could pray and summon a Vedic god and that god would grant her a son. When Pandu heard this he was ecstatic. He implored Kunti to use her boons. At her husband's insistence, Kunti prayed to god Dharma from whom she gave birth to Yudhishtira. Similarly, Bhima was born through god Vayu and Arjuna through god Indra. After these joyous births, Madri begged Kunti to share the secret mantra to pray and appeal to a god of her choice. Upon Kunti's parting with the secret, Madri prayed to the heavenly twin gods, the Ashvins, and obtained through them the twins Nakula and Sahadeva. These five were known as Pandavas.

Look mother — see what we won! (Adi Parva)

Approaching their house, Bhima shouted out to his mother that they had won a prize at a competition. Kunti, without even looking (and thinking that the prize was food that Bhima, whose appetite was already legendary, would devour alone) said, "Whatever it is, you must all share it!"

The following morning, the wedding took place at the palace (King Drupada was delighted that these "brahmins" were actually the Pandavas), and Draupadi was married to all five brothers! The arrangement was that Draupadi would be the wife of each brother for one year. If any brother saw Draupadi (even by chance) with another husband in private, the punishment would be banishment and exile to the forests for one year.

If you can't beat them, cheat them? (Sabha Parva)

Word that the Pandavas had survived the fire and were alive and well and that they had married princess Draupadi soon got around. Upon invitation from their uncle, the blind king, the Pandavas, along with Draupadi, returned home to their own palace at Hastinapura (present-day Delhi). A period of peace, fame, and prosperity followed. However, the Kauravas soon began scheming, and their maternal uncle Shakuni (Queen Gandhari's brother), an expert in dice games, was only too willing to help them out. The Kauravas knew that Yudhishthira had a penchant for gambling. With the permission of the king (and against the protests of Bhishma and other elders), the palace hall was arranged for a game of dice between the Kauravas and the Pandavas.

The stakes began with jewels and gold but grew to include stables, elephants, cows, Yudhishthira's army, his treasury, and his kingdom. Finally, in desperation (and drawing shouts of protests from the assembled elders), Yudhishthira staked Sahadeva, the youngest Pandava brother, and lost. Brother after brother was staked as though they were chattel, and each was lost. The last stake was Yudhishthira himself, and he lost. The Pandavas had become the slaves of the Kaurava men!

One more chance to win everything back (Sabha Parva)

Uncle Shakuni had a brilliant idea. He said to the loser, "You still have Draupadi. Why don't you stake her and win back everything? If you win, the Kauravas will go into exile for 12 years and spend the thirteenth year incognito. During that thirteenth year, if we are discovered, we will repeat the cycle. If we win, you agree to do the same."

The king, Queen Gandhari, Bhishma, and other elders were in shock at this proposal. But Yudhishthira, to the utter disgust of all, went along with it — and lost! The Pandavas had lost everything.

If you think this sad state of affairs has reached a climax, I am afraid you are wrong.

A lady's honor (Sabha Parva)

Duryodhana ordered his brother to drag the "slave" Draupadi to the court. The brother rushed to the inner apartments of the palace and told Draupadi that she was wanted at the king's court because the Pandavas had lost everything including themselves and her.

Draupadi, with a presence of mind surprising in such circumstances, asked whether Yudhishthira had lost himself before or after he had staked her. In her opinion, if he had staked her after losing himself, he would not have had the freedom to stake her.

Not caring a whit about the "technicalities," Dushasana began to drag Draupadi by her hair to the court. At that point, Draupadi revealed that she was menstruating and therefore could not appear in public. Her protests meant nothing to cruel Dushasana. He dragged her to the court anyway.

The disrobing of Draupadi (Sabha Parva)

What happens next is a source of shame that Hindus over centuries have struggled to understand.

Dushasana pulled Draupadi by her hair into the court and started to disrobe her saying that, as a slave, she had no rights whatever to protest. The Pandavas hung their heads in shame. Draupadi asked Bhishma how he could let this happen. Everyone was ashamed, but the brute continued to tug at her clothing.

A miracle to save her honor (Sabha Parva)

After losing faith in everyone around her, Draupadi simply brought her palms together and prayed to Lord Krishna. A miracle happened. As Dushasana pulled away Draupadi's garments, layer after layer, more and more layers manifested themselves, leaving Draupadi fully clothed. The brute was exhausted, and the hall contained pile after pile of clothing.

Off to the forests (Sabha Parva)

The king finally stopped this nonsense and granted freedom to the Pandavas, but Duryodhana insisted that they fulfill the rules of the game. And so the five brothers and Draupadi left the palace and the capital and proceeded toward the outskirts and into exile, which they would suffer for 12 long years.

Life among sages and demons and beasts (Aranya Parva)

Twelve years is a long time. Much happened that tested the character of the Pandavas. There was never a dull moment and a great deal of suffering for princes and the princess who would otherwise have been rolling in luxury. In the interest of space, I am choosing to present a single episode that took place as the twelfth year of exile was nearing its end.

One day a brahmin came rushing to the Pandavas and begged for help. He had, it seems, hung his fire kindling sticks on a low branch of a tree. A passing stag happened to stop and rub his body on the trunk of this tree and, in the process, the sticks got entangled in the animal's horns. The stag fled, struggling in vain to rid himself of this unwanted burden, and the more he shook his head, the more firmly the fire sticks got wedged in his antlers. The poor brahmin wanted the Pandavas to pursue the fleeing animal and recover the sticks. The Pandavas, believing that it was the duty of kshatriyas to provide any and all help and protection to those who practiced their *dharma*, went fully armed in pursuit of the stag. They soon caught sight of it, but all attempts to stop the animal failed. More running and huffing and puffing ended in the tiring of the party. Not only had the quest failed, but they ended up hungry, thirsty, tired, angry, and frustrated.

The brothers finally sat down under the cool shade of a large tree to rest. Naturally, they began to fret over the outcome of this relatively simple, uncomplicated task. Greater battles with their cousins lay ahead of them, and yet they had not been able to help a brahmin even in such simple circumstances.

Yudhishthira instructed Nakula to climb a nearby tree to locate any sources of water in the vicinity so that they could quench their thirst. Once up in the tree, Nakula informed Yudhishthira that, from a cluster of trees not too far off, he could hear the cries of water cranes. Yudhishthira suggested that Nakula go to the pond and fetch water.

After walking a short distance, Nakula located a beautiful crystal clear lake surrounded by trees, flowers, and birds. Overjoyed, Nakula's first instinct was to enjoy a cool drink himself. He descended to the water's edge, but just as he was about to scoop up some refreshing water, he heard a strong and clear voice of warning:

> *Do not dare to touch the water from this lake that belongs to me.*
> *You must first answer my questions and then you may drink or fetch.*

Thinking that he was hearing things due to sheer fatigue, Nakula ignored the warning, drank the water, and immediately fell dead.

When Nakula did not return, Sahadeva went to see what was delaying him. He arrived at the lake where Nakula lay as though asleep. Thinking to quench his own thirst, he heard the same warning, ignored it and, upon attempting to drink, also fell dead.

Now it was Arjuna's turn to determine what had happened. Armed with his Gandiva bow (which legend says was made by the god Brahma; see Chapter 7), Arjuna saw his brothers lying dead. Trying to quench his own thirst, he heard the same warning. Instead of ignoring the warning, Arjunja challenged the being to show itself and shot several arrows in the direction of the voice.

He only received further and sterner warning. Arjuna challenged the voice, saying, "Stop me if you can" and proceeded to drink the water and fell down dead. Some short time later, Bhima arrived and had the same fate.

Concerned about harm befalling his dear and powerful brothers, Yudhishtira went in search of them. When he arrived at the lake, he could not believe the dreadful sight before him. All four brothers dead on the ground! All his hopes were shattered now. How would he ever be able to recover his lost kingdom without them? He grieved for a while and then sought to determine the reason for these deaths. He noted that their bodies displayed no signs of violence from weapons and that there were no footprints anywhere. He decided that his brothers' killer must have been a supernatural being.

As he approached the water's edge to fetch some water to begin the last rites for his brothers, he heard a voice: "I am the cause of your brothers' death . . . you shall be the fifth victim if you do not answer my questions."

Yudhishthira asked, "Who are you? Are you a *rudra, vasu,* or *marut*? You must be strong to be able to put to death these powerful brothers of mine. Your feat is remarkable because neither gods, antigods, *gandharvas* nor *rakshasas* could stand up to my brothers. But why? What do you want? Noble one! Why are you here? Who are you?"

Note that all the beings named by Yudhishtira (whose names I have italicized in the previous paragraph) are forces of nature that represent wind, storms, and other elements found in the sky, the woods, and the earth.

The voice replied, "I am a *Yaksha,* Yudhishthira. May you prosper." Before Yudhishthira's eyes, a form appeared: a massive, tall body with grotesque eyes burning like the fire of the sun and a voice like thunder. It said, "I warned your brothers. But they would not listen to me. So now they are dead. This pool belongs to me, and unless you answer my questions, you shall not even touch this water."

Yudhishthira replied, "I have no desire to take what has been yours. Ask me and I will answer as best as I can."

The being, a forest spirit, asked Yudhishthira a series of riddles. For example: What is weightier than earth? What is taller than the sky? What is faster than the wind? What is more numerous than grass?

Yudhishthira's answers were Mother, Father, Mind, and Thoughts, respectively.

The questions went on and on, and Yudhishtira answered them all.

All such riddles and the answers have guided the lives of Hindus for thousands of years. For example, a child looking at the preceding riddles learns how mother and father are to be respected, how the mind works, and how thoughts arise — one after another too numerous to count — much like grass growing. In this way, the riddles in the *Yaksha Prashna* episode (which literally means "questions of the Yaksha") serve as a basis for the Hindu value system.

Brothers in disguise (Aranya Parva)

The Yaksha that appeared by the lake was Yudhishthira's celestial father in disguise. He wanted to test his son's strength in the context of character and values so that he could indeed win the war that was about to happen between the Kauravas and the Pandavas.

Satisfied with Yudhishthira's answers, he restored the brothers to life and asked them to proceed to the kingdom of Virata. There, the five brothers and Draupadi were to disguise themselves. Yudhishthira was Virata's brahmin counsel; Bhima, a cook; Arjuna, a eunuch dance instructor; Nakula, a stable boy; Sahadeva, a cowherd; and Draupadi, a hair dresser. This comic interlude comes as a relief between the hard years in the forests and the battle to come.

A last try for peace and plans for the battle (Udyoga Parva)

At the end of the 13 years, the Pandavas returned to the Kuru kingdom, and Lord Krishna was sent as an emissary to negotiate a deal between the Kauravas and the Pandavas. Krishna , trying to see whether peace could be established, asked the blind king Dhritarashtra first for half the kingdom for the Pandavas and as a last step just five villages. The king refused: Not even five villages would fall to the Pandava share. Each side began to assemble armies. The inevitable was about to happen: war.

The 18-day battle (Bhishma Parva)

The armies from each side were in battle formation with horses, elephants, and a variety of arms, medics, and other support systems. The location was a place still known as Kurukshetra, northeast of present-day Delhi.

As the battle was about to begin, Arjuna lost heart and declared that he had no interest in fighting a battle in which he had to kill his elders, friends, and teachers. In despair, he threw his bow down from the chariot. At this moment, Lord Krishna taught him the concept of dharma.

That lesson taught on the battlefield is the most sacred scripture of the Hindus — the Bhagavad Gita, which is the subject matter of the next chapter.

By the end of the battle in the *Mahabharata,* the Pandavas had won. The principal Kaurava kings and their supporters were all killed. The Pandavas were crowned, and they ruled justly for a number of years before relinquishing the kingdom and retiring. Arjuna's grandson Parikshit ascended the throne as Dwapara Yuga (the third period in the time cycle) was reaching its end. Nevertheless, the battle was so horrific and the carnage so great that the survivors openly wondered whether all that killing, violence, and hatred had been worth it.

Was it all worth it?

Imagine that you have just survived a battle in which everyone you know is either wounded or dead. An ocean of blood was shed. The lives of your uncles, brothers, friends, and most of your children have been shattered. You ascend the throne to rule. What joy can there be? Who won? What was won? Was it worth it? The debate goes on and on!

The questions continue, but the Bhagavad Gita straightens us out by teaching the reasons and the consequences. I cover that subject in the next chapter.

The Epics Today

The Hindu epics continue to be vital. Hindu children learn these stories from their parents and grandparents, and the themes and lessons within the tales serve as guidelines throughout their lives. Such guidelines help us understand the complexities inherent in human relationships; the havoc that results from jealousy, greed, and hatred; the beauty of love; the importance of skills; the need for dharma; the role of elders; the power of youth; the impact of war; and a whole host of issues that can all be summed up in one word: life.

The epic characters walk the streets of India (and the world) today. Televised versions of the epics still bring a whole nation to a halt as a wide cross-section of people stop everything to watch episode after episode. The grip is certain and permanent. The power of the epics is such that they have for thousands of years influenced the lives of Hindus around the world and will undoubtedly do so for another thousand years and more in keeping with the promise made by Brahma to Valmiki, that the story of Rama will be cherished by people as long as mountains stand and rivers flow. The same can be said for the *Mahabharata.*

Meeting the Puranas

A *purana* is an encyclopedic compilation of ancient stories, wisdoms, and tradition — both religious and secular. The contents of the puranas include god stories, the genealogy of kings, creation stories, advice on rituals, the caste system, and many secular topics. Their sacred character was assigned to them by naming as their author the same Vyasa who is considered to be the compiler of the Vedas (see Chapter 10), the epic *Mahabharata,* and the Vedanta philosophy (see Chapter 19). They are, in fact, of more recent origin; scholars date the puranas from the fourth century BCE to 1000 CE. But, not surprisingly, some parts of them may predate the Vedas.

There are 18 well-known puranas comprising some 400,000 verses *(shlokas).* The 18 may be classified into three groups of six each according to the particular god they glorify among the Hindu trinity. However, as is often the case in Hinduism, one purana does not glorify a particular god to the exclusion of the others. So in Brahma Purana, for example, you find verses in praise of Krishna and Vishnu as well as considerations of the caste system and hell! So, to be taken with a grain of salt, here are the three classifications:

- ✔ **On Brahma:** Brahma, Brahmanda, Brahma-vaivarta, Markandeya, Bhavishya, and Vamana Puranas

- ✔ **On Vishnu:** Vishnu, Bhagavata, Narada, Garuda, Padma, and Varaha Puranas

- ✔ **On Shiva:** Shiva, Linga, Skanda, Agni, Matsya, and Kurma Puranas.

Seeing how the puranas are structured

The puranas are structured in such a way that the contents are told by a narrator to an attentive listener. For example, the Agni Purana is presented to sage Vasishta by the fire god Agni who discusses a variety of topics including the worship of Shiva, Ganesha, and Durga; installation procedures for deities in temples; astrology; architecture; sculpture; and principles of grammar.

Influencing Hinduism

Hindu scholars believe that the accessibility of the puranas (in contrast to the much more complex Vedas and Upanishads) has been largely responsible for preserving the tenets and practice of Hinduism in spite of major turmoils both within Hindu society and resulting from external invasions and conquests. Hindu audiences assemble in the evenings in a temple hall or a village square to listen to professional storytellers. Children learn these stories from their parents and grandparents. Adults look to these treatises for instruction regarding conducting ceremonies and celebrations. And today, of course, stories of interest from the puranas are embodied in movies, dramas, dance dramas, popular fiction, television, and other media outlets. Tapes and CDs allow folks to listen to these puranas whenever they wish.

Chapter 13

The Song of the Lord: The Bhagavad Gita

. . . .

In This Chapter

▶ Understanding the basic message of the Gita

▶ Studying the dialogue between Lord Krishna and the hero Arjuna

▶ Driving home the Gita's crucial lessons

. . . .

*T*he Bhagavad Gita, *Gita* for short, is the Hindu scripture of scriptures, and it raises and answers life's persistent questions. The single most important reason that the Gita is revered by Hindus as the most sacred scripture is the implied promise that salvation can be earned, here and now. The Gita shows us that the right conduct of the individual matters — that the right action taken at the moment of need keeps the world in balance. The immediate cost may be high in physical terms, but good must — and will — prevail, and the good individual must act to make it so. The Gita teaches this and other important lessons through the story of a hesitant hero, Arjuna, facing — and ultimately fighting — a horrific war.

In this chapter, I share highlights of the Bhagavad Gita; cover the sacred teachings of Lord Krishna on the battlefield to the hero Arjuna; and explain how, through studying the Gita, one can achieve *moksha,* freedom from repeated births and deaths. The battlefield is called *Kurukshetra* (which is a city about 100 miles north of present-day New Delhi). In the scripture this battlefield is referred to as *Dharmakshetra,* meaning "the field of dharma" and implying the field where dharma prevails.

Getting Familiar with the Bhagavad Gita

The Gita is attributed to Vyasa, the same person who authored the epic called the *Mahabharata* and is credited with compiling the puranas, both of which

I cover in Chapter 12. The first chapter of the Gita begins roughly where the Bhishma Parva (the sixth book) of the *Mahabharata* leaves off; this chapter covers the preliminaries on the battlefield and climaxes with the shocking picture of a hero throwing down his cherished weapon and refusing to fight. The remaining 17 chapters of the Gita are Lord Krishna's charge to Arjuna (and humanity) regarding the concepts of duty, Reality, and various Yogic approaches — the charge to come to grips with life and make the right choices.

Here are the fundamentals to know about the Gita's structure and theme:

- ✔ **Structure:** The Gita is a complex treatise and extremely difficult to grasp. It is highly philosophical. The 18 chapters of the Gita are arranged essentially into three parts that focus on the individual soul, Brahman (the ultimate Reality), and the Yoga systems that, when practiced, lead to liberation.

- ✔ **Theme:** The theme of the Gita is that devotion is the best path to salvation. The Gita begins with Krishna dealing with Arjuna's uncertainty, which stems from his mistake in confusing the self with the body. Lesson one of the Gita is that the soul is eternal and cannot die. The next lesson directs the warrior toward his specific dharma or duty. Lessons on ideal character and right attitude follow. Gradually, Arjuna is drawn to recognize the Supreme Self. The seeker follows the path of duty, self-sacrifice, and knowledge, and he finally arrives at devotion. All paths are valid, but faith and love are the best. Finally, God's love for mankind and mankind's love for God will lead to salvation.

The Gita's Story: An Overview

"I will not fight."

Bhagavad Gita (Chapter II, Verse 9)

These were precisely the words (in Sanskrit, of course) spoken by the great warrior Arjuna to his charioteer, Lord Krishna, on the battlefield of Kurukshetra. The timing (right before a decisive battle was set to begin) couldn't have been worse, and the location (the very battlefield where the conflict would be fought) couldn't have been more inappropriate. (Refer to Chapter 12 for the back story leading up to this war.)

Arjuna, the symbol of hope and promise for the Pandava princes (the five sons of Pandu in the Kuru kingdom), arrived on the battlefield in a chariot driven by Lord Krishna. Back then, as now, the governing rule on a battlefield was kill or be killed. Arjuna had prepared for this battle for more than 12 years. Since boyhood, he and his family had suffered humiliation, insult, and injury at the hands of the Kauravas (the 100 sons of Pandu's brother, King Dhritarashtra). He had visualized this particular day since that long-ago day when a despicable attempt was made to disrobe his wife in public. (I explain that episode in Chapter 12 as well.)

Arjuna's refusal to fight was due not to fear but to confusion, despondency, and uncertainty. Many of the people on the other side of the battle were dear to him: the beloved patriarch Bhishma, his revered teacher Drona, his uncle Kripa, and a host of other family members and friends who had little or nothing to do with the cruelties inflicted on the Pandavas. He knew that loved ones on his own side of the battle would be lost in the fighting as well. Arjuna visualized the bloodshed and carnage and decided that he wanted no part of it. He understood and felt the futility of war, and the goal of winning to rule an empire suddenly seemed unimportant.

Despite his reluctance, Arjuna did fight after Lord Krishna taught him the whole truth about dharma. As a *kshatriya* (a member of the warrior class), Arjuna was duty-bound to restore dharma. He had to fight evil, no matter what the consequences were.

Yet Arjuna's dilemma is our own. He is not merely a figure of history; he is each of us. And the battlefield of Kurukshetra is not just a geographical location; every mind is such a battleground. You and I face conflicts and are called upon often to make choices in resolving them. Some choices are certainly unpleasant. Some choices are ones we hesitate to face (like Arjuna did) or refuse to face (like the blind king, Dhritirashtra, did).

The story of the battle begins with the blind king Dhritirashtra "viewing" the scene from afar with the help of his aide, Sanjaya. The king asks Sanjaya to tell him what his sons (the Kauravas) and the sons of Pandu (the Pandavas) are doing gathered to fight at Kurukshetra. This setting of the Bhagavad Gita immediately tells the reader that the battle to be waged is one in which good will strive against evil.

Hand-held television?

In the Gita, the blind king Dhritarashtra hears the developments on the battlefield through his trusted aide, Sanjaya. Sanjaya had received a *boon,* a gift from Vyasa (the author of the *Mahabharata* epic and the Gita), so that all he needed to do to see events and report in real time was to open his palms. This was how he gathered information and reported it to the king.

Amassing armies and discussing rules of war

Anticipating the great battle, the various kingdoms around India aligned themselves with one side or another. The Kauravas had assembled 11 *akshohinis* (army brigades) from their allies. They knew that the Pandavas had assembled only seven on their side. Each akshohini had about 22,000 chariots, an equal number of elephants, three times as many horses and riders, and about five times as many infantrymen. The totals on each side were huge:

✔ **Kaurava army:** 1,924,560 soldiers; 240,570 chariots; 240,570 elephants; 721,710 horses

✔ **Pandava army:** 1,224,720 soldiers; 153,090 chariots; 153,090 elephants; 459,270 horses

Representatives of both campaigns discussed and agreed upon the rules of war to ensure that a code of conduct was followed at all levels. These rules stipulated things as follows:

✔ Fighting can be only between equals who are similarly armed. (To put this rule in modern terms, you can't throw a hand grenade if the other side is using spears!)

✔ Fighting must end with sunset and be resumed at sunrise the next morning.

✔ You cannot fight someone who is wounded or who is withdrawing.

✔ Medics and suppliers (noncombatants) going through the field cannot be harmed.

Setting the stage for internal conflict

Wanting to take a good look at his enemies just before the war commenced, Arjuna asked his charioteer, Krishna, to place the vehicle in the middle of the armies. In fulfilling this request, Krishna could have simply given Arjuna a guided tour of the front lines and returned the chariot to its assigned place. But had he done so, the Bhagavad Gita would not have come about. Instead, Krishna placed the chariot exactly where it would arouse the strongest emotions in Arjuna. He parked it where Arjuna could get a close look at the two men he loved and respected most: Bhishma and Drona. In this way, Krishna set the ideal stage for Arjuna's inner conflict.

Seeing Bhishma and Drona, Arjuna, who until then had considered the entire Kaurava army his enemy, was suddenly overcome with grief. He protested to Krishna about the foolishness of fighting between kith and kin.

Arjuna then asked the fundamental question of the Gita, the question that set the ball in motion: "Of what use is kingdom, of what use is luxury, and of what use is this very life?" In so doing, he questioned life in its entirety. His focus shifted from the principle he was fighting for to the people he was fighting against — a whole different way of looking at war.

A host of closely related questions must be answered to gain knowledge of life and what life really amounts to — questions such as, "Why kill?" "Why till the land?" "Why rule a nation?" and "Why engage in trade and commerce?" Ultimately, the question is this: "Why do our duty?" The amazing thing about the Bhagavad Gita is that these questions aren't specific to Arjuna; they have been asked by billions of Arjunas born since the Gita was written and will be asked by the billions yet to be born.

You can have either me or my army

The two sides went around the country looking for support and adding to the thousands of soldiers ready to fight for them. It happened that the cousins Duryodhana (the eldest of the Kaurava princes) and Arjuna (a Pandava) arrived on the same day at Dwaraka town to ask for Krishna's support. Duryodhana arrived moments before Arjuna and was told that Krishna was asleep but that he could wait in the room. So Duryodhana went in quietly and sat on a chair near the head board. Arjuna entered and, with his reverence for Krishna, he first silently prostrated and then sat near the end of the bed. When Krishna awoke, he saw Arjuna first as the latter was sitting near Krishna's feet (the Hindu way of showing respect), and he saw Duryodhana soon after. He enquired from each of them the reason for their visit (as if the Lord didn't know!), and each said the same thing: They had come seeking Krishna's support for their side during the coming war.

Krishna gave them a choice. You can have only me and my support, or you can have the support of my whole army — one or the other. And he further stated that Arjuna would be the first to choose. Duryodhana protested that, because he had arrived earlier, he should have first choice. He feared, of course, that Arjuna would go for the whole army and Duryodhana would get stuck with one man!

Krishna said that while it might be true that Duryodhana arrived earlier, he (Krishna) saw Arjuna first upon waking. So Arjuna got to choose first, and his choice was Krishna, leaving Duryodhana to get the whole army of Krishna. The Lord wanted to serve Arjuna as his charioteer. Arjuna was the Lord's friend and devotee. This role that he inherited positioned the Lord in an extraordinary framework of serving a devotee and friend, counseling his favorite Pandavas, and playing a mediator if and when called for. This is what Hindus call *lila:* play by the Lord.

Amazing conversation on the battlefield

What followed Arjuna's attempt to withdraw was a conversation with Krishna in which Krishna exhorted Arjuna to do his duty and set aside all temptations and wrong notions that might come in the way of its performance.

The key parameter Krishna referred to is dharma — and in particular, *kshatra dharma,* which applied to Arjuna. A *kshatriya* (member of the warrior caste) is bound to protect dharma and fight to restore it when an imbalance favors evil. As rulers and defenders of the land, kshatriyas have no other choice. In the situation that Arjuna found himself in, dharma had been grievously violated (see Chapter 12).

To provide a simple introduction to the ideas brought out in the 18 chapters of the Gita, I present the main points in the following dialogue that I have imagined taking place between Lord Krishna and Arjuna:

Arjuna (A): I will not fight.

Krishna (K): But you must.

A: And why?

K: Because it is your dharma. You are a kshatriya. Your dharma is to protect dharma. You really have no choice. Each of us has a duty to perform to make sure the society functions normally. What will happen if your farmer neighbor refuses to till the land and if your policeman neighbor decides to quit?

A: But I love Bhishma, Drona, Kripa, and all of them. How can I kill them?

K: I know you love them and that is great. And you are not killing them.

A: What? You just asked me to fight. You know when I do fight, most likely they will die.

K: What die are their bodies. You can never kill them if you understand that their true identities are really their souls and not just bodies. Souls never die.

A: How do we know that?

K: That knowledge comes from knowledge of the self.

A: So not only do you want me to act, but you also want me to obtain knowledge?

K: Yes. Because action must always be driven by knowledge. In the present context it is the knowledge about Brahman, soul, dharma, devotion, and states of consciousness.

A: What is the difference between action and knowledge-driven action?

K: The difference is vital. Knowledge-driven action is devoid of selfish motive.

A: You mean I don't need any motive?

K: No, I mean you are motivated, but your focus must be entirely on the action. You must act without any concern for the results. In this way, you perform your duty. You stay detached.

A: If detachment is key, then why do I not simply renounce everything and withdraw?

K: No. I mean detached dynamism. Here detachment pairs with dynamism. They are like two sides of the same coin. You don't run away from responsibilities. Detached dynamism allows you to perform your duty in a selfless manner. It calls for total commitment to duty with all the energy and passion one can throw in to perform that function and yet remain unconcerned about the fruits of such action. That is dynamic and that is detachment. Throughout all this action you remain devoted to me.

A: Tell me about devotion.

K: Simply relating every action to me — that is devotion.

A: Krishna, who are you really?

K: I am the Self and seated in the hearts of all beings. I am the beginning, the middle, and the end of all beings.

A: How does one worship you?

K: With faith. Whatever is sacrificed, given, or performed or practiced without faith is of no use here or hereafter.

A: Krishna, I shall abide by your word.

The 18-day battle

The battle between the Kauravas and Pandavas raged for 18 days. Each day, the commanders were designated and announced openly so that both sides knew who was in charge until they were killed. Each side developed strategies to protect its commanding general, and each side tried to figure out how to kill the other side's general.

As the battle neared its end, Arjuna's brother Bhima fought Dushasana — the Kaurava son who had treated Draupadi so cruelly after the Pandavas lost her in a bet (see Chapter 12). Bhima split Dushasana's belly and invited Draupadi to drench her hair in Dushasana's blood. The sight must have struck terror in the hearts of the onlookers, but the war raged another day until Bhima killed the equally cruel Duryodhana as well. By the end, all the principals were dead, and the battlefield was strewn with severed limbs, raw flesh, blood, bones, and vultures. It was a ghastly end indeed, but the Pandavas won.

Key Lessons Woven Through the Gita

The action in the Gita centers on Arjuna's hesitance and eventual acceptance of the need to fight, as well as the horrific 18-day battle that ensues. But the Gita is not really about the action at all. Instead, it's a theological treatise that explains how salvation can be earned. These lessons appear throughout the 18 chapters through the conversation between Krishna and Arjuna. Table 13-1 lists each chapter and gives a very brief description of the lesson it contains.

Table 13-1		Lessons in the Bhagavad Gita
Chapter	*Title*	*Lesson*
1	Arjuna Vishaada Yoga	Arjuna's grief and uncertainty on the battlefield are not unlike our own conflicts in our own battles.
2	Saankhya Yoga	One must identify oneself with the soul. It does not die.
3	Karma Yoga	One does his or her duty through selfless work.
4	Jnaana Yoga	Selfless action driven by knowledge defines a sage.
5	Sanyaasa Yoga	Action offered to God is better than renunciation.
6	Dhyaana Yoga	He who simply does his duty without caring for results is a Yogi.
7	Jnaana Vijnaana Yoga	A Yogi's mind has little interest in worldliness. It is attached to God alone.
8	Akshara Brahma Yoga	Brahman is the Supreme and is the soul in everybody. He is imperishable.
9	Raajavidya Raaja Guhya Yoga	Consecrating every action to the Lord is the royal road to self-realization and knowing Reality.
10	Vibhhoti Yoga	Krishna is the Self seated in the hearts of all beings.
11	Vishva Roopa Darshana Yoga	Krishna is Brahman encompassing every thing, every being, and every non-being. The sight of the Cosmic vision must be alarming.
12	Bhakti Yoga	Complete surrender to the Lord is the way.
13	Ksetra Kshetrajna Yoga	Prakriti (Nature) and Purusha (Supreme Soul) constitute everything.

Chapter	Title	Lesson
14	Guna Traya Vibhaaga Yoga	Transcending the three qualities — *satva* (serene), *rajas* (restless), and *tamas* (inert) — leads to *moksha* (salvation).
15	Purushottama Yoga	One must cut the tree of entanglement with the axe of detachment.
16	Daivaasura Sampad Vibhaaga Yoga	Traits of the divine and its opposite are learned.
17	Shraddhaa Traya Vibhaaga Yoga	Whatever is offered or sacrificed without faith is of no use here or in the hereafter.
18	Moksha Sanyaasa Yoga	Renunciation and sacrifice are synonymous.

The ideas that are presented in each chapter of the Gita are prescriptions that are relevant *only* if an individual has thought out and set a goal for life. For the Hindu, the goal is *moksha:* liberation or salvation that frees the individual from repeated cycles of births and deaths. If and only if the aspirant seeks that goal honestly and in good faith, then Krishna's teachings provide a broad framework to help prepare the individual to reach that goal. The teachings of the Gita are therefore addressed to spiritual aspirants.

Such an aspirant must be able to distinguish between Reality and its opposite and have the will to reject the unreal. Total commitment to the goal of liberation is a requirement. In addition, the prerequisites include training to control the senses and the mind and to develop a philosophical outlook and a clear focus. Clearly, these are very difficult constraints imposed on the individual. A strong body and a strong mind are therefore essential to walk the path of the Gita.

In the following sections, I explain the Gita's two most important lessons.

Dharma is the only basis

A conflict. Choices. Conflicting choices. These dilemmas are timeless. At this very moment, each of us may be experiencing them. The only difference is the nature and scope of conflict.

The conversation between Lord Krishna and Arjuna triggered by Arjuna's decision to quit begins with a warning that such weakness on Arjuna's part does not bode well for a kshatriya. Kshatra dharma leaves no room for a warrior to quit a fight. The fight was for dharma, and whatever it takes to restore dharma to its rightful place is the right choice.

This mantra that dharma needs to be protected so that it can protect you is etched into Hindu thought and memory. Countless experiences and stories are part of the Hindu heritage, and Hindus understand that there is no compromise insofar as asserting that the final arbiter in each and every conflict is the supremacy of dharma. Without dharma as the basis, a Hindu considers life as meaningless.

How to attain moksha

The goal of studying, understanding, and practicing the principles taught in the Gita is *moksha,* freedom from repeated births and deaths. Life is compared to a pipal tree, which appears to have no beginning and no end. The branches of this majestic tree reach down and go deeper into the ground. The roots come up and become one with the drooping branches. The tree symbolizes our entanglement in this world. Only the axe of detachment can cut down this tree of entanglement. The means of disengaging such entanglement in order to attain moksha is the subject matter of the Gita.

In the Gita, Lord Krishna presents a variety of Yogic paths for an aspirant to follow. Karma Yoga is suited to the young and Jnana Yoga to the matured, while Bhakti Yoga can be practiced at any age, but there is no restriction except the will to learn, act, and know. The end goal is the same. The following sections briefly discuss these different paths, which I explore further in Chapter 21.

The path one chooses to practice depends on a variety of factors, the most important being one's own temperament. While it may appear on the surface that one type of yoga is easier than another, the general belief among experts is that they are all equally difficult or easy. Practice of any of these disciplines aimed at self-realization is preferably done under the direction of a qualified yogi. Also, the notion that a Jnani does not do Karma Yoga or Bhakti Yoga is not quite accurate. Each type of yoga involves some of the other. To perform duty, one needs knowledge, and to gain knowledge is itself a performance of a duty. Any of these and other forms of yoga require devotion and divine grace.

Selfless service: Karma Yoga

Karma Yoga is the way of action. The work implied here is duty. As taught by Lord Krishna, doing your duty is the mandate of this yoga. But it is more than simply doing your duty. In performing that work, you should make no claim to the fruits of your labor. You have the right only to work — selfless work. Furthermore, you need to remain detached.

Reconciling the story with the principle of nonviolence

Mahatma Gandhi was once asked what he expected his son to do if someone abused and attacked the father. The Mahatma, without any hesitation, answered that he expected his son to spring into action and do whatever necessary to restrain the attacker. His answer showed that nonviolence, while a noble objective to live by, needs to be looked at from a realistic perspective. Lines have to be drawn and respected if we are to be part of a civil society. The strong and powerful need to exercise restraints, especially when it concerns the weak.

As I explain in Chapter 12, the Pandavas agonized for 12 years with the hope that a war could be prevented. The choice was to spend the rest of their lives as slaves to the Kauravas. They exhausted all avenues to gain their share of the kingdom. The case for war was clear.

The work in this context is, in the view of the Gita, one of the four social tasks ancient Hindus defined as essential to preserve the social order. (In the Gita, Krishna urged Arjuna to do his duty to preserve social order.) These four primary tasks (see Chapter 5) are

- Works devoted to building intellectual capital.
- Works devoted to defending the land and its people against enemies within or out. (This was Arjuna's role as a kshatriya.)
- Works devoted to creating and developing industry and commerce.
- Works devoted to growing food to feed its people.

It is not easy to simply perform such duty. Certain special training and a set of qualities are prerequisites; thus Karma Yoga's key words are self-control, selflessness, service, calm bearing, intense activity, nonattachment to results (dynamic detachment), and skill. Desire-less action dedicated to God is the basis of Karma Yoga, and it leads to purification of mind and to freedom (liberation).

The action in the context of Karma Yoga is defined as *action-less action.* Action is expected to result from action-less-ness. One way of understanding this concept is to think of a mother comforting a baby. There is perfect synchronization between what the caressing hands are doing (action) and the corresponding feeling in the mind and the heart of the mother. The mother has poured out her heart in the process. It is *as if* nothing is being done. That is the secret of Karma Yoga. One should feel no burden when one's heart is fully engaged with the mind as the service is performed. When we take on a task and do it under the parameters of Karma Yoga (duty, skill, intensity, dynamic detachment, joy, and so on), then the energy required is minimized. And it is then action-less-action! Such work indeed is worship.

The way of knowledge: Jnana Yoga

While Karma Yoga is one way to attain self-realization, the way of knowledge is devoted to knowing one's own self. The main purpose here is to cultivate the mind and emotions to shift the identification of the self with the body toward identification with the soul.

The mind, according to this yoga, needs to be trained to know and realize the self. The means of such training are developing detachment and a passion for freedom, truth, and meditation. This path requires considerable studies of scriptures, serving seers and learning under their guidance, and deep meditation. The focus of the Jnana yogi's prayer is to gain intelligence, wisdom, and efficiency in order to see and enjoy the light of that knowledge.

The royal way: Raja Yoga

Raja Yoga is considered the royal road to self-realization. This approach requires strict adherence to certain rules and practices of living one's daily life, including such things as physical exercises and breathing and meditation techniques. Raja Yoga stipulates that the aspirant practice nonviolence, moderation, cleanliness, austerity, focusing on Reality, breathing exercises, and concentrating the mind on the self through meditation. The eventual goal of the aspirant is to reach what is defined as a state of superconsciousness in which one experiences (even briefly) a state of bliss as one's own self unites with the Supreme Self.

The way of surrender: Bhakti Yoga

Bhakti means "divine love." A bhakta is a devotee. Bhakti Yoga is the way of surrender to the Lord. This yoga is in the form of love, a sort of infatuation. Its primary objective is for the devotee to realize the self through submission of all action, all speech, and all thoughts to the chosen godhead. It is love, pure and simple, with no strings attached. The choice of godhead, Krishna assures us, is immaterial; worship of God in a form is as valid as a formless one.

The popularity of the epics and the stirring and sublime poetry of the Gita have served to elevate the path of Bhakti in Hinduism. Much of the Bhakti movement in the last 1,000 years has centered on Krishna as the object of love, worship, and surrender.

Part IV
Hinduism in Practice

The 5th Wave   By Rich Tennant

I believe noble thoughts come from all directions. If I could just figure out where noble taxis come from...

In this part . . .

How does faith get translated into practice on a day-to-day and month-to-month basis? In this part, I show you how Hindus have formulated rituals to perform from the very first day of a baby's life, through childhood and youth, and later as householders and all the way toward the very end of life. Devout Hindus offer prayers daily at home. Home altars are common, and I describe a variety of worships — some formal and many informal. In addition, Hindus visit temples to "see" God and "be seen" by God. I describe a variety of Hindu festivals and many pilgrimage centers spread throughout the subcontinent of India.

Chapter 14

Worshipping at Home

. . . .

In This Chapter

▶ Discovering Hindu ideas about worship

▶ Conducting mealtime worship

▶ Offering prayers morning and night

▶ Focusing on deities

. . . .

*H*indus worship a variety of gods and goddesses in a variety of ways in a variety of settings and at different times during a day. While orthodox Hindus adhere to a strict schedule and pay attention to details prescribed by tradition, the majority of Hindus simply acknowledge a higher power and use a variety of gestures and salutations as they go through their daily routines. As they pass in front of temples or other worship centers, for example, they may pause momentarily and close their eyes in a few seconds' meditation before they move on. But home is where most Hindus keep up the formal family tradition of worship.

In this chapter, I discuss the daily religious practices that devout Hindus perform at home. For information about worship at temples, head to Chapter 15. Chapter 16 covers the festivals and holydays.

My goal in this chapter is to give you an idea of the rituals and steps involved in Hindu worship at home. Whether each set of steps in this chapter is followed strictly or modified depends on individual preferences based on family tradition and the time available each day for such practices.

Components of Hindu Worship

For most Hindus, worship is a priority in life. That being the case, worship is not reserved for a particular day or week; it's a daily routine, built into the mindset of Hindus and prescribed by family tradition and belief system. Hindu festivals, temples, rituals, observances, music, clothes, food, and social gatherings are principally the external expressions of this basic belief.

Faith is the critical element in all rituals and Hindu religious practices. Without faith, these rituals and practices are meaningless. In the Bhagavad Gita (see Chapter 13), Lord Krishna makes this very point to Arjuna:

> *Whatever is sacrificed, offered or performed and whatever austerity is practiced without faith, it is falsehood, O Arjuna. And, further, it is of no value either here or in the hereafter.*

In the following sections, I provide basic information about Hindu prayers, altars, and rituals for home worship.

The prayers

Prayers may have different objectives. Some Hindus pray for enhancement of their faith and commitment. Some may pray for specific reasons such as for a loved one's recovery from illness, the smooth delivery of a baby, or a family member's safe journey. The Hindu calendar (called *Panchangam* in Sanskrit) provides auspicious times and dates for certain prayers based on the year, month, position of the sun, phase of the moon, and season and correlates the same with respect to festivals and rituals. Here are just a few examples:

- ✔ On a New Moon day, you offer your respects and *oblations* (offerings) to your family's departed ancestors.

- ✔ On the Full Moon day, called *Poornima,* you worship Lord Satyanarayana, a popular deity who is believed to be a combination of the Hindu Trinity (Brahma, Vishnu, and Shiva).

- ✔ A particular date may commemorate the birthday of a deity, such as Rama or Krishna.

The bottom line is that prayer is an integral part of Hindus' daily lives.

Two important steps or procedures are basic to all prayer rituals and are often repeated. One uses water and the other air. I explain them next.

Procedures using water: Achamana

Hindu prayer rituals include using water to purify the immediate space and performing what is called *achamana,* which involves these steps:

1. Using a ceremonial spoon known as *uddharana* and your left hand, scoop water from a ceremonial cup and dispense it into your right hand, which is cupped by drawing the index finger in and holding it by the thumb.

2. Chant *achyutaaya namaha* (I salute god Achyuta) and take one sip of water.

3. Scoop more water from the ceremonial cup into your cupped hand, chant *anantaaya namaha* (I salute god Anantha), and take a second sip of water.

4. Scoop more water from the ceremonial cup into your cupped hand, chant *govindaaya namaha* (I salute god Govinda), and take a third sip of water.

Note that the names of gods used here are different names of Vishnu.

Procedures using air: Pranayama

A sacred mantra (chant) known as *Gayatri* is meditated upon during different times in prayer rituals using a controlled breathing technique known as *pranayama*. The mantra is translated as follows:

> *Om. That which pervades earth, sky, and heaven, which is worthy of worship, that has no beginning; that which is the light of wisdom and truth; Let us meditate on the radiance of that divinity. May that brilliance help inspire and illuminate our minds. That One which represents water, light and is the quintessence in all things; May that almighty spirit pervading the earth, atmosphere, and heaven bless us with enlightenment.*

While meditating on this mantra (saying the words in your mind), you follow these steps:

1. Close your right nostril with your right thumb (with the fingers naturally bent slightly inward except for the middle finger, which is drawn completely in toward the palm).

2. Draw air through the left nostril as long as you can.

3. Then block the left nostril with the ring finger as you release the air through the right nostril.

4. With the left nostril still blocked, draw air through the right nostril.

5. Now block the right nostril with the right thumb, unblock the left nostril, and release the air through it. After you release the air thus through the left nostril, you've just completed one pranayama.

I offer these steps so you can visualize what prayanama involves, but if you want to practice this technique, you should refer to a Yoga book or a teacher.

The arrangement of an altar

Most Hindu households set up an altar (or shrine) at a special place in the home dedicated to offer prayers. This area can be elaborate or simple. For example, some households may reserve a shelf in the bedroom or the kitchen for daily worship. Large households may set aside a separate room with a tier of shelves or a *mantap:* a four-pillared wooden gazebo-like structure, within which a statue of a deity stands. If an altar is not permanently set up inside the home, Hindus put one up for special occasions when they perform a *puja* (worship) and invite friends and extended family members to participate.

Regardless of the size of the altar, this shrine is always in the inner part of the house that is less exposed to noise and traffic than other living quarters. Such a location provides a sense of privacy and sacredness. The altar also generally faces the eastern direction.

You find the following objects on a Hindu altar in most homes of devout Hindus (see Figure 14-1):

- ✔ A clean cloth to drape over the altar
- ✔ A picture of the main god or goddess to be worshipped, as well as pictures or statues of the family godhead and guru
- ✔ Two stainless steel or silver vessels for water and a metal spoon called an *uddharana*
- ✔ A cloth piece to symbolize clothing
- ✔ *Kumkum* (the red powder that Hindu women use on their foreheads) and *haldi* (turmeric) in small cups
- ✔ Jewelry, to serve as the symbolic offering
- ✔ *Akshata* (a dry mixture of turmeric-tinted uncooked rice) in a cup
- ✔ Sandal paste, incense sticks, and camphor
- ✔ Fresh flowers, fruits, coconut, and leaves on plates, as well as fruit juice in a cup
- ✔ Lamps with wicks soaked in oil or *ghee* (clarified butter)
- ✔ An *arati* plate (a metallic plate containing in it a small cup or spoon-like receptacle into which a small lamp with wick and oil or a few crystals of camphor are placed and lit at the conclusion of a puja)

The rituals

Worship ceremonies may be simple or elaborate and take from just a few minutes to an hour or two. A simple ceremony may involve no more than the devotee (and his family) standing in front of an altar, lighting and placing an incense stick at the altar, and uttering a couple of prayer mantras before leaving home in the morning. An elaborate ceremony, on the other hand, can last longer, use many objects of symbolic importance, and follow a lengthy series of prescribed steps. The remaining sections of this chapter describe such ceremonies.

Figure 14-1:
A typical
home altar.

Pray, Eat, and Pray! Mealtime Worship

In the Hindu epic called the *Mahabharata* (see Chapter 12), prince Yudhishthira is quizzed by the Yaksha (a forest spirit) with this riddle: "Who is happy?" Yudhishthira answers this way: "That person who is free of debt, not in constant travel, and who eats a frugal, satisfying hot meal in his own home every evening." In this section, I explain Hindu mealtime rituals and the rituals associated with the monthly fast day.

Following mealtime procedures

Orthodox Hindus, especially males in the brahmin (priestly) caste, are brought up to regard eating as a ritual. For the two major meals of the day — lunch and supper — they begin with the ritual known as *parishechanam*. This ritual follows these steps:

1. Pour a couple spoons of sanctified water into your cupped right hand.

2. Sprinkle this water over the entire set of food items served (on a banana leaf or perhaps a plate), circling the items three times clockwise and chanting and addressing the food itself: *You are the Truth. I circle you with dharma.*

   The intent of this mantra is to create a boundary around the food with sanctified water to ward off any bad vibrations.

3. Sip the remaining drops after chanting *Let this be the nectar spreading through the food inside.*

   Amrita (nectar) is considered to be the preferred drink of the gods. The intent of this chant is to pray for infusing nectar throughout this food.

4. Take no more than a grain of rice (or other staple) from the banana leaf (or plate) and swallow it without chewing. Do this five times, one after another, as offerings to each of the wind elements inside the body that control various bodily functions: *prana* (main breath), *samana* (digestive system), *vyana* (circulatory system), *udana* (respiratory system), and *apana* (eliminatory system).

5. Now it's time to eat!

6. Indicate the end of the meal by sipping a few drops of water and chanting, *Let this protective nectar infuse the food eaten.*

A night to fast: Ekadashi

Some days, Hindus just don't eat, at least not a full meal. The eleventh day on the Hindu lunar calendar is known as *Ekadashi.* Each month, that day is set aside for contemplation and fasting. (**Note:** Fasting doesn't mean what you probably think. Hindus, at the end of that day, can look forward to a light meal of delicious snack items, warm milk, and sweet drinks.)

Typically, when a wife or mother serves only a light meal on the evening of Ekadashi, she cooks up a feast the next day (Dwadashi). An orthodox Hindu family, after fasting on Ekadashi, will enjoy that sumptuous meal on Dwadashi after completing morning *ablutions* (washing, bathing), getting dressed, and worshipping at home.

All meals that are eaten as part of worship contain only vegetarian items. In a typical South Indian home, the dishes include items like seasonal and seasoned curried vegetables; *sambar* (a thick soup prepared with spices, lentils, and a vegetable); and a milk-, fruit-, or cereal-based sweet dish. The dishes do vary from region to region in India, but when they're part of worship, they remain vegetarian.

Praying Morning, Noon, and Night

Devout Hindus begin and end the day with prayers. Here, I explain the mantras they use upon waking and through the rest of the day until bedtime.

A simple morning prayer

Upon waking, most Hindus ask forgiveness for stepping on Mother Earth by chanting a mantra that translates this way: *I offer my salutations to the Consort of Vishnu, Mother Earth, asking her to forgive me for stepping on her, whose body is clothed with oceans and mountain ranges.*

Next, Hindus open and look at the palms of their hands, chanting the following: *At the tip of my fingers resides Lakshmi, Saraswati in the center of my palms, and Govinda at the wrist. Thus I view my hands with reverence in the morning.*

Now the day can begin. After a bath and before breakfast, many Hindus offer a simple *puja* (worship) by standing in front of the altar, lighting an incense stick, and chanting a mantra or two. An example of such a mantra is this: *May Brahma, Vishnu, and Shiva along with the planets Sun, Moon, Mars, Mercury, Jupiter, Venus, Saturn, Rahu, and Ketu grant this to be a good day for me.*

(*Rahu,* the eclipse, is represented as a mouth that threatens to swallow the sun and moon. His image in temples, a head with no tail, never faces that of the sun or the moon. *Ketu,* the comet, is the unlucky trailing tail with no head attached. These are malign influences that need to be appeased by invocation and prayer, along with the benign "planets.")

At this point, many Hindus are ready to be on their way. But the orthodox need to do more, as the next section explains.

Sandhya vandanam: Worship for orthodox Hindus

Sandhya refers to that particular period of time when the day breaks and the sun rises. The same word is used to identify the time when the sun sets. *Vandanam* means "salutations." Thus, *sandhya vandanam* is a celebration saluting the sun god. Orthodox Hindus perform this celebration three times every day: at sunrise, noon, and sunset.

The ceremony is based in the Vedas and involves no physical form of a deity. No altar is required, and it can be performed in the open as long the environment is conducive to worship (it's quiet and clean). All that is needed is a cup of water and a spoon. The ceremony requires the worshipper to stand, sit, and turn toward the four directions during different parts of the puja.

Before the ceremony

Before beginning the worship, orthodox Hindus follow specific instructions that include minute details, such as the following:

✔ Washing hands and nails 12 times

✔ Rinsing the mouth 12 times and brushing their teeth

✔ Immediately after doing an achamana (refer to the earlier section "Procedures using water: Achamana"), taking a bath while chanting a declaration that the bath is being taken under the orders of the Almighty and to please the good Lord Narayana (another name for Vishnu) in order to absolve all sins

✔ Invoking and saluting the river Ganges while pouring water on their bodies and completing the bath

The worshipper then dons clean clothes and applies denominational marks on his forehead and other parts of his upper body, as I explain in Chapter 4.

Meanwhile, the lady of the house prepares herself and the family to get ready for the morning puja and cleans the areas around and inside the prayer room by lighting an incense stick or two along with a lamp and setting up the altar with puja materials and flowers for offerings. The housewife also typically decorates either the front steps of the house or the entrance to the puja room with what is called a *rangoli* pattern drawn with chalk or rice flour; you can see a typical rangoli pattern in Figure 14-2.

Figure 14-2:
A rangoli
pattern.

The principal steps

The worshipper starts with achamana (explained in the section "Procedures using water: Achamana"). Then he follows these steps (note that each chant involves the names of gods who are all forms of Vishnu):

1. Using the right thumb, touch the right and left cheeks while chanting *Keshavaaya namaha* and *Narayanaaya namaha* respectively. The translation of this chant is "I salute Keshava and Narayana." (The other chants in this list have the same meaning addressed to the other names of Vishnu.) This is a typical salutation to a godhead.

2. Using the ring finger and chanting *Maadhavaaya namaha, Govindaaya namaha,* touch the right and left eyes, one at a time, with eyes closed.

3. Touch the right and left nostrils with the index finger while chanting *Vishnave namaha* and *Madhusudanaaya namaha.*

4. Touch the right and left ears with the little finger while chanting *Trivikramaaya namaha* and *Vaamanaaya namaha,* respectively.

5. Touch the right and left shoulders with the middle finger while chanting *Sreedharaaya namaha* and *Hrisheekeshaaya namaha.*

6. Finally, using all fingertips, touch the navel and head while chanting *Padmanaabhaaya namaha* and *Daamodaraaya namaha.*

The belief is that these contacts with the right-hand fingers energize the seats of energy in the upper body.

7. Say this prayer to remove all obstacles in the way of this ceremony: *I meditate on Vishnu clothed in white, the color of the moon, four-armed, of pleasant aspect, so that all obstacles may be lessened.*

The worshipper then declares his intention through a chant to perform the ceremony by specifying the time (morning, noon, or evening). After doing so, the worshipper follows these steps:

1. Perform the pranayama three times (see the earlier section "Procedures using air: Pranayama.")

2. Sprinkle a few drops of water on the head while uttering a chant in praise of water itself.

3. Do an achamana and sip water (see the earlier section "Procedures using water: Achamana") while making prayers to banish any anger from yourself and asking for forgiveness for any sins committed the previous night.

4. Say a prayer to the Supreme Being.

5. Stand up and offer a palmful of water (facing east in the morning, north at noon, and west at sunset) while chanting the pranayama (Gayatri) mantra.

6. Sit down and declare that you, the worshipper, are indeed Brahman, followed by an achamana.

7. Salute, by chanting each name, each of the nine planets and the forms of Vishnu named in steps 1 through 6 of the preceding list. Dispense water, as you chant, by pouring it into the cupped right palm and offer it through the fingertips by emptying the slightly bent hand.

8. Chant the Gayatri mantra in a meditative pose (facing east in the morning, north at noon, and west at sunset).

9. Worship the very word Om by

- Touching the head and meditating on Brahman

- Touching the upper lip and meditating on Gayatri

- Touching the chest while meditating on the Supreme Soul

- Touching the head again to salute the Seven Sages (see Chapter 9)

- Touching the chest to show reverence to the fire god Agni, wind god Vayu, god of waters Varuna, and the chief of gods Indra

10. Perform three pranayamas.

11. Meditate on Gayatri.

12. Meditate on and chant salutation to the sun god.

13. Salute gods that protect each direction, spaces above and below, and the Hindu Trinity.

14. Salute Yama, the judge of the dead.

15. Conclude with a dedication offering everything that was done by your deeds, mind, and speech to the Almighty.

This completes the worship ceremony for an orthodox Hindu.

Ready to call it a day? Bedtime prayers

At bedtime, Hindus say another prayer to ward off bad dreams. Some Hindus chant a praise to several forms of Vishnu as follows and then go to sleep: *I meditate on Achuta, Keshava, Vishnu, Hari, Soma, Hamsa, Janardhana, Narayana, and Krishna in order to rid myself of bad dreams and sleep at peace.*

Formally Worshipping a Deity

Many families learn how to conduct a formal worship to their family god/goddess by watching their elders. These ceremonies use simple Sanskrit chants even though the family members may not be able to read or write Sanskrit. (It's not uncommon to see worshippers use notes written in the worshippers' own language.)

Pujas (forms of worship), such as the one that follows, may take place on birthdays, anniversaries, or other special occasions. Sometimes a priest may be invited to come and perform the puja. Some householders prefer to do a puja to their family godhead daily at the end of the day.

In the following section, I show the steps used to conduct a simple and typi-cal worship ceremony by the family without assistance of a priest.

The worship begins by invoking the godhead, followed by a series of invitations, prayers, and offerings described by the Sanskrit word *shodasha upacharas,* meaning "16 offerings." The following sections take you through the worship of goddess Lakshmi to show how Hindus perform a typical 16-step puja.

Prayers to Ganapati, guru, and the family godhead

Before starting the puja, you have to contemplate Ganapati (Ganesha), the lord of obstacles, to ensure that no obstacles interfere with a smooth perfor-mance of the puja rituals. Thus, with folded hands, you say the following: *So that the ceremonies we are about to undertake proceed to completion without any obstacles, we contemplate on Mahaganapati.* (**Note:** Hindus always chant the equivalent of these words in Sanskrit.)

You also invoke the *grhadevata,* the family godhead, who bestows protection to the family at all times, by saying *I respectfully contemplate our family godhead.*

Finally, you pay respect to the family guru (see Chapter 9) and offer prayer before beginning the ceremony by saying *Salutations to the preceptor who is verily Brahma, Vishnu, and Maheshwara (Shiva) and who personifies the Supreme Being.*

Shuddhi (cleansing)

To be sure that any and all evil tendencies are removed from the worship room, start with a prayer to Shiva whose very invocation is believed to clear out any troubling vibrations. Say *I salute the Lord of the Southern direction who is the very embodiment of the sacred symbol Om and of pure knowledge and eternal peace.*

Next, invoke and invite the seven sacred rivers to fill the metallic vessel. (A typical vessel is a rounded, narrow-necked urn or bowl.) You use this water, now sanctified, to cleanse and offer throughout the worship. Start pouring water from one vessel into the smaller one as you say *O Ganga, Yamuna, Godavari, Saraswati, Narmada, Sindhu, and Kaveri waters, please be present in this place.*

After you receive the sacred waters, symbolically cleanse your hands by offering a spoonful of water into the hands of the other worshipers and by wiping the hands with reverence as you say *May anything unholy become holy, may all lower tendencies depart, cleansing both inside and out as we remember the Lord.*

Prayer of invocation to Goddess Lakshmi

Say this prayer to invoke the Goddess Lakshmi:

> *I worship Mahalakshmi, daughter of the king of the Milky Ocean, queen of the abode of Mahavishnu, who is served by the consorts of all the Gods, who is the one light and point of origin of the universe, through whose benign grace Brahma, Indra, and Shiva attained their exalted positions, who is Mother of the Three Worlds, who is called Kamala, and who is the beloved consort of Mukunda.*

The 16 upacharas

Now you're ready to invoke Mahalakshmi and offer upacharas — in other words, to receive the goddess and make offerings with reverence.

1. **Avahana — Greeting and welcoming:** With folded hands, focus on the picture of the deity as you say *I offer my salutations to Goddess Mahalakshmi* (you repeat this before each step). Then offer a few grains of *akshata* (turmeric-tinted uncooked rice) with your right hand such that the grains fall on the picture gently as you say *I offer an invocation to you.*

   Be sure to make the offerings using your right hand only and with your palm facing upward.

2. **Aasana — Offering a seat:** Offer akshata as before such that the grains fall on the altar as you say *I offer a seat for you.*

3. **Padyam — Washing the feet:** Offer an uddharana-full of water at the feet of the deity or picture as you say *I offer water at your feet.*

4. **Arghyam — Washing the hands:** Offer an uddharana-full of water to the hands of the deity or picture as you say *I offer water for your hands.*

5. **Aachamanam — Offering water to drink:** Offer again an uddharana-full of water to the hands of the deity or picture as you say *I offer water to quench thirst.*

6. **Madhuparkam — Offering a sweet drink:** Offer fruit juice or honey-sweetened beverage as you say *I offer some sweet drink.*

7. **Snaanam — Bathing:** Symbolically offer water to bathe or pour water over the deity to bathe as you say *I offer clean water to bathe.*

8. **Vastram — Offering clothing:** Symbolically offer a clean piece of cloth to represent gifts of clothing, and say *I offer clothing.*

9. **Aabharanam — Offering ornaments:** Symbolically offer a jewel or two (a necklace or a bangle) to be placed around the neck of the statue or in front of the picture of the goddess while saying *I offer jewels to you.* You use the Aabharanam only for goddesses. For male gods, you use the Yagnopaveetam (offering the sacred thread) and say *I offer the sacred thread.*

10. **Gandham — Offering perfume (sandalwood paste):** Apply to the forehead some sandal paste as you say, *I offer sandal paste.* Then apply some kumkum to the forehead as you say, *I offer kumkum to you.*

11. **Pushpam — Offering flowers:** Offer flowers or petals to the picture or the image of the deity, saying *I offer flowers in worship.* Then with folded hands say the several names of Lakshmi as follows: *I salute Mahalakshmi who is known as Kamala (lotus lady), Ramaa (beautiful lady), who is Mother of the Universe, daughter of the Lord of the Milky Ocean, who sees everything, and who is sister of Chandra (Moon).*

12. **Dhoopam — Offering perfumed incense:** Offer incense by motioning incense smoke with your right hand toward the altar, saying *I offer fragrance in worship.*

13. **Deepam — Offering a lighted lamp:** Lift the lamp and show it to the picture or deity such that it illuminates the face and say *I offer sacred light.*

14. **Naivedyam — Offering food:** Lift the plate of fruits, leaves, and flowers in reverence and offer them saying *I offer a variety of flowers, leaves, and fruits.* Then lift the cover off the *prasadam* (food offered to the god), such as a cooked dish of sweet rice, and offer it as you say *I offer delicious food to you.* Then sprinkle a few drops of water with the uddharana on the food as you hail the various wind elements in our bodies that promote digestion. The final hail is to the creator Brahma. Continue to offer water as you say *I offer more water as you partake the foods.*

15. **Suvarna – Offering gold:** Offer a coin as you say *I offer gold to you.*

16. **Pradakshina — Circumambulation and salutation (prostration):** Stand up and do a *pradakshina* (circumambulation) three times turning to your right, saying *Whatever sins I have committed in all my lives may all of them be absolved as I circumambulate in worship.*

The easiest way to understand these steps is to imagine that you've invited someone whom you love and deeply respect to your home. What would you do? You'd prepare your home to receive her, make special dishes to offer her, and perhaps buy a gift or two. In short, you'd think of ways to show her that you respect her and to offer her what you know she likes in order to make sure she's happy. These are the same kinds of things that Hindus do in the rituals they follow to worship a god or goddess.

Conclusion

You complete the puja with an *arati:* a metallic plate containing a small cup or spoon-like receptacle into which a few crystals of camphor are placed and burned. Use your right hand to lift the arati with the burning flame and wave it up and down in an elliptical form clockwise to light up the deity's face, while you ring a ceremonial bell with your left hand. When that is done, take the arati plate around so that the devotees can receive the blessing by reverentially cupping their hands downward and receiving the warmth of the flame and touching their eyes with the cupped hands inward.

As the arati is being performed, the devotees may sing devotional songs depending on the family practice. You conclude the puja ceremony by saying:

> You alone are our mother and father
> You alone are our sibling and friend
> You alone are our knowledge and prosperity
> You alone are everything to us my Lord my Lord

> Whatever I have performed through my action,
> speech, thought, knowledge, or my natural habit,
> may all that be surrendered to *Srimannarayana* (another name
> for Vishnu).

The *prasad* (offered food) may now be distributed and enjoyed after chanting the Shanti Mantra:

> May Brahman protect us
> May we dine together
> May we work together with great energy
> Let us be illumined together
> Let us live in harmony
> Peace, Peace, Peace!

Chapter 15

Worshipping at Temples

*H*indus have been worshipping in a community setting since the fire altars of the Neolithic age (6000–4000 BCE). The earliest temples were probably constructed of wood to house a particular deity, and there are still many famous caves with natural rock formations revered as images of gods. (Two examples are the Amarnath caves dedicated to Shiva and the Vaishno Devi cave in Jammu dedicated to Shakti). Such caves are popular pilgrimage destinations.

While there is no way to date the cave shrines, elaborate rock-cut temples in Ellora (in Western India) date from the fifth to tenth century CE. These temples and monasteries were carved vertically from the hillside, sometimes from the top down, by Hindus, Buddhists, and Jains. Together, they form an ecumenical neighborhood. Today, they are a UNESCO World Heritage Site.

For at least a thousand years, temple complexes have been built with soaring towers, colonnades of carved pillars, and larger-than-life sculpted marble and granite images. In the city of Trivandrum in South India, for example, you can see an 18-foot-long stone sculpture of Padmanabha (a form of Lord Vishnu) in repose on a huge serpent. This temple was flourishing long before Vasco da Gama (the first modern European visitor to India) arrived in India in 1498. Of course, not all temples are this ornate. Exquisite hill-top temples, often near the source of a river, and city and village temples that are simpler in style and smaller in size flourish throughout India. Temples built after 1600 CE are usually based on the classic designs of the earlier period.

Despite the variety of Hindu temple designs, their planning and construction follow certain guidelines originating in the Vedas and *Shastras* (ancient Sanskrit manuals). Specific rules must be observed in choosing a principal deity and associated deities; selecting the materials for sculpting the statues to be installed for worship; choosing the right month, day, and time to break ground; preparing the deities for installation; performing a host of other related tasks; and sanctifying the shrine.

This chapter presents the scriptural basis for planning, building, and sanctifying temples, as well as worship practices prescribed in ancient manuals.

Studying Temple Architecture

A Hindu temple is known as *devasthanam* in Sanskrit, meaning "abode of God." (In northern India, the word *mandir* is more commonly used.) In other words, Hindu temples aren't merely places where devout Hindus go to worship; they are the earthly homes of the gods.

The specific source of architectural rules and guidance for Hindu temples is known as *Vastu Shastra* (a "manual for dwelling places"). It is the architectural manual relevant for the construction of Hindu homes and temples — a vast volume of knowledge accumulated over the millennia to guide and accomplish the building of terrestrial homes for the gods.

While Vastu is used to develop a construction plan for a temple, a related manual, the *Shilpa Shastra,* is used by *shilpis* (sculptors) who select and carve out images in wood, brick, marble, and granite based on procedures spelled out in the Vedas (see Chapter 10). Each architectural pillar, *plinth* (pedestal), or other section has a name and specified size in proportion to the whole. Every decision made related to how to construct a temple is traced back to the specific denomination of the temple benefactors and devotees (see Chapter 4); the choice of the presiding deity; and the style of temple (northern or southern; a distinction I explain later in this section).

The following sections describe the key parts of a temple and explain what rules apply to its construction and use.

The overall structure

Ancient Indians held that the whole universe is made up of five elements: sky (or *ether* where the gods lived), air, fire, water, and earth. The central importance of the planet Earth, called *Bhumi Mata* ("Mother Earth") and equated with nature, is that all five elements can be found here together. Also, when Brahman, the Supreme Soul, expanded into matter (Prakriti) and spirit (Purusha), as I explain in Chapter 19, these two together generated all physical, spiritual, animate, and inanimate forms in existence.

Based on this fundamental concept, the temple plan is visualized in elaborate mathematical patterns that begin with a square *garbha griha* (main sanctum) and expand outward. The resulting grid pattern develops from 8 or 9 squares named after Vedic gods (with Brahma at the center) to a *Vastu mandala* (geometric pattern) of 64 or 81 squares, each named after gods (including gods of directions), goddesses, and planets. Within this mandala, the pattern of a human form (Purusha) is accommodated with the head in one corner and the torso and lower part laid out along the axis (see Figure 15-1). The navel on this form locates the *sanctum complex:* a sacred room that houses the presiding deity. (***Note:*** This pattern is not evident on the site but is always envisioned in the plan. In addition, not all squares need to be filled.) When the presiding deity stretches out, its feet indicate the main entrance.

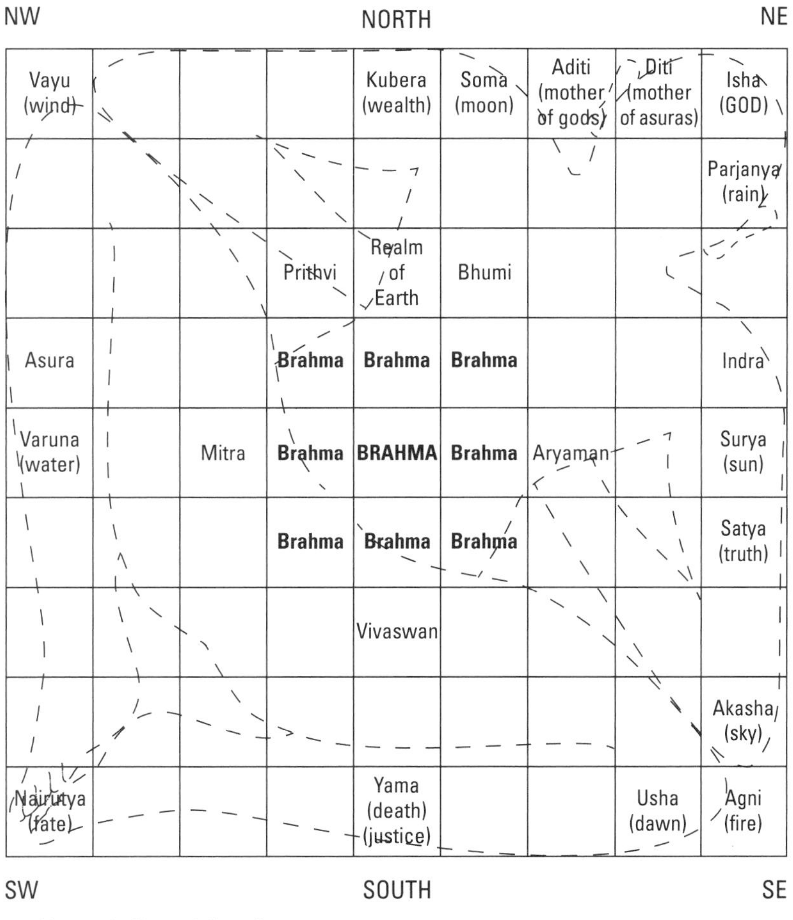

NW			NORTH				NE
Vayu (wind)			Kubera (wealth)	Soma (moon)	Aditi (mother of gods)	Diti (mother of asuras)	Isha (GOD)
							Parjanya (rain)
		Prithvi	Realm of Earth	Bhumi			
Asura		Brahma	Brahma	Brahma			Indra
Varuna (water)	Mitra	Brahma	BRAHMA	Brahma	Aryaman		Surya (sun)
		Brahma	Brahma	Brahma			Satya (truth)
			Vivaswan				
							Akasha (sky)
Nairutya (fate)			Yama (death) (justice)			Usha (dawn)	Agni (fire)

| SW | | SOUTH | | SE |

Key to dedicated directions:

Northeast: Direction of power; ruler is Isha (God/Supreme One)
East: Direction of good fortune; ruler is Indra (King of gods) with Surya (Sun)
Southeast: Direction of fire; ruler is Agni (Fire god)
South: Direction of darkness; ruler is Yama (Judge of the dead)
Southwest: (Nairutya): Direction of fear; ruler is Putna (Demoness)
West: Direction of uncertainty; ruler is Varuna (Lord of waters)
Northwest: Direction of strength; ruler is Vayu (Wind lord)
North: Direction of the mother (earth); ruler is Kubera (Yaksha, lord of wealth)

Figure 15-1:
The overall layout of a temple.

Key areas and structures

Some of the features of the great ancient temples in India include stone sculptures, 1,000 or more elaborately carved pillars, 4,000-foot-long corridors, grand entrance towers soaring more than 100 feet, towers above the sanctums, sculpted walls, corridors within corridors, carved doors, and courtyards. Walking and winding from the outermost to the innermost corridor, the visitor finally arrives at the *sanctum sanctorum:* the main sanctum housing the presiding deity. Of course, not all temples are this grand. But some are, and they are famous pilgrimage centers too.

Here are some of the areas and structures you may find in a Hindu temple:

- ✔ **Garbha griha:** This is the sanctum sanctorum, where the presiding deity resides. An essential requirement is that the presiding deity face the eastern direction. The morning sun lights up the temple entrance, and the deity can thus "view" the sunrise as priests chant sacred mantras to welcome the morning and praise the Lord.

- ✔ **Towers:** A tower placed above the main sanctum is patterned on the idea of the legendary Mount Meru, a sacred axial mountain at the navel of the universe around which all else rotates, and is usually adorned with a decorative metallic urn called a *kalasha.* This tower and the entrance towers of a temple complex are built to specific mathematical proportions.

- ✔ **Multiple sanctums:** Some ancient temples, located on many acres of land, have several sanctums housing different deities that correspond to or complement the presiding deity. Temples dedicated to Vishnu, for example, may have a sanctum for Krishna or other Vaishnavite gods.

- ✔ **Mandapas:** These rectangular, pillared structures are developed, when needed, to enlarge the facilities. They extend from the main sanctum to the south and east.

- ✔ **A rectangular pool commonly referred to as a *tank*:** This pool is used principally for ritual bathing purposes by the devotees. It can also be used for rituals that need to be performed close to a body of water.

- ✔ **A stambha:** This tall decorative pillar is close to the main entrance and is believed to be a cosmic pillar connecting the earth with the heavens.

- ✔ **A hall (called *yagna shala*) with a fire pit at the center:** This area is used for elaborate fire rituals called *homas.*

- ✔ **Sculptures:** The deities installed for worship are the subjects of the main sculptures inside the temple. Other sculptures — such as those of minor gods and goddesses, guardians of doors, and characters from Hindu epics (see Chapter 12) — as well as a variety of decorative motifs may all be seen around the temple complex.

Figure 15-2 shows a famous temple to Meenakshi (the fish-eyed consort of Shiva) at Madurai in South India. This temple features nine spectacular towers *(gopurams):* four grand entrance towers located at cardinal points, as well as towers above the sanctums of each shrine. The devotees entering at one of these towers walk around, always clockwise (sunwise), as they maneuver corridor after corridor converging to the principal sanctums. The sanctums are arranged in such a way that the visitor has to go through several corridors passing small shrines and niches that house minor gods and goddesses before arriving at the main sanctum.

Figure 15-2:
The Meenakshi temple at Madurai in South India.

Photo by Government of India Department of Tourism

In the garbha griha, the presiding deity Meenakshi resides. There is a separate sanctum for Shiva and a pavilion to Nandi (the bull who is Shiva's vehicle).

Within the Meenakshi temple complex is also a tank known as *Lotus tank* that devotees may use to bathe before entering the sanctums. In addition, the Meenakshi temple includes a thousand-pillared hall used on special occasions for worship outside the sanctums to allow large gatherings to sit and participate in ceremonies such as a divine wedding.

A divine wedding

Traditional temples, especially in southern India, include among their rituals a wedding ceremony of the presiding deity with his consort(s). In the case of the Madurai Meenakshi temple, the presiding deity is female, so the consort is Lord Shiva who has a temple of his own within the temple complex.

The wedding ceremony is full scale, taking most of a day. It starts with the procession of the "groom" toward the wedding hall accompanied by his "family and friends" and received by the "bride's family and friends." The bride(s) and groom are metal processional replicas of the deities. Every ritual that is part of a typical Vedic ceremony is practiced, and the ceremony concludes with a procession of the wedded couple followed by a great feast. It is common for devotees to offer a variety of gifts to the "groom" and "bride(s)" that will serve as donations to the temple.

Principal differences in northern and southern traditions

The basic differences between temples in North India (referred to as *Nagara style*) and South India (referred to as *Dravidian style*) are the design of the towers and the material and style used for the permanent, installed statues.

- **Design of the towers:** The southern style of architecture generally uses a trapezoidal tower design, while the northern style is narrower at the base and somewhat conical.

- **The sculptures of the deities:** The sculpted deities in the Dravidian style (known also as Hoysala or Chola style) are almost always made of stone (granite or black stone), whereas the northern tradition is to install deities sculpted out of marble.

The rituals from groundbreaking to sanctification

A temple complex can function as a traditional Hindu temple only if it is sanctified using a specific series of rituals that are based in scriptures known as *Agamas.* The rituals are conducted by trained priests and are tailored to the particular denomination of the temple benefactors and devotees.

- **Ground-breaking rituals:** Before temple construction can begin, religious rites take place on the site when ground is broken. This ritual, known as *Bhumi puja* ("groundbreaking ceremony"), is conducted to honor and placate Bhumi Mata (Mother Earth). Offerings are placed into the ground at or close to the location of the temple premises.

These offerings become more elaborate and specific to the gods when the foundation stone is laid. At the foundation of each sanctum, just below where the deity will be seated, special worships take place with offerings made of grains, symbolic gold and silver foils, turmeric, kumkum (red powder), and a copper foil with names of devotees etched on it.

✔ **The preliminaries:** As temple plans are prepared, the community holds regularly scheduled meetings. Community members discuss the progress of the project, conduct worship ceremonies to the presiding deity (using either a picture or metallic replica), and pray for the safe journey of the sculptures from their site of origin (normally in India) to their destination site. When the sculptures are in transit, it is usually a trying period for the community. (*Note:* If any damage occurs during transit, that sculpture cannot be used in the sanctification rituals I describe later in this list.)

For the completion of the temple in Middletown, Connecticut, 13 sculptures were packed with extreme care and shipped from Bangalore, India, by truck to the port city of Madras; by ship to Singapore and from Singapore to Seattle; by train from Seattle to Boston; and by truck from Boston to Middletown.

✔ **Preparatory rituals:** After their journey, the sculptures are worshipped for the first time through a series of preparatory rituals prior to installation. As priests and devotees chant, the images are readied to "rest" for four days in containers filled first with water, then a day later with flowers, and later with raw rice. Finally, the deities are left in their containers under sheets as though asleep.

✔ **Energizing and installing the deities:** Following the preliminary steps, the sculptures are readied for the ceremony known as *Prana Pratishtapana,* the ritualistic process of evoking the life force into the sculptures. In Middletown, the deities were energized through rituals held at fire altars set up outside in the open. These were elaborate fire ceremonies. First, each deity, while still lying in a container, was worshipped. Then priests lit a torch (whose cloth had been soaked in *ghee,* clarified butter) with the fire from the fire altars and, while chanting, carried the torch from one empty sanctum to another to purify the space. Only after all these preparations had been completed were the deities installed, one after another, in their own sanctums during the five days set aside for the purpose with special worships, feasts, and music concerts. Note that all these ceremonies are based on *shastras* (rules) relevant to the particular deity and corresponding tradition.

✔ **Sanctifying the deities:** Five priests direct the sanctifying proceedings over five days following the strict rules laid down in the manuals known as Agama. Such sanctification infuses energy into each of the installed deities. These steps are the basis for Hindus to believe that the sculptures can be invoked during appropriate ceremonies to represent living gods.

Touring the Satyanarayana Temple in Middletown, Connecticut

In the Middletown, Connecticut temple, the presiding deity is Satyanarayana and the sanctum housing that deity faces east. On each side of the principal sanctum are separate sanctums to his consorts Lakshmi and Bhudevi.

In the Middletown temple, the principal deities (Satyanarayana, Lakshmi, Bhudevi, Ganapati, and the Navagrahas) are all carved out of *Krishna Shila* (black stone from the Indian state of Karnataka). Satyanarayana, Lakshmi, Bhudevi, and Ganapati stand between 6 and 8 feet tall. The Navagrahas are about 14 inches high each except for the sun god, which is about 18 inches.

To take a tour of this temple, follow the temple plan shown in Figure 15-3 as you read the following list. (For more information on these gods and goddesses, refer to Chapter 7.)

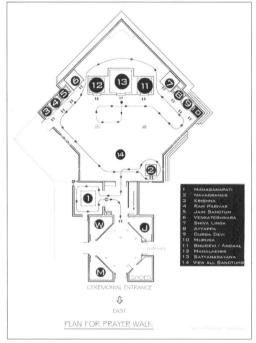

Figure 15-3: Temple plan for the Hindu temple in Middletown, Connecticut.

Illustration by Barun K. Basu, AIA

✔ **1 – Mahaganapati:** The sanctum for Ganapati (or Ganesha) is the first shrine worshippers and visitors come to, located just outside the main hall to the left as you enter, and facing north. The elephant-headed god, Remover of Obstacles, is sought out by parents with children on their way to college or those seeking or beginning a new job or a new venture.

✔ **2 – Navagrahas:** The next shrine, to the right as you enter the main hall, is dedicated to nine planets or heavenly bodies: sun, moon, Mars, Mercury, Jupiter, Venus, Saturn, Rahu (eclipse), and Ketu (comet).

Ancient Hindus believed that the life of each human was, to some extent, influenced by the position and movement of planets and other cosmic bodies at the precise moment of birth. Therefore, the nine planets are included as an essential part of all major worship. At this sanctum, Hindu worshippers circumambulate (walk around) the nine individual deities, which are arranged on an octagonal base at chest level with the sun at the center, and offer flowers, fruits, and perhaps a coin as they pray to the whole ensemble. Some worshippers sponsor a special *puja* (worship) to all the planets including ritual baths (with milk, honey, buttermilk, and water) followed by chanting of the 108 names of each of the nine planets.

✔ **3 – The Radha-Krishna Shrine:** Krishna is an avatar of Vishnu (see Chapter 8). He plays a key role in the epic called the *Mahabharata* (see Chapter 12) and teaches the epic hero Arjuna the lessons revealed in the most sacred Hindu scripture, the Bhagavad Gita (see Chapter 13). He is worshipped by all Hindus irrespective of their denominations. Hindus recall this savior god's promise to appear as needed in times of crisis. (***Note:*** Radha, Krishna, and the images in the Ram Parivar, described in the next paragraph, are made of white marble.)

✔ **4 – The Ram Parivar:** This ensemble includes the hero of the epic *Ramayana* (see Chapter 12) along with his wife Sita and brother Lakshmana. In this grouping, Hanuman, the monkey god, sits at Rama's feet with his head bent in reverence. Hindus pray that their sons grow up as brave as Rama and his brothers and as loyal and courageous as Hanuman. Girls are blessed to grow up as virtuous as Sita.

✔ **5 – The Jain Sanctum:** Two Jain saints, Rishabhdev and Mahavir, are installed in this sanctum for worship by Jains. (*Jains* follow a faith called Jainism, which began in India and shares many Hindu core values.)

✔ **6 – Venkateshwara Sanctum:** This sanctum houses Venkateshwara, a popular form of Vishnu. Devotees make vows to visit this deity if a certain plea or prayer is granted. (See the story of my first haircut in Chapter 17.)

Venkateshwara is Lord of Tirupati, a famous temple and pilgrimage center in the Indian state of Andhra Pradesh. Literally millions of people from India and abroad visit this temple to seek Venkateshwara's blessings. Devotees make vows and offer prayers asking for male progeny, a good marriage, a big promotion, and so on. In return for fulfilled wishes, they come to Tirupati and, in a typical example, offer their hair if that was part of their vows. (The result is a huge business in hair exported abroad earning millions in revenue.)

✔ **7 – Shiva Sanctum:** This sanctum houses the linga form of Shiva (refer to Chapter 7). This powerful god is one of the Hindu Trinity, and most religious ceremonies begin with a prayer to Shiva to ward off all bad vibrations from the area.

✔ **8 – Ayyappa Sanctum:** Ayyappa is a popular god for Hindus from the state of Kerala. Millions worship him during a festival at the winter solstice called Makara Sankranti (see Chapter 16).

✔ **9 – Durga Sanctum:** Durga is the shakti form of Devi (goddess) whose awesome power is directed toward those who violate dharma and whose compassion is directed toward her devotees (see Chapter 4). From this goddess, Hindus seek protection from enemies and illnesses.

✔ **10 – Murugan Sanctum:** Son of Shiva, this popular god (sculpted in granite) is the object of worship of Tamilian Hindus. His vehicle is a peacock, and the sanctum includes his consorts Valli and Devasena. He is worshipped by devotees seeking mental peace.

✔ **11 – Bhudevi Sanctum:** The Earth goddess resident of this sanctum is worshipped by devout Hindus every morning seeking her grace and compassion. She represents plenty and fertility (see Figure 15-4c).

✔ **12 – Lakshmi Sanctum:** Goddess of wealth and wellbeing, Lakshmi (shown sitting on a lotus throne in Figure 15-4b) is worshipped by all Hindus, especially those seeking wealth and success in business.

✔ **13 – Satyanarayana:** Satyanarayana, shown in Figure 15-4a, is the presiding deity of the Middletown temple. He is considered to be the very incarnation of the Hindu Trinity, Brahma, Vishnu, and Maheshwara (Shiva), worshipped by millions of Hindus worldwide. Hindus seek his merciful gaze and ask for his blessings for their families, community, country, and the whole world.

Figure 15-4: Sculptures of Satyanarayana, Lakshmi, and Bhudevi.

a   b   c

Photos by Asha and Stephen Shipman

About the Navagrahas (the nine heavenly bodies)

While it is true that ancient Hindus focused inward while trying to unravel the mysteries of the self or life on this earth, they also turned their attention to the study of the cosmos. They believed that the life of each human was, to some extent, influenced by the position and movement of planets and other cosmic bodies at the precise moment of birth. The horoscope drawn up at birth was and often still is seen as a basic guide to future trends and general character, and it is often consulted at the time of prospective ventures or betrothals.

Nature — water, fire, earth, wind, trees, flowers, mountains, the seasons, food crops — is an important aspect of Vedic ritual and prayer. The invocation of sacred rivers, fire-making, and ref-erences to the year, month, day, season, position of the sun, and phase of the moon are all integrated into specification of time and space during sacred ceremonies. In this context, the nine *grahas* (planets or heavenly bodies), called the *Navagrahas,* are included as an essential part of all major worship. Every major step in the celebration of life — the naming of a child, the first haircut, the first day of school, the thread ceremony (religious confirmation), puberty rites, marriage, housewarming, and even the start of a venture — includes a ceremony of worship directed to the Navagrahas. Navagraha *puja* (worship) is an integral part of Satyanarayana puja.

What may be a tour to non-Hindus is actually a prayer walk to devotees. At each of the locations mentioned in the preceding list, devout Hindus utter specific prayers. If you're ever in the Middletown, Connecticut temple, you can find these prayers in my book *Prayer Walk,* which welcomes and guides visitors to the temple.

Reviewing Temple Ceremonies

The practice at all sanctified temples is for the priest in charge to open the sanctum door at dawn, clapping his hands three times. The next steps involve cleaning, as well as assembling materials such as fresh flowers, fruits, fresh water, and other paraphernalia needed. If the plan is to perform a ritual bath, then additional materials including milk, honey, buttermilk, ghee, and juice also are assembled. It is not unusual for community members to be present to assist the priest, but in general, no one other than the priest is allowed inside the sanctums. After all preliminaries are taken care of, worship can begin, regardless of whether any devotee is present.

A few words on Hindu temple protocol

Almost all religious spaces have rules about the conduct and demeanor of people visiting them. Hindu temples are no different. So if you are visiting a Hindu temple, please keep these points in mind:

- ✔ You must remove your shoes upon arrival at the temple.

- ✔ No smoking is allowed. Nor can drugs, alcohol, or meat products (meat, fish, eggs, poultry) be brought in or consumed on the temple premises.

- ✔ Please remain quiet and contemplative inside. Worshippers may recite the appropriate prayer(s) silently, especially if other people are present. No loud noises, beepers, or conversation! (Please turn off your cell phone before entering a temple.)

- ✔ If a puja is in progress, you may stay, participate, and receive the blessings and offering (prasadam). Otherwise, you may pray and/or observe and proceed to the next sanctum.

- ✔ Worshippers may circle the shrine three times clockwise, keeping the main sanctum to their right, and prostrate before leaving the temple. Flowers and fruits may be offered or left just outside the sanctum, before circling the shrine. Please do not touch the vigrahas (images).

Daily worship

The daily rituals vary, but in general prayers are offered consistent with the time of day: at sunrise, at noon, and at sunset.

Morning worship includes chanting of *suprabhatam:* hymns in praise of the deity and glorifying the morning that is holy. This worship praises the Lord and sets the stage for other rituals. A chant of 108 names of the Lord, as described in the next section, concludes with an *arati:* a plate with a flame waved up and down clockwise in front of the deity at the conclusion of a worship (refer to Chapter 14).

The different worship rituals use additional chants from different scriptures, such as the Vedas. In the morning, the additional chants come from the Rig Veda; at noon, they come from the Yajur Veda; and at night, the Sama Veda (see Chapter 10). Occasionally a devotee may show up with a new car and request a puja to be performed for it! The priests oblige and do a worship ceremony asking gods to bless the vehicle to ensure safety and performance.

Salutations using 108 or 1,000 names

Orthodox Hindus, particularly in southern India, used two sets of chants commonly practiced and chanted at home but mostly used at temples in front of the deity being worshipped. These chants are salutations to the godhead using either 108 names or 1,000 names.

So what is special about the number 108? There is no clear answer and all sorts of convoluted explanations. Here, for example, are a few facts that may or may not have had an impact:

✔ The distance between Earth and the sun is 108 times the diameter of the sun.

✔ The distance between Earth and the moon is 108 times the diameter of the moon.

✔ There are 108 stitches in a baseball. (Okay, this one could not have been a factor!)

All major and some minor gods (and goddesses) are described with 108 names, as well as 1,000

(Sahasra Nama) names. Using Lakshmi as an example, her 108 names/attributes include: Well-wisher of all life, Supreme Soul, Speech, Lotus, Purity, Auspicious, Inauspicious, Nectar, Fulfilled, Golden, Wealth, Strong, Radiant, Bright wife of the sun, Light, Earth, Earthborne, Wife of Vishnu, Beautiful-eyed, Granter of wishes, Intelligent, Sinless, Nine-Durgas, Wife of Hari, Sorrowless, Nectarlike, Remover of miseries, Abode of morality, Kind, Mother of the universe, Beloved of god Padmanabha, Virtuous, Fragrant, Giver of boons, Sister of the moon, Doer of auspicious things, Mother of the universe, Remover of poverty, Earth's daughter, Protector, Lover of palaces, Daughter of the milky ocean, Vishnu's chest jewel, Consort of Vishnu, Kali, Friend of the Trimurti.

Hindus don't necessarily stop at 108 names. They have a thousand ways of praising a godhead.

Chanting the names of God

Worshipping Hindu gods, especially in temples, includes almost always a chanting that is known as *Ashtoththara Shata Namavali,* meaning "chanting the 108 names." All major gods/goddesses are greeted with a set of 108 names frequently chanted by priests at temples and by devotees. The event is called *archana,* meaning "offering of praises." When these worship services are conducted, the devotees and their families stand in reverence in front of the sanctum while the priest chants the names one at a time, offering a few petals of flowers or a few grains of *akshata* (raw rice tinted in turmeric, an auspicious symbolic offering).

In South Indian temples, the archana is commonly sponsored by a devotee family to celebrate an event (the birth of a child, passing an examination, a new job, or marriage, for example).

If there is a front office at the temple, you can buy a ticket to have the archana performed for a fee (currently $11 at the temple in Middletown) and take it to the deity of your choice and present it to the priest in charge. He will then ask you for your name, lineage, birth star, and the name of the person for whom this worship is being offered. For example, you may tell him the name of a newborn. (The lineage represents what Hindus call *gotra,* the name of the sage your family spiritual lineage is traced back to.)

With these details established, the worship begins. Each chant starts with the sacred symbol Om followed by the particular name of the god or goddess, followed by the Sanskrit word *namaha,* which means "I salute." Using the goddess Lakshmi as an example, the chant would be *Om prakrtyai namaha.* Translation : "Om I salute Nature." Nature is one of Lakshmi's names, and this chant means "O Lakshmi, You are Nature and I salute you as such."

Special days for individual deities

Certain days are considered special for certain deities. For example, Friday night is a time to welcome and worship Lakshmi, the goddess of good fortune and well-being. Mondays are for Shiva. Full moon nights are celebrated with an elaborate worship of Satyanarayana. Worships also are conducted after eclipses.

Temples are set to perform elaborate pujas to these deities on special days and nights as well as on days that mark a festival (see Chapter 16).

A sample worship (puja) ceremony

The most popular worship ceremony at the temple in Middletown, Connecticut, is the special puja performed each month to the presiding deity Lord Satyanarayana. This occurs on the full moon night. It begins in the early evening and concludes a couple of hours later. The ceremony includes 32 distinct steps that represent a total worship. It includes prayers to nature (Earth, planets, directions, conch), demigods (protectors of primary entrances and doors), Shaivite gods (Shiva, Ganapati), Shakta goddesses (Bhudevi and Lakshmi), and Vaishnavite gods (Vishnu). The ceremony also integrates offerings of dance and music.

After all the rituals and ceremonies are conducted by the priests, the devotees offer their own service through singing in praise of the deities. These are devotional songs sung together as a group with someone leading and accompanied by musical instruments. This gives individuals their own voice to express deep feelings about God through songs they learned while young. This activity also brings people together as a community.

You may wonder why the penchant for outward expression. Hindus offer two explanations. First, a deity helps focus the mind on God. The ritual involved in worship is a step toward eventually rising above mere form to reach the formless. Second, worship at a temple allows for contact with a community of like-minded people and provides the semblance of an organized activity. Nevertheless, Hindus strongly believe that religion is a matter between the individual and the maker. Life goes on with a delicate balance among these conflicting beliefs.

Chapter 16

Holydays and Festivals

In This Chapter

▶ Celebrating the first holydays of the year

▶ Observing spring, summer, and fall festivals

▶ Noting the impact of regional festivals

The eager anticipation by young and old! New clothes! The gathering of extended family members! The exchange of gossip and gifts! All these facets add to the color, fun, and frolic of the holidays. And the food? Ah yes! Although the religious rituals appropriate to each occasion are the most important aspects of the holidays, the climax is really the meal.

The most important driver determining the size, scope, and ritual in a festival is the family tradition, which explains why these observances vary so much from region to region and sometimes within a region. Non-Hindus can feel confused by this variety, struggling to see a unifying principle beneath it all. But Hindus simply accept the diversity —even relish it — and don't mind if the family next door practices the same festival in a different manner. The word *uniformity* hardly exists in the Hindu world! But don't worry; in this chapter, I help you figure out the fundamentals about Hindu festivals and holydays.

As you read this chapter, keep two points in mind:

✔ The underlying theme of all festivals is the same: the triumph of good over evil and establishing and restoring dharma (moral order).

✔ Festivals fall into three main categories: those commemorating the birth or triumph of a god or goddess, those celebrating a lunar or solar event, and those celebrating a harvest.

Festivals Celebrated Throughout India

All the festivals listed throughout this chapter are observed by Hindus irrespective of where they live or what language they speak. However, certain regions emphasize some festivals and are known for special celebrations that attract people outside the region. Table 16-1 lists the festivals that are celebrated throughout India.

Table 16-1	Timetable of Hindu Festivals	
Festival	*Commemorating*	*Season*
Makara Sankranti	Winter solstice and harvest	Winter
Shivaratri	The night of Shiva	Winter
Ramanavami	The birth day of Rama	Spring
Varshapirapu, Yugadi, Gudi Padwa	The lunar new year and spring equinox	Spring
Holi	Harvest	Spring
Krishna Janmashtami	Krishna's birthday	Summer
Ganesha Chaturthi	Ganesha's (Ganapati's) birthday	Summer
Navaratri	Celebration of the devis: Durga, Lakshmi, and Saraswati	Fall
Diwali	Hindu festival of lights	Fall

Makara Sankranti

Makara Sankranti is both a harvest festival and a celebration of the winter solstice. *Makara* is the name of the zodiac phase the sun enters into in mid-January. Sometimes this festival is simply referred to as *Sankranti.*

Hindus view the winter solstice as the time when Surya, the sun god, returns from his journey south, and his journey in a northern direction begins. The journey south is called *Dakshinayana,* and the journey north is referred to as *Uttarayana.* The six months it takes for this journey to end so that the direction may change to north from south is the equivalent of a single night for the gods. In essence, therefore, the six-month night of the divine ends, and Makara Sankranti marks the dawn of a new day — a new sixth-month day of the gods (because one year for us humans equates to one day for the gods).

This celestial event provides a green flag for individuals and families to undertake important or auspicious events. For example, in many parts of India, no marriages are negotiated or performed until after Makara Sankranti. And the epic *Mahabharata* (refer to Chapter 12) tells us that the patriarch Bhishma, who was severely wounded in the war during the Dakshinayana period, waited until Uttarayana began to relinquish his body. He had received a boon (that's another story within another story within the main story!) that allowed him to choose the time of his death.

As with most festivals, Sankranti celebrations vary from one region to another. The sections that follow provide a sampling of the activities and traditions. In the various Makara Sankranti celebrations you can see the emphasis that Hindus place on the worship of nature, such as the sun, cattle, and regenerative forces of life. (Check out Chapter 3 for more on Hindu beliefs about nature.)

Along the sacred rivers of India

During Makara Sankranti, a dip in a nearby river at sunrise is a must for devout Hindus. At the sacred rivers — such as the Ganges and her tributaries in northern India, the river Godavari in Maharashtra, and the river Cauvery in the south — very large crowds gather, and devotees offer flowers to the river and lift handfuls of water toward the sun in a prayerful gesture of offering.

One extraordinary festival event, known as Kumbha Mela, takes place only every three years at the confluence of three sacred rivers: Ganga, Yamuna, and Saraswati at Prayag in the Uttara Pradesh province. In 2001, over a period of six weeks during this festival, 70 *million* people bathed in the rivers. (Read more about this special event in Chapter 18 where I cover the Hindu pilgrimage story.)

In Karnataka

Karnataka is one of the southern states of India with more than 61 million people. The capital is the well-known city of Bangalore where every major U.S. corporation has an office. The city of Mysore is 80 miles away and is the location of the famed Navaratri ("nine nights") festival, which I describe later in this chapter.

Harvesting the winter crop in Karnataka, Hindus pay respect to an important factor in any successful agricultural season: the cattle. Cows and bulls are bathed and their horns polished and painted with bright colors and topped with glittering gold dust. They are decorated with flowers, garlands, and bells, and new ropes are used to handle them.

In the evening at a central location in the village or town, the cattle and their handlers assemble and then walk in procession, led by musicians playing pipes and drums. Along the way, the cattle and their handlers jump, one by one, over a fire built at an intersection. This act symbolizes triumph and purification as both man and animal come through the fire. All evils are warded off, and the handlers and their cattle are ready for a new season. When the procession reaches its designated end and the cattle are brought home, an *arati* is performed to them and they are given food to eat. (I explain the ritual step of arati in Chapter 14; a plate with a small flame at the center is ceremoniously waved in a clockwise direction in front of the entity being worshipped.) Worship ceremonies take place in local temples, and sweet rice (called *sakkarai pongal*) is the food offering shared by all.

During this festival, in which everyone is brought into a mood of expectation, enthusiasm, and gaiety, man worships the animals, expresses gratitude, and demonstrates harmony with nature.

In Tamilnadu

Tamilians, the majority of whom live in the South Indian state of Tamilnadu, celebrate this winter harvest holiday over four days and refer to it as *Pongal* instead of Makara Sankranti. You may have heard the word *pongal* used to refer to a dish of rice porridge, but in this context, Pongal is the name for the celebration. The four days of Pongal are

- **Bhogi Pongal:** Bhogi Pongal celebrates Krishna and comes about because Krishna decided to teach a lesson to Indra, King of Heaven, who had become arrogant when millions worshipped him on Pongal. Lord Krishna ordered his cowherds to worship Mount Govardhan instead. Indra was furious and sent huge rainstorms. Lord Krishna simply lifted up the whole mountain, used it like an umbrella, and sheltered the cowherds, the farms, and the cattle. Indra recognized this feat as that of Krishna, begged forgiveness, and prayed to be allowed back into the festivities. And so on this Pongal day, Krishna is worshipped for allowing Indra to continue to send rains at the proper seasons to grow abundant food. Bhogi Pongal is also a day to clean out unwanted items from the house and burn them.

- **Surya Pongal:** Surya Pongal is dedicated to the sun god. To honor him, Hindu women use rice flour to draw elaborate rangoli patterns on the floor in front of their homes. (Flip back to Chapter 14 to see an illustration of a rangoli pattern.)

- **Mattu Pongal:** This day celebrates cattle and came about because of Shiva's anger at his vehicle Nandi, the bull. Shiva instructed Nandi to go to Earth and tell humans to get an oil massage and bath every day but eat only once a month. Instead, Nandi announced that Shiva commanded humans to eat every day and get an oil massage bath once a month. Furious, Shiva cursed Nandi to be born on Earth and toil with his offspring to raise food so that people could eat every day. Benefiting from this curse, we show our gratitude by decorating cattle and worshipping them on Mattu Pongal day!

- **Kanu Pongal:** Kanu Pongal is a day of pure family revelry. On this day, sisters honor their brothers for being there for them and offering protection. Kanu Pongal is also the day to see and be seen, so young and old dress in their finest and spend time out and about in public places, making this a perfect day for parents to scout for prospective sons- or daughters-in-law. And of course, young adults are also on the lookout for prospective spouses!

Shivaratri: The grand night of Shiva

Shivaratri is a solemn celebration of Shiva, one of the Hindu Trinity (refer to Chapter 1). During this holyday, devotees (mainly Shaivas; see Chapter 4 for more information on the various Hindu sects) stay up all night fasting, praying, meditating, and worshipping in the belief that doing so absolves them of all sins.

Shivaratri falls on a moonless night in February or March in the dark waning moon fortnight. Some Hindus believe that on this day, god Shiva married Parvati. Others believe that this was the day of Shiva's cosmic dance of creation *(Tandava nritya).*

Simplicity is the guiding principle during this festival, from the rituals to the foods, and contemplation and meditation are the order of the day. The most familiar representation of Shiva is the iconic *lingam* — a phallic symbol. Temple priests, on behalf of devotees, offer elaborate ritual baths, followed by an arati, to the lingam every three hours. Flowers, kumkum powder, and bilva (bael) leaves are offered. (Bilva trees are commonly found on the grounds of Shiva temples, and the leaves are highly valued by the Hindu medical system of Ayurveda.)

The highlights of this festival include holding a night-long vigil, singing *bhajans* (rhythmic phrases in Sanskrit or local vernacular in praise of gods) that praise Shiva, repeating *om namah shivaya* (Om, I salute Lord Shiva), participating in temple worships until morning, and breaking the fast with a final worship and frugal meal.

Ramanavami: Rama's birthday

Ramanavami is nine days of festivities in April (the Hindu month of Chaitra) that celebrate the birthday of Rama, an avatar of Vishnu and hero of the *Ramayana* (see Chapter 12). During Ramanavami, it's customary, especially in the south, to read the poet Valmiki's version of the epic in Sanskrit. (I introduce you to Valmiki in Chapter 12 as well.) On the ninth day, the entire festivity reaches a climax with a great feast. Skillful storytellers relate the nearly infinite substories that bring the theme back and forth to the main story, the *Ramayana.*

Rama is usually portrayed as a handsome young warrior armed with a bow. In Chapter 7, I show you *Ram Parivar:* the popular pictorial grouping of Rama with his wife Sita, his brother Lakshmana, and Hanuman the monkey god. Rama stands with Lakshmana on his right (also armed with a bow), Sita on his left, and Hanuman kneeling at his feet.

During this festival, temples perform ceremonial divine weddings of Rama to Sita. These weddings use brass or bronze images of the two (known as *utsava murthis,* or processional images) and are performed in great detail. After the wedding, the images are carried out in a public procession.

Festivals marking the spring equinox and lunar new year

New Year celebrations have always had a religious undertone among Hindus. This event, which is called different names, is not celebrated on the same day by all Hindus. Family traditions, as well as whether a family follows a lunar calendar or solar calendar, determine the timing of the celebration:

✔ Tamilians observe *Varshapirapu* (birth of a new year) in mid-April

✔ Kannadigas (people from Karnataka, who speak Kannada) and Andhras (Telugu-speaking folks from Andhra Pradesh) celebrate Yugadi in mid-March.

✔ Maharashtrians call this celebration *Gudi Padwa* and observe it in mid-March.

✔ People in northern India consider Diwali, which occurs in late October or early November, as their New Year celebration. For more on this festival, see the later section "Diwali."

Regardless of what this celebration is called or when it is celebrated, all practices include worshipping at home or a temple followed by a special feast. A special feature in some parts of India is to make sure everyone gets a taste of a mixture of *jaggery* (brown sugar) and leaves of bitter *neem* (a tree from the mahogany family) to drive home the point that life in the New Year will include both sweet and not-so-sweet experiences.

Dressing down for the occasion: Holi

Holi, a festival celebrated all over northern India, is essentially thanksgiving for the end of the winter crop harvest of wheat. During this festival, you'd be wise to dress casually when you step out of your house. You are liable to be met with shouts of *"Holi hai!"* ("Holi's here!") and a shower of red, orange, or yellow color by pranksters (your friends and neighbors, dressed in their worst) ready to throw or spray colored powders or water on one and all. This is a free-for-all fun time, caste no bar, for men and women.

Krishna Janmashtami: Krishna's birthday

If one Hindu god's name is known and recognized throughout the world, it's Krishna, an avatar of Vishnu (see Chapter 8). The most observed celebration during the summer is Krishna's birthday.

Krishna's birthday, known as *Janmashtami* (as well as *Krishna Jayanti* and *Gokulashtami*), is celebrated on the eighth day *(ashtami)* in the darker fortnight of the month Bhadrapada (August/September), in the middle of the monsoon season. The festival celebrating Krishna's birth occurs in the late evening to late night because Krishna is believed to have been born at midnight.

Indian summers begin with torrid heat: In the northern plains, it's a dry, scorching 100 to 120 degree F; the coastline gets a soggy, humid 90-degree heat. Beginning around the end of March, this heat continues unabated until relieved by torrential monsoon rains in late June. During the hot season, few major festivals are conducted, and even weddings cease from mid-March to mid-April.

Janmashtami is a popular festival celebrated throughout India and other parts of the world. In temples where the presiding deity is Krishna, the rituals begin in the evening with a variety of worship ceremonies that include a royal bath *(abhishekam)* for the deity followed by dressing the deity with new colorful clothing, flowers, and jewelry. *Harikathas* (tales of Krishna rendered by professional storytellers) and music concerts all culminate with the grand finale comprising lighting camphor in an arati plate and waving it up and down ceremonially three times clockwise as priests chant prayer mantras at midnight. A small baby statue of Krishna in silver is set up in a decorated cradle and rocked during the final arati and treated to lullaby songs.

In South India, you can tell that a family is celebrating Janmashtami just by looking at the front door step in the family home. You'll see a drawing of the two small feet of a child decorating the front in a rice flour rangoli pattern. The joy and anticipation resemble that felt at the birth of a baby in the family!

And the food? Where to begin? Janmashtami is my favorite holiday because no festival excels this holiday in the number of delicious items prepared! Families, especially those with children, prepare 15 or more delicious sweet and savory special dishes. These are mostly finger foods. In a popular arrangement in Iyengar households (those from a subsect of the Vaishnava denomination; see Chapter 4), one of each item is tied to a piece of string and hung from a low ceiling frame in front of the altar specially set up for worship that night with a cradle, pictures, and small statues of baby Krishna. Celebrations include an evening *puja* (worship) and chanting from sacred scriptures.

Ganesha Chaturthi: Ganesha's birthday

Ganesha Chaturthi falls on the fourth day *(Chaturthi)* in the second (brighter) fortnight of the Hindu month of Bhadrapada (August/September), near the end of the monsoon season and close to the autumnal equinox. This all-India festival is especially popular in Mumbai and the western Indian state of Maharashtra. It celebrates the birthday of Ganesha (also known as Ganesh, Ganapati, Mahaganapati, Vinayaka, and Vighneshwara), one of the few major godheads who is a combination of man and animal form. Even Westerners who have little exposure to Hinduism recognize the elephant-headed god (see Figure 16-1).

Figure 16-1: Ganesha, the elephant-headed god.

Photo by Asha and Stephen Shipman

Irrespective of the region of India, irrespective of special affiliation to any aspect of Hindu religion, Hindus offer their first prayer to Ganesha, Lord of Obstacles, before any auspicious tasks are undertaken. Hindus believe that Ganesha's blessings at the start of an endeavor will help the rest of the mission to proceed smoothly and without incident. For example, most concerts of Indian classical music begin with a composition in praise of Ganesha. This genial, kindly god occupies a very special place in the hearts of Hindus, and almost all Hindu households and places of business display his picture or statue in a prominent setting.

Although Ganesha is a favorite of Hindus worldwide, the festival celebrating his birth is especially popular in Maharashtra in the tradition begun by Lokamanya Balgangadhar Tilak (1856–1920), considered to be the father of the *swaraj* (Indian freedom) movement. To this day, the ten-day festival takes place in grand style, attracting millions to Maharashtra's capital Mumbai, and this religious fervor unites Hindus everywhere as no other festival does.

Beginning the celebration: The homecoming

The festival begins with buying and bringing home a clay sculpture of Ganesha, colored in gold, yellow, pink, and red, from the market and installing it at home in an inner room, along with all the paraphernalia needed to perform daily worship ceremonies. Then each day during the celebration begins with worship to Ganesha. When the festival is held in a temple, the daily worship continues with *darshans* (visiting the divine) by devotees, a storytelling session, a music concert, and a concluding brief worship ceremony at the end of the day.

Send-off ceremony

The ten-day celebration ends with a send-off ceremony called *visarjan* in which the image of Ganesha is immersed in a body of water, preferably a sacred river or lake. In Mumbai, the former Bombay, this ceremony becomes an amazing public spectacle in several parts of the city in which a gigantic Ganesha is mounted on a moving chariot. The decorated throne is drawn through the streets by thousands of followers who finally carry it down to the beach and launch it into the ocean.

Navaratri

Navaratri ("nine nights") is part of the ten-day event that begins on the first day *(Prathama)* of the bright half of the lunar month of Bhadrapada–Ashvayuja (September or October, depending on the lunar calendar). A concluding festival is tagged on to the tenth *(Dashami)* day known as *Vijayadashami* (Victorious Tenth Day) and pertains to victory of good over evil in the context of local lore. In between are sandwiched worships and celebrations directed toward the *devis* (principal Hindu goddesses): Durga, Lakshmi, and Saraswati.

Based on the Hindu calendar, the current practice is to worship Durga on the first three nights, Lakshmi on the second three nights, Saraswati on the seventh night, and Durga on the eighth night *(Ashtami)* celebrating her killing the demon Mahisha Asura (refer to Chapter 7 for that story). The ninth night is *Ayudha Puja* dedicated to the worship of martial arms and implements — namely guns, vehicles, elephants, and horses.

The Navaratri festival combines fun and frolic, grace and dignity, community involvement and participation, religious fervor and worship, display of power, plenty and pageantry, and connection with epics and legend.

On the last day of the festival is the Vijayadashami, a celebration of the victory of good over evil. The victory is realized in hundreds of stories from the two epics, the *Mahabharata* and the *Ramayana* (see Chapter 12). For example, Hindus celebrate (from the *Ramayana*) the victory of Rama at Lanka, his grand entrance to his realm after 14 years in exile, and the rescue of Sita, as well as (from the *Mahabharata*) the recovery of precious arms that the Pandavas had hidden in the shami tree. All are cause for celebration and a triumphant display of power and plenty.

The most famous Navaratri: Dasara in Mysore

Although Navaratri and Vijayadashami are celebrated throughout the Hindu world, the Dasara at Mysore is without question *the* celebration that has made a mark on Navaratri celebrants around the world. (Think Times Square on New Year's Eve spread over ten nights!) No city celebrates this festival better than Mysore. Each night during Navaratri, the entire boundary of the famed Mysore Palace is illuminated with thousands of electric bulbs. (It's often called a sight for gods to see.)

The presiding deity in Mysore is Chamundeshwari, a form of Durga also known locally as *Mahishasuramardini,* slayer of demon Mahisha of local lore from whom the name Mysore is derived.

To pull off this grand celebration, the Karnataka state government goes all out, involving upward of 150 to 160 high-level officers of the government (you can only imagine the number of assistants in each such office). The result? The usually laid back, somewhat sleepy town comes alive and greets thousands of visitors with activities and events, including hundreds of games (soccer, volleyball, badminton, regional sports called khokho and kabaddi, wrestling, and so on), juried competitions, concerts, and dances, all culminating in the grand finale on the tenth day.

In Mysore on the tenth day, the Vijayadashami procession — beautifully decorated elephants, horses, chariots, men in uniform, government officials, and prominent citizens — assembles on the palace grounds and then winds its way through the town to the indigenous shami tree to the tune of many bands.

When the *maharaja* (king) ruled, he would sit in the *howdah* (a specially designed throne-like seat that fits on the back of an elephant) on the royal elephant and the entire procession would wind its way a couples miles from the palace to the *Banni Mantap* (a gazebo type of structure) where the shami tree is worshipped. Then the maharaja would "slay the demon" by chopping down a banana tree with the ceremonial sword, and the festival would be over.

Celebrating Vijayadashami in North India

North India in general and Delhi in particular celebrate Vijayadashami as Rama's victory at the battle of Lanka by erecting huge effigies of the demons Ravana, Kumbhakarna, and Meghanada (see Figure 16-2). At the climactic moment, an individual playing the role of the hero Rama shoots flaming arrows and the effigies catch fire and burn, symbolizing to all that dharma has been restored once again by their beloved king!

Photo by Government of India Department of Tourism

Navratri at Wesleyan University, Connecticut

Lest you think that this festival is celebrated only in India, consider an example closer to home. Navaratri at Wesleyan is a tradition established there in the 1960s by Professor Robert Brown and two music teachers (professors Tanjore Visvanathan and Tanjore Ranganathan visiting from India). A series of concerts are arranged several evenings during a week in the fall, kicking off the entire season with a student performance.

For a glimpse, go to any search engine and type *Wesleyan Navratri YouTube 2009* and listen to students performing. The festival concludes with a puja performed on the last day to goddesses Durga and Saraswati. It's traditional for teachers to give a brief lesson to their students after the puja.

The doll festival

As part of the Navaratri festival, many families, especially in rural areas in India, celebrate a doll festival. The doll festival is called Gombe Habba or Bombe Habba in Kannada (*bombe* and *gombe* mean "dolls," and *habba* means "festival"), Kolu Pandigai in Tamil Nadu, and Bommala Koluvu in Andhra Pradesh. The festival serves as a vehicle to introduce children to the world of animals, myth, legends of ancestors, and the modern world.

The doll festival is celebrated in the United States partly as a way to help children remember and enjoy the great events from their heritage. Through the doll festival, Hindu children get to see traditional folk art renderings of musical instruments, soldiers, elephants, horses, chariots, and scenes with a host of details depicting traditional stories and teaching them about life in India and the past with all its wonders and grandeur.

A bit of nostalgia: Setting up the dolls

Since the days before Sesame Street and radio and television — in fact even before electricity — Gombe Habba (the festival of dolls) has been celebrated. Gombe Habba was mostly for young girls, but young men helped because it required setting up. Beginning in the morning, the men in the family would set up a tier of steps much like the bleachers in a stadium, using wooden planks about 15 to 20 inches wide, 8 to 10 feet long, and about an inch or so thick. After the steps were covered with white sheets, they were ready for dolls to be arranged on them according to size.

In my own home, these rows extended all the way up to just under the paintings and embroidered framed pictures at the level of the ceiling. I and my brothers helped my elder sisters arrange the 100 or so dolls, which had been stored upstairs nicely covered in paper or old clothes. At the ends of the top boards we placed two life-size monkeys of just the right color and with the right look of curiosity. The other dolls were made of porcelain, wood, brass, and wires, and included horses, elephants, men and women wearing traditional and modern clothing, dogs and cats, and a wide variety of other animals. And on the side was a smaller set of tiers on which we arranged musical instruments and books to celebrate the Saraswati Puja on the seventh night of Navaratri. And on the sides of this small tier rested a rifle and a saddle for horses, ready for Ayudha Puja.

By noon, all the arrangements were complete and the dolls would be in their assigned places, ready to be viewed. In the evenings, neighborhood children — young girls who looked like dolls themselves, dressed in fine silks of green, blue, red, and pink — came and sat on mats spread in front of the staircase of dolls. The children were urged to sing and were given small toys, as well as a mixture of sugar crystal, fried *chana dal* (lentils that look like yellow split peas), and chunks of dry coconut mixed with sesame. It was a sight to see: these beautiful girls, dressed in their finery, moving about in the neighborhood visiting their friends and relatives. No television program comes close to providing the joy and peace that the doll festival brought, and life in the village became richer because of Navaratri.

Diwali

Diwali is India's festival of lights. The literal meaning of the word *diwali* is a "row of lamps." Earthen lamps (small enough to fit in a child's palm) are still used in rural India. Filled with a couple tablespoonfuls of oil and a cotton wick, they're lit and arranged in a pattern or rows on a home's or public building's threshold, roof edges, window sills, and front porch. In urban areas, electric bulbs are used. The row after row of these lights, in every building, proclaim a happy occasion for one and all. The event is celebrated in the Hindu month of Kartika in the dark fortnight that falls in late October or early November.

So, what does Diwali celebrate?

✔ **The return of the epic hero Rama to his kingdom after 14 years of exile:** North Indians associate the Diwali festival with Rama. They consider Diwali to be the day when he made his triumphal entrance to his capital Ayodhya after 14 years of exile (see Chapter 12). Legend has it that the overjoyed citizens decorated their homes and lit hundreds of lamps to greet their king.

✔ **Dhanalakshmi, the goddess of wealth:** Merchants and businessmen worship Lakshmi in the form of Dhanalakshmi (Lakshmi, the goddess of wealth) during the Diwali festival. In fact, businesses use this special day of celebration to close the books for the year and make preparations to begin the new fiscal year. The day is believed to coincide with the emergence of the goddess from the milky ocean during the great churning event when gods and demons churned the ocean to recover the many precious items that had been lost during the great flood. (I tell this story in Chapter 8.)

In addition to the rows and rows of lamps or light bulbs, fire crackers are lit and displayed by children. Wearing new clothes and jewelry is a must, as is distributing a variety of sweets. The excitement among clothing and jewelry merchants is palpable as they expect to make a lot of money during the week before Diwali!

The Diwali season is also a bonanza for those who sell sweets. Many varieties of aromatic, colorful, and delicious sweets are made fresh just for this season, and thousands of pounds of these delicacies are bought and distributed among family and friends. In large cities, the whole city erupts with gaiety, color, smiles, and sweets.

Regional Festivals

Among the thousands of villages and towns from Kanyakumari in the southernmost tip of India to the northern state of Kashmir in the Himalayas, and from Mumbai on the west coast to Calcutta on the east coast, many regions in India lay claim to one episode or another from an epic or a purana (god stories of the ancient past) that took place in their own region. This event may have led to the construction of a temple and installation of a deity, a special day to celebrate the event, a special form of worship, or a challenging sporting event, all of which may grip a community and create a tradition specific to that location.

The age-old traditions are preserved in these regional festivals, although a modern touch has been integrated here and there. This chapter (or this book, for that matter) is not long enough to cover all these festivals. Instead, I have selected representative festivals for each region.

In the northern region: Karva Chauth

The Himalayas serve as an impregnable boundary in the north of India, but the western passes and coastal region were wide open for visitors and invaders. The resulting historical events, languages, and corresponding literature have had a significant influence on what people in the region conceived, adopted, and adapted as celebrations. The northern states covered here include Uttar Pradesh and Rajasthan.

Uttar Pradesh, and northern India in general, set aside a day in the dark half of the month of Kartik (October) for married women to pray for the wellbeing of their husbands. Women observe a strict fast on this day, which is called *Karva Chauth*. This is also the day for a wife to be seen at her very best, much as she was at her wedding. Young women, especially those newly married, spend time and money to get their hair done and decorate themselves with *mehendi* (patterns traced with colorful vegetable dye on their hands and feet; see Figure 16-3) and jewelry. In addition, nothing is spared in terms of the lavishness of bright colored silks, colorful bangles, and finery. Some newlyweds choose to wear their wedding dresses and jewelry, adding an item or two of their latest buys. (Local merchants anticipate this fact and stock their shops with silks and jewelry for the days before the celebration.)

Figure 16-3: Mehendi.

Photo by Sushma Gupta

Worship of Shiva, Parvati, and Ganesha begins early in the morning before sunrise when the newly married woman is served a meal by her mother-in-law, thus allowing the fast to begin promptly at sunrise and last until moonrise. In return, the new bride presents a gift basket to the mother-in-law on behalf of her own family. Thus the stage is set for peace and plenty all around.

Legend has it that Shiva advised his wife, Parvati, not to be afraid when he was not around, and he suggested setting aside a day on which she could fast and pray to rid herself of all apprehensions. Thus the practice of worshipping Shiva and Parvati at this time came about.

At the end of the day, women traditionally gather in a friend's or relative's house and prepare for the evening puja, which involves setting up an altar and a karva for each lady. (The *karva* is a silver, brass, or copper pitcher full of water with a red string tied around the pitcher's neck.) Songs are sung, and offerings of fruits, flowers, sweets, water, incense, or light in a lamp are made to the deities of Shiva, Parvati, and Ganesha. An elderly lady may read a story of the Karva Chauth legend, a tale of what befell a wife who broke her fast too early. At the end of the puja, the assembled ladies view the moon through a sieve or through the end of their sari. Later the husband is viewed, sometimes also through a sieve, which ends the fast. A feast follows.

Western region: The elephant festival

Rajasthan, the land of maharajas, camels, elephants, and men and women decked in the colorful Rajasthani style, has developed indigenous festivals reminiscent of the glorious past with a touch of the modern. Great palaces, for example, are now first-class hotels with a thriving tourism industry.

Rajasthanis celebrate their indigenous strengths: elephants, camels, and turbans! The elephant festival at the capital city of Jaipur in February is the occasion to show off these large but graceful animals. Elephants are scrubbed clean and decorated with colorful hand-loomed silks and cotton cloths and glittering gold ornaments (even anklets and bells). These animals are then led in a spectacular procession joined by equally bedecked camels, horses, and folk dancers. This state festival attracts thousands of visitors from within India and abroad.

Jaipur makes the most of the festival by adding games such as polo and even a tug of war between an elephant on one side and competing men on the other! And of course a competition to show off turbans of different styles adds to the fun and excitement of this desert region. Some of these activities take place on full moon nights with the desert in the foreground adding another dimension to Rajasthan's glory.

Rajasthan literally means "the land of kings," and the state lives up to its good name. The associated pomp, pageantry, grace, and grandeur are visible everywhere. The grand fortresses and palaces of Jodhpur, Udaipur, Ajmir, Bikaneer. and a wide variety of Rajasthan towns and cities of lore have now become excellent tourist spots. Walking down any street, you'll see men with the Rajasthan brand turbans on their heads and women in colorful dresses. And elephants and camels add to the imagery and impression that visitors carry in their minds as they tour the state and return home.

Southern region: The Vairamudi, Rajamudi, Kavadi, and Onam festivals

The culture of the south is influenced by its relatively peaceful past. Because it has had fewer onslaughts of invaders than the north, the ancient practices are preserved essentially intact.

Celebrating the diamond crown (Vairamudi)

The Vairamudi festival is purely a SriVaishnava (Iyengar) event. (See Chapter 4 to find out about this Hindu subsect.) It takes place once a year in March/April in the otherwise sleepy town of Melkote in Karnataka. More than 200,000 visitors flock to the town for this event.

Vairamudi refers to a jeweled crown studded with diamonds of extraordinary brilliance. (*Vaira* means "diamond," and *mudi* means "head gear" in Tamil.) Srivaishnavas believe that this crown has never been seen in daylight because of its brilliance. On Vairamudi day, this crown is placed on the head of the presiding deity Cheluva Narayana (adorable Lord Narayana, a form of Vishnu) at the Melkote temple, and a grand procession takes place at night.

All year, the crown is housed in a sealed box in the treasury at Mandya, the district headquarters. On the day of the festival, it is guarded by a contingent of security officers in a special car and driven 22 miles to Melkote. It arrives at sunset on the outskirts of town. It is ceremonially met by the high priests, all SriVaishnavas of the temple, along with principal personages of the town. Strict temple honors are presented to the sacred crown: *poornakumbham* (a silver vessel filled with water resting in a bed of uncooked rice), flowers, fruits, and garlands are part of what the priests and assistants carry on decorated silver plates to receive the crown amid sacred chants. This whole assemblage is considered to represent the goddess Mahalakshmi.

The heavily guarded procession moves from the village outskirts to the temple, and the unopened box is set in front of the sanctum of SriRamanujacharya, the founder of the Vaishnava sect, for four hours until nightfall. No one — not even the chief priest — is allowed to see the vairamudi until Lord Cheluva Narayana is crowned. (The designated priest is believed to perform the crowning all alone with his eyes covered by a silk cloth.)

After some important preliminary ceremonies, the procession then winds through the streets of Melkote and is watched by thousands who pack every nook and corner of the town. This celebration goes on until the early morning hours when the Lord returns to the temple. The great day comes to an end, and Melkote prepares to anticipate another grand procession the following day with the Rajamudi, which I explain next.

Rajamudi: Celebrating the king's crown

Rajamudi literally means the "king's crown" and refers to a crown studded with precious jewels offered to the Lord Cheluva Narayana by Raja Wodeyar (1578–1617), ruler of the former state of Mysore. The Rajamudi procession takes place the day after Vairamudi, and the *darshan* (divine visit) of the Lord is enjoyed by devotees who throng to Melkote to take it all in on successive days. A devout Vaishnnavite, Raja Wodeyar is believed to have entered the *sanctum sanctorum* (the sacred room that houses the principal deity) on the last day of his life and never come out.

With the grand processions over and the festivals coming to an end, Melkote resumes its peaceful and quiet religious life until the next year. These grand events are a reminder of ancient glory, of a time when this region of India supplied gold, diamonds, and other precious gems to the Roman Empire 2,000 years before the mines in South Africa and Australia were in operation.

In Tamilnadu: The Kavadi Festival

This festival is observed every January in the southern Indian state of Tamilnadu, in the vicinity of Murugan temples. *Kavadi* is a light wooden structure; for example, a pair of woven baskets tied to the two ends of a pole and carried on the shoulders of a devotee. Kavadi devotees carry such contraptions and appear entranced and not themselves as they pierce their bodies with silver needles from cheek to cheek, or get hooks put on their backs that are attached to chariots that they then pull (see Figure 16-4). No blood appears visible to the naked eye, and these devotees do not even wince as they carry out vows made during the preceding year in return for a prayer answered or a favor granted by the presiding deity, Shiva's son Murugan.

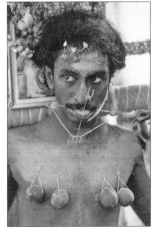

Figure 16-4:
A Kavadi
devotee.

© Alain Evrard/Getty Images

In what is called *Agni Kavadi,* the devotee walks barefoot on a bed of hot coals to the repeated shouts of encouragement from the onlookers, intense music, and shouts of high praise to the Lord. The devotee emerges unscathed! It may be called a state of ecstasy with no visible connection to the world around.

Kavadi is one of the archaic remnants that persist in Hindu practice: a trial of the body in order to gain grace or fulfill a vow. Those of the particular faith in which such practices are prevalent do, without doubt, understand and respect this approach. The general feeling is that the pain experienced by the body is nothing compared to the grace of the Lord they seek. For example, if the life of a loved one has been spared because of a vow to carry a kavadi, then the bodily pain experienced when fulfilling that vow is worth it. It is an act of supreme devotion to Lord Murugan and a display of intense love for the Lord. Some people may wonder at these practices, but you can find parallels in some other religions in which the faithful don't hesitate to hurt themselves in their quest. They are undertaking a form of worship.

Kerala: The Onam Festival

The South India state of Kerala celebrates Onam: a state festival celebrated on a grand scale over ten days in September. The main focus is welcoming the beloved King Mahabali, whose reign in legendary days was much admired by the ancients of Kerala. In Chapter 8, I tell the story of King Bali, who grew overly ambitious and wished to displace the chief of gods, Indra, as king of heaven. Vishnu, disguised as a brahmin dwarf, visited Bali and received three boons from the welcoming king. Vishnu asked Bali to grant him the space that would occupy no more than three of his paces. Vishnu took one step to cover the entire earth, another to cover the entire sky, and with the third he stepped on Bali's head and banished the king to the underworld. Bali was granted a visit to his beloved kingdom and his people every year, and Onam is that time. Vishnu is also worshipped at this time.

With so many flowers in bloom, the festival begins with elaborate flower decorations in front of each dwelling, which signal a welcome mat for the ancient king. Cleaning homes, taking early baths, and visiting a favorite temple in the vicinity are all part of the festivities.

The ten days provide an opportunity for different cities and towns in Kerala to enjoy elaborate processions of elephants, boat races, archery contests, prize fighting, Kathakali dance drama performances (a famous type of theater special to this region) under the auspices of the Kerala Kala Mandalam (Kerala Arts Circle), and elegant clap dances performed by beautifully dressed young women, all capped by great feasts. The main feast is called *Onasadhya,* in which 13 dishes, all vegetarian, are prepared and served on banana leaves and enjoyed by folks sitting on mats and chatting as they share each other's company for a sumptuous meal.

Eastern Region: The Jagannath Rath Yatra Festival

Puri, an ancient pilgrimage center, sits right on the Bay of Bengal, and the great Jagannath temple is near the beach. This twelfth-century temple celebrates the Puri chariot festival (the Jagannath Rath Yatra Festival) each year, attracting a large number of pilgrims from within India and abroad.

The festival takes place in July when the three temple deities — the principal deity Jagannath, his brother Balabhadra, and their sister Subhadra — travel on three chariots (see Figure 16-5) from the city of Puri "on vacation" to a location known as Gundicha barely 3 miles away in the countryside. This festival of chariots of three deities is about ten centuries old. Each year the Puri chariot festival attracts more than a million spectators from different parts of India and abroad.

Figure 16-5: Chariots in procession at Puri.

© STRDEL/Getty Images

Over the centuries, certain families have always built the chariots, and they retain that right to this day. Constructing the wooden chariots and the horses "pulling" the chariots takes about three months, and the builders follow age-old specifications: The largest chariot (Jagannath) must have 16 wheels, the mid-size chariot (Balabhadra) must have 14, and Subhadra's chariot must have 12. The footprints of these great chariots are respectively 35, 33, and 32 square feet. So that the millions who throng to have a look can recognize them individually from afar, the fabrics for each chariot must use a specific color combination. The principal deity Lord Jagannath's chariot is yellow and red, his brother Balabhadra's is red and blue, and the colors on Subhadra's chariot are red and black.

From Jagannath to juggernaut

You undoubtedly have heard of the word *juggernaut*. The word is derived from the name of the principal deity in the very famous temple at Puri. The name of the presiding deity is Jagannath, meaning Lord of the Universe. It is rumored that stories of the horror of occasional serious accidents (when someone got caught under the huge wheels of the chariots and was badly hurt or crushed to death, for example) were reported in the British press as human sacrifices made to a terrible deity called Juggernaut.

Chapter 17

Cradle to Cremation: The Life-Cycle Rites

"*W*hen are you going to have this child's hair cut?"

Pointing at me, my grandmother posed this question to my father "for the thousandth time" when I was nearing seven. She was referring to a ritual called *Chudakarma* (known as *Mundan* in Hindi) marking a child's first haircut, which typically takes place between the ages of 1 and 3. (The delay in my case was due to a vow that this very grandmother had taken, that the first haircut of her first grandson would take place only at the temple of the family deity Lord Venkateshwara at Tirupati. The delay? Tirupati was about 200 miles away from my village and, back in those days, not easy to get to.)

This haircut was a serious matter because it constituted just one of the traditional 16 sacraments *(samskaras)*, or rites of passage, prescribed for Hindus. These rites occur throughout a Hindu's life, beginning with conception and ending with cremation. Although each rite pertains to a specific time and life event, they all seek to purify and strengthen the body and mind of the candidate of the rite.

In this chapter, I present the series of prescribed rituals and celebrations observed by ancient Hindus and comment on those that are still in vogue.

A Quick Look at the 16 Ceremonies

The rites for the 16 ceremonies are prescribed by the *Grihya Sutras* (manuals of domestic rites). These texts provide a set of rituals and associated mantras with specific instructions for the family to follow. Table 17-1 lists the generally accepted traditional 16 ceremonies and provides a bit of information about them. Notice that many are seldom practiced today.

Table 17-1		Sixteen Ancient Hindu Rites of Passage	
	Sanskrit Name: Intent	**When Performed**	**Notes**
1	Garbhadana: Promoting conception	Soon after wedding	Prayers for progeny, advice from elders; generally not practiced anymore
2	Pumsavana: Obtaining a vigorous male child	Between second and fourth month of pregnancy	Ceremony may be combined with the Garbhadana
3	Simanthonnayana: Smooth delivery of the baby	Usually the seventh month of pregnancy	The hair-parting ceremony
4	Jatakarma: Cutting the umbilical cord	Immediately after birth	Generally not practiced anymore as a ceremony
5	Namakarana: Naming the baby	Eleven or 12 days after birth	May be limited to immediate family
6	Nishkramana: Baby introduced to close families	Between the twelfth day and the fourth month after birth	A social event now
7	Annaprashana: First feeding of solid food	Six months after birth	Guided by family traditions
8	Chudakarma: First haircut	Between age 1 and 3	Mostly for boys in some families; for both genders in others
9	Karnavedha: Piercing the ears	Between the seventh and tenth month after birth	Mostly for girls in some families; for both genders in others
10	Vidyarambha: Beginning education, first lesson	At age 5	Teaching the alphabet, kindergarten
11	Upanayanam: Initiation into Vedic studies	Age 8, 11, or 12	Thread ceremony celebrated

	Sanskrit Name: Intent	When Performed	Notes
12	Vedarambha: Beginning Vedic studies	Soon after or within the year after Upanayanam	Mostly observed by renunciates who learn under a guru
13	Samavartana: Returning home	After Vedic studies (used to be at the age of 18 years)	No longer an established practice
14	Vivaha/Shadi: Wedding	Formerly after returning home from Vedic studies but now entirely dependent on individual and/or family	Guided by individual family preferences
15	Vanaprastha: Retirement	Used to be after grandchildren grew up, but now up to the individual	Formerly involved forest dwelling; today individual choice
16	Anthyeshti: Rites upon death	The day of or day after death	Funeral rites practiced almost without exception

Observing Prenatal Rituals

From the moment a family learns that a young wife is pregnant, the news and excitement spread quickly. Women begin to plan the nine-month-long celebration. Dates are set and priests are summoned to perform a set of prenatal ceremonies. Parents and grandparents of the pregnant lady offer prayers to their family godheads, not only for a smooth delivery but also for a male progeny, a wish driven by certain socioeconomic and religious reasons, as well as to ensure that the family name will be preserved for yet another generation.

The prenatal samskaras include the following:

- The conception ceremony (Garbhadana)
- Prayers for a male progeny (Pumsavana)
- The ceremony to protect the fetus in the womb (Simanthonnayana)

The performance of these events varies, depending on the traditions of the family, from purely religious observance to completely social gatherings and parties. Often the extended family and circle of close friends are also included in the festivities. Special prayers and visits to temples are not uncommon. Some families skip the first two samskaras entirely, begin with the third, and then focus on ceremonies past the prenatal ones, which you can read about in the later sections of this chapter.

Conception: The Garbhadana

The intent of the Garbhadana ceremony is to caution the couple to maintain a balance in their views about faith and life so that physically and mentally they are prepared to bring another life into this world to carry on their name. This ceremony emphasizes love, good habits, a clean and healthy body, and strong values, to provide a firm foundation for a baby.

Although many families skip this ceremony entirely, orthodox families may seek the assistance of a priest to perform a homa during the first month of pregnancy. The *homa* is a fire ceremony with offerings of grain, incense, ghee, and so on, in praise of Vedic gods Indra, Soma, and Agni, and in praise of nature (the wind, earth, air, water, and so forth). The priest also blesses the couple as they embark on the journey to bring on another life.

Praying for a male child: The Pumsavana

Between the second and fourth month of pregnancy, the Pumasavana is performed. The specific purpose of this ceremony is to pray for a male child. Ancient Hindus observed this ceremony by preparing concoctions made from several herbs to feed the mother-to-be in order to sustain her health. Modern families usually skip this ceremony entirely or add it to the third ritual.

Hoping for a smooth delivery: The Simanthonnayana

Occurring during the later part of a pregnancy (usually the seventh month) — and only during the first pregnancy — Simanthonnayana (or Simantham) involves purification and protective rites aimed at assuring the safe birth of a baby while cheering and congratulating the mother-to-be. (**Note:** In Gujarat and some parts of northern India, this ceremony is known as Shrimant, Khodo Bharavo, or Godh Bharai.) Historically, the earlier stages of this ceremony have been organized and performed by female relatives and friends of the family. These earlier stages included putting bangles on the mother-to-be's hands and tying flowers in her hair.

In the Simanthonnayana ceremony, which takes place on a full moon day, a tiny bundle is assembled. It consists of a porcupine quill (symbolizing the desire for sharp intellect for the baby), a small bunch of unripe fig fruits (the large number of seeds in the fruit symbolizing fertility), and three darbha grass leaves (symbolizing humility). Everything is tied together with a turmeric-tinted triple-twisted thread.

The husband uses the quill to part the wife's hair, stroking the part gently from the front to the back of the head three times. As the husband strokes her hair, he chants three mantras, which translate roughly to these:

- ✔ Stroke 1: Parting the hair of my wife, I pray that our progeny live to old age.
- ✔ Stroke 2: I praise the mother-to-be as beautiful as a full moon night.
- ✔ Stroke 3: I pray for the impending birth to be smooth and as free of pain as the movement of a needle through a cloth being sewn.

This display of affection constitutes the core ceremony and serves as a public acknowledgement to relatives and friends of the husband's paternal relationship with the unborn child.

Prayers are offered to household gods, such as Dhatri (lord of the world), Raaka (presiding deity of the full moon), Sinivali (presiding deity of the new moon), and Prajapati (lord of progeny). The husband offers prayers for health, wellbeing, courage, wealth, prosperity, and longevity on behalf of his wife. The husband garlands his wife and applies *sindhur* (red powder like kumkum) on the parting of the hair.

The ceremony concludes with felicitations. Ladies from both families come forward to perform a ritual combing of her hair, adorning it with flowers. They apply kumkum on the mother-to-be's forehead, put bangles on her wrists, and fill her lap with symbols of prosperity (uncooked rice, fruits, sticks of turmeric, betel leaves, betel nuts, dry coconut cut into halves, brown sugar, a few coins, and other gifts according to custom). They then perform an *arati:* a concluding ritual that uses a plate with a flame that is waved clockwise three or more times in front of the worshipped; see Chapter 14.

The mother-to-be and her relatives reward the ladies in turn with bangles and flowers. This colorful and enjoyable domestic ceremony is concluded with a series of blessings to the couple by the priest and the assembled elders.

Observing Childhood Rituals

After enjoying the prenatal ceremonies, the parents-to-be and their families eagerly await the birth of the baby. After the baby is born, a multitude of ceremonies follow. These include rituals for naming the baby, taking the baby out of the home for the very first time, the first feeding with solid food, the first haircut, and piercing the ears.

Cutting the umbilical cord: Jatakarma

Upon delivery, an extraordinary ceremony known as Jatakarma used to be performed by the ancients just before the umbilical cord was cut. Although no longer performed today, the Jatakarma ceremony was of extreme significance to the ancients. It included prayers for the following:

✔ **Intellect for the new baby:** The father chanted the Gayatri mantra (see Chapter 14) and, using his ring finger, "fed" the baby with a drop or two of *ghee* (clarified butter) and honey.

✔ **Long life for the newborn:** The father, while "feeding," whispered into the baby's right ear that her life would be long much like the fire fed by fuel, the oceans fed by rivers, and so on.

✔ **Strength:** Blessings were chanted for the baby to live a strong and healthy life of a hundred years.

Immediately after these steps, the cord was severed and the baby brought to the mother for her to begin breastfeeding.

Why did this ritual come to an end? Because the umbilical cord is now cut by a midwife or a doctor even in remote areas. It simply ceased to be a ritual.

Naming ceremony: Namakarana

The next important ceremonial event is Namakarana, giving the baby a name. In the old days, this ceremony took place 11 or 12 days after birth. In modern days, however, it happens much earlier because the parents have probably already chosen a name, especially when they know the baby's gender even before it is born. Plus, modern-day requirements include registering the birth at the hospital. For these reasons, the name is given shortly after birth, and the ceremony itself may come within a couple weeks, on a day and at a time recommended by a priest. The baby's name is written on a bed of rice, and the father whispers the name into the baby's right ear. The assembled elders bestow blessings upon the baby as well as the parents, and the ceremony is complete.

The first outing: Nishkramana

Between the twelfth day and the fourth month, the baby is taken on its first outing. The object of this ceremony is to "introduce" the baby to the outside world. For the first time, the baby is taken out of the home to meet with close relatives and to see the sun, the moon, the stars, and so on. The goal is to make the baby aware of the world outside its immediate environment.

Drawing up the horoscope

Devout Hindus pay a lot of attention to the precise time of birth because they believe that the life of the newborn is influenced by the exact position of the planets (see Chapter 15) at the time of birth and their subsequent movement.

An elder, knowledgeable in astronomy or astrology, may be invited to draw up a horoscope for the baby on which the birth date, time, birth star, constellation, and so on are marked. Many families use this information when their child is ready to get married, comparing the horoscopes of the potential couple for compatibility and suitability.

The first solid food: Annaprashana

About six months after birth, it's time to add solid food to the infant's diet. This event provides another opportunity to invite elders in the family for a ceremony. During the Annaprashana, it's customary to prepare festive food to offer to the family deity and elders and then to feed a small quantity of cooked rice to the baby.

The first haircut: Chudakarma

This ceremony generally occurs when the child is between the ages of 1 and 3 years old, but traditions vary from family to family and region to region.The process includes wetting the head; offering a prayer to the razor (praising it and asking that it not injure the child — remember, Hindus worship everything!); inviting the barber to begin; chanting Vedic verses while cutting the hair; and expressing wishes for a long life, prosperity, valor, and even progeny for the child. A series of offerings is made to Agni (god of fire) in an elaborate fire ceremony.

Piercing the ears: Karnavedha

The day when a child's ears are pierced is considered special and worthy of celebration. Therefore, the ear piercing ceremony is a tradition that has remained in most families, even though the Grihya Sutras don't include it. The purpose of the ceremony is considered to be ornamental, although some references claim that certain diseases or conditions, such as hernia, can be avoided through ear piercing. Both boys' and girls' ears may be pierced, but this tradition varies from family to family and region to region.

Getting Ready for Adulthood

The rituals described in this section were all practiced by ancient Hindus. Most modern Hindus skip the Vidyarambha and Vedarambha (which makes the Samavartana ceremony irrelevant). However, they prefer to perform the Upanayanam ceremony for boys.

Initiating a child into learning: Vidyarambha

Traditionally, formal education at the primary level began when a child was 5 years old. In a typical Hindu household in ancient days, Sanskrit was the spoken language. The child would have listened to Sanskrit mantras chanted at home and elsewhere. To initiate the child into learning how to read and write, a teacher was brought in, and an auspicious day was selected when the sun was in the northern hemisphere (past mid-January). The child, bathed and groomed, sat in front of the teacher, who faced east. The teacher used a golden pen to write the alphabet letters on a silver plank and had the student read them. Afterward, salutations to godheads such as Saraswati (goddess of learning), Lakshmi (goddess of well-being), and Narayana (a form of Vishnu) were written, and the student read these. Then education continued under the watchful eye of a teacher until the child was ready to begin the study of the Vedas.

Families that could not afford a silver plank and a gold pen used raw rice spread on a wooden plank for this purpose, and the words were "written" using the index finger. None of this is relevant today because a child at that age is perhaps texting on a cell phone already!

The thread ceremony: Upanayanam

This ceremony, which takes place at age 8, 11, or 12, is part of a child's preparation to enter adulthood. Even today, this sacred step is considered essential, especially among *brahmin* parents (those from the priestly or intellectual class; see Chapter 5).

Ancient Hindus prescribed this step as a passport for boys to the study of sacred texts under guidance. (Girls did not — and still do not — go through the thread ceremony.) Study of the Vedas was considered a serious and essential step toward adulthood, and this ceremony confirmed the student's commitment to education and the quest for Truth.

Upanayanam means "to lead or bring one closer to the truth," and this ceremony allows the young person to wear a sacred thread, known as *yagnopavitam,* for the first time and forever after. This investiture of the sacred thread is the equivalent of a license that allows the individual to officiate at ceremonies after appropriate training. The sacred thread itself is an assembly of three strings tied together at a knot called *brahmamudi* ("knot of Brahma"). Each string represents a quality *(guna)* — satva (pure), rajas (active), and tamas (inert) — that constitutes one's life on this earth.

At this stage of life, the young person connects with the community and obtains a broader outlook on life. In ancient times, when a pupil went to live with a guru (teacher), as was the custom, his daily food was obtained through alms. In this way, the community's support was essential and helped cement the relationship among the guru, fellow students, and the local populace. Also, the student derived a debt to society that needed to be discharged later by serving the community.

The Upanayanam ceremony inducts the candidate into what is known as *Brahmacharya,* a state of celibacy over the period when the young person commits to a life of learning the Vedas under a guru. The ceremony involves these steps:

1. A boy has his head shaved; puts on a loin cloth and grass *(darbha)* girdle; and picks up a staff, a *kamandalu* (vessel to drink water from), and a loose upper garment. All these items are symbols of purity, discipline, humility, and life on the road.

2. The initiate is instructed to stretch the string tight with the knot of Brahma at the top, right palm up, and the lower part held with the left palm facing down. He is then asked to repeat a mantra that translates as follows:

   This, the most sacred thread, is sanctioned by Prajapati (Lord of Progeny) himself and is considered sacrosanct. This, the symbol of purity, shall enhance my longevity and bring strength and vigor.

   Immediately after chanting the mantra, the young man is instructed first to wear the thread as a garland and then to insert his right arm through the loop such that the string rests on the left shoulder draping across the upper body from left to right.

3. The climax of the ceremony occurs when the guru, the student, and the student's father huddle secretively behind a curtain as the father whispers into the right ear of the initiate the Gayatri Mantra. Here, I provide the translation of this sacred mantra:

   Om. That which pervades earth, sky and heaven, which is worthy of worship, that has no beginning; that which is the light of wisdom and truth; Let us meditate on the radiance of that divinity. May that brilliance help inspire and illuminate our minds. That One which represents water, light and is the quintessence in all things; May that almighty spirit pervading the earth, atmosphere, and heaven bless us with enlightenment.

The avowed purpose of this secrecy is to prevent unfit people from hearing the mantra. The teaching of the sacred Gayatri Mantra is called *Brahmopadesham* (Brahma's counsel). After learning the mantra, the student is accepted as "twice-born."

4. The student shares a last meal with his mother before leaving home. During this meal, the young man actually begs for food for the first time from his own mother by bending his head down and asking *bhavati bhikshaam dehi* ("kindly give me alms"). The pupil sits together with his mother and eats that meal.

The Upanayanam ceremony is similar to initiation ceremonies such as confirmation and bar and bat mitzvahs. In ancient times, the prescribed age for this rite was the eighth year for brahmin boys, eleventh year for kshatriyas (members of the warrior caste), and twelfth year for vaishyas (members of the trading or commerce class). Nowadays the ceremony is performed mainly for brahmin boys as early as age 12 and anytime up to right before the wedding ceremony. See Chapter 5 for a discussion of the caste system.

Going away to study the Vedas: Vedarambha

For ancient Hindus, the studies began in earnest at this point. The goal was to learn the four Vedas (refer to Chapter 10), but the studies included these categories as well:

- **Vedangas:** Branches of the Vedas — one of them, for example, being Sanskrit grammar

- **Upangas:** Subbranches, which require study of the more complicated texts called *Darshanas* (see Chapter 19)

- **UpaVedas:** Subsidiary Vedic texts that teach subjects such as *Ayurveda* (health science)

- **Brahmanas:** A section of the Vedic literature that expounds the mantras from the Vedas (see Chapter 10)

The ceremony could take place either on the day of the Upanayanam ceremony or shortly after, but certainly within the year of the Upanayanam. It began with instructions from the father that advised the student to follow strict guidelines during the course of studies, such as daily salutations to the guru; celibacy; cleanliness and hygiene; daily prayers and fire rituals; strict adherence to dharma; obedience to the guru as long as his instructions did not violate dharma; control of anger; moderation in eating, sleeping, and speech; no intoxicating liquids or foods; and the practice of yoga and meditation.

Upon the child's acceptance, the events were set in motion and the student was off to the guru's residence.

Completing education: Samavartana

With the permission and blessings of the guru, after a brief ceremony of taking leave at the guru's residence, the young man returned home, fully educated and ready to take on the responsibilities of a householder.

Becoming a Householder with the Marriage Ritual: Vivaha/Shadi

With very few exceptions, most Hindus enter marriage (*Vivaha* in Sanskrit or *Shadi* in Hindi) at a "suitable age" seeking an alliance with a "good family." The Hindu wedding ceremony is based on Vedic traditions and rituals that originate in the Rig Veda, the earliest of the four ancient Sanskrit books of knowledge that form the basis of Hinduism (refer to Chapter 10). All the rituals that comprise the wedding ceremony, directly or indirectly, charge the couple to strive for what are known as four aspects: *dharma*, *artha* (worldly knowledge), *kama* (love), and *moksha* (liberation). The rituals, which date back at least 5,000 years, form a significant dramatic sequence and used to take five days. Modern families have condensed them to a single day.

Following is a typical program, which covers the essential steps and satisfies the time-honored Vedic tradition. Note that during the ceremony, all mantras and dialogues are spoken in Sanskrit.

1. **Receiving the groom and his family: Baraat/Swagatham**

    The groom and his family arrive with great fanfare and are received by the bride's family at a designated entrance and escorted to the *mantap* (wedding canopy) or stage.

2. **Invocation: Veda Mantras**

    The ceremony may begin with a recitation of Vedic chants. The recitation is followed by purification of the site using mantras that invoke the sacred rivers marking the venue as a sacred space.

3. **Honoring the groom: Vara Puja**

    The bride's father (or a designate) declares his intention to welcome and honor the groom and his family. A short dialogue follows with the groom agreeing to proceed.

4. Garlanding: Jayamala

The bride is escorted to the sacred space by her maternal uncle(s) and friends. She indicates her choice by garlanding the groom. He in turn garlands her to show his consent.

5. Declaring the lineages: Pravara/Hasta Milap

The ancestral lineages of the two families are announced. The bride's father unites the couple by joining their right hands.

6. Declaring the space and time: Sankalpam

The bride's father declares his intention to give the bride away and specifies the time and space of the event.

7. Giving the bride away: Kanyadanam

The bride's mother pours water over a coconut held by the bride, groom, and bride's father. (The coconut sits on the palms of the bride's father. His palms rest on the palms of the bride, which in turn rest on those of the groom.) This step consecrates their union and symbolically passes the daughter to the love and care of her new family.

8. Tying the wedding necklace: Mangala Sutra

The groom ties an auspicious necklace blessed by both families around the bride's neck. This necklace is the principal seal or bond between the bridegroom and the bride.

Note: In most South Indian traditions, this ceremony is considered the climax in the series of steps. After this step, the couple is considered to be husband and wife.

9. Fire Rituals – I: Agni Homa

A sacred fire *(Agni)* is lit to receive offerings and to stand witness to the couple's vows. Holding hands, the couple pledge their love to each other. Into the fire, offerings of grain, herbs, clarified butter, incense, and sandalwood are made to symbolize the sacrifice of all the couple's worldly possessions to God's grace.

10. Fire Rituals – II: Mangal Phera/Laaja Homa

The couple offer parched rice into the fire as a symbol of the first hearth of their new home together. With garments "knotted" (meaning the ends of their garments are connected), the couple circle the fire four times, pledging to lead lives guided by *dharma* (moral law), *artha* (worldly knowledge), and *kama* (love), leading to *moksha* (liberation).

11. Seven steps: Saptapadi

The bride and groom take seven steps around the fire, while they recite the customary vows and pledge their eternal friendship to each other. Indian Civil Law recognizes marital status as lawful only upon completion of the seventh step around the fire altar.

12. Seven blessings: Ashirvadam

Seven blessings by the officiant and the assembled conclude the ceremony. The couple seek the blessings of all elders, family, and friends as they embark on their new life together.

For more information on Hindu weddings, visit my website `www.indianweddings.us.com`.

The implication in each step of the wedding ceremony is that the couple adhere to a dharmic life. In fact, immediately after the groom ties the *mangala sutra* (the auspicious necklace), the father of the bride charges the groom that he shall not cross the boundaries of good conduct in leading the life of a householder. Only after the groom responds saying that he shall not do so, the bride moves to the groom's left, indicating that they are now husband and wife. Similarly, the priest charges the bride to lead a virtuous life.

Getting Ready for Retirement: Vanaprastha

Ancient Hindus understood that there is an end to life and that even the most important relationships one develops throughout life — relationships to spouses, children, and friends, all of which may be extraordinary and loving — are temporary. The ancients didn't frown upon enjoyment in this life, but realism dictated that they begin the process of detachment when grandchildren arrived and grew up. No particular age was stipulated, but older people were encouraged to withdraw from worldly attachments. This stage was defined as *Vanaprastha*.

The prescription was to retire to a forest *(vana)* hermitage. Saying goodbye to the family included the wife, whose care was entrusted to the grownup children, unless she also wanted to go along. The rule was to live among other seekers — of solace, knowledge, peace, and freedom. Service to others — to needy people, animals, and nature — became the key in this concept. What was once a give-and-take became about only giving.

But those were the ancients! Today, the grandparents in New Delhi may move to New Jersey and spend the rest of their lives with their son or daughter and grandchildren. What was once the call from a forest may now be a park-like setting in a nursing home. The whole concept is essentially (but not absolutely) a thing of the past.

Upon Death: Anthyeshti

The Anthyeshti rites are performed on the day of or the day after a Hindu's death. In this section, I explain some of the fundamental Hindu beliefs about death.

In the Yaksha Prashna episode of the epic *Mahabharata* (refer to Chapter 12), the Yaksha asks Prince Yudhishtira this question: "What is most amazing?" The prince replies, "Every day creatures die and yet everyone thinks he lives forever. What can be more amazing?"

The death of the body, but not the soul

When Hindus speak of death, they refer only to our bodies. To the Hindu, there is no death of the soul. Only the body dies; the soul never dies. According to the Bhagavad Gita (see Chapter 13), the soul is spirit that a sword cannot pierce, the fire cannot burn, the water cannot melt, and the air cannot dry. The soul, it says, is free, unbounded, holy, pure, and perfect. The Hindu's goal is to avoid rebirths so that the individual soul merges with the Supreme Soul. The merger is what Hindus call *moksha:* liberation.

Cremation rather than burial

Most Hindus choose to dispose of the body, after its death, through cremation — usually within a day. The ashes are collected, and on the fourth day they are disposed of in a nearby stream, one of the sacred rivers, or a sacred body of water. Jawaharlal Nehru (1889–1964), the first prime minister of India, left instructions that his ashes be strewn symbolically across the whole of India by spreading them from an airplane.

Many families celebrate the departed life on the twelfth day with a feast to mark the day when the soul achieves release.

Chapter 18

Taking a Pilgrimage

. . . .

In This Chapter

▶ Understanding the Hindu urge to go on pilgrimage

▶ Identifying the major pilgrimage destinations on the Indian subcontinent

▶ Sorting out the legends and beliefs behind Hindu pilgrimage sites

. . . .

A few decades ago, if you had asked a Hindu about vacation plans, the reaction may have been something like "Vacation? What's that?" The concept of taking time off to travel just for the fun of it was alien. And holidays were understood to mean *holy* days, which Hindus observed as such. When Hindus did travel any distance, they referred to their journeys by the popular word *yatra,* which means "pilgrimage." A *Teertha Yatra* is a sacred journey.

Such a yatra, for example, could be to the famous Venkateshwara temple at Tirupati (see Chapter 7) or to Melkote to participate in the annual procession of the Lord Cheluva Narayana adorned with a diamond crown (see Chapter 16). These are just two of the thousands of pilgrimage places or events open to Hindus. Some pilgrimage centers are regional and attract mostly locals. Some are well-known to the Hindu world in general and attract pilgrims from around the world.

In this chapter, I provide you with the basic information on Hindu pilgrimages, including why (to worship at sacred sites), how (by foot, bus, and other means of transportation), where (a short list of the more common destinations), and when (on dates dictated by celestial events, festivals, and so on). I also take you on a pilgrimage to major centers.

An Overview of the Pilgrimage Experience

When undertaking a pilgrimage, Hindus translate their religious fervor and beliefs into action as they plan, prepare, and embark on journeys to their favorite destinations. There is a great deal of variety in how these pilgrimages are undertaken. A pilgrimage can be as simple as a single family going to a major shrine or as awe-inspiring as hundreds of thousands of pilgrims from multiple places of origin converging at a single location. Along the way they sing, dance, and chant high praises to the deity they will visit and worship a few days or weeks later. In the following sections, I provide an overview of what makes a good destination for a pilgrimage, why and when Hindus take pilgrimages, and what kind of transportation pilgrims use.

Websites, airplanes, luxury coaches, call centers, national highways, special trains, local buses, and improved education and economy have combined to meet the challenges of a growing multitude of people engaged in pilgrimages. Modern life has not reduced Hindu interest in sacred places. Instead, more education and more money have meant better, faster, and more frequent opportunities to visit them. This increased interest strains the infrastructure, but state and federal governments have responded to meet the challenge. Pilgrimages are not a thing of the past for Hindus. Many, if not most, vacations are still spent that way.

Discovering pilgrimage destinations

Christians and Jews have the Holy Land, Buddhists have Bodh Gaya, and Muslims have Mecca. But what about Hindus? What is their one pilgrimage center? There isn't one — there are hundreds! The exact number is hard to pin down because Hindu pilgrimage destinations include temples, rivers, mountains, waterfalls, and a host of major and minor locations that may have legends associated with them.

The idea of connecting with the land and the nation is built into Hindu pilgrimages from early times. In Chapter 9, I introduce the famous eighth-century saint Shankaracharya who was the founder of the Advaita Vedanta philosophy that I discuss in Chapter 20. Shankaracharya traveled to the four corners of India to rejuvenate Hinduism, and he founded four Vedanta centers *(Char Dham)*: Rameshwaram in the south , Dwaraka in the west, Badrinath in the north, and Puri on the east coast. Together, they essentially define the geographic shape of India and are major pilgrim destinations to this day.

See Figure 18-1 for a map of India that pinpoints cities that are famous pilgrimage centers. Table 18-1 names the cities, the states where they are located, and the focal point of interest, along with the prime date or event that attracts Hindu pilgrims.

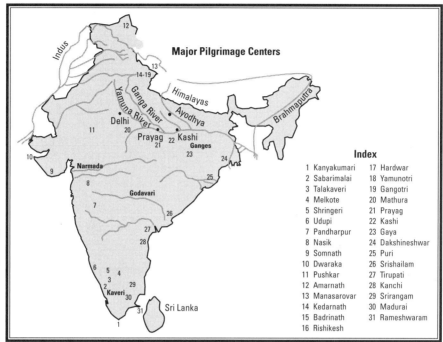

Figure 18-1: A map of India showing major pilgrimage destinations.

Table 18-1	Major Hindu Pilgrimage Centers		
Destination	**Location**	**Focus/Feature**	**Preferred Dates**
1. Kanyakumari	Tamilnadu	Kanya Devi/Vivekananda rock; Tiruvalluvar statue	Year-round
2. Sabarimalai	Kerala	Ayyappan hilltop temple; apparition of divine lights	Winter solstice
3. Talakaveri	Karnataka	Kaveri River; the river surges into a pool at an auspicious moment	Sun enters Tula (Libra), mid-October
4. Melkote	Karnataka	Vairamudi/Diamond Crown Procession	Mid-January
5. Shringeri	Karnataka	One of four Shankaracharya Centers	Year-round
6. Udupi	Karnataka	Lord Krishna temple	Year-round

(continued)

Table 18-1 *(continued)*

Destination	Location	Focus/Feature	Preferred Dates
7. Pandharpur	Maharashtra	Vithoba shrine; Warkari walking pilgrimage	Twice yearly in June and November
8. Nasik	Maharashtra	One of four sacred sites for Kumbha Mela; near source of Godavari	Mid-August every 12 years
9. Somnath	Gujarat	One of 12 Jyotirlingam sites; Somnath temple	Year-round
10. Dwaraka	Gujarat	One of 7 sacred cities for moksha; 170-foot-tall Krishna temple, one of the Char Dhams	August (Krishna's birthday)
11. Pushkar	Rajasthan	Site of Pushkar fair; temples around lake	Kartik Purnima (October–November full moon)
12. Amarnath	Kashmir	Ice linga in cave waxes and wanes with the moon	Shravana month (July–August)
13. Manasarovar	Tibet	Sacred lake in the vicinity of Mount Kailash (Abode of Shiva)	Year-round not including winter
14. Kedarnath	Uttaranchal	Shiva temple	March–October
15. Badrinath	Uttaranchal	Narayana (Vishnu) temple; one of four Char Dhams	March–October
16. Rishikesh	Uttaranchal	City of ashrams and yoga schools; Swami Shivananda ashram	March-October
17. Hardwar	Uttaranchal	Gateway to Himalayan temples; one of the four sites for Kumbha Mela	March–October
18. Yamunotri	Uttaranchal	Source of the Yamuna river	March–October
19. Gangotri	Uttaranchal	Source of the Ganges river	March–October

Destination	Location	Focus/Feature	Preferred Dates
20. Mathura	Haryana	Krishna's birthplace	Mid-August
21. Prayag	Uttar Pradesh	Confluence of Ganga, Yamuna, Saraswati; site of Kumbha Mela	Mid-January
22. Kashi/ Benares	Uttar Pradesh	Vishwanatha temple; one of the cities that grants moksha	Year-round
23. Gaya	Bihar	Center for memorial rites	Year-round
24. Dakshineshwar	West Bengal	Kali temple; Ramakrishna Paramahamsa Belur Math	Year-round
25. Puri	Orissa	Jagannath/chariot festival	July
26. Srishailam	Andhra Pradesh	One of 12 Jyotir lingams	Year-round
27. Tirupati	Andhra Pradesh	Lord Venkateshwara/ Balaji temple	Year-round
28. Kanchi	Tamilnadu	Shiva, Vishnu, and Devi temples	Year-round
29. Srirangam	Tamilnadu	Lord Sriranganatha (Vishnu) temple	Year-round
30. Madurai	Tamilnadu	Meenakshi Amman temple complex	Year-round
31. Rameshwaram	Tamilnadu	Shiva temple; Rama Sethu (bridge to Lanka)	Year-round

Table 18-1, although incomplete, does include the most sought-after destinations for Hindu pilgrims. It also covers the interests of all denominations, the easy and difficult treks, and generally covers the geography of India. It does not and cannot include all regions and centers.

Rivers and bodies of water

Worshipping nature is integral to Hindu theology. Water, in particular, is part of every Hindu ritual. When ancient Hindus saw wide rivers (like the Godavari) flowing gracefully or narrow streams (like the Alakananda) rushing along with great energy, they felt a sense of awe and reverence.

Ancient Hindus visualized seven major rivers as goddesses, and they named them Sindhu, Ganga, Saraswati, Yamuna, Godavari, Narmada, and Kaveri. Then they named their own daughters after them. These rivers spanned the length and breadth of India. The first four — Sindhu (Indus), Ganga (Ganges), Saraswati, and Yamuna — flowed in the north; Godavari and Narmada in the central part of India; and Kaveri in the south.

To the ancients, these rivers were not simply the source and sustenance of life; they were sacred and worthy of worship. Therefore, pilgrim destinations today include sources of sacred rivers and temples located on their banks. Wherever two or more rivers converge, the location acquires special significance and attracts millions of pilgrims.

In all sacred rites (refer to Chapters 14 and 15), the first step after the initial chants in praise of gods is to invoke the seven most sacred rivers and pray that they manifest themselves in the water to be used throughout the ceremony.

Mountains

The Hindu belief that godheads dwell on mountaintops makes mountains destinations for pilgrims. Mountains become sacred not only because they house gods but also because they have offered shelter to great saints as they engaged in deep meditation. Further, certain rivers (such as the Ganga and Yamuna) are "born" at mountains and descend to the plains below.

Mountains considered sacred in India include the Himalayas in the north; the Vindhya mountains, which are 700 miles long and divide the northern plains from the Deccan Plateau; Mahendra in the northeast; the Malaya mountain range in the southwest; Sahyadri and Raivataka in the west; and the Aravali mountain range in the northwest.

Locations associated with events from the sacred texts

"See that lake?" a Hindu may ask, pointing to a sparkling body of water. "It was near that very lake that Rama rested with his wife Sita and brother Lakshmana."

"See that huge tree? That is where the Pandavas hid their powerful weapons while in exile."

"Can't you see that line of rocks in the sea? That is the bridge the monkeys built for Rama to cross over to Lanka so that he could rescue his wife from the demon king Ravana."

"Kashi, city of Benares, is where Shiva is believed to have gone through severe austerities!"

Legend after legend after Hindu legend includes locations that have historical and religious significance. Any of these locations can inspire a pilgrimage.

When I discuss the story about the churning of the milky ocean (refer to Chapter 8), I refer to four places in northern India where a few drops of the nectar of immortality are believed to have fallen. (Another version of the legend says that the nectar rescued from the churning effort was hidden in these places.) These four locations (Char Dhams) have become pilgrimage centers attracting millions of Hindus every three years. The four locations are Prayag, Hardwar, Ujjain, and Nasik. The festival itself is called Kumbha Mela.

The world's biggest religious meet

Imagine the sight of 70 million Hindus all celebrating in one place at one time. Millions of ordinary Hindus and hundreds of thousands of religious personages are among the crowd, including renunciates called *sadhus, swamis, fakirs, sanyasins,* and *mendicants*. Everyone is dipping in the water at the confluence of three sacred rivers: the Ganga, Yamuna, and Saraswati, at Prayag in the province of Uttar Pradesh. Imagine the sounds of conches, drums, pipes, cymbals, shouts of praise, and Vedic chants from millions.

While a gathering this massive may be hard to imagine, it actually happened. In its broadcast on April 28, 2010, the British Broadcasting Corporation described the Kumbha Mela celebration at Prayag as the world's biggest religious meet.

Choosing a mode of transportation

In the past, many Hindus embarked on pilgrimages via *bullock carts* (ox-driven carts) or dangerously crowded buses. These days, you're just as likely to see pilgrims arrive at sacred spots in comfortable luxury coaches, private chauffeur-driven cars, and airplanes. Still, for a large number of folks, walking (as a group) continues to be a popular means of going on a pilgrimage because it combines fellowship, visiting, and worshipping en route to reaching the final destination. In fact, this walk itself *is* the pilgrimage, after which the throng breaks up and each individual or small group gets in line to enter the shrine or destination site.

Considering reasons for a pilgrimage

Just as there are thousands of destinations for pilgrims to journey to, there are as many motives. Some Hindus go on a pilgrimage to fulfill a vow undertaken when a certain prayer was granted, and some go just to be part of a community of like-minded devotees to a particular tradition or godhead. Some undertake the pilgrimage as a spiritual quest. Others go fully expecting all their sins to be washed away as they bathe in a sacred river or circumambulate a legendary hillock. Gaining religious merit is the common objective.

All these motives are powerful, and at the heart of each are an intense belief that a beneficial outcome can result from a sacred journey and the compelling urge to make an intimate connection with a godhead hundreds or thousands of miles away from home.

Pilgrimages are undertaken by all the different groups in Hindu society, irrespective of the region, caste, denomination, and economic status.

Picking a good time for a pilgrimage

The timing of a pilgrimage is dictated by a number of things: celestial events (such as, for example, when the sun enters Capricorn), festivals (such as the diamond-studded crown procession at Melkote, or Krishna's birthday at Mathura), and the need to fulfill a vow at a time that's convenient to the family (such as those traveling to Kashi; see the upcoming section "Taking a trip to Kashi before death"). A time-honored tradition among older Hindus is to go on a yatra upon retirement in order to, among other things, gain religious merit. These days, young people may combine a vacation and a pilgrimage.

Pilgrimages are made easier these days with modern conveniences like better transportation, more comfortable accommodations, and competent medical facilities should the need arise. In fact, a large travel industry has sprung up to meet the specific needs of those going on a pilgrimage. These services plan the entire trip, and the travel packages include transportation, accommodations, admission tickets . . . everything right down to the food that will be served, based on the preferences of the group that signs up!

Genuine pilgrims

Yuriko Ikenoya is a Japanese lady who came to India three decades ago for a visit and settled there as a disciple of Vinoba Bhave, a *Gandhian* (disciple of Gandhi). She says she is a *pucca Warkari*, meaning a genuine pilgrim as she undertakes a walkathon from Alandi (a town about 100 miles south-southeast of Mumbai) to the shrine of Vittal (a form of Krishna) in Pandharpur about 150 miles southeast of Alandi. She is referring to a thousand-year-old tradition begun by Maharashtrian saints from the western Indian state whose capital is Mumbai. These saints, named Dnyaneshwar (from the thirteenth century) and Tukaram (from the seventeenth century), undertook the pilgrimage to worship at the temple of Vittal. Their followers, known as *Warkaris,* keep up the practice.

Each year the Warkaris, carrying the sandals that the great saints had worn and worshipping these representations daily, begin their journey at the towns Dehu and Alandi and continue on foot. At each village they pass along the way, they are joined by hundreds more. Because the sandals are put in decorated *palanquins* (covered sedan chairs that are called *palkhi* in the Marathi language), this tradition has derived the name *Palkhi.*

Currently, the number of these Warkari pilgrims has swelled to about a half million. The journey takes 15 days, beginning on the eleventh day of the Hindu month of Ashadh (June/July). A similar pilgrimage takes place again in the month of Karthik (November/December). Singing, dancing, socializing, praying, eating, and camping together, the pilgrims reach Pandharpur, worship, and then return home by buses or trains.

For more details, or to listen to Yuriko Ikenoya talk about this pilgrimage, type the words "Warkari pucca" in any search engine.

The long road to Manasarovar, the lake of the mind

Manasarovar translates to "lake of the mind"; *manasa* is "mind" and *sarovar* is "lake." This lake is supposed to have been formed by the mind of Brahma in the vicinity of Mount Kailash, the abode of Shiva in the Himalayas. The sources of four great rivers are found in the vicinity of this mountain: the Indus (Sindhu); the Sutlej; Gogra, a tributary of the Ganges; and the Brahmaputra. Hindus believe that drinking the water from this lake at about 15,000 feet above sea level washes off sins of a hundred lifetimes and leads one, upon death, directly to the abode of Shiva.

In 1931, Krishnadevaraya Wodeyar IV, the maharaja (ruler) of the Indian state of Mysore at the time, undertook a journey with nine of his trusted assistants to this lake in the lunar landscape of Tibet in the Himalayas so that he could take a dip in the icy waters and circumambulate the mountain of Shiva. The group left their pleasant city on June 18, 1931, and traveled more than 1,700 miles one way by train, ponies, mules, and on foot through hills, valleys, and steep and treacherous passes with some trails no more than 3 feet wide. They went through sun and clouds, rain, and winds that blew hot and cold. Living in tents didn't deter them from their singular, sacred goal.

They were back safe and sound in their beloved city on September 7, 1931, a full 80 days after they left, much to the relief and admiration of the maharaja's subjects. Even now, eight decades later, this *yatra* (pilgrimage) is considered difficult and dangerous.

On the Road: Touring Important Pilgrimage Sites

Every Hindu recognizes the most popular destinations such as those discussed in this section, and they travel by special trains, buses, cars, and sometimes by foot to get there. In this section, I'll be your guide through a series of these popular pilgrimage destinations.

Your journey begins at a lake in Rajasthan and proceeds through a selection of sites shown in Table 18-1. Even though I provide descriptions of these centers based on a thematic view, a systematic pilgrimage would more closely follow the map in Figure 18-1, which leads you in a clockwise circumambulation (*Parikramana* or *Pradikshina*) around India. Enjoy the sights and sounds!

Around the Pushkar lake in Rajasthan

The Pushkar Fair is the largest festival in Rajasthan, a state in west central India. Festivities begin with the Cattle Fair, one of the largest in India, where 20,000 cattle, as well as camels and other draft animals, may be traded. The working fair is both accompanied and followed by camel, bullock, horse, and donkey races; bullock decoration; and horse dancing. The traditional fair that follows features turban tying and moustache competitions; cattle exhibits; and folk, classical, and devotional music. Ballads, folk dramas, and dramatic storytelling entertain the crowds. On average, 200,000 people take part in the annual fair and the pilgrimage, which have also become a tourist attraction since the 1970s.

Peak time for the pilgrimage is the full moon in the month of Kartik (mid-October to mid-November). The town of Pushkar lies among sand dunes. Five hundred temples are said to encircle the lake: These include one of the very few temples to Lord Brahma the Creator, where he is said to have performed a *yagna* (sacrificial fire ceremony) in the company of Shiva and Vishnu.

Major Pushkar pilgrimage destinations include a temple constructed in 1150 CE to Varaha, the boar avatar of Vishnu, and the Savitri Temple located on the highest hill above the town of Pushkar, which is dedicated to a wife of Brahma. The water, devout Hindus believe, bestows liberation on all who bathe in it and drink it. Pilgrims bathe in the lake water throughout the two festival weeks. They also perform a ritual called *Parikramana* around the lake. At dusk, lighted lamps made of leaves *(pattals)* are floated on the lake. The bank has 52 flights of steps leading down to the water.

Taking a trip to Kashi before death

Kashi translates as "shining city." It is the city of Shiva. Visiting Kashi is the equivalent of taking a crash course in Hinduism. Everything about life — and death — is seen here.

Every square inch of space in Kashi is considered holy by Hindus; even the air is considered holy. The city has more than 2,000 temples — there's one around every corner — most of them dedicated to Shiva. The main shrine is that of Vishveshwara (Lord of the Universe — Shiva). The city reverberates with the chant of *Om Namah Shivaaya* ("Om, Salutations to Shiva") everywhere — near every temple, large and small. Mendicants, the poor, the rich, the beggars, the high and the low; men, women, and children; the sick, the dying, the weak, and the strong — people of every description are found in Kashi. Likewise, all sorts of animals — cows, dogs, crows, and on and on — can be found there.

A pilgrimage to Kashi can be overwhelming. Mark Twain described the city as older than history, legend, and tradition all put together. In short, Kashi personifies Hinduism.

Kashi is also known as *Varanasi* because it is situated between the river Vaarana in the north and river Asi south of the city, both of which empty into the Ganges. Between these two rivers stretches a long ridge, crammed from its top height to the river edges with temples, palaces, small plazas, steps, narrow alleyways, and a famous vista seen in paintings and photos.

Kashi is also the city of death — good death, that is. According to Hindu belief, those who die here go directly to heaven. It is not uncommon for some ailing and elderly Hindus to ask their children to bring them to Kashi so that the parent can die in the holy city. When you visit Kashi, you see funeral pyres on the banks of the river in the vicinity of temples. Another common sight is that of relatives of the dead descending the 50 or 60 steps from the cremation grounds to the edge of the water all along the river and then bathing in the Ganges after the last rites have been administered and the funeral pyre is lit.

Why do Hindus throng to Kashi? In addition to the promise of a good death and immediate entry into heaven, Kashi is also known as the holy place a Hindu must plan to visit. It is the best known of the seven cities named in the *Garuda Purana* (an ancient scripture relating the dialogue between Lord Vishnu and his vehicle, the eagle Garuda), which have the special power to grant salvation *(moksha)* to those who visit and worship there.

The seven cities

Hindus believe that they will receive moksha if they visit these cities during their lifetime:

- **Ayodhya** is the City of Rama (of *Ramayana* fame; see Chapter 12) in North India.

- **Mathura** is the city where Lord Krishna was born, also in North India (less than 100 miles southeast of Delhi).

- **Maya,** also known as Hardwar, is where the sacred river Ganga (Ganges) enters the plains of India. (This is also one of the four places where pilgrims throng to attend the Kumbha Mela festival, described earlier in this chapter and in Chapter 16).

- **Kashi** stands out as the most sought-after destination by Hindus. The popular question is "What can you *not* get here at Kashi?" implying that one can attain all the four aims of Hindus: dharma, artha, kama, and moksha.

- **Kanchi,** or Kanchipuram, in southern India is close to the city of Chennai and famous for its several major temples of Vishnu, Shiva, and Devi.

- **Avantika,** also known as Ujjain, is another city famous for Kumbha Mela pilgrims.

- **Dwaraka** is the coastal city in the state of Gujarat from where Lord Krishna ruled his kingdom.

Ayodhya, Mathura, and Dwaraka are places of special interest to Vaishnavite pilgrims because the deities there are forms of Vishnu, while Maya (Hardwar), Kashi, and Avantika (Ujjain) are dedicated to Shiva. See Chapter 4 to read about Hindu denominations and Chapter 7 to learn about Hindu gods and goddesses.

Traveling to Rameshwaram, the Kashi of the South

Located on an island at the eastern tip of the peninsula in southern India, Rameshwaram is known as the Kashi of the South. Hindus believe that a visit to Kashi in the north is incomplete without a corresponding visit here. The bridge to Sri Lanka that Rama used to cross over to battle with the demon king Ravana originated near this island. Legend has it that Rama, after slaying Ravana, wanted expiation from the sin of killing a brahmin. (Yes, Ravana was a demon, a king, *and* a brahmin! See Chapter 12 for the details.) So Rama worshiped Shiva at this island before he returned home.

The temple here, famous for its 1,000-pillared corridor, is dedicated to Shiva and is one of the four destinations of pilgrims known in Hindi as *Char Dham:* four abodes of the Lord that attract 250,000 pilgrims each year. The other three are at Dwaraka (in the west), Badrinath (in the north), and Puri (in the east). These four centers were established by Adi Shankaracharya, the founder of the Hindu philosophy known as Advaita (see Chapter 20). A pilgrimage to these four centers covers all of India and is known as a *Parikramana*. It is the equivalent of the circumambulation (clockwise walkaround) Hindus do when they visit a temple.

Visiting Kanyakumari

Kanyakumari is a beautiful and peaceful town located at the southernmost tip of India at the confluence of the Arabian Sea, the Indian Ocean, and the Bay of Bengal. An extraordinarily beautiful sculpture of the deity Kanyakumari (a form of goddess Parvati) is the main attraction of pilgrims. The other, equally significant attraction for Hindus is the three-decade-old memorial to Swami Vivekananda (refer to Chapter 9) built on a rock just yards away from the shore. This was the rock on which the Swami meditated before he left for America to attend the World's Parliament of Religions in Chicago in the fall of 1893. Recently, a 133-foot statue of the Tamil poet saint Tiruvalluvar has been added at this site.

Queuing up to worship at Tirupati

Tirupati is about 120 miles from Bangalore and 100 miles from Chennai in South India. The 12-centuries-old shrine there is a complex of about 10 square miles situated on seven hills. Pilgrims on foot climb about 4,000 steps to reach the Sri Venkateshwara temple at the hilltop. Alternatively, cars and free buses may be used.

Not too long ago, pilgrims traveling to the famous shrine at Tirupati in the state of Andhra Pradesh could count on a long wait in queue. The wait is still long, but it's much more pleasant these days. Pilgrims enter a modern building, register, obtain a token that states the time for *darshan* (sacred viewing) of the Lord, enjoy free food, rest and relax, and watch on television the religious services taking place inside the temple complex. Continuing infrastructure improvements by the temple administration and the use of advanced technology and organization have helped to better manage the influx of 50,000 to 100,000 pilgrims each day. On special occasions, visitors swell to an incredible 500,000.

If you want to have free darshan, you may wait anywhere from one to ten hours after registering. For a fee of 300 Indian rupees (about $7), the wait may be reduced to between 45 minutes and 1.5 hours. At the very entrance to this temple, you check in your shoes and step into a cool drain of running water to wash your feet. You then begin the walk toward the *sanctum* (the area in and around the chamber that houses a deity) through many corridors in a clockwise direction.

Inside the *sanctum sanctorum* (the holiest chamber in a temple that houses the presiding deity) is an 8-foot-tall sculpture of Venkateshwara, a form of Vishnu, in *krishna shila* (black stone) and highly decorated with silver, gold, flowers, and a crown. Pilgrims enter this area for darshan and are ushered out less than a minute later. The darshan takes place between 2:30 a.m. and 1:30 a.m. the next day.

Pilgrims from every corner of India come to Tirupati. For Hindus from abroad, this shrine counts as a must-visit. For more information about this shrine, visit www.tirumala.org or simply type Tirupati in any search engine.

Honoring Lord Krishna at Mathura

Mathura, 90 miles southeast of Delhi, is the birthplace of Lord Krishna. Situated on the banks of the sacred river Yamuna, it is one of the seven towns that can grant moksha to a pilgrim/devotee.

What makes pilgrims throng to Mathura? This region is studded with places and events surrounding the life of Lord Krishna. Gokul, the town where Krishna grew up, is nearby. The Keshava temple here features an underground chamber where Hindus believe that Krishna's parents were jailed and where Devaki, his mother, gave birth to him (refer to Chapter 7). Brindavan, the garden-like setting where Krishna's playful pranks and tricks took place, is only 9 miles southeast of Mathura. Another legendary location, Govardhan, is only 18 miles from Mathura and refers to the mountain Lord Krishna lifted to protect the residents from the onslaught of rain brought about by Indra (Chapter 16 has that story). Brindavan is the Indian headquarters of the International Society of Krishna Consciousness. Mathura also serves as the center for the *bhakti* tradition, a Vaishnava tradition of surrender to the Lord as personal savior (see Chapter 4). The number of visitors swells on the birthday of Krishna in August.

Performing your own last rites at Gaya

Gaya, a town situated 60 miles from the city of Patna in the state of Bihar, is a pilgrimage center that attracts several hundred thousand pilgrims each year. A temple for Vishnu dominates the center.

An *asura* is a being considered to be ambitious and aggressive, unlike its opposite kind, the demigods and gods. An asura by the name of Gaya had acquired the blessings of Vishnu, who concluded that Gaya was a noble soul and declared that anyone who touched him attained salvation. Disturbed by Gaya's special power, other gods unleashed an onslaught on him. The abuse included putting a rock on Gaya's chest in order to kill him. Gaya sought Vishnu's protection. Vishnu appeared and assured him that all the gods, including himself, would stand at the head of Gaya forever if he only agreed to relinquish his body. Gaya readily agreed, and Vishnu stepped on his chest. This is the rock on which the "feet" of Vishnu were imprinted and housed at the Vishnu temple.

It's a sad tale of abuse due to the gods' jealousy, but Gaya's miserable end has led to a beneficial result: the belief among Hindus that they will receive moksha when they perform their own last rites at Gaya.

At the Himalayan abodes

Hindus believe that the spectacular Himalayas are indeed *Devalayas,* the abode of gods. Pilgrims, even older ones, take on these difficult trips undaunted by the weather, tough terrain, and high mountainous region. They visit Shiva and Vishnu temples after bathing in nearby lakes, collecting water from the sources of the sacred rivers Ganga and Yamuna, and offering the same when the gods are bathed during worship. Many travel a thousand miles or more and return fulfilled.

Hardwar, the gateway to Vishnu and Shiva temples

Two words that look alike — Hara and Hari — represent two distinct Hindu gods. Hara is another name for Shiva, and Hari is another name for Vishnu. For the same location at the foot of the Himalayas (which now goes by the name *Hardwar*), Vaishnavites say Haridwar and Shaivites say Haradwar. (*Dwar* in Sanskrit is "door.") This location is supposed to be the door (gateway) to Vishnu (located in the shrine at Badrinath) or Shiva (located in the shrine at Kedarnath).

Hardwar and Rishikesh are popular destinations of Hindu pilgrims. The Ganga (Ganges) descends 12,800 feet rapidly from the Himalayas before it touches the plains here and flows rapidly through these towns on its long journey of 1,200 miles to the Bay of Bengal (Ganga Sagar) in the east.

Worship of Ganga is a popular practice of pilgrims. It is common to make or buy a palm-size "boat" made of leaves, put an oil-soaked wick in it, light it, and float it on the river. At night thousands of these lamps bobbing up and down and rapidly moving along evoke a pleasant reverential feeling among visitors.

The holiness of this area becomes evident as soon as you get off at the train station because of the variety of holy men in saffron, either alone or with disciples, wandering about and on their way out of town and into the forest for meditation.

The area contains numerous sites where pilgrims can bathe, worship, and meditate. All sites have some special connection with an event or two from the *Ramayana* and the *Mahabharata* epics (refer to Chapter 12). For example, you find a temple for Bharata, the younger brother who ruled Ayodhya when the elder brothers, Rama and Lakshmana, were in exile. (This may be the only temple for Bharata in the world!) You also find a site where brother Lakshmana chose to cross Ganga and built a rope bridge; today, in its place is a beautiful suspension bridge for pedestrians. Decades ago, I stood on that bridge, which is outside of the town and away from the hustle and bustle. It was very peaceful, the only sounds being the river flowing and birds chirping. Beyond the bridge was an ethereal landscape of tall, slender trees, mist, and caves, unseen but occupied, where gurus dwelt and meditated. The solitude, peace, and quiet all hint at a world beyond, the world that a Hindu believes is the real one. To experience this feeling of what lies beyond, pilgrims come by the thousands to this place!

Here Swami Shivananda, whom I discuss in Chapter 9, meditated and trained many disciples (including Swami Satchidananda of Woodstock fame), later going around the world to spread his message of divine life. The Divine Life Society, which is active throughout the world today, owes its origin to this remote area in the Himalayas.

Many pilgrims come to Hardwar, proceed to Rishikesh, and complete their pilgrimage after traveling to Kedarnath and Badrinath, which I describe next.

The Shiva temple at Kedarnath

The Himalayas at this location rise to a height of 23,000 feet, and the Shiva temple is at 11,780 feet. This part of the Himalayas is known as *Rudra Himalaya,* referring to Rudra (Shiva). Shiva is represented here in the form of a *linga* (stone) — one of the 12 most sacred lingas in the land. (See the sidebar "The Dwadasha [12] Lingas legend.") Kedarnath is also held as holy because the Advaita saint Shankaracharya reached the end of his life here. A building nearby marks his *samadhi* (grave site).

The spires at the top of the Kedarnath shrines appear to reach the sky. The location is covered in snow during winter. Therefore, the temple opens in spring when the sun enters the zodiac sign of Mesha (Aries) and closes when the sun reaches Vrishika (Scorpio) in late fall. During the Kumbha Mela festival at Hardwar (when the sun is in Aries), the pilgrims in 2010 swelled to millions. (You can see some footage on YouTube: Type in "Kumbha Mela Hardwar.")

The Vishnu temple at Badrinath

Hindus believe that the pilgrimage to Kedarnath is incomplete without a visit to Badrinath (and vice versa). Badrinath is on the route the Pandavas took before they ascended to heaven (refer to Chapter 12). It is also close to the place where King Pandu was cursed when he mistakenly killed a sage couple enjoying each other disguised as deer. This is also the area where Draupadi (wife of the Pandavas) fell in love with a special flower and sent Bhima to fetch it.

At more than 10,000 feet above sea level, Badrinath has several sacred lakes and ponds for bathing by pilgrims before entering the temple to Narayana (Vishnu). The town is situated on the banks of the river Alakananda, and the temple is at the center of town. Almost in front of the temple is a hot water spring called Taptakunda suitable for bathing. Twenty-five steps lead to the main entrance of the temple that rises to 45 feet above. The *gopuram* (tower) above the sanctum is made of gold, and the deity is 3 feet high made of *saligrama shila* (sacred black stone), sitting on a throne, and adorned with a gold crown.

Amarnath

This cave temple in the Himalayas is 86 miles northeast of Srinagar, capital of Kashmir. An ice linga naturally forms each month inside this cave at 13,000 feet above sea level. The linga begins to form on the first day of the bright half of the moon and reaches its full size of 12 feet by full moon. It reduces its size gradually after full moon and loses all its height by new moon.

The journey to the cave is difficult, but pilgrims do make it starting at Srinagar and visiting a variety of holy places along the way. Each year, thousands of pilgrims travel to the Amarnath cave led by the *Shankaracharya* of Kashmir Mutt (a religious leader in the lineage of Adi [the first] Shankaracharya who heads up the monastery known as Sharada Peetha) during the Hindu month of Shravana (July/August). The cave is 50 feet wide, 55 feet long, and 45 feet tall. Pilgrims offer their own *puja* (worship) because there are no priests serving the cave temple. In 2010, the number of pilgrims reached 600,000.

The Dwadasha (12) Lingas legend

Once there was a contest between gods Brahma and Vishnu about who was the better of the two. Shiva was asked to settle the issue, and so he appeared in the form of a pillar of light. He asked the contestants to go find the extremities of the light, saying that whoever did so would be the better of the two. Brahma, in the form of a swan, flew upward, and Vishnu, in the form of a tortoise, dove downward. Years later, Brahma appeared with a flower called Ketaki which had told him that it had been offered as worship to Shiva at the very top. Brahma therefore claimed that he had seen the topmost extremity. Vishnu appeared and admitted that he could not find the extremity. Shiva was angry at Brahma for not telling the truth and cursed him with never having a temple in his name. But Shiva admired Vishnu for being honest. "Light has no end" was the message!

Hindus believe this pillar of light manifested itself in 12 places, where it is represented by the short, cylindrical stone structure called a *linga*. The 12 places became holy as the locations where Shiva appeared as light. In addition to Kedarnath shrine, the other 11 shrines are located at Somnath (Gujarat), SriShaila (Andhra Pradesh), Ujjaain (Madhya Pradesh), Omkareshwara (on the banks of the sacred river Narmada in Madhya Pradesh), Bhima Shankara (Maharashtra), Vishweshwara (Kashi), Trayambakeshwara (on the banks of Godavari in Maharashtra), Vaidyanath (Bihar), Nageshwar (Dwaraka, Gujarat), Rameshwaram (Tamilnadu), and Ghushmeshwara (Ellora, Maharashtra).

When Shiva denounced Brahma for pretending to reach the end of Shiva's pillar of light, he declared that the Creator would have no temples in India. But the yagna Brahma conducted in the company of other members of the Trimurti (Hindu Trinity) may have absolved him sufficiently to allow for at least *one* temple; refer to the section "Around the Pushkar lake in Rajasthan" in this chapter to read about it.

The hilltop pilgrimage to Sabarimalai

Each year, millions of devotees of Ayyappa (see Chapter 15) travel from all parts of India to Sabarimalai in the south Indian state of Kerala. Sometimes the expected number of pilgrims gets so large that as many as 400 special trains are provided by Indian Railways to convey the pilgrims to the nearest town, Pampa. Once in Pampa, pilgrims have only one way to reach the temple on the hill: walking — for about two to three hours.

Women between the ages of 10 and 50 are not permitted beyond Pampa because the godhead Ayyappa is a bachelor! Pilgrims practice austerities (abstinence, vegetarian food, non-alcoholic drinks, fasting on selected days, and so on) for 41 days before they begin travel to the holy site. From the base, they must climb 18 steps to reach the shrine at the top. The temple is open daily only from mid-November to mid-January. During other months, the temple opens for just a few days in the middle of each month.

The highlight of this pilgrimage is the sighting of *Makara Vilakku* ("makara lights"). These special divine lights are believed to appear annually on the winter solstice day (when the sun enters Capricorn) on the Ponnambalamedu hill across from the mountaintop temple. They are seen by about 40 million pilgrims.

Pilgrimage to where rivers are "born"

As I mention earlier in this chapter, rivers are sacred to Hindus. Worshipping them and bathing in them is common to Hindu pilgrims. What is more special is to travel to the very location where the water of the sacred river originates.

In the next sections, I give three examples: two, Gangotri and Yamunotri, are in the Himalayas where the sacred rivers Ganga and Yamuna are born. The third is Kaveri in southern India.

Gangotri and Yamunotri

Just less than 10,000 feet above sea level, Gangotri is close to India's northern border with Tibet. Near this little town of fewer than 1,000 people, the Ganges emerges — at about 14,000 feet up in the Garhwal region in the Himalayas. A temple to Ganga in this town is open between May and November.

Yamunotri is the seat of the river goddess Yamuna, also close to the Tibetan border and not too far from Gangotri.

Pilgrims bathe in the earliest stretches of these rivers and collect the water to offer in worship when they visit Kedarnath and Badrinath.

Bathing at the source of sacred Kaveri

Pilgrims arrive at the town of Talakaveri in Coorg province in the southern state of Karnataka to celebrate *Tula Sankramana* (when the sun enters Libra) at the source of the sacred river Kaveri, the Ganges of the south. The Coorg region (known as *Kodugu* in Kannada) is where the river is "born" and flows southeast through the states of Karnataka and Tamilnadu, irrigating thousands of acres of rice fields and generating electricity on its way to the Bay of Bengal in the east.

Rising at Talakaveri in the Brahmagiri hills of Kodagu, this source of Kaveri attracts thousands of pilgrims in mid-October each year. On the Tula Sankramana day, at the precise moment when the sun enters the zodiacal house of Libra, water gushes out as a fountain and fills a large pool. This event is considered to be holy and cause for celebration and a dip in the holy water. People of Kodugu who gather at this spot collect the water in bottles and take it home to be used on special religious occasions. A spoonful of this water is fed to the dying, which is believed to grant them *moksha* (liberation).

Part V
Delving Deeper into the Hindu Concept of Reality

The 5th Wave   By Rich Tennant

VEDANTA

"I think you're on to something here."

In this part . . .

Fair warning: The material in this part is somewhat more complex than that in other parts of the book. Here, I take you deeper into Hinduism by discussing the ancient Hindus' thirst for knowledge and insistence on finding a rational basis for understanding Reality. I describe what Reality means to Hindus and how it relates to attaining *moksha* (salvation). I also walk you through the ways ancient Hindus used logic, the atom-based physical universe, and the inner universe in their attempts to understand Reality. *Vedanta,* a philosophy that revolutionized and helped bring about a Hindu renaissance, is the focus in this part.

Chapter 19

The Six Schools of Thought: The Darshanas

In This Chapter

▶ Understanding the great urge to seek the Truth

▶ "Seeing" Reality: The Darshanas

▶ Opening the toolbox of the six different paths

The Hindu word *darshana* means "seeing." Hindus often say they are on their way for a darshan (or darshana) when they visit a temple. The implication is to "see" God in the deity they are about to worship. Hindus also commonly use the word *darshana* when they go to see a holy person or a village elder. In this context, it means a respectful visit.

But Darshana is also a philosophy that means seeing at a deeper level — seeing Reality. Six different approaches to seeing Reality have been recognized as ancient schools of Darshana philosophy. This chapter examines these approaches and introduces the six schools (Darshanas) that provided a theoretical foundation for Hindu thought.

Seeing or believing — which comes first? If indeed "seeing is believing" as the old saying goes, optical illusions like the mirage effect refute the seeing. If believing is seeing, the thinking person can take offense because that minimizes the requirement of the rational approach. The Hindu says that you must see. Whether you believe or not is entirely up to you.

As you may expect, the discussion gets a little complex in this chapter — and indeed in this entire part of the book. What makes the material complex is the attempt to blend *metaphysics* (philosophy dealing with abstract concepts of Reality) with the essentially scientific reasoning of these approaches. These approaches are based on the application of logic and an atom-based description of substances to define physical reality in terms of a mind, body, soul connection. I try to keep the chapter as simple as possible to convey the basic principles supporting these concepts.

A Guide to Understanding the Darshana Philosophies

The Darshanas were developed in the post-Vedic and post-Upanishadic period (approximately from 500 BCE to 500 CE). To provide a firm rational basis for Hinduism, every conceivable variable relevant to Hindu thought was included in the studies: dharma, moksha, karma, Prakriti, purusha, logic, Truth, mind, matter, body, soul, self, death, the material world and its composition, and Vedic dictums. (Refer to Chapters 1 and 3 to understand what such terms mean.)

Distinguishing between realities

Ancient Hindus defined two levels of reality. One reality is what you can experience through your senses — for example, what you see or touch. The book you are reading, the roses in your garden, the floor under your feet, and the roof over your head — even the mountains and oceans — all are real in the sense that they have a physical reality. But a higher level of reality is *absolute reality* — Reality with a capital R.

Absolute Reality is defined as that which is not subject to change. Within that context, the book is not real, nor are the roses, the floor, the roof, or even the oceans and mountains — because they all change. They come into being, they exist, and then, eventually, they are no more. For this reason and in this context, Hindus declare that *this world is not real.*

So then what is Real? Truth. Truth does not change, decay, or die. It was there before, it is there now, and it will always be there. Thus seeing Reality is the equivalent of seeing Truth.

The aim of the six schools of Hindu philosophy is to search for Reality and to determine ways to reach that goal. These schools seek to know fundamental truths — those of a *metaphysical* nature (meaning they deal with things that can't be experienced physically) — and to realize these truths through direct experience, as explained in the following sections. The result is not just theory but a no-holds-barred approach to the following:

- Attaining realization of our selves by understanding our relationship with the external world

- Learning to distinguish between appearance and Reality

- Learning to control the body and mind in order to recognize the true self

Introducing the sutras

Six schools, each led by a different sage, approached the quest for Truth much the same way that a scientist goes about seeking scientific truth — with complete freedom to inquire, doubt, and question without prejudice or dogma. The Darshana sages were not scientists, yet their studies fulfilled the rigor stipulated for scientific inquiries. Each of the six schools of Darshana presented its ideas in treatises known as sutras. The word *sutras* means "strings." These treatises have survived in their earliest form because they were originally conceived as *aphorisms* (concise statements of principles). Hindus look upon them as representing pearls of wisdom on a string.

These six sutras and the associated sages are listed in Table 19-1.

Table 19-1	The Six Sutras of Darshana Philosophy	
Sutra	*Associated Sage*	*School of Thought*
Nyaya Sutras	Gotama (second to first century BCE)	School of logic
Vaisheshika Sutras	Kanada (sixth to fourth century BCE)	Atom-based school of physical reality
Samkhya Sutras	Kapila (fourth century CE)	School of matter and spirit
Mimamsa Sutras	Jaimini (third century BCE)	Veda-based school
Yoga Sutras	Patanjali (second century BCE)	School of Yoga: training of the body, mind, and soul
Vedanta Sutras	Badarayana (fourth century BCE)	School of the One

You can read more about each of these schools of thought in the later section "The Six Different Ways to View Reality."

The general approach of the Darshana philosophies

The approaches seemed to demand the impossible to attain the ultimate goal: salvation and freedom from the cycle of births and deaths. Achieving such a goal required reasoning logically regarding belief statements, understanding clearly the physical world, and exploring the concept of spirit and the mechanics of the human body. The vigor and rigor of the efforts needed to match the anticipated result. And they seemed to.

The inquiry required a high level of intellectual curiosity and debate regarding life's persistent questions, pursued according to the following dictates:

- ✔ Don't accept anything at its face value. Question it, doubt it, debate it, argue about it, and challenge it.

- ✔ Find the answer by yourself. Do not depend upon anyone else.

- ✔ Use logic, develop an understanding of the most basic elements of the material world, and distinguish between matter and spirit.

Only by following this process, according to these proponents, would it be possible to gain knowledge and be free.

Beginning with the root cause of human suffering: Ignorance

By posing questions about the source of human unhappiness, pain, and misery, and doubting obvious/traditional answers, the Darshana sages focused on defining the root cause(s). What did they mean by obvious/traditional answers to a malady? Take a string of bad luck as an example. An obvious response in ancient times may have been a sacrificial offering of a chicken or goat to a local deity. Another example would be a serious illness in the family; a remedial measure may have involved undergoing a painful penance to appease a deity. The Darshana thinkers viewed such responses as less than rational.

The ancient sages were seeking rational answers. The answer they found was this: The root cause of all human suffering is ignorance or false notions. Ignorance is, in the sages' view, at the very source of our miseries. In this context, ignorance refers to a lack of knowledge of our selves. The sages insisted, therefore, that acquisition of knowledge is the only weapon and powerful antidote against suffering.

Knowledge, for the Darshana sages, meant freedom. Freedom meant understanding one's self, knowing oneself to be part of the divine, and earning release from the cycle of rebirths. With this in mind, the different Darshanas all had the same goal of dispelling ignorance, of finding a way to guide the mind in its quest for knowledge and the ultimate release of the soul. Only the sages' methods differed.

Pursuing belief by doubting everything

In the Darshana schools, inquiry begins with doubting seemingly obvious beliefs. The Darshana philosophers refused to accept, at face value, rituals, sacrifices, and worship as prescribed in the Vedas unless supported by rational thinking or a theoretical foundation that answered fundamental questions about life.

Early Vedic wedding rituals, for example, involved the sacrifice of a cow. Later, this practice was modified by simply bringing a cow to the ceremony and making a declaration — "Release the cow" — at a certain point in the celebration. Was it the principle of *ahimsa* (nonviolence) that led to the change? Did the influence of Buddhism effect the change? We don't know, but the point is that change did occur, and it resulted from questioning accepted practices and making thoughtful amends. On the other hand, in the same Vedic ceremony, the sages decided to keep intact the clear and unmistakable charge to the couple that they have become friends as they complete taking seven steps around a fire altar. The sages thought it through and decided that friendship must be the basis of conjugal union and retained the emphasis. The practice remains to this day!

Clearly, those who were bent upon exploring a rational basis for the philosophy of Hindus wanted debate and discussion. They were playing and playing hard at the boundary between faith, theology, and metaphysics on the one hand and critical thinking on the other. And not even the Vedas — the holiest of Hindu sacred texts — were exempt from this examination!

Teaching by memorization and dialogue

As aphorisms, the sutras could be easily remembered and transmitted, and this strategy helped preserve the inherent wisdoms, but it did not make them easy to understand.

The cryptic nature of these sutras comes about by virtue of their origin: the oral tradition. Students of Darshana were required to memorize the sutras, recite them before their guru, and enter into a dialogue. Such interaction between the teacher and the disciples helped expand and explain the intent and meaning hidden in these statements. Understanding the sutras is the equivalent of breaking a code to reveal the true meaning, which would then be used in discussion and debate. This memorization requirement was a great way to teach and train the mind of an aspirant.

Commentaries known as *bhashyas,* which came about through the discussions between teachers and disciples over generations, are abundant in Hindu literature and serve as indispensible tools to enhance our understanding of these literary masterpieces. The early sutras in the Darshana texts were purposely kept brief and cryptic in order to make oral transmission easy; as a result, additional commentaries that unraveled and expanded them to more intelligible messages were necessary. Great saints such as Shankaracharya and Ramanujacharya, for example, wrote commentaries on self-knowledge and Vedanta. Even these commentaries, although helpful, remained rigorous, which led to additional commentaries by their disciples to help unravel the meaning of the verses. Such effort continues to this day because the Darshana sutras remain beyond the grasp of many. So you are not alone! Understanding these inherently complex texts requires guidance from scholars. But this chapter is a good beginning.

The Six Different Ways to View Reality

The six Darshanas address aspects that help resolve the validity of beliefs and enhance our understanding of the world we see (the physical world) and the world that we don't see (the world of ideas, matter, spirit, body, and mind).

The school of logic: Nyaya

The Nyaya tradition is based on the Nyaya Sutras of Gotama, which were possibly composed in the first century BCE (or, as some scholars believe, the second century BCE). These sutras live on in the commentary of Vatsyayana, 500 years later. Nyaya attempted to train the mind through a logical sequence of (a) perception, (b) inference, and (c) comparison, backed up by the teachings of a knowledgeable person or by scripture. Nyaya proponents claimed that their approach proved the existence of the soul, karmic consequences, and rebirth (refer to Chapter 3 for a discussion of these concepts).

Nyaya is the science of logic and reasoning. Its goal is to obtain valid knowledge of the external world and its relationship with the mind and the self. Nyaya claims that one may rid oneself of all suffering by understanding and applying its technique to validate any proposition. It offers a set of tools to validate knowledge. It provides a rational basis for the analysis of fundamental questions leading to attainment of moksha. The principal aphorism states:

Pain, birth, activity, faults, and misapprehension — on the successive annihilation of these in the reverse order, there follows release.

Note the crisp and concise nature of the sutra. In Sanskrit, it has even a better ring to it; it sounds like a formula a student would memorize, understand, and repeat often to help oral transmission to the next generation.

Short of this "annihilation," man's sufferings in this world continue. This unending cycle begins with a false notion (about anything) that arises out of ignorance and, as can be seen in Figure 19-1, proceeds clockwise through a series of developments. Table 19-2 outlines the stages, using an example of four brothers who go to war to illustrate each stage. In this highly simplified and somewhat exaggerated scenario, I discuss the parameters of the Nyaya circle of Figure 19-1. Note that any rewards/punishments received (accolades, military honors, and so on) become the experience of the soul and are relevant only in determining the nature/quality of the next life.

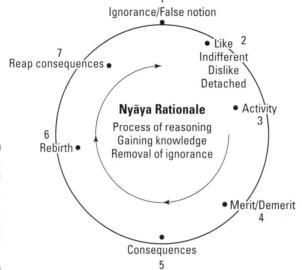

Figure 19-1:
The cycle of karmic consequence according to the school of logic.

Table 19-2	The Cycle of Karmic Consequence: Four Brothers Go to War			
Stage	*Brother A*	*Brother B*	*Brother C*	*Brother D*
1. Ignorance/false notion	Thinks war is an opportunity to travel	Thinks war is hell	Thinks war is a legal opportunity to kill	Thinks participating in war is duty to country
2. Like/indifferent/dislike/detached	Is indifferent	Dislikes	Likes	Detached
3. Activity	Joins the navy	Joins the ambulance corps	Becomes a sniper	Volunteers for battle as needed
4. Merit/demerit accrued by soul[1]	Demerit	Merit	Demerit	Neither
5. Consequences[2]	−	+	−	0
6. Rebirth	Yes	Yes	Yes	No

(continued)

Table 19-2 *(continued)*

Stage	Brother A	Brother B	Brother C	Brother D
7. Reap consequences	Reborn as a sea goose	Reborn into a family of educators and ministers	Reborn as a wolf	Freed from cycle

[1] *Merit or demerit is the experience accumulated by the individual soul. It is the aggregate of such experiences that determines the chances of rebirth or total salvation.*
[2] *The symbol + or – indicates whether another birth is warranted to reap the consequence of actions.*

The only way to break the cycle is to have no notion, but that is nearly impossible. The best alternative is to do one's duty without *any* concern for the result (Karma Yoga, which you can read about in the next chapter). Be therefore detached like brother D!

The basis of this approach is the recognition that human minds are vulnerable to illusion; by insisting on logic, this approach helps people distinguish Truth from its opposite. Therefore, Nyaya teaches how to think logically. Such training, if successful, should lead one to examine fundamental propositions and determine their validity. According to this school, conclusions in regard to any proposition can be reached only through doubting, questioning, reasoning, and arguments. With doubt as the driving force, illusions get sorted out and rejected, logically.

These are the subjects for study recommended by Nyaya:

- ✔ The soul *(atman)*
- ✔ The body *(sharira)*
- ✔ The senses *(indriya)*
- ✔ Object of the senses *(artha)*
- ✔ Intelligence *(buddhi)*
- ✔ The mind *(manas)*
- ✔ Activity *(pravritti)*
- ✔ Faults *(dosha)*
- ✔ Transmigration *(pretya-bhava)*
- ✔ Consequences or fruits of action *(phala)*
- ✔ Pain *(duhkha)*

The methodology of understanding the subject

The very first topic in the very first Nyaya sutra addresses the methodology or the means, *pramana,* for obtaining what it calls the *right measure, prama,* or knowledge about a subject. It answers the question about how one determines whether a certain piece of information or proposition is true and accurate. Nyaya recommends these four steps for this assessment:

1. **Perception by the senses:** What do you see, hear, and so on?

2. **Inference:** What do you make of your perception? This inquiry is further divided into five logical steps:

    1. Hypothetical statement or proposition (A house on the street is on fire.)

    2. Reason for the statement (Smoke is visible in different parts at the roof level.)

    3. Example that supports the observation (Where there is smoke, there is fire.)

    4. Application of the reason (This house is smoking.)

    5. Conclusion (Therefore this house must be on fire.)

    Upon this inference, the analysis proceeds to compare with any other earlier experience and any verbal authority to lead to a final conclusion.

3. **Comparison:** Is there anything comparable in your experience?

4. **Verbal authority:** Are you aware of any testimony or trustworthy reference to support the perception?

The core message is that you can train your mind to think logically to resolve an issue and draw rational conclusions. It presents a rigorous alternative — a scientific approach — to mere believing.

Nyaya strategy for analyzing a proposition

Other topics in the Nyaya sutra deal with a series of stages for establishing or denying a proposition or dealing with a controversial issue:

1. **Samshaya:** Express doubt about a proposition.

2. **Prayojana:** Define the purpose or motive for discussing the proposition.

3. **Drishtanta leading to siddhanta:** Present an illustrative example that leads to the established conclusion.

4. **Purvapaksha:** Consider the other side's arguments.

5. **Tarka — nirnaya:** Consider a hypothetical argument that refutes the objection and ascertains the merits of the proponent's case.

6. **Vada:** Engage in discussion and debate.

7. **Jalpa:** Wrangle or refute points just for the sake of doing so.

8. **Vitanda:** Raise frivolous objections or refutations or offer destructive criticism.

9. **Hetva-abhasa:** Point out the fallacy in the cause or fallacious reasoning.

10. **Chhala:** Engage in quibbling or guile.

11. **Jati:** Offer futile replies.

12. **Nigraha-sthana:** Put an end to all discussion by demonstrating the objector's incompetence and noting the vulnerable point in the opponent's argument. This is a post-mortem on the opposition, a necessary tool to finish off what has been learned in the course of the argument.

Do some of these steps sound harsh and too overbearing? It appears they were meant to because only by rigorous debate can the Truth be discovered.

The atom-based school of physical reality: Vaisheshika

While Nyaya provided tools to establish the validity of any proposition pertaining to Reality, Vaisheshika focused on the reality of the physical world and beyond. Vaisheshika defined nine substances that constitute matter. In addition to the five elements (earth, water, light, air, ether), they include time, space, soul, and mind. Vaisheshika further recognizes the many individual souls and the Supreme Soul — that is, the One.

According to this school, the most basic element in all material objects is the atom, which was considered to be indivisible, eternal (neither created nor destroyed), and extremely tiny (and therefore not visible to the naked eye and totally imperceptible to the senses). The combination of atoms leads to substances that in turn lead to the physical world as we know it.

The formation of the world through a series of integrations of atoms, and the subsequent disintegration of the world through an equally vast disintegration of the atoms, are believed to take place by the power of an unseen but extraordinary force known as *adrishta*. The essentially scientific reasoning used by Vaisheshika scholars to describe the physical world ties neatly to the presence of an unseen force that is critical to initiate the process of forming (and subsequently undoing) that physical world.

The proponent of Vaisheshika is known as sage Kanada. According to Kanada, atoms always existed, have no particular cause, and are therefore eternal. (Note the similarity between this and the concept of soul in Hindu thought.) Another feature worthy of note is that each atom has a uniqueness of its own, and this uniqueness, known as *vishesha,* lends the school its name.

Explaining evil

Every religion poses the question of how a merciful, kind, powerful, loving, and compassionate God can allow the levels of misery and suffering we see in the world. There are demons but no Satan in Hindu thought. The closest possible explanation is inspired by the Nyaya school: One reaps the consequences of one's action: good, bad, or indifferent. Any experience in this life is attributable to the soul's experience when it occupied another body in a previous life.

Vaisheshika considers the following seven categories as the components of Reality:

- Substances *(dravya),* such as earth, water, and so on

- Properties of substances *(guna),* such as color or pleasure

- Action *(karma),* such as expansion and contraction

- General properties *(samanya),* such as properties of a certain species

- Particularity *(vishesha),* referring to differences that distinguish one substance from another

- Intimate relations among these *(samavaya),* referring to the inherent relation between atoms and the resulting material — for example, the greenness in a green leaf

- Nonexistence *(abhava),* such as nonexistence of fragrance in a flower yet to bloom

Individual souls and minds are included in the category of substances. Some substances are atomic. Some are eternal. Some, like souls, are both. Vaisheshika's thesis is that an unseen force known as *adrishta* is responsible for the world to emerge based on an aggregation of atoms. Individuality and karmic consequences (in the atom-based souls) are at play here, and the knowledge of creation and subsequent disintegration at the end of an era *(yuga),* when all will simply fall back to the original categories, is the knowledge that leads to "seeing" Reality and salvation.

The more recent knowledge that the atom is divisible and is itself made of even tinier components doesn't negate the main thesis of the school. What holds the "indivisible" atom together is now known to be an extraordinary electromagnetic force, which is released when the atom is split.

The school of matter and spirit: Samkhya

Unlike Nyaya and Vaisheshika, which attempt to provide an analytical basis for what is, the school known as Samkhya (also often spelled Sankhya), developed by sage Kapila, focuses on understanding the basics of how it all came about.

The Sanskrit word *samkhya* derives from *samyag akhyate,* meaning an attempt to explain the whole. The aim is to consider the entire universe and our connections with it. An understanding of the Samkhya approach to Reality begins with *Prakriti,* defined as the great producer.

Defining Prakriti (matter)

Sometimes the word "nature" is used to describe Prakriti, but it is only one of the many meanings of the Sanskrit word. Another word commonly associated with Prakriti is "matter." Nature and matter are useful in developing an understanding of the concepts inherent in Samkhya, as long as you keep in mind that Prakriti encompasses much more than those two words convey. The root word is *prakaroti,* meaning something that evolves or produces. It can be seen as a primal essence.

Prakriti is non-conscious, not intelligent, and made of three materials known as sattva, tamas, and rajas:

- *Sattva* materials comprise a host of highly desirable properties (qualities) such as awareness, happiness, gentleness, illumination, calmness, and a certain lightness.

- The qualities that govern a *tamas* material are the opposite, comprising (for example) sloth, sorrow, roughness, obstruction, darkness, inertia, and heaviness.

- *Rajas* material possesses qualities that make it vibrant — full of activity, passion, anxiety, and pain.

If you think that these qualities *in total and in some combination* define life, you're on to Samkhya's viewpoint. When these materials are in balance, nothing happens and nothing is produced. But any imbalance is enough to motivate Prakriti to produce. Different entities (a clod of clay, a worm, or a monk) are produced based on the magnitude and proportions of the three materials, much the same way an alloy is produced depending upon the quality and quantity of each contributing base metal.

Defining purusha (spirit)

What is the source of any imbalance that sets a course for Prakriti to begin to produce? It is purusha! *Purusha* is pure spirit, pure consciousness; it is passive with no qualities attributed to it. Purusha is an absolutely neutral but extraordinarily powerful presence. It is simply there with no feelings, no attachment; it is totally immune to pleasure and pain, and it's inactive.

What exactly is purusha? Look upon purusha as the soul, which has a subtle connection with a living body (matter). T*he living* comes about because of that connection — that is, the presence of the soul. By definition, therefore, there are an infinite number of individual purushas.

The union of Prakriti and purusha

Purusha's mere presence causes excitation in Prakriti, leading to an imbalance in the three qualities (sattva, tamas, and rajas), which in turn leads to production of a great variety of entities (beings, things). The level of the imbalance depends on any experience present in the particular purusha.

For example, if the particular purusha (think soul) was of a good person in the previous life, then experience in that life would have the quality of sattva predominant. The result of any interaction between this particular purusha and Prakriti would then include the sattva element in any output. The extent of this element will have profound influence leading either to release or rebirth.

Prakriti produces without any apparent *direct* aid from purusha. The radiance of purusha is all that is required. But the results are extraordinary. They lead to production of intelligence *(buddhi);* the "I" ness *(ahamkara),* which is the ego; the faculties of action, thought, and sense; and subtle atoms and the gross elements (ether, air, fire, water, and earth).

An infinite number of individual purushas exist, unlike the one Prakriti. This Samkhya approach leads to the well-known concept called Dualism, or *Dvaita,* which maintains distinct identities between Purusha (Universal Soul) and purusha (individual soul). Prakriti (matter) evolves, and Purusha (spirit) manifests. Science tells us that such evolution took thousands of centuries, beginning probably with a single cell and reaching an age where humans as we know them evolved. There are infinite purushas interacting with Prakriti. Perhaps the earliest such interaction may have resulted in microbes. All such knowledge forms the basis to understand the relationships between the different contributing factors to our outer and inner world.

The Veda-based school: Mimamsa

Sage Jaimini, the proponent of Mimamsa, insisted that the path to seeing Reality was already clearly laid out in the Vedas. Neither rationalism (the reason-based Nyaya and atomic-based theory of Vaisheshika) nor the personal god of theism had any appeal for him. He claimed that neither reason nor a god was needed to see Reality; therefore, in essence, the Vedas served that role entirely. A supreme being, according to Jaimini, may exist but is not needed for that purpose!

Some have defined Hindus as those who accept the authority of the Vedas, and this belief is rooted in Jaimini's assertion that the Vedas contain all that is necessary to know and practice dharma (right conduct) through the rituals prescribed there. Dharma is the focus in this system, and the very first aphorism in his sutras clearly states: *athato dharma jignasa*; "Next therefore is the inquiry into dharma."

Jaimini emphasized the power of the *mantras* (words and their sounds combined in chanting), and this feature gives credence to a Chinese proverb: "The echoes of a word once uttered vibrate in space to all eternity." (How true, and how critical it is for us to think before we speak!)

Notwithstanding its somewhat less than philosophical and, I may add, apparent unscientific character, Mimamsa's aim was to raise and address doubts in regard to rituals and sacrifices. It delved into identifying what it considered to be apparent discrepancies in the Vedic texts and attempted to resolve them.

The methodology Mimamsa uses to identify and remove the discrepancies in the Vedas has parallels in Nyaya. It begins with a statement of a proposition. Then it raises a doubt about its correctness and discusses the erroneous approach to treating the question. Following that is a refutation of the erroneous approach by what Mimamsa claims as a true argument, and the process concludes with stating the result of the investigation. So although this school insists that "the Veda needs no authority, but it is eternal," its methodology follows a logical process of inquiry and debate.

Nyaya, Vaisheshika, and Mimamsa no longer survive as separate schools, although many of their methods and concepts have been adopted by later and even contemporaneous denominations and schools of thought. Reverence for the Vedas and dharma, for example, a hallmark of Mimamsa, has been absorbed into Vedanta and mainstream Hinduism.

The school of Yoga: Training the body, mind, and soul

Yoga Darshana, attributed to sage Patanjali, is based on the acknowledgement of a supreme being, a Supreme Soul as the only Reality. The goal is to train the body and mind to reach a level of perfection that leads to the merging of the individual soul with the Supreme Soul. (*Yoga* means "union" in Sanskrit.)

The first step in Yoga is to train a healthy body to support and contain a healthy mind. A series of body postures *(asanas)* have been developed to keep the body supple yet strong. This system is known as *Hatha Yoga.* Clearly Hatha Yoga can be practiced as beneficial physical exercise without any direct connection to religion — and many non-Hindus practice it for just this reason. (In fact, the only common connection with Hinduism, if any, comes about when the students may, at the end of the class, chant the familiar monosyllable Om!)

Hatha Yoga in the West

Hatha Yoga is now very popular in the West, and in the United States it's not uncommon to find a yoga teacher with a few adherents even in small towns. Even mainstream health clubs now offer classes in yoga on a regular basis.

The general trend is to be gentle in assuming the body postures and not strain the body unduly, even though examples of extreme contortions of the body as practiced by a few easily get the attention of the press and the public.

Where Hinduism may come into play is in training the mind through meditation — through, for example, advanced techniques of concentration (Raja Yoga). To train the mind through meditation, Hindus offer silent prayers or maintain focus on a chosen deity. (Millions of non-Hindus who practice meditation choose a different focus of their choice.)

When Hindus meditate, their goal is to train the mind to develop what is known as *vairagya,* suppression of all passions. The method proposed is concentration on a chosen image or sound or on nothing. The goal is to empty the mind of all thought and attain a state of being that is both at peace and still alert. This concentration is accomplished through restraint *(yama),* rituals *(niyama),* body postures *(asana),* breathing techniques *(pranayama),* control of senses *(pratyadhara),* control of mind *(dharana),* contemplation *(dhyana),* and reaching a state of trance *(samadhi).* The focus is inward to both the body and the mind because, the argument goes, what we seek outside is already within us.

The school of Yoga has survived until today because of its continued ability to deal with and support a structure that has not changed much through the millennia: the human body, in all its strengths and weaknesses. And the body supports the mind. And the mind supports the spirit within. Yoga in its several branches caters to all these needs. See Chapter 21 for details about Yoga's ultimate goal.

The school of the One: Vedanta

Attributed to sage Badarayana, Vedanta Darshana brings all the other philosophies together. The Sanskrit word *Vedanta* means "the end (culmination) of knowledge." Vedanta refers back to the pantheistic creed so eloquently stated in the Chandogya Upanishad: e*kam eva adwitiyam* (one and only essence without a second); refer to Chapter 11. This belief in One Supreme Being is the foundation of Hinduism, and without understanding it, Westerners may misinterpret the true spirit and meaning implied in the Hindu worship of many gods (polytheism).

Vedanta's allegiance is to the One — Brahman. Many great sayings *(maha-vakyas)* serve as the foundation of Vedanta. such as:

Brahma satyam jagan mithya: Brahman is the Reality, the world is false

Sarvam khalavidam brahma: All this is Brahman

That is why Swami Vivekananda (refer to Chapter 9) declared, "The living god is within you." In this school, there is no distinction between the individual soul and the universal soul. They are one and the same, leading to another great saying:

Tat tvam asi: Thou art That

This is the basis for the philosophy of Nondualism (Advaita). The "That" represents existence, knowledge, and joy all together and expressed as one thing with the Sanskrit words *sat-chit-ananda* or *sacchidaananda.* The "That" in Vedanta has no attributes or emotional content and is without beginning or end (eternal). *That* is Brahman.

Major branches of Vedanta that are still in existence include Advaita, Visishtadvaita, and Dwaita. You can read more about them in Chapter 20.

Chapter 20

Vedanta: The End of Knowledge

. . . .

In This Chapter

▶ Absorbing the end of all knowledge

▶ Understanding Dvaita, Advaita, and Vishishtadvaita

▶ Recognizing the unity in the diversity

. . . .

Someone saw God and asked, "Who are you?" God replied, "You."

This very brief dialogue dramatizes the mandate "Thou art That," which appears in the sacred texts called Upanishads (see Chapter 11). Because this mandate succinctly sums up all that the sacred scriptures called the Vedas (see Chapter 10) convey, I could end the chapter right here. But to absorb all that is contained in that truth, we need to know more. Who is thou? What is That? How art thou That?

That is Brahman. *Thou* is you. So you are Brahman. You are divine. The Hindu sages proclaimed that every human, in fact every animal, is, in its essence, divine. Therefore there is no difference between the inner you and the inner me. We are the same except for the different bodies and the different experiences. We are like passengers on a plane all heading to the same destination even as we live in different places and experience different things.

Having pronounced divinity in you, the ancient Hindu sages insisted that you are not a sinner. Swami Shivananda Saraswathi (1887–1963), a sage who founded a religious order known as the Divine Life Society, declared that bliss is your birthright. The Hindu idea of life on earth is that we need to enjoy it while performing our karma (duty) till the end, at which time the body dies but the soul lives on.

In this chapter, I look at the three main branches of *Vedanta,* which is a philosophy or school of Hindu thought that brings all other Hindu philosophies together (see Chapter 19). The three branches of Vedanta are Advaita, Dvaita, and Vishishtadvaita, and in this chapter I compare their similarities and differences. I also discuss how they differ from mainstream, polytheistic Hinduism and where they fit into the two main denominations, Shaivism and Vaishnavism (see Chapter 4), representing the worship of Shiva and Vishnu respectively.

This chapter outlines the Vedantic way of "seeing" Reality, which looks at the intricate relationship between an individual soul and the Supreme Soul and, particularly in the case of Advaita Vedanta, pronounces that they are the same.

The concepts presented in this chapter take you deep into Hindu philosophy. But make no mistake: The saints/sages/religious thinkers who developed these approaches to a spiritual life had no doubt that they can be practiced and, therefore, are practical. I try to make this subject as simple as possible.

While I introduce six separate Darshanas (schools of Hindu thought) in Chapter 19, I devote an entire chapter only to the Vedanta Darshana because the ideas from the other Darshana schools were gradually integrated into practical Vedanta. Vedanta is the philosophy that prevails today both in theory and practice.

Understanding the Basics of Vedanta

Vedanta is the *anta* (end or culmination) of *Veda* (knowledge). *Knowledge* here refers to the knowledge of Reality, Truth, and Brahman. Vedanta philosophy is the foundation of modern Hinduism.

The Vedantic system consists of three branches: Dvaita (Dualism), Advaita (Nondualism or Monism), and Vishistadvaita (Qualified Monism). These branches are based on a synthesis of knowledge presented in the three scriptures defined together as *Prasthanatraya:* the Upanishads, the Brahma Sutras, and the Bhagavad Gita. The Brahma Sutras, composed between 400 and 200 BCE by Badarayana, contain a set of aphorisms on Brahman.

Thou art That. If you and the next person and everyone and everything else are divine, how many divinities are there? An infinite number — that is, Brahman. Brahman contains all. If you believe you are divine (and Hindu sages say you must), your life on earth is governed by the divinity in you influencing your action, speech, and thought, all of which are divine. If everyone and everything behaved the same, all would be well; it would be heaven on earth with divine actions, divine speech, and divine thoughts all around.

Is heaven on earth an unattainable dream? No, say the sages. According to them, that is what life on earth was meant to be. Thou art That. We are therefore One. Trouble starts when we forget that inherent oneness, and the result is the imperfect world we see and live in.

Vedanta is not just theory. It is a practical — albeit challenging — mandate. It lays down an ideal before us, an ideal that is possible to attain. That ideal is to live the divinity in us. Vedanta asks us to elevate our lives to meet that ideal and to avoid the tendency to compromise the ideal. Instead we must stick to it, arranging our lives accordingly. Living the divinity within ourselves requires action with an essential caveat: Such action must take place amid inner calmness. This seeming conflict is insisted upon by the scriptures.

The Upanishads tell us that the philosophical ideas issuing out of such a high ideal were not always the outcome of sages thinking out their thoughts alone in distant caves. Some of the busiest monarchs were also responsible in shaping this knowledge base. The best example is the Bhagavad Gita, which is considered the greatest commentary on the Vedanta. The Gita was taught to Arjuna, a Pandava prince (refer to Chapters 12 and 13), on the battlefield of Kurukshetra.

The goal of life: Self-realization

Vedanta stresses that the single most important goal of life is the realization of our true nature. We must know ourselves, know who we really are. As simple as this idea may sound, attaining self realization is actually very hard because we are distracted by our external focus. Such external focus has undoubtedly helped humanity in many ways: the green revolution that helped grow food; the moon landing; advances in genetics, computers, medicine, and the Internet; and so on. Yet, such external engagement has also blinded us to the most fundamental need: to know who we truly are.

Although many a recent thinker has brought this lapse to our attention, it's not a new discovery. Hindu sages charged "Know thyself" *(Atmanam Viddhi)* centuries ago. So did thinkers in other cultures. The Greek version, *Gnoti seauton* (carved over the door to the temple of the Oracle at Delphi), and the Latin *Nosce te ipsum* mean the same. Hindus made a special effort to focus their attention inward for a different reason: They found the inner universe as equally fascinating and equally demanding as the outer universe.

The sages assured us that, when we know who we really are, we will then be able to assert the Truth. The Truth is stated in the *mahavakyas* (grand utterances) this way:

> *Aham brahmasmi* (I am Brahman)
>
> *Tat tvam asi* (Thou art That)
>
> *Ayamatma Brahma* (The extension of the self is Brahman)

According to the sages, the concept "I am God" needs to be revealed, understood, repeated, and repeated again until it becomes part of every human being's being. This alone affirms Oneness of the universe. This alone is considered the greatest truth of Advaita Vedanta. It is also Vedanta's goal, its mandate: Realize who you are.

Unity in diversity

According to Vedanta, the oneness, when realized, leaves us free. With the realization of our true identity — our oneness with everything and every being — outward differences in name, color, dress, speech, station in life, and so on simply become less important.

The path an individual chooses to realize the self and to reach God doesn't matter. Uniformity isn't needed because all paths eventually lead to the same Truth, which is why Vedantists are able to declare, "Truth is One but the wise may express it differently *(ekam sat viprah bahudha vadanti).*"

The Hindu is not concerned about how you reach this realization. He doesn't insist that you adopt his path. He is comfortable when you follow your own path. A Hindu's wish for you is that you be a better Christian if you are a Christian, a better Jew if you are Jewish, a better Taoist if you are a Taoist, and so on. No matter what path you choose, the Hindu believes that he will ultimately meet you when you both reach your goal.

Vedanta doesn't care who the individual is or what the individual believes in. It asks that we develop a perspective from whose height all differences, real and important though they may be, diminish until we're able to view unity, harmony, and beauty. Think of being in an airplane at 30,000 feet and looking down to see a beautiful, smooth terrain.

Is this universe real or an illusion?

Hindus commonly use the word *maya* to describe events, experiences, and observations that cannot be explained easily. *Maya* means illusion. With the assertion that the only Reality is Brahman and everything else is an illusion, the Vedantist is left with the burden of explaining these things:

- ✔ The practical existence of the world we see and feel

- ✔ A personal god we may adore and worship

- ✔ The individual souls we believe in and attribute to every being

- ✔ The manner in which we inherited a world full of problems admittedly originating from a pure and perfect source (Brahman)

The Vedantist attributes these things to the very source. According to Hindus, the Supreme Being launches existence as we know it — the illusion *(maya)* — for its own amusement *(Lila* — pronounced *lee la* — meaning amusement or play). Thus, what you and I see and experience day in and day out is *apparent* reality — not Reality. We live in this illusion until we learn of our own true identity. When we realize our true divine nature, the illusion is gone, and then we are free. We see clearly.

The example cited most often to explain *maya* is that of a rope lying in your porch or yard that, in the darkness, you mistake for a snake. Another way to look at it is to think of yourself as an actor in a play. The best actors lose their real identity for the duration of the play, but when the curtain closes, they are themselves again. They have regained their true identity. Your life is an act in a wonderful play, but you can end this act and return to your own true nature whenever you want. That return happens with knowledge.

Achieving happiness through spiritual enlightenment

The core message of the Vedanta is that human beings cannot achieve happiness by mere experience of physical pleasures obtained through acquisition of wealth. Such pleasures are temporary and cannot last long. At best, they guarantee you another turn on the wheel of rebirth. Vedanta aims at absolute happiness obtainable only through spiritual enlightenment. Such enlightenment alone is capable of cutting the link between endless action and corresponding consequences. When the individual soul (*jivatman*) is freed from this connection, it's liberated from the cycle and unites with the source, Brahman (*Paramatman*, the Supreme Soul).

As I mention previously in this chapter, one is free to follow any path one chooses to find God. The different Hindu denominations do not matter to Vedanta. It does not matter if one Hindu considers Vishnu to be supreme and another Hindu looks upon Shiva as supreme. Names and images do not matter to Vedanta. What matters most is to move away from darkness and move toward light — toward Reality. In this sense, Vedanta is both a religion and philosophy, reflected in the following Hindu prayer.

> *Om, lead me from the unreal to the Real*
> *Lead me from darkness to light*
> *Lead me from death to eternal life*
> *Om, Peace, Peace, Peace*

Brahman and the soul: The connection

Brahman, the Supreme Soul, is defined as pure consciousness. It is, in addition to many other things, birthless, deathless, beyond time, beyond space, and not bound by any laws of causation. Brahman defies description.

The individual soul in each of us is divine but is held in bondage of matter — enveloped, as it were, by several layers of consequences. The goal is to become free of this bondage. This view of the soul and the Soul has led to inquiries regarding the relationship, if any, between the two and the manner in which these two entities interact upon death of the body. Remember: Only the body dies, never the soul.

Vedanta insists that you should come face to face with any existences beyond those you sense. You begin by admitting that "I" does not mean your body, your mind, or your ego. "I" refers to the soul, which is not matter.

The message of Vedanta is this: If there is a Universal and Supreme Soul, then you should go there directly, see the Supreme Soul, and remove all doubts. There's no need to struggle in your attempts to believe — just realize. Use the ancient tools — logic, sorting out the physical world, the mind-body-spirit connection, self-discipline, and even devotion — in order to see your way (see Chapter 19).

Three philosophies that emerged from Vedanta

Three systems of philosophy emerged from considerations of Reality and the relationship between the individual soul and the Supreme Soul:

✔ The first philosophy is known as *Advaita* (Monism or Nondualism). It claims that Brahman is the only Reality. The proponent of this philosophy is the saint Shankaracharya.

✔ The second philosophy, known as *Vishishtadvaita* (Qualified Monism or Qualified Nondualism), can be described as Theism, which admits a personal God as ultimate Reality. The proponent saint of this philosophy is Ramanujacharya, who acknowledged that the Reality is indeed Brahman but allowed that individual souls as well as the universe are also real.

✔ Another philosophy, which is a branch of Theism, is *Dvaita* (Dualism). This system claims that the Supreme Soul and individual soul are indeed different. The proponent saint of Dvaita is Madhvacharya.

You can read more about each of these three saints in Chapter 9.

Some scholars believe that the three philosophies offer a process of evolution to reach God; Dualism (Dvaita) may be considered the first step, followed by Qualified Monism (Vishistadvaita), ultimately reaching Monism (Advaita). Of course, the adherents of Dualistic philosophies may not agree with this "evolution." Table 20-1 outlines the basic beliefs of each school.

Table 20-1	The Three Vedanta Schools		
Beliefs	*Advaita (Nondualism)*	*Vishishtadvaita (Qualified Nondualism)*	*Dvaita (Dualism)*
Proponent Saint	Shankaracharya	Ramanujacharya	Madhvacharya
Reality	Brahman alone	Universe and individual souls	Universe and individual souls
Illusion	Universe	None	None
Knowledge	Absolute	Relative	Relative
God	Brahman	Ishvara/Narayana*	Vishnu
Relationship between Supreme and individual soul	One	Qualified One	Different
How to attain realization	Knowledge (Jnana)	Bhakti-Jnana	Devotion (Bhakti)
Declaration	I am Brahman	I am all Yours (personal god)	I am your servant
Upon body's death	If eligible, soul merges with Brahman	Individual soul retains its identity	Individual soul retains its identify
Salvation	In death and momentarily in life	Only upon death	Only upon death

* Ishvara is a generic name for the Almighty. Narayana is another name for Vishnu.

The three Vedantic paths all have the same goal: reaching *moksha* (liberation, salvation) — that is, breaking free of the cycle of rebirth and death. All misery ends and the soul is at complete peace and bliss. Although all the philosophies share the belief in God, individual souls, and the associated fundamentals (such as the quest for knowledge, respect for nature, devotion, dharma, karmic consequences, and so on), differences among the three exist. The remainder of this chapter discusses the highlights of each philosophy.

The Advaita Philosophy: Nondualism

The word *dvaita* in Sanskrit implies two. Add the prefix –a, which essentially means "not," and you have the *Advaita* philosophy, which implies "not two." A more accurate definition of Advaita is *Monism,* which is a metaphysical view in which there is one and only one Reality with no component or independent parts. The Advaita philosophy refers to the One without a second (Brahman). The One has no form, no attributes, no qualities, and is an impersonal God. The One is everything. Everything is in the One. This concept is the core of Advaita philosophy.

Advaita makes no distinction between the subject and the object. Advaita says we are in the One, but we are not aware of it. Therefore, we cannot recognize that we are divine even though we are part of the One. Why? Because we are enveloped in sheaths of self-doubt, ignorance, and weakness. Even when we know of this connection or may even feel it to a degree, we are, by nature, distracted by everything else but the One.

This phenomenon is the equivalent of the temptation to rush toward a pile of coal when a pile of gold is within reach. The Hindu doesn't claim to understand why that is the case but knows that it is.

Advaita says that the aspirant must first become aware of the weakness and develop a plan to become strong and walk toward the light of knowledge. In other words, we must become what we inherently already are —Brahman.

Shankaracharya, the proponent saint of Advaita

Every Hindu recognizes the name Adi Shankara, which refers to the saint Shankaracharya, the proponent of the Advaita philosophy. Born in the sixth century CE, Shankara lived only 32 years, yet in that short time he made everlasting contributions to Hindu thought. At age 10, he was acknowledged by scholars as an intellectual giant having read, memorized, and written commentaries on complex scriptures. He was unhappy with his teachers who, he observed, did not practice what they taught. He saw Hindu society as materialistic and decadent. He decided to lead a monastic life and traveled the subcontinent four times, establishing four monastic sites. He assigned a Veda to each site for study, specialization, preservation, and propagation.

The famous *Peethams* (monastic centers also known as *Maths*) that he established at four cardinal points are as follows:

- Shringeri Math at Shringeri (Karnataka state in the south), which studies the Yajur Veda

- Dwaraka Math at Dwaraka (Gujarat state in the west), which studies the Sama Veda

- Jyothir Math at Badrikashram (Uttaranchal state in the north), which studies the Atharva Veda

- Govardhan Math at Puri (Orissa state in the east), which studies the Rig Veda

Each center continues to function to this day and is directed and managed by its own spiritual leader, also referred to as Shankaracharya. The original Shankaracharya's philosophy of Advaita has a strong foundation in the world today primarily due to the great support and propagation by the nineteenth-century saint Swami Vivekananda.

Distinguishing between the real and the Real

According to the Advaita philosophy, Brahman is the only Reality. All else is falsehood. *Real* is defined as that which has always existed, will continue to be forever, and does not change.

Advaita does, however, recognize that there is this world we see and live in. It knows that multiple forms, names, qualities, souls, bodies, and beings exist — the good, the bad, and the ugly. So why does it not acknowledge this obvious presence as Reality? Why insist that there is only one Reality?

Advaita recognizes this infinite variety within Brahman as real but not Real! In fact, it looks upon the world as neither real nor unreal. It is the rope and snake analogy (refer to the earlier section "Is this universe real or an illusion?"). The rope is seen, and thus it is real, but our perception of it as a snake vanishes the moment we realize the truth; thus, it was not Real. This is how Advaita reconciles between the One we don't see and the innumerable beings and objects we do sense.

Levels of reality in Advaita

This belief leads to redefining reality to help understand the Real by granting recognition to what the senses experience. At the lowest level, illusory appearances may be given a temporary status of some kind of reality. For example, the snake was "real" until someone realized that it was a rope. At a slightly higher level is our day-to-day experience, which Advaita grants has some kind of reality. For example, the car you are in is "real," although it is not, given the definition of Reality: that which has always existed, will continue to be forever, and does not change. The highest Truth lies in the One who is the One and Only Reality.

Ignorance is the barrier, and knowledge is inherent

Advaita, by definition, can't conceive of knowledge, the objects of knowledge, and the knower as separate entities because that would mean things and concepts can exist outside Brahman, which basically negates the whole premise of Nondualism. For that reason, knowledge, which is absolute in the eyes of Advaita, is already in Brahman — that is, in us. So why don't we all know everything we need to know about Reality and our true selves? Because the individual *jiva* (soul, atman) is encased in sheaths of ignorance, wrong identity, and ego — all of which put it in bondage. Recognition of this bondage of ignorance and a strong will to break it liberate the soul.

Allowing for knowledge-based devotion

Advaita does not ignore a common person's need for a personal god. Notwithstanding the abstract concept that insists on one and only one Reality, Shankaracharya introduced the concept by which Shaivites could worship individual gods, such as Shiva, Vishnu, Ganesha, Surya (sun), and Devi: Such devotion must arise out of *jnana* (knowledge).

To attain such knowledge, the sheaths of ignorance first have be removed, which, says the Advaita, is possible only through the help of a religious leader (guru). With these sheaths of ignorance destroyed, the *jivatman* (the individual soul) will realize its true identity and belong in Brahman.

A certain discipline is essential to remove ignorance. Certain practices under the direction of a competent guru will go a long way toward freedom. Through a disciplined life, one acquires a sense of discrimination, a sense of dispassion and perspective, and an intense desire for liberation. Listening to the guru, reflecting on the teachings, and subsequent contemplation are the prescriptions of Advaita.

Advaitins believe that Brahman can be reached during one's own lifetime. Shankaracharya claimed that he reached Brahman and described It as an ocean of nectar. Mind cannot conceive It, he said. After returning to human consciousness, he claimed to abide by the joy of the atman. Similar mystic experiences were described by Ramakrishna Paramahamsa (see Chapter 9).

Distinguishing between the Individual and the Supreme Soul: Dualism

Dvaita philosophy is Dualism, propounded by the thirteenth-century saint Madhvacharya. Madhvacharya posited what seemed practical and easy to feel and understand: We see the world. We see humans, animals, healthy, sick, wealthy, poor, high, low, rivers, mountains, and so on. These things are *all* real. Reality consists of not just One, as Advaita claims, but three entities: God, nature, and human souls, and all are eternal.

Madhvacharya claimed five differences (known as *pancha bheda*) as real:

- ✔ The individual soul is different from the Supreme Soul.
- ✔ The supreme godhead (Vishnu) is different from everything inanimate.
- ✔ One individual soul is different from every other soul.
- ✔ Any individual soul is different from anything inanimate.
- ✔ One inanimate entity is different from any other inanimate entity.

To Madhvacharya there was no need for abstraction. It was clear that we are humans and we live in a world with other humans. He didn't shy away from acknowledging this reality. In this way, Dvaita does not subscribe to Shankaracharya's abstract concept of the relationship of the individual soul and the Supreme Soul. Thus, Dvaita is easier to understand as it makes a clear distinction between the two fundamental entities: individual soul and the Supreme Soul. The following sections highlight key points of Dvaita.

Distinguishing between individual souls and the One

Unlike Shankaracharya, who insisted that ignorance makes us blind to unity with the Supreme Soul, Madhvacharya said that individual human souls are just that: human and souls. Every soul is different from every other soul, and not all souls have the connection to the One, which adherents of the Nondualist philosophy consider inherent. The Dvaita school divides individual souls into three categories:

✔ Those fit to be liberated through the grace of God and spiritual practices.

✔ Those who are interested only in the material world with little craving for a spiritual life.

✔ Those who are inherently evil and end in hell. Yes, in Dualism, hell awaits the inherently evil even if it is mainly a purgatorial interval before the next birth.

Dvaita's proponent saint: Madhvacharya

Madhvacharya was born in 1199 CE. Uninterested in studies at school, he pursued scriptural studies at home and developed an early desire for renunciation. He studied Vedanta under a guru who was an Advaitist. He began to develop his own view of Vedanta and wrote a commentary on the Gita. He traveled widely, engaging scholars and firming up his own ideas about Duality. He believed that all cannot attain moksha. Some will, most may not, and some will be subjected to damnation. Vishnu's Vaikunta (his abode, or heaven) was the devotee's ultimate goal according to Madhvacharya. For more on this saint, see Chapter 9.

According to the Dvaita philosophy, an individual soul has its own consciousness, willpower, and ability to learn, know, act, and experience joy. It is a mere reflection of God and, in that context, has some of God's attributes reflected in it. The individual soul is forever dependent on God. Each soul resident in a body is subject to bondage. Actions affect the soul — contracting it by bad karma and expanding it by good karma.

Liberation through devotion to Vishnu

The primary godhead of Madhvas (followers of the founder Madhvacharya) is Vishnu, who has these divine attributes: merciful, lovable, and taking human avatars and yet remaining the Almighty. Note that absolutely no evil attributes whatsoever are attributed to Vishnu. All other gods are Vishnu's reflections, except for Lakshmi, his consort, whom he has graced with his own powers and is therefore considered to be his equal.

Release from bondage occurs through many lives and depends upon the type of life led. Lives led with devotion to God following dharma (moral order) qualify for entrance to that heaven known as Vaikunta, the abode of Lord Vishnu. Short of this, the individual soul is subject to move, upon death of the associated body, to another body. This cycle can continue forever or until the soul qualifies for entrance to Vaikunta.

Vishnu's Vaikunta is full of happiness and is devoid of disease and death: It is the great end. No more births and deaths. Upon liberation, the individual soul retains its identity but becomes free of any suffering. Dvaita does not believe in liberation during one's lifetime.

We are servants of God

Some Dualists (both Dvaitins and Vishishtadvaitins) look upon themselves as servants of God. The word *dasa* means servant, and it's not uncommon to see such devotees sign themselves off as Dasa or Dasan in their correspondence with others. As vegetarians, their logic in not killing animals is that they shouldn't harm animals, which have souls and belong to God.

God, according to Dualism, descends to earth because of his love for the devotees. When the devotees speak of God, they're referring to the avatars of Vishnu and the promise of Lord Krishna in the Gita that he will manifest himself here on earth whenever there is decline of dharma (see Chapter 8).

The only way to have wishes fulfilled is to pray to one of the gods. Dvaitins are encouraged to offer worship to gods, all of whom (except for Lakshmi, who has the same status as Vishnu) are reflections of Vishnu. Icons are used in these worships to represent the godhead. Devotees are cautioned to look upon these icons as icons only, representing the true identity of gods. To do otherwise is to violate an important belief in the *difference principle,* which distinguishes between Vishnu and the icon, which is an inanimate object. To reach the real goal — salvation — prayers are said to Vishnu.

Reaching a Compromise: Vishishtadvaita (Qualified Nondualism)

Between Madhvacharya's distinct differences between individual souls and the Supreme Soul (espoused in Dvaita) and Shankaracharya's insistence on their oneness (Advaita), Ramanujacharya's philosophy allowed for a sort of middle ground. Hence the name *Vishishtadvaita,* which means Qualified Nondualism. In essence, Vishishtadvaita integrates the essentially philosophic approach of Shankaracharya with an emphasis on worshipping a personal God. The following sections outline the key points of this philosophy.

While Shankaracharya based his approach to worship and devotion *(bhakti)* on *jnana* (knowledge), Ramanujacharya argued that knowledge results from bhakti. The goal is essentially the same, but the order is reversed.

Allowing for a personal, loving God

Ramanujacharya, much like Madhvacharya, allowed for a personal, loving God. He argued that a personal God conceived as Brahman cannot be without attributes. So Ishvara (God), a substantive part of Brahman, with attributes of *satya* (reality), *jnana* (consciousness), and *ananta* (infinity), served as the basis to define a personal God.

The extraordinary dependence of devotees on God is unique to Dualism and can be a subject of criticism by others. This level of dependence, indeed surrender, is seen as a sign of weakness because, according to Advaita, we are divine. Advaitists maintain that such dependence is not unlike vines clinging to a grand tree for survival. To the Advaitist, we are that grand tree.

The relationship between the individual soul and the Supreme Soul

Ramanujacharya posited that both "It" (the Supreme Soul) and "I" (the individual soul) are Real. In essence, the individual soul is in the Supreme Soul but is not the same as It. Same but different is the theme here.

Ramanujacharya accepted Shankara's definition of Reality with a qualification. According to Ramanujacharya, Brahman is to the Cosmos what an individual soul is to the body. God, Nature, and Soul are three separate existences in one. God is considered the Soul, and all the individual souls and Nature are the body of God.

This approach retained the abstractness of Advaita to some extent by admitting that Brahman is the ultimate Reality but opened the door a little for another level of reality, which allowed a dependence (which requires two entities) as the One yielded to two. In this way, a devotee might relate to God and develop a loving relationship with God.

God exists with positive attributes

By allowing the other level of reality, Ramanujacharya was able to provide a means for devotees to recognize a Supreme Soul (Paramatman) with wonderful qualities, with extraordinary grace and compassion toward them. Being a Dualist means believing that everything about God is good. There is always light and no darkness in any consideration pertaining to God. All good and no evil: That is the summation of Dualism's thesis.

The proponent saint of Qualified Nondualism: Ramanujacharya

The tenth-century saint/reformer Ramanujacharya modified Shankaracharya's Nondualism to accommodate the thirst to find and worship a God with love. His approach was that a loving, compassionate, and merciful Almighty needs to be worshipped with love. The best path for an aspirant is surrender, he argued. This was consistent with a core message from the Gita. He developed a great following and took the opportunity to convert a large number of people of other castes into his SriVaishnava (brahmin) sect. He has been deified himself at Melkote in Karnataka state. See Chapter 9 for more on Ramanujacharya and Chapter 16 for celebrations related to him in Melkote.

Chapter 21

The Yogic Path to Salvation

*Y*ou may often hear that Yoga is good for you. That statement almost always refers to yoga exercises. But Yoga is more — much more — than yogic postures. *Yoga,* in Sanskrit, means union (it's linguistically related to the English word *yoke*). Yoga Darshana, a system of philosophy, sets out the steps by which a dedicated student can unite body, mind, and soul in the quest for salvation: the release of the individual eternal soul (atman) from the cycle of rebirths. The path to salvation is the realization of the soul's (the inner self's) true nature and goal: ultimate union with the Supreme Self, the Paramatman who is the basis of all being.

Yoga requires a teacher or guru to lead a student through the process. The ideal is a perfected body in a stilled mind, ready and receptive for the final revelation. The process involves physical exercises and postures *(asanas)* for the outer body; breathing exercises *(pranayama)* for the inner body; and meditation *(dhyana)* to bring calmness to the mind.

The physical, mental, and spiritual regimen worked out over the millennia by yogi masters is so scientific and so neatly fitted to the human condition that it is as valid and useful today as it ever was. Because it came into being long before most creeds, anyone — regardless of religion or world view — can practice Yoga on the physical and mental level. Many people these days practice Yoga at this level with immense benefit to health of body and mind.

In this chapter, I trace the beginnings of Yoga as a discipline; its proponent sage Patanjali and followers; the emphasis on a Yogic Tripod in the sacred scripture, the Bhagavad Gita; and the importance of Yoga in today's world. The topics I cover here that are related to physical aspects of Yoga are easily understood. But aspects of Yoga that deal primarily with spiritual discipline are less well-known and sometimes complex. I present them in a somewhat simplified manner.

More Than a Series of Postures: Yoga as Spiritual Path

As I explain in Chapter 19, Yoga is one of the *Darshanas,* the six traditional schools of Hindu theology developed roughly between 500 BCE and 500 CE and expounded on in famous commentaries over the next 500 years or more. The role of the Darshanas was to provide an intellectual underpinning to what had become a pyramid of religious ritual practices, largely in the hands of an entrenched priesthood. Meanwhile, the Darshanas and the Upanishads had resolved the all-important identity of soul and Supreme Soul (atman and Paramatman, respectively). What about the path to salvation offered by Yoga Darshana? It is the complete control, training, and testing of body and mind to be a fit temple for the soul.

Sage Patanjali, who lived circa the second century BCE, was the compiler of the Yoga Sutras, which form the basis of what is called *Raja* (Royal) *Yoga.* These sutras follow the philosophy of Samkhya Darshana (refer to Chapter 19) and form the practical aspect of that school of theology. In its emphasis on the strict training of body and mind (thoughts and senses) through rigorous postures, breath control, and meditation, Yoga is in a direct line from the more ancient Shramana tradition (ascetic life of rigor lived in forests) of individual physical effort and endurance. Patanjali connected this effort directly to the great goal of the era: the search for the Truth (of self and Self).

The Raja Yoga of Patanjali

The Yoga Sutras of Patanjali consist of 196 aphorisms or short memorable statements divided into four books *(padas).* These sutras form the basis of the later fully developed forms of Yoga Darshana. The following sections explain.

An intriguing seal

In Chapter 2, I discuss the archaeological revelation in 1921 India of a developed urban civilization (circa 2900–1500 BCE) in the valley of the Indus River. A significant finding in subsequent excavations was a tiny seal with an image that has teased scholars ever since. The central figure appears to be male, heavily bearded or with three faces, horned or in horned headgear, seated in a strikingly yoga-like pose. Is this where Yoga began? Possibly.

1. Samadhi Pada (Book of Perfect Concentration)

The Samadhi Pada, which has 51 sutras, defines Yoga as the disciplining and calming of the mind and explains how, when that step is accomplished, we will realize our true nature, which is boundless. This pada lays out clearly what liberation means and how Yoga can lead there.

11. Sadhana Pada (Book of Discipline)

This pada has 55 sutras. While Samadhi leads the aspirant to a blissful state, Sadhana addresses a rigorous system of practices classified into two yoga disciplines: Kriya and Ashtanga:

- ✔ **Kriya Yoga:** Kriya is the Yoga of effort aimed at achieving a specific result. It is also referred to as *Karma Yoga* (Yoga of action), detailed in Chapter 3 of the Gita, where Arjuna is urged to act without expecting any results (see Chapter 11).

- ✔ **Ashtanga Yoga:** Ashtanga is the eight-limbed set of disciplines aimed at specific goals, described in the following list. This entire set is also termed *Raja Yoga.*

  - *Yama:* Laws of life: nonviolence, truth, non-covetousness, celibacy, and non-attachment

  - *Niyama:* Rules for living: cleanliness, satisfaction, austerity, study of scriptures regarding God and the soul, and surrender to God

  - *Asana:* Postures

  - *Pranayama:* Breathing control

  - *Pratyahara:* Withdrawal of senses

  - *Dharana:* Concentration

  - *Dhyana:* Meditation

  - *Samadhi:* Oneness with the object of meditation

111. Vibhuti Pada (Book of Manifestation)

The Vibhuti Pada has 56 sutras. According to Patanjali, supernormal powers develop through *sanyama,* a special concentration of the mind with the object of meditation. These powers called *siddhis* (knowing the past and future, moving objects through sheer willpower, shifting atoms to cause moments of invisibility, and so on) are some of the magic moves that made ancient *rishis* (sages and saints) and yogis feared and respected. Patanjali advised against using them because such an exercise has consequences — namely, distracting the aspirant from the main goal and wasting otherwise needed spiritual energy — that compromise the goal of liberation.

IV. Kaivalya Pada (Book of Liberation)

This book, which contains 34 sutras, explains the nature of liberation through self-realization and attainment of what is called *dharma megha samadhi*. Scholars debate the exact meaning of the complete phrase. One interpretation is that such samadhi showers the aspirant with merit leading to freedom. Scholars continue to ask whether it refers to a rain of dharma on the enlightened soul, which then needs nothing more to attain the highest samadhi or oneness with the supreme boundless consciousness. This phrase is interpreted further to mean a state of boundless consciousness, of oneness with the universe. No doubt it is the peak of yogic attainment. The few who attain this level are called *jivanmuktas,* those who have achieved full enlightenment while still living in this turning world.

The main goal: Freedom from our lower selves

The first lesson in Raja Yoga is the distinction among "substances": mind *(manas),* ego *(ahamkara),* intelligence *(buddhi),* thought-waves *(vritti),* and material stored in the mind *(citta).* This is the broadest definition of "substance," and I refer to it in some detail in Chapter 19. All these features belong to the body and are therefore not Real — that is, they're not eternal. They are only reflections of true consciousness and will die with the body. Meanwhile, they do distract and delude us into supposing that they are functions of the self.

The mind uses intelligence to collect sensations from the body and perceptions through thought-waves. The mind assumes it, the mind, is the actor, the collector of impressions; the ego assumes that it is the knower, the doer of the action. Consequent sensations of happiness and pleasure or the opposite are phantom results and will keep us dissatisfied.

The next distinction is between all these material substances, which are temporary, and the individual soul, which is eternal. The purpose of Yoga is to first strengthen and tune the body into the instrument it is supposed to be. A strict regimen is prescribed for body and mind that includes lifestyle, attitudes, and behavior, as well as the familiar routine of body postures. The first result of such a regimen is a healthy body and mental attitude receptive to the final goal of freedom. Attaining freedom involves knowing the last distinction: between the self (individual consciousness) and the Self or boundless Cosmic Consciousness.

The role of a guru for serious practice

From time immemorial, the help of a guru has been recommended and sought for any serious study of religious thought or practice for the student of any age. The ancient *gurukulam* (resident school) system has been superseded by conventional schooling for young children, but many institutes for religious education flourish in India and now abroad. The extreme discipline for body and mind prescribed for Yoga requires a guide even at the lowest level of Hatha Yoga asanas or postures.

Centers for instruction in all forms of Yoga in India are often found in the great pilgrimage cities (see Chapter 18). Because Hinduism is not a centralized religion, a popular and effective teacher can also attract a large following. You may begin by taking classes as offered by any of these institutes, but the serious seeker is encouraged to take up, if only temporarily, the kind of lifestyle described in Patanjali's second book (The Book of Discipline) in order to prepare the mind. You need to start from where you are, as swamis often say.

The Yogic tripod: Karma Yoga, Jnana Yoga, and Bhakti Yoga

Picture this: Two sets of cousins of the Kuru race face each other on the first day of battle in what turns out be an 18-day war. The 100 Kaurava brothers (whose father is the reigning monarch, the blind Dhritarashtra) are challenged by their dispossessed cousins, the five Pandavas. Lord Krishna, avatar of god Vishnu, has agreed to be the charioteer for the Pandava prince Arjuna. Arjuna is leading the forces of good against the forces of evil, and Krishna is present to help him. However, the forces of evil have many good or worthy people fighting on the wrong side for their own justifiable reasons. Krishna steers Arjuna's chariot to the front between both armies; Arjuna balks not from fear but at the approaching horror of an era coming to a bloody end at his hands. He throws down his weapon and refuses to fight. The lesson begins.

In the Bhagavad Gita (see Chapter 13), Lord Krishna teaches Arjuna (and millions of Hindus who have followed) that devotion gained through duty, self-sacrifice, and knowledge is the best path to salvation. In doing so, Krishna emphasizes Jnana Yoga (the Yoga of Knowledge), Karma Yoga (the Yoga of Action), and Bhakti Yoga (the Yoga of Devotion).

Krishna's message from almost the beginning of the Bhagavad Gita is one of love: love of God for the devotee and the devotees' love or devotion that will help bind the soul to the Supreme Soul. Krishna makes it clear that although all three paths are good and effective in reaching the goal of salvation, Bhakti Yoga or faith is the easiest and best.

I use the phrase the "Yogic tripod" to emphasize the mutual interdependence of these three Yogas — Karma (selfless service), Jnana (knowledge of the self), and Bhakti (surrender to God), all aimed at self realization and liberation — to help maintain a certain level of balance in the aspirant.

Karma Yoga (Yoga of Action): Serving society through selfless service

Chapters II through V in the Bhagavad Gita cover Arjuna's immediate problem. Krishna tells Arjuna he must fight. Arjuna, he says, is mourning for those he cannot really kill. The real self is the soul, not the body. The soul will find another body like another set of clothes and be born again into another lifetime. Krishna expands on the imperishable nature of the soul and reminds Arjuna of his duty as a warrior to fight a just war. To die fighting in such a war would be his entry into heaven.

Krishna preaches the Yoga of Action as appropriate for a warrior but warns that the action must be accompanied by detachment from the fruits of that action. One's dharmic duty must be performed with no reward in view, with a mind that views victory and defeat as equal, without pain or pleasure. Krishna then teaches the ideal of man: unselfish, centered in self, firm and tranquil, with firm control over the mind and finding true knowledge. Such a person will find final bliss in Brahman.

Arjuna is momentarily confused with this gift of knowledge from Krishna. If knowledge is all, he asks, then why kill? At this, Krishna preaches against inaction. He explains how he himself must perform works in order to prevent the universe from falling into ruin. Arjuna, Krishna says, must perform his own warrior dharma for which he has been born.

Krishna further discriminates between what work is and is not, and how it is refined as ritual through renunciation, by serving others. He defines a yogi as one who can control his senses, breath, mind, and intellect; who is impartial; and who combines renunciation with right action.

Jnana Yoga (Yoga of Knowledge): Seeking union through higher knowledge

Chapters VI and VII of the Bhagavad Gita present the Yoga of Meditation and the Yoga of Knowledge *(Jnana)*. Krishna describes the yogi: celibate; living alone; eating frugally; sleeping just enough; preparing a clean area; spreading it with cloth, animal skin, and grass; sitting and holding the body erect with sight fixed; and concentrating on the divine with courage and perseverance.

Arjuna notes the all-too-common waywardness of the mind and asks what will happen if the well-meaning yogi fails in his goal. Krishna responds that success will come slowly after many attempts. The struggle for dharma will never be wasted. The yogi will have a blessed interlude in heaven after death and then be reincarnated to try again for perfection. Krishna urges Arjuna to become a yogi, seeking shelter in the Lord and practicing Yoga. He also is full of praise for the wise man and expresses his preference for the seeker after knowledge.

Bhakti Yoga (Yoga of Devotion): Seeking union through surrender

In Chapters VIII through XII of the Bhagavad Gita, Krishna reveals himself as the Supreme Soul, as Brahman, as the essence in all, the beginning and end of creation. This view is not the impersonal Brahman encountered in Sankhya Darshana (refer to Chapter 19), although so many elements of Sankhya philosophy appear throughout: the three gunas (qualities) that are infused through character and substance, for example, as well as Prakriti (Nature) and Purusha (Spirit). The remaining chapters deal with devotion, specifically devotion to Krishna himself in a form nothing short of Brahman.

Kundalini Yoga and chakras

Kundalini Yoga is rigorous and powerful — and magical. *Kundalini* means "the coiled one" and refers to serpent power. Also called *Laya Yoga,* the name is a nod to the well-known regenerative abilities of snakes, which made them a symbol of rebirth and renewal in many ancient cultures. *Chakra* means "wheel." The body is pictured as divided into seven planes of consciousness corresponding to nerve complexes along the spinal cord, and representing energy sources (see Figure 21-1).

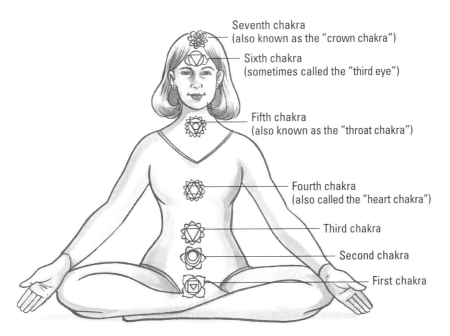

Seventh chakra
(also known as the "crown chakra")

Sixth chakra
(sometimes called the "third eye")

Fifth chakra
(also known as the "throat chakra")

Fourth chakra
(also called the "heart chakra")

Third chakra

Second chakra

First chakra

Figure 21-1:
Chakras.

The seven chakras are (1) Muladhara (base) chakra; (2) Swadhisthana (sacral) chakra; (3) Manipura (solar plexus) chakra; (4) Anahata (heart) chakra; (5) Vishuddha (throat) chakra; (6) Ajna (brow) chakra; and (7) Sahasrara (crown of head) chakra. When someone is seated in a basic yogic posture, the lowest center of consciousness, Muladhara chakra, is at the base of the spine. The life force is seen as a coiled sleeping serpent. With the use of mantras (chants) and intense *sadhana* (prescribed practice under guidance), the life force or inner self is moved up the spine, through three "channels" known as *ida* on the left, the right *pingala,* and the central *sushumna* channel. The life force moves past the heart to the top of the skull, where it blossoms into a thousand-petaled lotus. Different colors, shapes, numbers of petals, and sound syllables are associated with each chakra.

Breathing exercises *(pranayama),* correct posture, sound syllables, sacred diagrams (called *yantras*), and meditation are important components of this yoga. Kundalini concentrates on inner powers and improves circulation, memory, and intuitive and mental awareness.

In Chapter 9, I introduce you to Swami Shivananda Saraswathi, founder of the Divine Life Society. His 1935 book called *Kundalini Yoga* is a definitive source of information on this practice. Yogi Bhajan, founder of the 3HO (the Happy, Healthy, Holy Organization) in 1969, was the first to introduce Kundalini to the United States.

Kundalini is sometimes included in esoteric practices more commonly referred to as *Tantric Yoga,* which you can read about next.

Tantric Yoga

In Tantric Yoga, practitioners seek what are considered magic powers, the kind of knowledge credited to ancient yogi ascetics. This knowledge is separate from astrology, horoscope reading, and related forms of knowledge, which are considered within the mainstream in Hinduism and the province of scholars. And unlike the Yogas outlined in the section "The Yogic tripod: Karma Yoga, Jnana Yoga, and Bhakti Yoga," Tantric Yoga is really pursued only by *renunciates:* those who wish to pursue a spiritual lifestyle. Although sexual union is sanctioned as one of the ritual acts that can lead to a state of bliss in Tantric Yoga, it is not the goal and end-all, as may be perceived by many in the West.

The earliest forms of Yoga involved manifesting material objects from nothing, levitation, invisibility, shape changing, and even raising the dead. The Indian Rope Trick comes to mind, as do various feats of hypnosis and group hypnosis. These abilities were credited to the use of special secret chants, magic written and sound-syllables, hand gestures, sacred diagrams, chakras, and the like.

The holy atmosphere of the city of Kashi on the banks of the Ganges appears to have been a magnet for practitioners of a variety of yogas, especially Tantric Yoga. Visitors to Kashi (Benares) and similar sacred places of pilgrimage can still encounter proponents of the renunciant tradition from all origins, all ages, and varying conditions and abilities. On sacred occasions such as the Kumbha Mela, when much religious benefit is gained from dipping in the holy waters at an auspicious time (see Chapter 16), large numbers of such *sadhus* (religious mendicants) appear in public from their places of seclusion. Otherwise, the renunciant tradition, sometimes made fearful by the appearance of some of its practitioners, is more often now sublimated into a more spiritual practice.

Years of dedicated mind and body control can achieve the unusual. During experiments conducted at the Menninger Institute in the 1960s, Swami Rama (a visiting renunciate) was able to demonstrate such yogic powers as stopping his heart for 16 seconds, making an object spin from five feet away, and producing sleep wave patterns while awake (called Yoga Nidra). Yoga Nidra is one of the states of consciousness produced by the Omkara mantra (chanting of Om). These feats demonstrate some of the powers, called *siddhis,* referred to in the earlier section "The Raja Yoga of Patanjali." From the scientific point of view, they demonstrate what is biologically possible in terms of human brainpower and body.

Hatha Yoga – a guide

Hatha Yoga, the best known and most popular in the West, has been transformed over centuries into a systematic science. Following are brief descriptions of traditional Hatha Yoga exercises:

- Netra Vyayamam (eye exercise): Moving, cupping, massaging the eyes

- Nasagri Dhristi: Gazing at and focusing on the nose tip

- Soorya Namaskar: Sun salutations, as explained in the next section

- Meditative poses: Forms of Padmasana or Lotus pose, seated with legs folded

- Twenty to 25 intermediate poses including the Cobra (Bhujangasana) and leading into the Corpse pose (Savasana) and headstand (Sirshasana)

- Forty advanced poses, from elaborate stretching (such as the Shooting Bow pose) to a total scrunch-up of the body called *Yoga Nidrasana,* or Yogic Sleep pose

- Pranayama: Breathing techniques

- Mudras, or gestures, used in meditation: Figure 21-2 shows an example of such a gesture

- Kriya or cleansing rituals for the stomach, colon, nose, and eyes

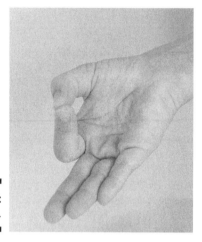

Surya Namaskar: Sun salutations

During the 1970s, in Bristol, Connecticut, the late Dipti Sen conducted Yoga classes at her Om Center. One of her special exercises, also taught by most Yoga teachers, especially for beginners, is the *Surya Namaskar,* a series of movements based on a prayer to Surya (also spelled Soorya), the sun god. Each movement involves setting and holding a pose, or *asana,* while breathing in; moving smoothly into another pose while breathing out, through 9 or 12 or 20 steps. Figure 21-3 shows the traditional 12-step method.

Each position is accompanied by a particular mantra:

- Om, Mitraya namaha: Salutation to the One who is the Friend of all

- Om, Ravayeh namaha: Salutation to the One who Shines on all

- Om, Suraya namaha: Salutation to the One who Guides all

- Om, Bhanaveh namaha: Salutation to the One who Illuminates all

- Om, Khagaya namaha: Salutation to the One who Soars faster than all

- Om, Pushneh namaha: Salutation to the One who Gives strength to all

- Om, Hiranyagarbhaya namaha: Salutation to the One who Promotes life to all

- Om, Marichayeh namaha: Salutation to the One who Gives light to all

- Om, Aditaya namaha: Salutation to the One who is most Powerful of all

- Om, Savitreh namaha: Salutation to the One who is the Source of life for all

✔ Om, Arkaya namaha: Salutation to the One who Transmits energy to all

✔ Om, Bhaskaraya namaha: Salutations to the One who gives enlightenment to all

Figure 21-3:
Surya
Namaskar
(sun saluta-
tions).

Illustration by George Herrick

Yoga in the United States from 1893 to the Present

Swami Vivekananda's famous visit in 1893 was a landmark in the introduction of Advaita Vedanta and the Yoga systems to the United States. A combination of the mid-nineteenth century New England Transcendentalist movement, the 1875 founding of the Theosophical Society in New York, and the liberal Unitarian impulse behind the World's Parliament of Religions in 1893 had prepared for an intellectual interest in Indian thought. Following his visit and an acclaimed three-year lecture tour throughout the United States, Vivekananda established the Ramakrishna Missions. Vivekananda is famous for his extensive lectures on Karma Yoga, Raja Yoga, Jnana Yoga, Bhakti Yoga, Vedanta (Advaita), and other topics that have all been brought together in *The Complete Works of Swami Vivekananda* (Vedanta Press) which I recommend reading. The Mission centers, named after his guru and sometimes after Vivekananda himself, also offer lectures and maintain bookstores.

Interest in Yoga ebbed and flowed through the following decades, more often connected with trends such as vegetarianism and with health and physical wellbeing. Yogi Ramacharaka was a prolific writer on all aspects of Yoga. Standout early texts include the works of Ernest Wood.

Paramahansa Yogananda's *Autobiography of a Yogi* (in print since 1946) is the foundation of the Self-Realization Fellowship, which teaches Kriya Yoga.

After World War I, the ex-Bengal Lancer, Francis Yeats-Brown, author of *Lancer at Large* (Garden City Publishing Co.), *Eight Steps to Yoga* (Blue Ribbon Books, Inc.), and *Yoga Explained* (Vista House), brought knowledge of Yoga to the street level, especially when his *Lives of a Bengal Lancer* (The Viking Press) became a Hollywood hit.

Following World War II, the American West coast and California became a destination. Christopher Isherwood emigrated from England and translated the Yoga Sutras of Patanjali with Swami Prabhavananda. Indra Devi, an early Yoga pioneer, settled in Hollywood in the 1950s and taught Yoga to movie celebrities. Beginning her career in dance and film, she lived in India for many years, studying yoga under the same guru as B.K.S. Iyengar and Krishna Pattabhi Jois.

From the mid-twentieth century on, a number of Yoga gurus have established well-known schools in the United States and have introduced new approaches. Swami Satchidananda (the guru who appears fleetingly in the film *Woodstock*), author of *Integral Yoga Hatha* (Integral Yoga Publications), arrived in 1966 and established his Integral Yoga Center and L.O.T.U.S. shrine. B.K.S Iyengar's *Light on Yoga* volume (Shocken) with its 200 asana photographs is now a classic.

As I mention in the earlier section "Kundalini Yoga and chakras," Swami Shivananda's 1935 book *Kundalini Yoga* inspired Yogi Bhajan's 3HO, the Happy, Healthy, Holy Organization in 1969. Swami Rama, author of *Enlightenment Without God (Mandukya Upanishad), Living with the Himalayan Masters,* and *Science of Breath: A Practical Guide* (all published by Himalayan Institute Press) founded the Himalayan Institute of Yoga Science and Philosophy in 1971.

Part VI
The Part of Tens

The 5th Wave   By Rich Tennant

"I'm always endeavoring to become one with all things, however, I'm going to make an exception with this fish casserole."

In this part . . .

No long sentences or detailed discussions in this part. Instead I provide brief lists highlighting interesting facts about Hinduism. Here, you find answers to ten questions non-Hindus often have about Hinduism, ten common Hindu prayers, and ten traditional pieces of advice or scriptural mandates that Hindus grow up learning.

Chapter 22

Ten Common Questions About Hindus

Q&A. Ancient Hindus encouraged it. In fact, there is a whole Upanishad called *Prashnopanishad,* the Upanishad of Questions. Six pupils came to a sage and asked him questions about Brahman. The sage asked them to practice *Brahmacharya* (celibacy) for a whole year while serving him at his ashram. They did so, and then the sage answered some tough questions about spirituality and Brahman. Well, I'm no sage and I don't insist on any condition.

So where did I get these questions? I sought out my non-Hindu friends and asked them to fire away. Here are some of their questions. (Interestingly, nobody asked, "Have you seen God?" Full disclosure: Not yet!) I hope these questions will inspire you to seek out your Hindu friends and pester them with more questions. I assure you, you will both learn in the process.

How Did Hinduism Get Started?

Ancient Hindus called their faith *Sanatana Dharma,* which means "eternal dharma." In other words, the faith, according to them, had no beginning. And in fact it had no founder. Hindus believe that the eternal truths that comprise their faith emerged from the penance of ancient sages and seers and were first "heard" by them. This experience was named *shruti,* meaning that which was heard by many sages and over many centuries. Further, Hindus believe that these truths were communicated orally from generation to generation. They were finally written down around 500 BCE (or earlier) and are known as the *Vedas.* The Vedas form the foundation of modern Hinduism. Other than those scriptures, there was no central Hindu authority then and there is none now; nor was there a particular person around whom the faith was based.

The word *Hinduism* has its origin in the word *Hindu* that ancient Persians used to describe the neighboring community that settled on the banks of the river Sindhu (Indus). Head to Chapter 2 for more on the origins of Hinduism.

Is Hinduism a Passive Religion?

Hinduism is most certainly not a passive religion. Hinduism is a dynamic religion. The two great Hindu epics, the *Ramayana* and the *Mahabharata* (see Chapter 12), would be only a few pages long were it not for the terrible battles fought to restore dharma. The entire Bhagavad Gita is devoted to convincing Arjuna to fight (see Chapter 13). There is no passivity here.

The impression of passivity that has prevailed over centuries may exist because of the perception of Hindus as "navel gazers." Focusing on one's navel or the tip of the nose is a recommended Yogic posture during meditation, and Hindus are interested in exploring the inner world to obtain knowledge of the self. Also, Hinduism does not have a strong missionary mandate to convert others, which may give the impression of passivity.

Are Individual Souls Unique?

Hindus believe that individual souls are unique. Their uniqueness comes about by virtue of the experiences accumulated during the soul's tenure in a body. Upon the death of one body, the soul occupies another, accumulating experience until the soul qualifies for total release. It is likely that, upon total release, the individual soul has no more connection with past lives. Total release is the end, when the soul becomes pure consciousness.

Holy Cow! Are Cows Worshipped (and Can Animals Reach Salvation)?

Hindu tradition reveres cows. The Rig Veda refers to the cow as a mother, which may be due to the fact that, for many millennia, cow's milk was actually the only available substitute for mother's milk for infants. Fire rituals to this day specify the use of *ghee* (clarified butter) in making offerings to Agni, the Fire God. And in rural areas, modest cottages and huts are still cleansed with cow dung to keep insects away, and cow dung mixed with rice husk and made into patties is a source of fuel for many villagers.

It is not clear when eating beef became taboo and forbidden among Hindus, but the prohibition has been in vogue for 25 centuries or more and continues to this day. Even Hindus who eat meat may hesitate to choose beef.

Salvation is the goal of humans who struggle through hundreds of lives before they attain *moksha* (release from life on earth). Animals have souls, but to achieve moksha, they have to be born as humans (based on their own karma) and then begin the process of working toward salvation.

Why Greet Friends with Palms Folded?

Bringing your palms together at the chest level and bending your head down is a Hindu's way of acknowledging the divinity in you. This casual greeting may follow a formal greeting and show of respect, such as prostrating in front of an elder or a deity being worshipped. This gesture helps bring the focus to the subject being respected and revered.

Why Break Coconuts at the End of Worship?

It is a tradition among Hindus to bring to a temple a plate of flowers, fruits, and a coconut as an offering. Fruits and coconut are considered a food offering to a deity being worshipped. At the end of the worship ceremony, either the priest or the devotee breaks the coconut into two and offers the pieces to the deity ready to be "eaten." Similarly the fruits are peeled and offered. This act is clearly a gesture. Another explanation suggests that the coconut offered represents the individual worshipper's ego. The ego is thus surrendered to the deity and upon worship, it is broken into two halves. The belief is that the worshipper is thus absolved.

What Is That Dot on Hindu Women's Foreheads?

In the past, only married women wore the dot to signify a happily married status. The dot was a must, and elderly women would admonish young women who failed or forgot to wear the mark. Today, the familiar dot on the foreheads of Hindu women is an auspicious sign of general wellbeing. When families visit other families, it is a common practice for the hostess to offer a plate containing a small cup of red powder to females when they are ready to leave. They respond by dipping their right-hand ring finger into the cup and touching their own forehead at the location of the dot.

Another explanation is that the location of the dot coincides with that of the "third eye" and helps bring the focus of anyone to that spot during casual or formal visits. The "third eye" between the brows is an energy center designated as a chakra (refer to Chapter 21).

Why Do Hindus Cremate the Dead?

Hindus do not believe in resurrection of the material body. They believe that, upon death, the soul, which truly represented the person, has departed. The body has no significance, and therefore no attempt is made to preserve it. While some Hindus do bury their dead, the most common practice is to cremate the body, collect the ashes, and disperse them in a body of water or other places of importance to the deceased individual.

Can You Convert to Hinduism?

You can convert to Hinduism if you so desire and if you find a guru who is willing to initiate you. Fundamentally, Hindus are not set up to convert others. If and when it does occur, the initiation is at a spiritual or philosophical level. If you want to practice Hinduism, you can do everything Hindus do and still remain in your faith, if you don't see any conflict. Hindus most certainly do not see any conflict.

How Can I Learn More About Hinduism?

If you want to learn more about Hinduism, my recommendation is that you read the epics, the *Ramayana* and the *Mahabharata* (refer to Chapter 12). You can also read books by and about Swami Vivekananda. After digesting these, you may attempt to study the Bhagavad Gita (see Chapter 13).

Chapter 23

Ten Common Prayers

In This Chapter
▶ Prayers for help and understanding
▶ Salutations to gods and goddesses

*W*hen you grow up in a Hindu household, you learn prayers and more prayers. You see your parents offer prayers, almost casually, throughout the day, seeking God's blessings — mostly for your wellbeing, your future, and your life. In conversations, you notice casual references to gods and goddesses and phrases such as "only His kindness" or "with His grace" or "with Her benevolence" and so on. Then there's the worship at home or at the temple where you hear even more prayers. For the devout, prayers begin as they rise in the morning and continue throughout the day in a systematic manner.

In this chapter, I list ten prayers most commonly used in Hindu households.

Forgive Me, Mother Earth

समुद्र वसनें देवी पर्वत स्तनमंडलें ।
विष्णु पन्निर् नमस्तुभ्यं पादस्पर्शम् क्षमस्वमें

samudra vasanē dēvī parvata stanamandalē
viṣṇu patnir namastubhyam pādasparśam kṣamasvamē

I offer my salutations to the consort of Vishnu, Mother Earth, asking her to forgive me for stepping on her, whose body is clothed with oceans and mountain ranges.

Looking at My Palms in the Morning

कराग्रे वसते लक्ष्मी कर मध्ये सरस्वती

करमूलेतु गोविंद: प्रभाते करदर्शनम्

karāgrē vasatē lakṣmī kara madhyē saraswatī
karamūlētu govinda: prabhātē karadarśanam

At the top of my palms resides goddess Lakshmi, goddess Saraswati at the center, and Lord Vishnu at the base. So shall we shall see them in our hands in the morning.

Please Remove All Obstacles

शुक्लांभरधरं विष्णुं शशिवर्णं चतुर्भुजं

प्रसन्न वदनं ध्यायेत् सर्व विघ्नोपशांतये

śuklāmbharadharam viṣṇum śaśivarṇam caturbhujam
prasanna vadanam dhyāyēt sarva vighnōpaśāntayē

I meditate on Vishnu who is clothed in white, the color of the moon, four-armed and smiling, to lessen all obstacles.

वक्रतुंड महाकाय सूर्यकोटि समप्रभा

निर्विघ्नं कुरुमेदेवा अद्य कार्येशु अद्यदा

vakratunda mahākāya sūryakōti samaprabhā
nirvighnam kurumēdēva adya kāryēśu adyadā

My Lord Ganapati, with a curved tusk and mighty body and with the brilliance of a million suns, please remove any obstacles in my tasks today.

Let This Be a Great Day

ब्रह्मा मुरारि स्त्रिपुरान्तकारि भानुश्शशी भूमि सुतो बुधश्च

गुरुश्च शुक्रः शनि राहु केतवह कुर्वंतु सर्वे मम सुप्रभातम्

brahmā murāri stripurāntakāri, bhānuśśaśī, bhūmi sutō budhaśca,
guruśca śukra: śani rāhu kētava: kurvantu sarvē mama suprabhātam

May Brahma, Vishnu, Maheshwara; sun, moon, Mercury, Jupiter, Venus, Saturn, Rahu, and Ketu grant this to be a good day for me.

Salutations to the Sun God

जपा कुसुम संकाशं काश्यपेयं महाद्युतिं

तमोरिम् सर्व पापघ्नम् प्रणतोस्मि दिवाकरं

japā kusuma samkāśam kāśyapēyam mahādyutim
tamōrim sarva pāpaghnam praṇatōsmi divākaram

Salutations to Divakara, the Sun God shining like the japa flower, descendent of sage Kashyapa, of great brilliance, destroyer of all sins and the enemy of darkness.

Let Us Meditate on the Radiance of That Divinity

ओं भूः ओं भुवः ओं सुवः ओं महः ओं जनः ओं तपः

ओगुं सत्यं ओं तत्सवितु वरेण्यं ।

भर्गो देवस्य धीमहि धीयोयोनः प्रचोदयात्

ओं आपो ज्योतिरसो अमृतं ब्रह्म ओं बूर्भुवस्सुवरों

ōm bhū: ōm bhuva: ōm suva: ōm maha: ōm jana: ōm tapa:
ōgum satyam ōm tatsavitu varēṇyam
bhargō dēvasya dhīmahi dhīyōyōna: pracōdayāt
ōm āpō jyōtirasō amṛtam brahma ōm būrbhuvassuvarōm

Om. That which pervades earth, sky, and heaven, which is worthy of worship, that has no beginning; that which is the light of wisdom and truth; Let us meditate on the radiance of that divinity. May that brilliance help inspire and illuminate our minds. That One which represents water, light and is the quintessence in all things; May that almighty spirit pervading the earth, atmosphere, and heaven bless us with enlightenment.

Let There Be Harmony

ओं सहना ववतु सहनौ भुनक्तु
सहवीर्यं करवावहै
तेजस्विना वधीतमस्तु
मा विद् विशा वहै
ओं शान्तिः शान्तिः शान्तिः

ōm sahanā vavatu sahanau bhunaktu
sahavīryam karavāvahai
tejasvinā vadhītamastu
mā vid viśāvahai
ōm śāntih śāntih śāntihi

May Brahman protect us, may we dine together, let us work together with great energy, let us be illumined together, let us live in harmony,

Om, peace, peace, peace!

Let Everything Be Surrendered to You

कायेन वाचा मनसेंन्द्रियैर्वा बुध्यात्मनावा प्रकृते स्वभावात्
करोमि यद्यत् सकलं परस्मै नारायणायेति समर्पयामि

kāyēna vācā manasēndriyairvā budhyātmanāvā prakṛtē svabhāvāt
karōmi yadyat sakalam parasmai nāryāyaṇāyēti samarpayāmi

Whatever I have performed through my action, speech, thought, knowledge, or my inclination, may all that be surrendered to the Lord.

Lead Me from Darkness to Light

असतोमा सत्गमया तमसोमा ज्योतिर्गमया
मृत्योर्मा अमृतं गमया ओं शांति: शांति: शांति:

asatō mā satgamayā tamasōmā jyōtirgamayā
mṛtyōrmā amṛtam gamayā ōm śāntih śāntih śāntihi

Lead me from the unreal to the real, lead me from darkness to light
Lead me from death to eternal life, Om peace, peace, peace

By Whose Grace the Mute May Become Eloquent. . .

मूकं करोति वाचालं पंगुं लंघयते गिरिं
यत्कृपा तमहं वन्दे परमानंद माधवं

mūkam karōti vācālam pangum langhayatē girim
yatkṛpā tamaham vandē paramānanda mādhavam

By whose grace the mute may become eloquent, the lame may leap mountains, to that blissful Lord I offer my salutations.

Chapter 24

Ten (Plus) Traditional Mandates

One thing you should know about Hindus: We give and get a lot of advice — from parents, teachers, close and distant relatives, siblings, friends, strangers, visiting swamis, wandering monks, fellow travelers on a bus, train, or airplane, beggars, and so on. It's as though all this knowledge is stored up and suppressed in these well-wishers, and then you show up, and the dam breaks with an outpouring of mantras, references to great men, their own experiences relating to your current venture . . . you get the picture. Only respect for elders prevents you from running away. So exercise care before you seek a Hindu for advice because you will no doubt receive it.

I hesitate, but then the urge to share with you all the advice I got overcomes me, and so I offer you these mandates, most of which come from a variety of scriptures and are aimed at the young. They are usually referred to as *subhashitams,* meaning proper and appropriate sound advice. Some may even sound familiar, having parallels in your own faith.

Worship Your Women

Women in Hindu religion are the true gatekeepers of *dharma* (right conduct) and culture. That is, of course, my opinion, but I am certain most of my Hindu sisters and brothers share it. The scriptures also say so. Specifically the verse, from the Manu Smriti, goes:

यत्र नार्यस्तु पूज्यंते रमंते तत्र देवताः

yatra nāryastu pūjyantē ramantē tatra dēvatāha

Gods are pleased where women are worshipped.

Hindu men will most likely tell you, "Yes, we know it" — and advise you to remember it.

Be Strong in Mind and Body

An unmistakable message of *Vedanta* (philosophical knowledge about spiritual life that follows on the most sacred scriptures of Hindus known as the Vedas) is one of strength. Swami Vivekananda (see Chapter 9) eloquently said that the greatest sin human beings can commit is to say that they are weak. Be strong, he said, advising us to develop muscles of iron, nerves of steel, and a mind made of the same material of which the thunderbolt is made. According to him, strength is life and weakness is death. And there is a reason for emphasizing such strength. It is driven by a Sanskrit saying:

नायमात्मा बलहीनेन लभ्य:

nāyamātmā balahīnēna labhyaha

This Atman cannot be realized by the weak!

Atman is one's self, and it requires a certain level of mental capacity and strength to realize the self. And an associated humorous poem confirms it:

अश्वं नैव गजं नैव व्याघ्रं नैवच नैवच

अजा पुत्रं बलिं दत्वा दैवो दुर्बल घातुक:

aśvam naiva gajam naiva vyāghram naivaca naivaca
ajā putram balim datvā daivō durbala ghātukaha

Neither the horse nor the elephant and never a tiger, it is the lamb that is offered in a sacrifice; even God destroys only the weak!

Work Hard

Ancient Hindus recognized the peril of sloth. The Hindu practices of getting up early in the morning before sunrise, preparing for morning worship, studying, and so on were all geared toward instilling a certain discipline. Farmers went out to the land to tend to one or another task early in the morning and worked through noon. Hard work was built into the daily routine. Hindus found the scriptural authority to work hard in a statement from the *Panchatantra* (a collection of Hindu fables written between 100 BCE and 500 CE) in Book II (see the story of the weaver named "Soft"):

उद्यमेनहि सिध्यंति न च मनोरथैहि
नहि सुप्तस्य सिंहस्य प्रविशन्ति मुखे मृगा:

udyamēnahi sidhyanti na ca manōrathaihi
nahi suptasya simhasya praviśanti mukhē mṛgāha

Accomplishments come from work, not by wishful thinking. No prey enters the mouth of a sleeping lion.

Company Is Important When. . .

A subhashitam I learned while taking Sanskrit in middle school states succinctly when having company becomes relevant:

ऐकस्तपो द्विरध्यायी त्रिभिर्गानं चतुष्पथ:
पंच सप्त कृषीणांच संग्रामो बहुभिर्जनै:

ēkastapō dviradhyāyī tribhirgānam catuṣpathaha
panca sapta kṛṣīṇānca sangrāmō bahubhirjanaihi

One to meditate, two to study, three to make music, four to travel, five to seven to work in the fields, and many many more for battle.

Work with Passion, but Don't Concern Yourself with Results

In the Bhagavad Gita (see Chapter 13), you can find this statement:

कर्मण्येवाधिकारस्ते मा फलेषु कदाचन

karmaṇyēvādhikārastē mā phalēṣu kadācana

You have a right to work — not to its fruits.

The scripture wants you to work hard, as if your life depended on it, but it warns you not to be concerned with the results. The reason? Work done without any selfish motive in the service of others is performing one's duty irrespective of what the outcome may be. Work is your right, and the rest is in God's hands.

Don't Bother If You Don't Have Faith

Ancient Hindus wanted to make sure that rituals, prayers, and worships did not become mere routines that lacked the fundamental faith required while undertaking these spiritual tasks. The corresponding message is found in the Bhagavad Gita:

अश्रद्धया हुतं दत्तं तपस्तप्तं कृतं च यत्
असद् इत्युच्यते पार्थ न च तत् प्रेत्य नो इह

*aśraddhayā hutam dattam tapas taptam kṛtam ca yat
asad ityucyatē pārtha na ca tat prētya nō iha*

Whatever is sacrificed, offered, or performed and whatever austerity is practiced without faith, it is falsehood, and of no value either here or hereafter.

Protect Dharma, and It Will Protect You

The mandate to protect dharma is one of Hinduism's most sacred. The strong attachment to the concept of *dharma* (moral order) is so ingrained in Hindu hearts and minds that it serves as a yardstick to determine whether an action is within the bounds of right conduct. It was evident as far back as the epic times that this mandate cannot be taken for granted. Dharma will protect you, of course, but only if you do your duty to protect it. This mandate is stated in the following crisp statement (found at the end of the story of Yaksha Prashna that I tell in Chapter 12):

धर्मो रक्षति रक्षितः

dharmō rakṣati rakṣitaha

Dharma protects those who protect it!

Don't Tell Pleasant Lies or Unpleasant Truths

सत्यं ब्रूयात् प्रियं ब्रूयात् न ब्रूयात् सत्यमप्रियम्
प्रियं च नानृतं ब्रूयात् ऐष धर्म: सनातन:

*satyam bruyāt priyam bruyāt na bruyāt satyamapriyam
priyam ca nānṛtam bruyāt eṣa dharma: sanātanaha*

Tell the truth and share pleasantness but don't tell an unpleasant truth. Don't lie, even if it is pleasant — that is the eternal dharma.

This verse found in *Manu Smrti* (Laws of Manu) expresses a practical guide to interpersonal relationships, but it's not meant to be interpreted literally. Sometimes sharing an unpleasant truth may be essential if doing so means preventing a disaster that may result otherwise. For example, if the kitchen is on fire, you'd shout.

Nonviolence Is the Supreme Dharma

अहिंसा परमो धर्मः

ahimsā paramō dharmaha

Nonviolence is the supreme dharma.

This mandate (originally from the epic the *Mahabharata* and made popular by Mahatma Gandhi) also is not meant to be interpreted literally. After all, the same epic (see Chapter 12) lists about a hundred reasons to go to war with the enemies of dharma. Dharma needs to be protected at any cost. Even Mahatma Gandhi, when asked by a reporter whether he expected his son to come to his aid in case he was attacked, without any hesitation replied in the affirmative. But barring such exceptional circumstances, practicing *ahimsa* (nonviolence) conforms with the Hindu philosophy of tolerance, peace, and oneness.

The Whole World Is Your Family

One learns from the Atharva Veda and Mahopanishad two of the least-known beliefs of Hindu ancestors:

अयं लोकः प्रियमतः

ayam loka: priyamataha

This world is to be loved.

Vedic sages declared this to be the case in the Atharva Veda (see Chapter 10).

अयं निजः परोवेत्थि गननं लघु चेतसां
उदार चरितानां तु वसुधैव कुटुंबकं

ayam nija: parōvetthi gananam laghu cētasām
udāra caritānām tu vasudhaiva kutumbakam

Myself, this is mine, that is yours, is a petty way of seeing reality; for those with noble consciousness, the whole world is a family.

You can find this in the Mahopanishad (see Chapter 11).

You May Have to Abandon Something You Care About

Sometimes you may have to sacrifice something or break a relationship to serve a greater cause. Sage Chanikya (350–283 BCE), who was considered an expert in the science of finance and served in the Hindu emperor Chandragupta's court, declared thus:

त्यजेदेकं कुलस्यार्थे ग्रामस्यार्थे कुलं त्यजेत्
त्यजेत् ग्रामं जनपदस्यार्थे आत्मार्थे पृथिवीं त्यजेत्

tyajēdēkam kulasyārthē grāmasyārthē kulam tyajēt
tyajēt grāmam janapadasyārthē ātmārthē pṛthivīm tyajēt

For the sake of a family you may have to disconnect from an individual, for the sake of a village you may have to abandon a family, for the sake of a region you may have to abandon a village, and for the sake of the self you may have to abandon the earth (earthly pleasures).

Index